Black Life and Culture in the United States

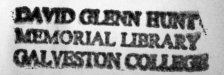

THOMAS Y. CROWELL COMPANY

NEW YORK · ESTABLISHED 1834

Black Life and Culture in the United States

Rhoda L. Goldstein

EDITOR

Acknowledgments

The publisher gratefully acknowledges permission to use the following: pages 31 and 75: excerpts from *African Religion and Philosophy* by John S. Mbiti, Praeger Publishers, Inc., 1969, copyright © 1969 by John S. Mbiti, reprinted by permission of Praeger and Heinemann Educational Books Ltd., London; page 160: "Little Girl, Don't You Know," from Bluesway album *Stormy Monday Blues*, copyright © 1967 by Pamco Music, Inc.; page 176: excerpt from "A Song of Praise," and page 177: "For a Lady I Know," both reprinted from *On These I Stand* by Countee Cullen, copyright 1925 by Harper & Row, Publishers, Inc., renewed 1953 by Ida M. Cullen, reprinted by permission of the publishers; page 177: excerpt from "Our Land," reprinted from *The Weary Blues* by Langston Hughes, copyright 1926 by Alfred A. Knopf, Inc., and renewed 1954 by the author; page 198: quotation from Ralph Ellison, reprinted by permission of William Morris Agency, Inc., on behalf of the author, copyright © 1971 by Ralph Ellison; pages 327-28: excerpt from *Mission Accomplished* by Ben Caldwell, first published in *The Drama Review*, Vol. 12, No. 4 (T40), Summer 1968, copyright © 1968 by *The Drama Review*, reprinted by permission, all rights reserved; pages 331-333: excerpt from *Ceremonies in Dark Old Men* by Lonne Elder, copyright © 1965, 1969, by Lonne Elder III, reprinted by permission of Farrar, Straus & Giroux, Inc.; page 339: "Black Art," reprinted from *Hopes Tied Up in Promises* by Julius E. Thompson, copyright © 1970 by Julius E. Thompson; page 348: excerpt from "The Saga of Sally Sue" by Deanna Harris, copyright © Sept. 1969 by *Negro Digest*, reprinted by permission of *Black World;* page 351: excerpt from "The Politics of Education" by Theodus Jowers, Jr., reprinted by permission of the author; page 354: excerpt from "Black Determination on Campus," by Donald M. Henderson, reprinted by permission of the author; pages 354-55: excerpt from "A Poem to Complement Other Poems," copyright © 1969 by Don L. Lee, reprinted by permission of Broadside Press.

Designed by Ruth Smerechniak

Manufactured in the United States of America

L.C. Card 74-146281
ISBN 0-690-14598-5

1 2 3 4 5 6 7 8 9 10

*For
our children*

ACKNOWLEDGMENTS

This collection of articles grew out of a course I coordinated at Douglass College. In order to decide what should go into a "first" course, an introduction to the study of the life and culture of Afro-Americans, I drew upon the critical thinking and advice of many people—colleagues, students, and community activists. A number of those who shared in some of the initial discussions are represented in this volume, namely, Cecelia Drewry, Lennox Hinds, William M. Phillips, Jr., Emily Alman, Ann Lane, Geoffrey Hendricks, Samuel Proctor, and Karen Predow. These individuals raised crucial questions, suggested speakers, and gave willingly of their ideas and support. It is difficult to thank them adequately. As the course and the book developed, other participants displayed genuine interest in the project. Alphonso Pinkney was especially helpful and encouraging.

My indebtedness to the people whose contributions are included in this volume is great. Their unusual cooperation and commitment made it possible to complete the manuscript well on schedule. Since all of the pieces were being written specifically for this book—with most based in varying degrees on previous lectures—it became necessary for contributors to work closely with me. Their willingness to spend hours in telephone discussion, to engage in long work sessions in some cases, and to carefully attend to my written communications demonstrated the involvement of the contributors in the success of this venture.

Patricia Thornton was my undergraduate assistant and Mathew Greenwald my graduate assistant for the Life and Culture course. The myriad number of detailed tasks required of them were undertaken with enthusiasm and good will. They helped in many ways to make the book possible. Mrs. Angie Bilotta, sociology department secretary, did much to facilitate my work. Kathleen Jordan was also involved in this undertaking from beginning to end, starting with her initial interest in it as a Douglass student. Although in graduate school at the time the course was given, Miss Jordan agreed to type the tapes of the lectures and most of the final copy. The accurate transcripts were extremely useful to a number of contributors in the rewriting process. Miss Jordan provided more than technical aid—wit, wisdom, criticism, meticulous attention to detail, and always warm support. Her involvement in the book was probably as great as my own.

The course itself was made possible through the generosity of Dean Margery S. Foster of Douglass College, who provided money for guest speakers from a special fund. Former Dean Frances Healy and her successor, Dean Nancy Richards, were also instrumental in certain aspects of the funding. Douglass College librarians were uniformly helpful.

Finally, I should like to thank my husband, Bernard, and my children—Mary, Meyer, and Helena—for their patience and forbearance during my total involvement in this work. They were extremely considerate and took pride in my efforts.

Contents

CONTENTS

xi

Illustrations

RHODA L. GOLDSTEIN

Introduction

How does one begin to grasp the elements—the suffering and overcoming, the deprivations and creativity, the cruelties of oppression and the warmth of community, the forces giving rise to self-pride and to self-hate, the hope and desperation, the fear and the courage—that would describe the life of black people since their arrival on North American shores? How does one describe the transformations, losses, and continuities in culture since Africans arrived here: men and women of different physical types, speaking different tongues, coming from different nations? Here they were thrust into differing expeirences on the whims of chance, becoming field servants, house servants, artisans, and freemen, and being dispersed through North and South, cotton plantation and tobacco field, small plantation and large.

How did the fate of these black people become an inexorable part of American history—and how was it possible to distort and ignore their role for so long? How is it that whites who, living at a later period, had missed the terror of slave revolts could so easily underestimate the significance of Nat Turner? How could moralistic America brand John Brown a madman rather than a saint? How could Frederick Douglass, the escaped slave turned abolitionist, the first sit-in'er, be so little known to our schoolchildren? How could Marcus Garvey be dismissed as a criminal or misguided fool? And in our time, why was Fred Hampton shot down in bed by a barrage of police bullets, and Muhammad Ali deprived of his heavyweight crown? How did the people who were enslaved, deprived of their human identity, lynched as dangerous and stereotyped as satisfied, survive to develop not one but two cultural renaissances in the present century? How does one explain the divergent currents of thought, plans, and proposals currently being advanced to achieve black liberation? As others have wondered out loud, how does one explain the resilience of these people?

One book cannot, of course. But rather than apologize for adding yet another to the growing shelf of "black experience" books, I am glad to offer this one. It provides one more attempt to get at the richness, complexity, beauty, and pain of Afro-American life.

It could only be with a sense of humility that I, a white sociologist, would undertake to edit a book on Afro-American life and culture. Certainly I have been listening to black people well enough to understand and share in the concern they express when white people study or write about them. The issue is complex and requires more discussion than is appropriate here, but it is not to be dismissed lightly. Indeed, at a recent national convention of sociologists the official black caucus made very clear that this was a matter of prime concern. Anyone who does not yet know why *will* know when he has finished reading what the authors of this volume have to say. Without continued and continuing informal guidance from individuals who are a part of the group that the book is about, I would not have undertaken to edit it.

Actually, the work developed quite naturally out of a course that I coordinated at Douglass College in the spring of 1970. The previous year my department had agreed that such a course should be developed and had gone through the necessary bureaucratic procedures to institute it. Next came the problem of who would teach it and how it should be presented. Colleagues, students, and persons active in the black community helped me decide that one function of such a course would be to fill the many gaps in knowledge left by centuries of white-oriented, in many cases anti-black, education. It would have to be taught by those who had expert knowledge of Afro-American life. To have validity, such a course would have to be relevant to the issues of today, but it would also need to retrace black history. Following the lead of black Americans intent on reexamining their origins and their heritage, the course would have to develop comprehension of the relevance of the past to the present. Indeed, "the relevance of the past to the present" became the theme of the course, and was developed in a lecture by Lennox S. Hinds, an activist-intellectual whose community experience had directed him toward the study of law. We began with an examination of the historical roots of black life and culture and moved toward analysis of the social, cultural, and political movements of today.

Since we lacked a well-developed program of African and Afro-American studies in our college at the time, the course was designed to cover a wide range of disciplines and to reflect as well as possible the varied political stances now present in black America. Guest lecturers were invited, each of whom could give but an introduction to his or her particular field and suggest areas for further study. So, for example, despite the fact that Henry N. Drewry and Ann J. Lane were teaching courses in black history at Princeton and Douglass, respectively, and had command of their subjects in depth, they each agreed to interpret a basic experience— in the one case American slavery, and in the other the Civil War and Reconstruction—in the brief period of one lecture. This book, then, is based largely on the lectures that were given by these and other scholars, artists, and activists, and it represents the approach just described. It is a survey, an introduction to the study of Afro-American life and culture.

As the field of scholarship in Afro-American life develops, its vastness and depth become more and more apparent. We had to select from the possible range of topics that might be included, omitting, for example, one that has been much written about and discussed by sociologists—the black family. We could not begin to discuss black literature either— an omission justified somewhat by the many books available in this field. However, the reader will find various authors touching on these subjects; for example, a fellow sociologist, Bill Phillips, poignantly describes the pressures on the black family in his discussion of survival techniques. Herbert Aptheker uses the writings of black poets and authors to demonstrate that the theme of self-pride and Afro-American "superiority" is not new. And, of course, Cecelia Drewry's paper on black theatre deals with one form of writing. Throughout the book extensive references are made to black poets and authors who have influenced the thinking of the contributors. Almost all those who lectured for the course at Douglass College are represented here, and many rewrote and edited extensively for the reading audience. A few additional pieces were also commissioned in areas deemed important. All the work is printed here for the first time.

My perspective is one of developing an appreciation of the life and culture of black people. It is now permissible for blacks to write of their own culture and identity with pride, to be "biased" in favor of themselves. But the white social scientist may feel constricted by the demands of objectivity, and may try to carefully balance the weaknesses and strengths of black communities. To do this would require the presentation of statistics on health, mortality, illegitimacy, welfare—all the things that social scientists have been wont to do. But sociologists, like historians, are learning that much of their past analyses were facile, oversimplified, and at times biased when they dealt with black Americans. Sensitivity combined with folk knowledge and self-knowledge enable black people to question some "scientific" findings designed to prove their inferiority or to describe their innermost life. Ralph Ellison, in his *Shadow and Act,* describes his uneasiness at the way Afro-American life has been presented and his wish to show another perspective:

> From the very beginning I wanted to write about American Negro experience and I suspected that what was more important, what made the difference lay in the perspective from which it was viewed. When I learned more and started thinking about this consciously, I realized that it was a source of creative strength as well as a source of wonder. It's also a relatively unexplored area of American experience simply because our knowledge of it has been distorted through overemphasis of the sociological approach. Unfortunately, many Negroes have been trying to define their own predicament in exclusively sociological terms, a situation I consider quite short-sighted. Too many of us have accepted a statistical interpretation of our lives and thus much of that which makes us a source of moral strength to America goes unappreciated and undefined.

The book is intended to be, in part, a platform for what a number of varied black people, who have studied it and lived it, have to say about aspects of the black experience. Many of them I have come to know and respect over the years. The individuals I met while preparing the Life and Culture course were uniformly cordial and cooperative, and eager to see this book in print. Indeed, many helped in its formulation. Some of the scholarly contributors are part of black history themselves. But in addition I have included some pieces by black writers, and one by a white writer, who were selected especially because of their roles in the community. Non-academicians who spend their time working with black communities can frequently provide us with knowledge and insights not otherwise obtainable. It is not always recognized that pragmatic insights tend to find their way into scientific analysis, rather than science providing practitioners with the answers. For example, it is true that the concept of the ghetto as a colony was used by psychologist Kenneth B. Clark and others; but only after it was found creditable, picked up, and used by community activists did it find its way into respectable scientific journals. It now replaces the former designation of black ghettos as "pathological" communities. And so we have chosen authors who come from varied backgrounds and who contribute various types of knowledge. This seems more valuable than bringing together pieces of homogeneous style.

Given the burgeoning cultural revolution in Afro-America, I had to be selective in dealing with the arts. The writings on black art by the artists James Denmark and Frank Bowling and on black theatre by Cecelia Hodges Drewry help to illustrate the ferment going on in cultural fields. Dr. Drewry places the evolving black theatre in its various forms within a social-historical-political framework and takes us beyond the present into anticipation of the theatre of the future. Bowling, who is a critic as well as an artist, was asked to offer his analysis of the question, "What is black art?" In doing so, he raises basic issues about the standards and perspectives that are currently being applied to black endeavor.

One part of the cultural renaissance consists of reexamining the links between black peoples all over the world. This strong focus of interest is represented in a number of selections. To help us begin at the beginning, we include a selection on African art by Geoffrey Hendricks. Colin Palmer, in his description of certain aspects of the slave trade, makes more vivid the circumstances surrounding the dispersion of African peoples.

As black studies develop, it becomes increasingly clear

6

that national boundaries are no longer sharp delineators of black experience. Julius Waiguchu was asked to do a general piece on links between Africa and the United States. He traces intellectual and cultural ties, but has also chosen to provide a theory that, from a sociological point of view, dares to be very controversial. The continuity of black experience is also becoming evident in the field of linguistics: new strides are being made in the discovery of African forms in the speech patterns of North and South Americans. I was fortunate in being able to add to this collection a piece by Ivan Vansertima, in which he traces connections between the languages and folklore of Africa, the Caribbean, and the United States. Vansertima joined the Douglass College African and Afro-American Studies program after the Life and Culture course had been given. Esi Sylvia Kinney, in her selection on music and dance of the Americas, illustrates the better-known mutual influencing of the music of black people throughout various continents.

In politics as well as in culture, black people are crossing national boundaries. Some Afro-Americans are beginning to call themselves Africans; at the least, black leaders here are trying to develop contacts with their brothers in the Caribbean and in African countries. In fact, several of the contributors to this volume spent part of the summer during which it was being written in African or Caribbean countries. While quite a few of the authors are settled, for the moment, in New York or New Jersey, they come from such varied backgrounds as Guyana, Trinidad, Jamaica, Kenya, New Jersey, Texas, Virginia, and New York City's Harlem.

In contrast to this international focus, we also consider a local setting. In a 1964 article appearing in *Phylon* I tried to point out some of the interrelationships between civil rights activities at various levels: local, state, and national. As a participant I was able to see how the August 28, 1963, March on Washington brought together different local and national groups. I considered it appropriate to have the book include a blending of local, national, and international perspectives. As the movement for black liberation gains momentum, faces reaction, and surges forward, it is reflected in every community in America. Here we use the most obvious local situation, Douglass College, part of Rutgers University in the state of New Jersey, to gain insight into the desegregating process on American campuses. The effort to bring greater numbers of black students and some black culture into universities gained national attention in 1968 and 1969, when major campuses witnessed student demonstrations. Emily Alman, in writing about Douglass and Rutgers, brings the issue into local perspective, and shows the preconditions for, and stages leading up to, the revolt of the black students. She also brings out the marginal position of the small handful of whites who have always allied themselves with the cause of black freedom.

Samuel Proctor, formerly president of two black colleges, and now at the Rutgers Graduate School of Education, deals generally with some of the issues in the education of Afro-Americans. As has been noted, the book includes several other pieces by faculty members of Rutgers University. Given the interest and knowledge available (and graciously shared) on our own campus, I frequently did not find it necessary to seek outside experts.

Two men, Theodore Taylor and Ronald Copeland, bring to bear their experiences in activism, especially in Somerset County, but also in other parts of New Jersey. The concept of black power has been described many times, but Copeland gives us a fresher view by explaining how local community leaders responded to the need for a new philosophy to replace the faltering goal of integration. The reader will find that some of the themes suggested by Taylor and Copeland are echoed in the writings of academicians. Taylor refers to the various anecdotes told about black encounters with whites in the South, and the humor made out of daily tragedy; and Henry Drewry tells such a story in his introductory remarks about the writing of black history.

When the Reverend Ralph David Abernathy, president of the Southern Christian Leadership Conference, came to talk on our campus, he was universal. He could easily refer to New Jersey as "up South" and see his audience nodding in agreement. Traveling throughout the country, Dr. Abernathy knows what he will find in each black community and what will have to be done in each white community. Support for black persons under attack, concern with justice at the hands of courts and the police, the quest for housing, employment, and political power—all these things are obviously pressing concerns throughout the nation. People all over the country know what Dr. Abernathy is talking about, and many of the older folks in numerous communities have walked with Ralph Abernathy and Martin Luther King, Jr. Dr. Abernathy re- wrote his presentation completely for the purposes of this book, understanding our wish to include an inside and inti- mate account of the growth of the civil rights movement and the role of Dr. King, as well as our desire to make available knowledge about the now less-publicized programs of non- violent activists.

Concern with black liberation is evident throughout this book, although the authors differ as to the best way it can be attained. As Alphonso Pinkney carefully delineates the varieties of current nationalist thought, he makes clear that it is the method rather than the aim that is disputed. I think I can speak for all the authors of this volume, black and white, in saying that despite differing approaches all are con- vinced that change is necessary. Many have played activist as well as scholarly roles. To give just a few examples: Doug- lass students were excited at the prospect of hearing Herbert Aptheker's lecture, well aware of his contributions to the rediscovery and recording of black history. (They were not disappointed!) They were interested in hearing the account of desegregation at their own college, as told by one who played a major role in effecting it. The daily pressures on community leaders like Len Hinds, Ron Copeland, Ted Tay- lor, and Dr. Abernathy are such that finding time to put their lectures into writing became a difficult chore.

The reader will find that a number of writers deal with the question of class versus race. Some take the position that class interests predominate over those of race, and that racism has been used as a tool. Sam Proctor expounds the case for including the black middle class in the struggle against discrimination. Ralph Abernathy, despite his deep understanding of the motivations of other types of militants, does not change a lifelong stance of promoting justice through love and creative nonviolence.

The authors deal with both black pride and black suffering, and a balanced and sensitive interpretation of these elements is most difficult to achieve. Survival techniques were developed in a hostile world, but black pride existed throughout all the suffering. Cultural nationalist thought takes account of these elements: there is a search for a proud past, which sometimes is pursued back through the centuries to Africa, but which can also be discovered in the reexamination of Afro-American history. There is a rejection of everything white, including alliances with whites, since "white culture" is that of the European oppressor. The flavor of such thinking is well expressed in excerpts taken from term papers written by my students Audrey C. Arthur, Deborah Bankston, and Karen Predow. They are representative of the many black students who take strong separatist positions and who would deplore the seemingly "integrationist" approach of some of the authors. The continuing dialogue of separatism versus integration can be observed throughout the history of black thought. Hinds analyzes this dialogue in the concluding essay, criticizing those leaders who fail to base their programs on an analysis of history and rejecting cultural nationalism as a solution.

Whether the freedom of persons of African descent lies only in permanent physical and psychological separation from white people; whether it lies in a revolution of all the oppressed; or whether there are other alternatives, only the future can tell. An appreciation of the life and culture of black people is a prologue to our understanding of what the future holds.

A Note on Semantics

In the area of race, semantics becomes subject not only

to logic, to "accepted" usage (in the black and white worlds), but also to political interpretation. We had taped the original lectures and provided our authors with these as a working base. In revising their manuscripts, several changed the usage of the word "Negro" or "black," in either direction, for reasons of their own. My students and I have been capitalizing the word "black," but not "white," and some of the authors prefer this form. Herbert Aptheker provided me with a logical reason for this usage, but in many cases it is an emotional choice. Looking over recently published works of highly committed blacks (for example, articles published in *The Black Scholar* or Bobby Seale's recent book, *Seize the Time*), I note that the lower-case letter is used for "black." The editors of the widely read Yale symposium *Black Studies in the University* discuss this issue, stating:

> Because of the current debate concerning the proper descriptive terms for people of African ancestry in the Americas, be it black, Afro-American, or Negro, considerable uncertainty exists over correct usage and capitalization. In an arbitrary effort to create uniformity in this volume, the following editorial decisions were made: use of Negro conforms to the present convention, and Afro-American complies with the same rule. Black is capitalized only when it appears as part of a proper name.

I decided to follow this precedent, as far as possible, with one exception. The selections from the writings of black students at Douglass retain their own, deliberately chosen, usage.

Suggestions for Reading

The Selected Bibliography at the end of the book is a composite of readings recommended by various authors. Sources included at the end of some chapters give fuller references for works quoted in the text, but are not necessarily recommended to the reader.

2

IVAN VANSERTIMA

African Linguistic and Mythological Structures in the New World

I shall try to present in this essay an outline of the oral tradition Afro-Americans have inherited in the New World—a tradition very much alive in the way many Afro-Americans speak and in the way also many of them think; a tradition enshrined in the language and mythology of black folk; a tradition which, in spite of its many locations and variants, has a common root, a common ground in the linguistic and mythological structures of Africa. It is my intention to trace a number of threads back to those structures.

Enormous misconceptions have grown up in this country about the patterns of English that black people speak in this hemisphere and the patterns of myth to which many of them subscribe. I would like to set fire to these misconceptions and bring some light to bear, at least in the field of language and myth, on what in essence constitutes our inheritance from Africa and the way in which we have transformed and refashioned that inheritance under the peculiar sociological and psychological pressures of the New World.

Let us look, first of all, at the variants of English spoken by black communities in the Americas and the Caribbean. One would readily assume that these dialects of English, separated as they were by great distances in time and space, and developing as they did among the transplants of different African peoples, would have very little in common. In fact, barring surface differences in vocabulary, these variants of English exhibit a common deep-structure, which has been retained like a mark and stamp upon the psyche of the Afro-American, and which, at a certain level, unites Afro-Americans scattered throughout this hemisphere and the world.

I, for one, coming from the coastlands of Guyana in South America, have never met a Gullah Negro from South Carolina or the Georgia coast. A vast ocean lies between us which we have hardly crossed, my Gullah brother and I, since the days of the Middle Passage. Yet when I read Gullah in the folktales, so faithfully recorded by Ambrose Gonzalez, something turns on in me like a second ear, something reechoes the words and structures of that dialect within me like a submerged speaker and tongue. What, you may ask, is that something? What is really moving and playing, like a drummer in shadow, behind me?

There have been many answers to that question, most of them misleading. The myths that have sprung up in the Americas to explain the origin and characteristics of Black English are legion. These myths are rooted not only in profound prejudice against black people, but in a profound ignorance about Africa. I feel one must restate some of these myths and examine them against the facts of a more recent and objective scholarship in order to place Black English within its proper historical and cultural perspective.

Myths About Black English

It has been said that the slaves who came here from Africa came here speaking a savage gibberish. Slowly they began to acquire a civilized form of communication, but because of their intellectual inferiority or physiological differences they failed to acquire the language properly. Their thick lips and oversized tongues got into the way of the English and murdered it. As a result, a strangled substandard brand of English evolved. Even a writer like Ambrose Gonzalez, to whom we owe so much for the recording of the Gullah dialect, subscribed to this myth.

While admitting the extraordinary richness of the oral tradition, the wit and charm of the Gullahs' dialect, Gonzalez in his book *The Black Border* had this to say of the way they spoke:

> Slovenly and careless of speech, they seized upon the peasant English used by some of the early settlers . . . wrapped their clumsy tongues about it as well as they could and it issued through their flat noses and their thick lips as so workable a form of speech that it was gradually adopted by the other slaves . . . with characteristic laziness these Gullah negroes took short-cuts to the ears of their auditors, using as few words as possible, sometimes making one gender serve for three, one tense for several and totally disregarding singular and plural numbers. . . .

Knowing nothing of linguistics and therefore unable to appreciate the nature of the phenomena before him, although his ears were as sharp and accurate as a modern microphone and tape, Gonzalez made fun of the Gullah Negro.

I quote briefly from his glossary of Gullah published half a century ago.

> "Uh" is the dominant note upon which the speech of the Gullah is pitched. With "uh" he boastfully proclaims the pronoun "I." He greets his brethren as "budduh" or "buh," his sisters as "sistuh" or "tittuh." Sweet potatoes he roasts and eats as "tettuh." His father, mother, daughter are "Farruh," "murruh," "daa'tuh"; his ever is "ebbuh," his never is "nebbuh," forever "fuhrebbuh"; his answer is "ansuh," his master is "mastuh," his pastor is "pastuh" (and so is his pasture). His either is "edduh," his neither is "needuh." If in daylight he falls asleep in an open place, the vulture's wing that hovers over him will cast a "shadduh." . . . Mother is "mauma," master is "massuh" . . . the white man is "buckruh" and the Negro is "nigguh." His feather is "fedduh," his weather is "wedduh," his measure is "medjuh," his pleasure is "pledjuh." And if, in pleasantry or wrath, he cries out upon a passing compatriot, he scornfully apostrophizes him "Yuh Gullah nigguh!"

To an ear like that of Gonzalez it seemed as though these Africans had come out of the House of Babel itself. The Europeans who first penetrated Africa came across countless tribes speaking what seemed to them countless unrelated tongues. There was no rhyme or reason, they thought, to their mutually unintelligible patter, no connecting structural framework or design. The truth was, however, that Africa, like Europe, had about three grand linguistic designs. Almost all the languages of Africa can be placed into three main families. These are the Sudanic, the Bantu, and the Hamitic.

African Language Families

Blacks of the American hemisphere come almost wholly from the first two families. The Sudanic family dominates a considerable part of the West African coast and embraces such languages as Twi, Ewe, Yoruba, Wolof, Temne, Mende, Mandingo, Ibo, Nupe, Efik, Mossi, Jukun, and Kanuri. Some

Afro-Americans come from the Lower Congo, which is Bantu-speaking—the Bantu family of languages accounting for a great part of East and Central Africa. (There are, of course, considerable differences between the East and West African languages, between the Sudanic and Bantu families, but also important resemblances.) The point I want to make here is that what appeared to the European to be bewildering differences among the speech of the tribes of the West Coast (the focal area of the slave trade) were in reality local variations of a deep-lying structural similarity. Under the surface of differences there existed certain basic patterns, patterns which were to assert themselves like engineering blocks and architectural blueprints when it became necessary for the slaves to build a bridge of communication between the European and African tongues.

Black English and White American Dialects

It has been said that the forms of English spoken by black people in America owe nothing to Africa at all, that in fact Black forms of English are no different from dialects of English spoken by lower-class white groups, and that all the non-standard elements in Black English can be traced to an earlier English used and dropped by American settlers or still partly in vogue among lower-class American whites. Strangely enough, this theory was advanced in America by linguists who thought they were doing the blacks a great favor. They were putting forward this theory of the non-difference between white and black dialects of America to prove that, where language was concerned, the blacks were no different from the whites. This was their misguided but well-intentioned attempt to establish equality among the races. They believed that this could only be done by denying diversity among the cultural subgroups of America, as if the very existence of difference in the use of English by blacks indicated their inferiority, and only the denial of that difference could establish their claim to equality with the users of standard English. Integration of the black and white elements of America meant for them the standardization and uniformity of peoples, rather than the coexistence of diverse but equally valid culture-groups. They sought to negate ethnic and cultural plurality, which is America's greatest heritage.

They found support for their theory by concentrating largely on the vocabulary of black and white dialects. As I shall show, quite a number of words in American speech that we have come to take for granted as being of English derivation or indigenous Americanese are, in fact, of African origin. But even forgetting these words, since it is true that the main vocabulary of American blacks is non-African, the crucial African element to watch is not vocabulary at all, but a grammatical base, a syntactical structure. It is the African structure underlying the top layer of Anglo-Saxon words which accounts for the peculiar combinations, patterns, and transformations in the speech of peoples as far apart as the Guyanese of South America, the Gambians of West Africa, and the Gullahs of Georgia.

Cultural Deprivation Myth

The latest myth about Black English—as late as the 1960s—is that its use or retention beyond a certain age indicates arrested development. This myth blames the failure of a great number of blacks to gain a mastery of Standard English on some sort of cultural deprivation or social deficit. It sees the problems of learning and mastering Standard English as related to a whole range of social problems— the disintegration or lack of black family structure, poor motivation, underdeveloped linguistic and cognitive abilities, and the alleged inability of the black to delay gratification. In other words, we have come to that sorry pass when certain sociologists and linguists are beginning to look upon the speaking of non-Standard English as a pathological phenomenon, as an illness to be cured rather than as a ground of systematic differences to be examined in historical perspective.

17

History of Black English

Let us therefore look briefly now at the history of Black English. When and where did it originate? How did it come to the American hemisphere? Why are its variants so similar in structure, although they are dispersed over vast areas and have developed completely out of touch with each other? What constitutes the main ground of distinction between its grammatical features and those of Standard English?

I mentioned earlier that there were hundreds of languages along the West Coast of Africa, but that they fell into one or two families. The major differences between them, therefore, were lexical (that is, differences in the words they used). They possessed, however, a number of similar phonological (sound) and syntactical (grammar) systems. When, therefore, people from various African tribes and regions came into contact, they would, without any significant shift in basic phonological and syntactic structures, make use of the words from one or the other languages in order to communicate. The Africans devised bridge-languages to carry them across considerable areas of territory. This kind of bridging process leads to what linguists call "pidgin languages"—pidginization is a process that occurs when a common language is needed for contact and trade.

The Portuguese were the first Europeans to trade with Africa. These Portuguese seagoing traders would have had to acquire a new language at each port-of-call, which was an impossible task. The Africans solved the problem for them by absorbing Portuguese words, casting them into African phonological and syntactical molds, reworking the language, and regularizing it anew to suit themselves. Black Portuguese thus became the world's first trade language. In fact it became the first worldwide lingua franca. It was so effective as a means of communication, utilizing a minimum number of linguistic rules to convey a given message, that it was used also in China, India, and Japan.

It came to the New World in the early sixteenth century,

when African workers arrived in Spanish and Portuguese colonies. It flourished on both sides of the Atlantic for two centuries, and then the Dutch ousted the Portuguese and Black Dutch became the next major trade language of the world. It is interesting to note that white South Africans today speak a kind of Black Dutch, although they would most vigorously deny it. Black Dutch was a major element in the development of Afrikaans.

Black French came along in the same way, as the French moved into the world trade market on a large scale. Today Black French is spoken in all the French islands of the Caribbean. The Black French of Haiti and that of Mauritius are remarkably alike, although they exist half a world apart and although they have never been in contact. Evidence like this from other black dialects makes it very clear that black linguistic forms in the New World have substantial relationships to African linguistic history and development.

Black English emerged in the seventeenth century, when the English gained power in the Atlantic and moved into Africa, establishing a fort on the Gold Coast. Black English, however, did not come about merely through the collection of English and African languages. The earlier bridge-languages the Africans developed—Black Dutch, Black French, and especially Black Portuguese—had a lot to do with its emergence. By the end of the eighteenth century Black English was established at a number of points along the West African Coast, from Gambia to Biafra.

Black English in the New World

It was brought to the United States direct from Africa or via Jamaica (the main way station for slave transportation from Africa to the New World), either by the original slaves or by those who followed in the next three and a half centuries. The evidence seems to suggest that Black English did not originate here in isolated pockets. The similarities between its variants are so striking as to make it unlikely that they emerged as independent developments. Black Eng-

19

lish originated largely in Africa rather than in the New World. Some Africans already knew this English when they came here, and the common colonial policy of mixing slaves of various tribal origins so that they could not converse and conspire with their compatriots in their own native tongues forced them to fall back on a common lingua franca—BLACK ENGLISH—for use on the plantations of America and the British Caribbean.

Black English, of course, has undergone many changes, more here in America (where the physical and cultural presence of whites has been massive) than in the Caribbean (where the dominant physical presence is black). Its most distinct form in America, comparable with Caribbean Black English, is along the coastal areas of Georgia and South Carolina in the form of Gullah. It is only natural that over the centuries its vocabulary has taken in more and more Anglo-Saxon words and jettisoned more and more African words. But, despite the eroding of Black English in this country, several African features are still present. I would like to touch on some of those features.

Some Characteristics of Black English

There is the absence of gender (distinction between "he," "she," and "it") in some Black dialects. In Jamaica, for example, when I say *him prappa fraish,* I may be referring to a man or a woman. Likewise, in the Gullah speech, when I say " 'im" or "he," I can mean "he" as well as "she" or "it"; as in the Tar-Baby story, "Brer Rabbit keep on axing *'im,* en de Tar-Baby *she* keep on saying nothin'."

This absence of gender distinction is a feature of Bantu languages. Another feature of Bantu which appears in Black dialects is the absence of the connecting link between subject and predicate in certain constructions. For example, we have "he is black" in Standard English, but "he black" in Black English; "Who is he?" in Standard, "Who he?" in Black.

Then there is the distinction between second person singular (*you*) and second person plural (*yuna*) in Gullah that you find in the Krio language of Sierra Leone. In the Caribbean and in the United States the equivalent of this is "you" for singular and "you-all" or "y'all" (or "allya" in the Caribbean) for plural.

There is no obligatory marker in Black English dialects for the plural ("one cent," "ten cent"), no obligatory marker for the possessive ("teacher-book" for "teacher's book"), no obligatory marker for the third person singular of verbs ("he work here" for "he works here"). These omissions are not just due to sloppiness or mere simplification. They have correspondences with grammatical features in a number of African languages. The absence of the phoneme *th*, for example, in Black dialect is matched by a corresponding absence of that sound in African languages.

English is not a tone language, but African influence has introduced intonational ranges to mark differences in meaning. For example, the man from the Caribbean can be saying that something is possible or impossible according to the tone he uses for the word "can": "I can do it" (positive—short *a*), "I caan do it" (negative—prolonged stress on the *a* with falling pitch of the voice).

Another African feature of Black English is the use of specific phrases to announce beginnings of sentences—for example, "dig," "look here." The word *dega* has similar use in Wolof; *de* and *eh,* in Swahili.

There are other, more technical distinctions also, but I would like to deal with what is considered to be the most prevalent aspect of African grammatical features in Black English. That is the peculiarities of the verb system. Verbs in West African languages—and I would say the same is true of Bantu languages in East Africa—seem to focus more on what we may call the "mode of action" rather than on "the time of action." African verbs are best thought of in terms of their aspect, that is, in terms of whether the action they indicate is habitual or completed or conditional or obligatory, and so forth, rather than whether it is in the past, present, or future. Now don't misunderstand this simplification, for some people have got the funny idea into their heads that the Africans do not have any concept of time. The concept of time among the Bantu, in fact, is perhaps the most complex and profound time concept in any culture. What one is speaking about here is not an absence of time concepts, but a shift of focus onto other features of the action rather than a primary concern about the time of the action. This feature has left its mark upon Black English.

Thus, in the sentence "Dat man, he be fishing" we are in the presence of a construction that has no equivalent in the English verb system. It does not mean the same thing as "Dat man fishing" or "Dat man, he fishing." It is not indicating a man in the act of fishing at a particular point of time, but is speaking of a man who professionally or habitually fishes. It describes an action along a continuum of time. If the "be" is deleted in this sentence, then it reverts to the familiar and simple present tense.

African Words in American English

There are other aspects of the verb that could be examined, but let us look at lexical Africanisms, that is, African words that have found their way into Black English—indeed, words that have penetrated even into White English. Surface vocabulary is not as important as deep-structure grammar, but it is amazing to learn how many popular Americanisms which we take for granted are of African origin.

I will mention just a few in passing from the language of Wolof: "O.K." from the Wolof *waw kay* ("all right," "certainly"); "dig" from the verb *dega* ("to understand"); "sock," as in the sexual exhortation "sock it to me, baby," from a similar-sounding verb in Wolof, meaning "to beat with a pestle"; "jam" in "jam-session" from the old slave dances and assemblies, *jaam* being the Wolof word for slave; "guy" for person, again from Wolof, and also "cat" with the same connotation (in the combination "hep-cat," or "hippi-cat," for someone who is with it, who is seeing and feeling it like it is, we have the Wolof correspondence *hipi-cat*, meaning "a person who has opened his eyes"); also, "bug," as in "jitterbug" or "book-bug," meaning a person dead keen on something, has a similar-sounding form in the Wolof language that means "to desire, to like exceedingly."

Black English, said its detractors, was a criminal and delinquent form of English in that it strangled the King's English. In fact, today it is giving a new lease on life to English, which has begun to dry up at its source. In the ghettos of America the rich oral tradition of the blacks is continually throwing up combinations that hit one right between the eyes and catch fire immediately on everyone's lips.

It is not only in the spontaneous speech of the folk, but in the conscious art of black writers from America, Africa, and the Caribbean that forms of Black English are emerging, giving to Standard English a new freshness and vigor, magic and ebullience. Amos Tutuola of Nigeria, for example, writes a Black English not unlike, in parts, the creolized English Africans took with them to the New World several centuries ago. Using this language, which sounds like the speaking voice on the page, he writes one of the most remarkable epics of modern times, comparable in its archetypal depth and visionary quality to the *Iliad,* the *Epic of Gilgamesh,* and the *Aeneid.* Now that the centuries of a black oral tradition are finding expression in a written literature, that literature is beginning to explode confines imposed upon it by the fossilized formulas and structures of "non-oral" peoples.

FOLK MYTH

If, in the field of language, speculations as to the nature and depth of African influence upon New World dialects have been biased and confused, in the field of the folk myth they have been no less so. Since European and Asian folktales were published long before African tales appeared in print (the first tale to be published from sub-Saharan Africa appearing in 1828), it was assumed that any tale found in the African oral tradition which bore a structural resemblance or even surface resemblances to a European or Asian folktale had its origin in Europe or Asia and had diffused to Africa. Early scholars like Theodore Benfey came to the conclusion that folklore originated in India and spread from there to the rest of the world. Others, contending that "culture runs downhill," put forward the theory that Africans "recognizing the superiority of stories from more 'advanced' societies than their own" borrowed and appropriated them.

Conclusions based on the latest research into the folktale are equally absurd. Daniel J. Crowley, in a recent essay, "African Folktales in Afro-America," reports on efforts being made to trace the origin of the world's folktales. An enormous Tale Type Index has been devised, which numbers and documents the occurrences of every version of every tale type whenever it has been reported; and a Motif Index, which documents the motifs of tales, has also been set up. For these purposes a *tale type* may be defined as the structure or plot or dramatic outline of a story, and the *motifs* as the characters, objects, or incidents therein. The type is a constant— that is, a fairly fixed dramatic structure or configuration of events; the motif is a variable, a constantly changing surface feature, with different characters, objects, and incidents being employed in different versions or variants of the same tale type. It is assumed by scholars using the Index that a single tale type has a single point of origin. The possibility of two culture areas replicating independently the same tale type is a coincidence too remote for them to consider. Motifs, however—the free elements within the tale nucleus or type —are seen to be both repeatable and replaceable. It is appreciated that considerable motif replacements go on within the type as it diffuses to other places and other cultures. Take the method of divining a thief. Divination in a European culture may be by "sitting on a Bible" or "cutting the cards." This feature in a tale traveling to Africa may be replaced by "reading the bones," tapping a magic drum, or looking at images in a pool of water.

At present the Tale Type Index has validity only for Euro-Asian cultures. It cannot be extended to deal with Central

Africa, the North American Indian, or Oceania, since each of these major culture areas would need an index based strictly on its own cultural traditions. Yet, in spite of this admitted limitation and weakness, scholars are using the Index to arrive at conclusions as racially myopic as ever.

For the purposes of illustration, let us look at the Robber-Bridegroom tale type. This type may be outlined as follows: (a) a girl obstinately refuses all suitors; (b) she is wooed by an animal in human form and at once accepts him; (c) she is warned (usually by a brother) and disregards the warning; (d) she is about to be killed and eaten, but is saved by the brother whose advice she disregarded.

In medieval European folklore the Robber-Bridegroom usually takes the form of a wizard, while in African folk traditions he is an animal. But the structural type is the same. What the type expresses, I believe, is the primal fear of a virginal innocence within the human family being ambushed and despoiled by masked terrors in nature. Such a similarly structured response, in terms of myth, could have sprung up, I contend, quite independently in any culture. Using the Index with its built-in assumptions about a single point of origin for a tale type, and having earlier literary evidence of the type's existence in Europe, the researcher jumps to the conclusion that the type had its origin in Europe and diffused to Africa. This is not to deny that a number of European and Asian folktales have traveled to Africa and reappeared in traditional African dress, but the traffic in tales has certainly not been one-way. Aesop's fables, which diffused widely across Europe, came originally from Africa. Luqmān, the Arab fabulist, spoken of with approval by Muhammad in the twenty-first chapter of the Koran, is said to have been an Ethiopian—that is, a Negro—slave. His stories were passed on to Greece, where he was known as Aithiops, and this was taken to be his name and turned into Aesop.

Working without a knowledge of African archetypes or the indigenous prototypes of African folktales, Western scholars have been all too eager to dismiss African originality and to see striking parallels and correspondences with Euro-Asian models as clear evidence of borrowing from Europe or Asia. But at the level of the myth there are bound to be, however culture-specific the particulars, certain personae and primal events of the human psyche projected onto the stage of the tale in similar dramatic combinations.

What I find even more suspect and shallow are the conclusions arrived at by recent researchers with respect to African retentions in New World folk mythology. On the basis of a study of folk motifs they seek to prove that African influence on the folk myths of Afro-Americans is insignificant. What was happening a decade ago in linguistics is now happening in the field of folklore. In the same way as the linguists sought to show that European elements had completely wiped out the African elements in New World dialects —putting up a persuasive case by shifting focus from grammatical patterns to surface vocabulary—these folklorists are shifting focus from mythological structures to surface features of objects and incidents (motifs) to show that very little that is identifiably African survives in Afro-American folktales.

The following quotation from Daniel Crowley's essay is revealing. (The bracketed insertion and italics in the quote are mine.)

> Black Americans have taken about one-quarter of their tales from British and/or white American sources, which because of overlap together provide some 94 separate motifs or 41 per cent of the total motifs told by black Americans. Only one single black American motif (B210-I—Person frightened by animal successively replying to his remarks) is reported in Clarke's Guinea coast study [Clarke incidentally has documented 793 motifs as occurring on the Guinea coast of Africa, of which only 52 he claims are to be found in the Caribbean Index]. . . . *Thus, with only 9 per cent of Caribbean motifs traceable to Africa and with only one proven motif known among black Americans, ancestry, whether biological or cultural, does not seem to be . . . significant . . . in the transmission of Tales.*

On the basis of a motif count Daniel Crowley dismisses African "cultural ancestry" as a "significant" factor in the folk mythology of Afro-Americans. The conclusion not only contradicts his own dictum that the motif is a doubtful criterion, "notoriously untrustworthy," but flies in the face of the most obvious reasoning and even the most cursory examination of the facts. A motif count of zero would have established nothing about the significance of African influence, for motifs, let it be repeated, are mere surface manifestations of content. Even such major motifs as the dramatis personae change when they travel from one continent to another. The East African or Bantu *Sungura* (Hare) becomes the Brer Rabbit of North America (there are no rabbits in Africa). The land-tortoise of Africa is a water-tortoise (Brer Tarrypin) in America. In the Caribbean the Annancy stories are peopled by creatures who do not feature in the African prototypes and are indigenous to the Caribbean: John-Crow, Chicken-Hawk, Sea-Gaulin, Candle-Fly, Crab, and Tarpon. The original inspiration of these tales in the mythological imagination and architecture of fantasy in Africa cannot be dismissed simply because the surface features that appear (objects, creatures, incidents) in a new geographical and cultural environment give the traditional bones of the tale a new fleshing. Once again, it is like the words of the New World spun from our tongues to the tune of an ancestral grammar. The relevant questions, therefore, as I see it, are these: What are those African archetypes that have survived and persisted in the New World? What new function do they serve, and in what new forms and shapes (motifs) are these structures (tale types) expressed in Afro-America?

African Archetypes in the New World

It is interesting to note that animals dominate the folk archetypes of Africa. It is suggested that this is so because Africans humanize animals; they conceive of them as human beings in disguise, either human spirits moving in

beasts after death or human witches or shamans assuming
the forms of the beasts in some magical metamorphosis.
While such beliefs may indeed be found among African peoples, it is absurd to conclude, as some anthropologists do, that
the African is incapable of making a distinction between
the animal and the human. Alice Werner, in an early twentieth century study of the African and Caribbean folktale,
remarks on the human feature one constantly finds in Bantu
folklore.

> The hare and the elephant hire themselves out to hoe a
> man's garden. The swallow invites the cock to dinner
> and his wife prepares the food in the usual native hut
> with the fireplace in the middle and the *nsanja* staging
> over it. The hare's wife goes to the river to draw water
> and is caught by a crocodile. The tortoise carries its
> complaint to the village elders assembled in the smithy.

Because of these human characteristics, Miss Werner assumes that the African so literally takes the animal as a
human that he lacks the capacity to visualize the animal in
the abstract—that is, as a symbol for concrete aspects of the
human condition. Stereotyping the "native mind" as one of
a childlike and naively literal cast, Miss Werner upbraids M.
Henri Junod, author of *Songs and Tales of the Ronga,* for
attributing a subtler purpose to the African's use of his
animal myth-material.

> M. Junod overrates the conscious artistic purpose in the
> narrators of these tales. The native mind is quite ready
> to assume that animals think and act in much the same
> way as human beings. This attitude makes it easy to
> forget the outward distinctions when they appear as ac-
> tors on a stage.

Once again we see how the best scholarship in the field
(Miss Werner's work is commendable for its thoroughness
and scope and its wealth of comparative data) is overlaid by
traditional racial prejudices and preconceptions.

An analysis in depth of the main elements in African folktales will show that animals are involved in a shadow-drama

of the human world. They are dream figures through which personality traits, values, or power relations of groups—commoner and king, slave and master, the weak and the strong, the powerful and the suppressed—may be reflected in a dreaming drama of the social world, within which dream and drama the figures are invested with a fluidity and metamorphic quality denied them in the more rigidly structured social world, so that they often seem to reverse and overturn their given social role or condition. It is this capacity of the dream figure (animal archetype) to overleap and overturn an oppressive social condition that makes the personae of the tales (Annancy, Rabbit, Tortoise, etc.) take on a heroic cast and revolutionary function.

This role reversal and revolutionary function of certain African folk heroes account for their enormous popular appeal among the slave communities of the New World. Annancy, for example, the Spider Deity of the West Africans, divine trickster and shaman, plays the remarkable role of the outlaw and con man in Caribbean society. He does not subscribe to the laws and moral values of that society. Secretive, elusive, cunning, deceptive, sometimes cruel and treacherous, he is the Transcendent Criminal, avoiding through his legendary agility of wit the onerous and unfair burdens imposed upon his fellows, nearly always one step ahead of Brother Lion or Brother Tiger, the predatory lords and overseers of the jungle. In one tale he even tricks Brother Death, though he sacrifices a generation of his progeny in the contest.

The psychological value of Annancy's role in the Caribbean slave society has not escaped all investigators, though they have been led into certain conclusions that are inconsistent with a full appreciation of Annancy's real function and meaning. Rex Nettleford, for example, in an introductory essay to *Jamaican Song and Story,* makes the following observations:

> In Jamaica this descendant of the West African semi-deity seems to take on special significance in a society which has its roots in a system of slavery—a system

> which pitted the weak against the strong in daily confrontations. . . . It is as though every slave strove to be Annancy and he who achieved the Spider-form became a kind of hero. . . . This picaresque character misses no chance for chicanery . . . as though he lives in a world that offers him no other chance for survival . . . to cope with an unstraight and crooked world one needs unstraight and crooked paths.

It would seem clear from this passage that Nettleford understands the profound relationship between Annancy's ACT and the slave's DREAM.

Yet, in the very same passage, he commits the error of associating, in a very literal way, Annancy's characteristics with features of the Jamaican character.

> Annancy . . . expresses much of the Jamaican spirit in his ostentatious professions of love, in his wrong-and-strong, brave-but-cowardly professions of bluff, in his love for leisure and corresponding dislike for work, in his lovable rascality. . . .

Here are echoes of the slaveowner's slander of the naturally resentful and reluctant slave: "dislike for work," "love for leisure," "cowardly," "lovable rascality." This patronizing attitude is unworthy of such an astute critic as Nettleford. The "black" character of Annancy does not represent the character of Jamaicans in that sense at all. Jamaican children, brought up within a puritan ethic, utter an oath of purification—*Jack Mandora me no choose none*—when they narrate Annancy stories, the oath being a plea to the doorman at heaven's door to absolve them of responsibility for Annancy's wickedness. What we are really face to face with in Annancy is what I would call a black innocence. He is loved and lovable because his "evil" liberates rather than oppresses. He assumes aspects of evil in order to elude and conquer a condition of evil.

In this respect one is reminded of a West African deity, Legba, who seems to fuse with the configuration of Annancy in the Caribbean. Like Annancy he is a divine trickster, an impish rogue, but free of the fiendish malevolence that characterizes satanic beings in Christian cosmology. John Mbiti, in his *African Religions and Philosophy*, points out:

> The Devil is not the terror he is in European folk-lore. He is a powerful trickster who often competes successfully with God. There is a strong suspicion that the devil is an extension of the story-makers while God is the supposedly impregnable white masters, who are nevertheless defeated by the Negroes. . . . So different is this tricksterlike creature from Satan as generally conceived, indeed, that he is almost a different being. To account for the difference we turn again to that character in Dahomean-Yoruba mythology, the Divine Trickster and the god of accident known as Legba, the deity who wields his great power because of his ability to outwit his fellow gods. . . .

Legba "opened the gates" for the other gods. Annancy opened the gates of the slave plantation through feats of wit that metamorphosed the bound and impotent slave into a free and triumphant animal. These mental acrobatics (the wiles of Annancy) are a parallel phenomenon to the physical acrobatics of the *Limbo,* a Caribbean dance in which the symbolic freeing of the slave is achieved by what is almost tantamount to a metamorphosis of the body.

In this dance a bar or pole is set up against the advancing body of the dancer. It cramps his movement; it fences his horizon. The dancer must by some feat of unlimbing evade that obstruction. He cannot leap over it, for this would not be in keeping with the meaning of the dance, the bar representing a reduced physical and psychological space, being progressively lowered until, if one were to visualize it over the whole scale of the dance, from its highest to its lowest points of suspension, it would be seen to simulate the rungs of a prison cell. In order to issue under and through this bar or fence, the *Limbo* dancer must so dwarf and contort and fluidify his body as to bring his rigid bundle of limbs ultimately into line with the lowly stature of his knees. Annancy leaped over the bars of the slave plantation through tricks and stratagems and magical metamorphoses of the mind; the *Limbo* dancer sought escape under the bars through a corresponding trick of the limbs, metamorphosis of the body.

Annancy, of course, has a number of other functions in West Africa. He is the keeper of the gourds of wisdom in one tale; he is the spinner of the web of heaven in another. What underlies this complexity of forms and roles are just those features of the African archetype that serve the most crucial psychological function in the Caribbean situation. The Annancy folktales in Jamaica have even been used to preserve certain historical events (among the Maroons, for example) in a disguised and symbolic form.

What has seldom been remarked upon is the fact that West African archetypes, like Annancy, are almost the exclusive inheritance of the Caribbean and the Guyanas, whereas East African or Bantu archetypes feature largely in the tales of the American South. This is accounted for by the fact that the blacks of this hemisphere did not come, as is still popularly believed, wholly or mainly from West Africa. The Guinea coast was just the transit center for slaves. Most African slaves of the American South were from the Lower Congo, whose people were largely in the Bantu culture complex. There is evidence, too, that during the first quarter of the nineteenth century slaves were frequently imported from Mozambique and other parts of the eastern coast. "Mombasas" (Kenyans) are known to have been mentioned by the Negro slaves in Cuba, and many cargoes of slaves were smuggled from Havana into the southern states after the import trade was declared illegal.

This partly explains why the Bantu Hare (Brer Rabbit in the Uncle Remus tales) and Tortoise should be such prominent figures in American Negro folklore.

Observe closely the qualities of Hare (Rabbit). He occupies a disadvantageous position in the animal world. Extremely vulnerable, without a heavy hide, claws, beak, or sting, his fragility is counterbalanced by an extraordinary sensitivity (huge antennae for ears) and a lightning nimbleness (fleetness of foot). Though he may seem, therefore, an easy prey to the larger animals, the potential for outmaneuvering them belies his apparent fragility. In the body and spirit of Hare, therefore, is crystallized a subtle and delicate radar for scanning the potential peril (which he averts) and the potential possibility (which he exploits) in a given situation —a situation usually (in those tales most native to the tradition) of menace from the Mighty. A typical tale told by Uncle Remus is that of Brer Rabbit and Brer Lion, in which Rabbit is invited to offer up his life for Lion's supper and is so adept in his survival strategy that Lion dies wrestling with his own fearful shadow.

The tortoise is another symbol of the underdog in Bantu mythology. In fact he is more popular than the hare in some parts of East Africa. His main virtue is his capacity to endure, for he can live longer without food than any other animal. He moves with a painstaking slowness, but with the sureness of the sun in motion across the streets of the world, and this impresses itself upon the Bantu mind as the unrelenting and invincible doggedness of an elemental force. The brooding silence and secrecy of the tortoise also invest him with a suggestion of craft and cunning and mystery. He hides his innards under a shell in the way the black had to hide his true face and feelings in the Americas under shells and veils and masks of deception in order to carry and conceal the horror at the heart of his daily life.

Some interesting tales are told of Tortoise. Perhaps the best known is that of the Great Race, but to me the most significant is the tale of the Famine, of which there are innumerable versions. During the Famine the animals searching for food come across a tree, previously unknown, full of ripe fruit. They send messenger after messenger to the owner of the tree to ask its name. The name of the tree has a mystical significance (the fruit cannot be picked or made to fall without its precise utterance), but the messengers all forget it. Only the tortoise remembers, and he lifts the curse of hunger from the land by felling the fruit. But though he is the only one in the jungle who can relate himself back to a total

33

awareness of origins (the name of the tree being the name of the tribal ancestress), the other animals turn on him and refuse him a share of the fruit. The tortoise in some versions is smashed to pieces and is put together by the ants. On regaining his pristine strength he uproots the tree, with all the animals eating their fill in its branches, and they perish in the Fall.

The psychological value of this tale to Afro-Americans hardly needs to be underscored. The slave in the Americas may identify the smashing of the tortoise to pieces with his own dismemberment and fragmentation, the denial of its due share in the fruits of life with his own social deprivation, and its Samsonian uprootment of the Tree on the recovery of its strength as a prophetic indication of his ultimate release in a cataclysmic act of vengeance and revolt.

In some strange way what has survived of Africa in the Americas may be important not only to a discovery of what lies behind the Afro-American but also to a rediscovery of certain areas of the African himself. After the Mogul invasion of China in the thirteenth century so much of Chinese culture became fragmented and dispersed that it was necessary to look to Japan for many of the lost outlines of Chinese civilization. Such a living museum of African structural elements, a complement of both the Eastern and Western halves of that continent, resides in the oral tradition, the folk language and folk myth of Afro-America.

SOURCES

CROWLEY, DANIEL, "African Folktales in Afro-America," in John S. Szwed, ed., *Black America*. New York, Basic Books, Inc., 1970.

GONZALEZ, AMBROSE, *The Black Border: Gullah Stories of the Carolina Coast*, 1922. Reprinted: Columbia, S.C., The State Printing Company, 1964.

HARRIS, JOEL CHANDLER, *Nights with Uncle Remus; Myths and Legends*. Boston, Houghton Mifflin Company, 1911.

JEKYLL, WALTER, ed., *Jamaican Song and Story*. New York, Dover Publications, Inc., 1966.

MBITI, JOHN S., *African Religions and Philosophy*. New York, Frederick A. Praeger, Inc., 1969.

SHERLOCK, PHILIP, *Annancy, the Spider-Man*. New York, The Macmillan Company, 1962.

TAYLOR, ORLANDO, "Historical Development of Black English and Implications for American Education." Washington, D.C., Center for Applied Linguistics, Presented as paper, Ohio University, July 15, 1969.

WERNER, ALICE, *Myths and Legends of the Bantu*. London, Frank Cass and Company, Ltd., 1968.

3

GEOFFREY HENDRICKS

African Art

The traditions of African art below the Sahara span several thousand years and are as relevant to the black American as European art, from classical Greece to Picasso, is to the white American. In school one learns of the greatness of Michelangelo, but what does the student learn about the greatness of Ife sculpture? Even in Harlem's schools, are these traditions part of the standard curriculum? Perhaps especially not there. Such is our racism and ignorance. It is time the situation changed.

Art Is Vital in African Life

Life flows. Man is born, grows to sexual maturity, reproduces, dies. He depends on the land and vegetation and on the animal world for his existence, for food and shelter. He must interact with his fellow man as part of a family, and of a larger group. The farmer plants, cultivates, and harvests his crops in seasonal rotation. The animal world has the same cycle of birth, reproduction, and death as man, and the hunter counts on its continuity. These rhythms are basic to life and have been celebrated in the religion, rites, and rituals of the African from ancient times. Art was a vital part of this celebration and was knit tightly into the whole fabric of African tradition and life.

The sculptor was in touch with spirit forces within himself and in nature. When a tree was cut down to provide wood for a carving, the spirit of the tree was respected, and augmented the power of the image carved from the wood. The present-day white American levels forests for paper to print advertising to sell the population objects they neither want nor need—both paper and object then being tossed away to pollute the environment.

Such African men were not off tinkering with spaceships to "conquer" distant planets, nor making machines to manufacture artificial foods. They felt the forces of things growing in the earth and the changes going on in their own bodies, and they structured dances and ritual to guide and encourage these forces. An enemy was tangible—a drought, a plague, or a person from another area, dealt with directly in combat, or through magic—not an abstraction like Communism. An enemy might be killed and his vital force captured and directly incorporated. Cannibalism has existed in parts of Africa, as elsewhere. But though its Christian counterpart, the eucharist—which imparts Jesus' power through the token wine and wafer—seems more "civilized" to some, be-

37

ing more symbolic, the civilization which to a large extent embraces this form of worship is also capable of other abstractions: commercialism, genocide, and massive tampering with the natural order and its processes. Man's savagery and irresponsibility, it seems, increase in proportion to the decrease in personal connection—to places and to other human beings. Who winces at a term like "overkill," after all? Those who do are put down as malcontent neurotics. One does not experience the departing life force of ten thousand individuals when a bomb is dropped, only the energy of the bomb exploding. Connection, direct experience, and personal responsibility fall away, leaving abstraction and empty values. Has man in America lost touch with the spirit forces driving nature? He has a lot to learn from the art, ritual, and religion of African tradition.

A story from the Kalahari Desert, told by Laurens Van der Post in *Patterns of Renewal,* dramatizes this loss of connection. A Bushman had a wife whom he had caught when she came down from the stars, and all went well between them till he looked into the forbidden basket she brought with her. Seeing nothing in it, he laughed at her, and so, sorrowfully, she left him and returned to her home in the stars. It was not so much that the man had looked into the basket, explained the teller of the tale; the shameful thing was his inability to see all the beautiful things she had brought with her, for these were the very intangibles—the vibrant, intuitive forces—that make up the living ground from which the tradition of African art springs; from which modern, "rational," Western man has allowed himself to be divided.

History and Continuity

To the tradition-conscious cultures of Africa, continuity was of the utmost importance and tantamount to survival. The spirits of dead ancestors lived on in carved figures. Man was the custodian of forces from the past, and it was his duty to relay them, intact, to future generations. The very oral nature of the teachings kept them vital. All matters of importance were kept alive in memory and ceremonially transmitted, not stored away in volumes and forgotten.

An example of the phenomenal extent and precision of such oral records is seen through the work of Emil Torday, who recorded the telling of Bushongo (Bakuba) history early in this century. The major events in the reigns of all one hundred and twenty-four *Nyimi,* or kings—a time span of well over a thousand years—were recounted, and the historical accuracy of the account was corroborated by the dates of two natural phenomena: a total eclipse of the sun described in the reign of the ninety-eighth *Nyimi,* which occurred on March 30, 1680, directly over the Republic of the Congo (Kinshasa), and, in another reign, the passage of a comet over the area in 1863.

Oral history places the arrival of the Bushongo people at their present location in the Congo around the sixth century A.D. Sculpture of the Bushongo exists from the beginning of the seventeenth century, when Shamba Bolongongo, the ninety-third *Nyimi,* ruled during a period of cultural development and peace. He himself, a philosopher-king with a strong humane sense, is reputed to be the one to have instituted a tradition of royal portrait statues. There are extant statues of nineteen *Nyimi,* including Shamba, and each shows the ruler sitting cross-legged, with objects symbolizing accomplishments of his particular reign. Thus the history of African peoples is reflected in their art.

Early Art and Architecture

It is becoming increasingly clear that black Africa has a great and rich past. Considerable archaeological work carried out in Nigeria, for example, has uncovered cultures dating from the distant past. The oldest so far discovered comes from Nok, located in northern Nigeria, and goes back to the fifth century B.C. Excavations over a wide area have brought to light many terra-cotta heads, some life-sized; fragments of whole figures, and animals. Here was a thriving culture contemporaneous with that of the ancient Greeks and Etruscans.

About the thirteenth century A.D., or earlier, the Ife in southwestern Nigeria were producing portrait heads in both bronze and terra-cotta, modeled with strong sensitivity to the planes of the face, and more lifelike than we find elsewhere in Africa. Often these represented the *Oni,* or ruler. Some are covered with a linear vertical scarification that follows and accentuates the facial contours. The technique of bronze casting itself was carried to great heights. Europeans, coming across these pieces, found them so extraordinary that they wanted them to be of European origin, coming from the Mediterranean, perhaps Greece, or at least Egypt; but the work is black African.

Benin art follows that of the Ife, and like Ife art is a court art under the control of, and glorifying, the *Oba,* or king-god. Bronze casting is again the major medium, and thousands of plaques in high relief, as well as many heads, figures, figure groups, and animals such as leopards and birds were made to decorate the palace and city. Bronze casting was learned from the Ife and brought to Benin during the reign of the *Oba* Oguola around the thirteenth century by Ighe-igha, who came to occupy the position of a patron saint to bronze casters.

The first European contact with these people occurred in 1472, when a Portuguese navigator came upon Benin City. After this, Portuguese are represented in scenes on the plaques, and several ivory belt masks are crowned with small Portuguese heads. European expeditions continued throughout the seventeenth century—the span of Benin's great period—and accounts of these trips are vivid; a Dutchman describes the splendor of the city as rivaling that of Amsterdam. An expedition early in the eighteenth century found the city in ruins. It was rebuilt, only to be destroyed again by the British in a punitive expedition in 1897. A British officer had been ambushed and killed; and in reprisal Benin City was burned to the ground and two thousand bronzes were taken back to London as plunder: a whole city and its treasures in exchange for the life of one white soldier.

A sixteenth- or seventeenth-century Benin bronze in the Museum of Primitive Art in New York (see illustration on page 44a) is representative in this work. The frontal pose of the attendants flanking the equestrian *Oba*, the use of size to signify importance and rank, and the background treatment of quatrefoils and stippling are found extensively in these reliefs. The high coral necklace and headdress worn by the *Oba* are signs of his power.

Along the Lower Niger River stylistically different bronzes have been found. Carbon-14 tests show these to be from the middle of the ninth century A.D., predating the Ife work and pointing to a more complex cultural situation. Metal casting continues to this day in the area around Ghana, Dahomey, and Nigeria.

Stone carvings dating back to the sixteenth century survive in two areas of Nigeria. In Esie, a little north of Ife, some eight hundred standing, sitting, and kneeling stone figures, about a foot and a half in height, are kept in a special grove. Each year they are honored by sacrificial festivals to gain their assistance in assuring the fertility and well-being of the land and the people.

In eastern Nigeria, in the Cross River area of the Ekoi culture, there are some three hundred stone monoliths, up to five feet in height, in the centers of old villages. They are memorials to the ancestors, and each year are decorated with chalk and palm-leaf girdles for a festival in honor of their spirits. They are made of hard basalt, and the carving of human faces on them is very shallow, sometimes only incised, sometimes simplified and abstract. In overall shape they are phallic, and each has a pronounced protruding navel—strong images of the potency of the ancestors and the continuity of generation.

Other old stone carvings have been found in Sierra Leone, the Congo (Kinshasa), and elsewhere. In Sierra Leone the Mende use such carvings in their rice fields to insure a good harvest. Ruins of old cities in different parts of Africa also evoke a past of great richness. At Zimbabwe in Rhodesia, for example, where impressive fifteenth-century walls still stand, pottery remains have been uncovered dating from the third century A.D., indicating the span of civilization at that site.

Europeans coming across these early examples of art and architecture have tried to deny their African origin. Could the Ife heads be Greek or Egyptian? Did someone come from Europe to teach Benin and the Ife the art of bronze casting? Were the Benin bronzes influenced by the Renaissance through the early Portuguese explorers? Was Zimbabwe a Phoenician settlement? Such speculations are groundless nonsense. These works of art are all African in origin. It is the white Westerner who, having forced the African into slavery and exploited his country, is compelled to deny the black man his great culture and venerable past. This is the lie of the "white man's burden"—of "bringing civilization to the naked savage"—and it has been rationalized, fictionalized, and justified jealously for centuries. But times are surely changing.

Traditions of African Sculpture

The many traditions of African sculpture are found across West Africa from Guinea to Nigeria, up to Mali, and along the coast; they extend through Cameroon and Gabon into Central Africa and throughout the Congo (Kinshasa) and beyond. This is a culturally rich and varied area that still reflects a basic homogeneity. Images range from almost total abstraction to extremely sensitive realism; surfaces from highly polished, smooth hardwood to composites of varied materials; and yet most of the sculpture is wood, represents animals and people, and is made to be used in a larger context—in dance, ritual, and religion.

African art is a total art. To look at a mask intelligently, one must realize that it is worn, that it is only a part of the costume, that the person wearing it might be on stilts or coming out of the forest at nightfall; that the wearer of the mask will be dancing, and that there will be music, drums, singing, or the telling of a legend to accompany the action. The one object is integrated into a whole religious ritual. Ancestor figures, carved vessels, fetish figures, stools, and other objects also function as parts of a larger context. The art dealer's showroom where these masks are bought and sold as speculative financial investments is a long way from this world.

A clan developed its own tradition, sometimes influenced by neighboring ones, sometimes strikingly different. In Gabon, the Fang and Bakota exemplify independent styles of neighboring cultures. Both make mortuary figures that are placed in containers for skulls to protect the spirits of the deceased. The Fang carvings, strongly three-dimensional, are expressive images in wood, with long cylindrical torsos, short legs that hang over the side of the container, rounded shoulders and hips, pronounced foreheads, and compact protruding jaws; whereas Bakota figures are among the most abstract flat forms found in African art. They are decorated with incised brass and copper covering the wood, and are placed within the basket of skulls so that the sculpture becomes head and arms, and the basket, the body of the guardian spirit. In both traditions these objects serve the spirits of the deceased; they express continuity within the culture in the presence of death, as do the basalt monoliths from the Cross River area described previously.

Ancestors play a major role in African society and religion, their spirit energy being needed and invoked at various rites during the year. The health and prosperity of the society depends upon their cooperation. Figures are carved to contain the spirits of the ancestors, and in some cases the carvings are kept in the home, while in others they are cared for by a priest. In Mali the Dogon people will often carve a seated couple to hold these spirits. This primeval pair will be kept in a cave sanctuary and brought out at an annual festival to the dead, when they help to increase the fecundity of the living and are themselves entertained, fed, and given offerings. However, when a person dies, his body is placed in the cave next to the carved figures so that the spirits of the dead can be joined.

The nature of Dogon carving can be seen in the ritual vessel with equestrian figure (see illustration on page 44b).

43

Dogon ancestor figures are stylistically similar to that of the rider. Symmetry, large masses contrasting with thin linear forms, an almost cubistic abstraction, and incised, repeated surface patterns are all characteristically Dogon. This vessel was used ceremonially, and it, too, is probably related to rites for the dead, for it is reported that in the past human flesh was eaten out of such a container by a priest.

Masks are also used in funeral rites. Among the Ibo in eastern Nigeria, the Mmwo Society masks of white-faced female ancestor spirits are worn at both the yam festivals and at funerals. Again, a meeting of death and fertility.

For the beginning of life, objects are made to safeguard pregnancy and birth. The Baluba in the Congo (Kinshasa) carve mendicant figures holding bowls. These *Kabila* figures are placed outside the door of a house right before childbirth to insure a successful delivery. The Ashantis of Ghana carve simple dolls with disklike heads and small simple bodies, known as *Akua'ba,* that are worn by a woman during pregnancy.

Masks: Variety and Function

Masks come in many shapes. The Poro Society mask from the Dan culture in Liberia is worn on the front of the face; the Bundu Society mask from the Mende culture in Sierra Leone is a helmet covering the whole head; and the mask of the goddess Nimba, worn by the Baga in Guinea, covers still more of the person, coming down over the shoulders, while the mask's legs are held to help support the weight. Eye holes on the Nimba mask are between the breasts, and the goddess's head is solid (see illustration on page 44c). The Bobo in Upper Volta have masks that are held by a beardlike handle in front of the face, with a flat decorated board extending as much as six feet above the person's head. The *Epa* masks of the Yoruba in Nigeria may be four or five feet high and of great weight, depicting a mythological scene with a dozen figures on top of a helmet—yet an intricate dance will still be performed by the wearer. The costume

44

Oba and attendants, Bini plaque, Benin, Nigeria, 1550–1680, bronze, h. 19½".

(Museum of Primitive Art, New York, photo by Charles Uht)

Left, Malevolent fetish figure, Bakongo, Congo (Kinshasa), wood and other materials, h. 23⅛". *Right,* Dogon ritual vessel with lid surmounted by equestrian figure, Mali, wood, h. 33¾."

Left, Poro Society mask of the Dan, Liberia, wood and other materials, h. 8⅛". *Right,* Bundu Society helmet mask of the Mende, Sierra Leone, wood and raffia, h. 13¾".

(Museum of Primitive Art, New York, photos by Charles Uht)

The goddess Nimba: Baga shoulder mask, Guinea, wood, h. 46½".

(Museum of Primitive Art, New York, photo by Charles Uht)

Poro Society mask of the N'gere, Liberia, painted wood and other materials, h. 12½".

44d

extending down from the mask can include grass skirts, strips of bright-colored fabric, capes, beadwork, and bells, and it can be as dramatic as the mask itself. Some masks, embodiments of spirits, are handed down from one person to another, each person serving in his turn as guardian for that spirit. Other masks are made by a specialist in the art of carving, while still others are carved by the individual wearer. So the nature of the mask is varied.

In Guinea, Sierra Leone, and Liberia, on the coast of West Africa, two secret societies (one male, one female) control the rituals dealing with the major aspects of life. The influence of the societies cuts across tribal and national boundaries. The male Poro Society is usually linked with the Dan and N'gere cultures in Liberia, and the female Bundu Society with the Mende in Sierra Leone, but both extend throughout the area. Secret societies exist throughout black Africa; for instance, in eastern Nigeria there is the Ekpo Society of the Ibibio, and in the Congo (Kinshasa) the Kifwebe Society of the Basonge. These societies perform innumerable functions, including the initiation of adolescents into adulthood. The initiation rites are long and strenuous ordeals, carried on in the forest, away from the village; and the rites, like the societies themselves, are segregated as to men and women. When initiation camps are held, the traditions, history, and customs of the society are passed on. This is the time when an individual is initiated sexually, and when he will be circumcised where this custom prevails. It is an ordeal that tests the strength and endurance of a youth; he enters as a child and returns as an adult. It is a major rite of passage.

The principal mask of the female Bundu Society (see illustration on page 44c) is worn at these rites by the officials, especially as the initiates are being brought back to the village. The conical shape and the compact, low placement of the features are characteristic of this type of mask; so, too, are the representations of folds of fat—symbolic of wealth —around the base. The unfolding shapes at the top of the mask are suggestive of sexual forms, and appropriate to the occasion.

In the Poro Society masks are made for a wide range of roles, from that of police officer to doorkeeper to comic (a baboon), and the mask is seen as actually performing the function it illustrates. For example, with a judicial mask, the wearer sits as judge in a dispute, but it is the spirit of the mask that adjudicates. The mask is feminine, the wearer male, creating a balanced situation signifying judicial impartiality. These are ancestor masks, passed down from generation to generation. Masks are also made for legendary figures, and for specific functions, such as the killing of certain animals. The expressive range of Poro masks can be seen in comparing the Dan mask with the N'gere mask (see illustrations on pages 44c and 44d).

Some secret societies, including the Poro, can be very brutal in their practices. This can be easily understood in the light of African history. Many of these societies developed during the slave trade to expose informers and attempt to maintain the society and its traditions against destructive outside forces: brutality countered by brutality.

The dry grasslands of Mali and Upper Volta are the source of a basically homogeneous group of artistic traditions known as Western Sudanese. If one were to compare work from two major traditions in this area—the Dogon and the Bambara, for example—this stylistic unity would be clear to see. Dogon art was examined earlier in relation to ancestor figures and the vessel with equestrian figure (see illustration on page 44b). Bambara art might be familiar in the well-known antelope headdresses, which will be discussed shortly. Art from both peoples emphasizes simple curved shapes, incised geometric surface patterns, symmetry, and a feeling for negative spaces. Some of these elements of style might have been strengthened through an association with North African art, in which there is likewise an extensive use of abstract pattern and perforated form. There is a long history of Sudanese contact with North Africa through trade, and Moslem missionary activity—a relationship which has been steadily resisted by the sub-Saharan groups, but which nevertheless seems to have exerted some influence stylistically.

At planting time for the Bambara of Mali, men from the Chi Wara Society go out into the fields in pairs, each wearing an antelope headdress, one representing a male animal, one a female, the rest of their bodies covered by a long grass costume, and they perform a dance to encourage those who are planting, to insure crop fertility and sufficient rain, and to reenact the mythical birth of agriculture. The dance includes zigzag movements and great leaps into the air in imitation of the antelope, movements that also correspond to forms in the headdress.

The Baga from Guinea are linked with the Bambara and Dogon culturally and stylistically. In the recent historic past they migrated from the grasslands of Mali to the rain forests of the coast, but naturally took their traditions with them. Compare the example of Baga art on page 44c with the work from the Dogon to see how this is so.

Nimba, fertility goddess and patroness of maternity for the Simo Society of the Baga, appears at puberty rites, at funerals, and when the rice is harvested. She emerges out of the forest on these occasions, and seeing her must be a most impressive sight.

Our attention in this article has centered more on West African art than on Central African art, which is not to deny that Central Africa is equally rich culturally. The Congo is one of the greatest areas in the world for wood sculpture. A form common to the Lower Congo is the fetish, or power figure, used for magical and judicial purposes. Powers within the figure are activated by various means: nails pounded into the figure, a mirror to be looked into, or objects hung from the figure (see illustration on page 44b). The fetishes found in Bakongo art show a strong realism and project sensitive facial expressions.

Under the impact of colonialism, the slave trade, Christian and Moslem missionary efforts over the past few hundred years, and twentieth-century industrialization, it is no surprise that the force of these traditions is either dead or rapidly dying out. Nowhere, perhaps, does a mask or ritual object still generate the sense of danger and respect comparable to what the contemporary Westerner feels toward radio-active forces, although at one time this was surely so.

Quite apart from strong new traditions that are being developed by the contemporary African artist, copies of the old images are now being made to sell to the tourist, but these copies have no ritual force or importance. It is in the traditional objects still in existence from the past that the power is projected. Here it is that the cultural roots of the contemporary black American and African rest.

SOURCES

FAGG, WILLIAM, *African Tribal Images*. Cleveland, Cleveland Museum of Art, 1968.

———*The Art of Central Africa*. New York. New American Library, 1967.

———*The Art of Western Africa*. New York, New American Library, 1967.

FRASER, DOUGLAS, *Primitive Art*. New York, Doubleday & Company, 1962.

LEUZINGER, ELSY, *Africa; The Art of the Negro Peoples,* translated from the German by Ann E. Keep. New York, McGraw-Hill Book Company, 1960.

Metropolitan Museum of Art, *Art of Oceania, Africa and the Americas from the Museum of Primitive Art*. New York, 1969.

TROWELL, MARGARET, and Nevermann, Hans, *African and Oceanic Art*. Harry N. Abrams, Inc., n.d.

VAN DER POST, LAURENS, *Patterns of Renewal*. Wallingford, Pa., Pendle Hill Pamphlet, 1962.

WINGERT, PAUL, *Primitive Art, Its Tradition and Styles*. Cleveland, World Publishing Company, 1962.

4

ESI SYLVIA KINNEY

Africanisms in
Music and Dance
of the Americas

This description is intended to give an overall view of some
aspects of African art forms which have survived in the
New World. The Americas were populated by slaves who
were gathered from the interior of Africa as well as the
West African coast from Senegal to Angola. Some are even
reported to have come from the east coast—from Mozambique and perhaps Ethiopia. The trade to the New World

49

lasted about three hundred years, roughly from the middle of the sixteenth to the middle of the nineteenth century.

The Problem of Cultural Retention

After the first generation of Africans had produced off-spring in America, the retention of their African heritage became problematical. The conflicts arising from miscegenation, a different environment, loss of contact with Africa, and the attitudes of the slave masters contributed, among other factors, to great changes in the general life patterns of the Afro-Americans. Frequently ethnic groups were so mixed that not only was verbal communication limited but also other aspects of group identity, such as unified styles of singing, choreography, and expression in plastic art. The result was, in many cases, a mélange of African plus European language and art forms and what can safely be called "pan-African art forms."

Some groups of Africans successfully broke away from the slavers and isolated themselves in the American forest regions. Wherever this occurred, the traditional African culture remained fairly well intact, and survivals are still very apparent. Other instances of strong survivals are to be found in areas where large numbers of a particular ethnic group were taken and were able to make a great impact on their fellows; where slaveowners were more tolerant of the slaves' way of life; and where the slaves were easily able to syncretize elements of their culture with that of the European and/or the Amerindian. (In syncretism, the foreign elements are selectively absorbed into the culture.) Due to the presence of these favorable factors, a greater measure of retention can be observed in South America and the West Indies than in the United States, where it is much more subtle and subliminal.

It is axiomatic that culture is not static, but is ever changing. In some instances, however, the Afro-American has clung to certain elements of his heritage so tenaciously that they have remained for all intents and purposes basically unchanged. This is frequently exemplified in ritual, and here complete historical examination of the relevant West African customs must, of necessity, be continued in those places in the Americas where they have been to some extent fossilized. It is also well known, but nonetheless a very worthwhile field for further detailed research, that some Afro-Americans were able to return to their motherland and thence again to the New World. Many of these visits appear to have had the motivation of seeking lost information concerning ritual practices. Thus some reinforcement was added to the persistence of Africanisms.

The Retention of African Rhythm

Rhythm is the most striking aspect of African music, with drumming displaying it in its most complex form. African dance responds to this rhythm and makes visible its complexities. The body of the dancer or group of dancers incorporates both the subtleties and the more direct dynamics of expression, translating them into movement which corresponds to the music. One dancer can metaphrase—that is, duplicate exactly—all the rhythms of an entire drum ensemble by using the several parts of the body simultaneously. Or the dancer can paraphrase the rhythm, by moving in complementary or contrasting rhythms. Frequently paraphrasing and metaphrasing operate concurrently in the dance when the assembly is in the form of leader-chorus. Then the choreography may also conform to an antiphonal-responsorial style, which is spatially identical to that style of vocal music, the call and response pattern, in which a soloist sings an exclamation and a reiterative chorus responds at regular intervals (the melodic line of the soloist frequently overlapping into the chorus line).

These rhythmic complexities were transferred to the New World and are known to exist in full scale in North, South, and Central America. Where the music has been altered, its complementary dance has followed suit; however, the complexities have not necessarily diminished even in the United States, where the degree of hybridization is at its greatest.

The total performance is thought of as a whole in Africa—

that is, music, dance, costuming, and masking. While this concept has been retained in America, much of the associated material culture has been lost. There is little plastic art, and frequently materials for costuming, including customary local dress, have become unavailable or for other reasons have disappeared.

Areas of Strongest African Retentions in the Americas

Localities where Africanisms are known to be strongest are found in northern Brazil, Surinam (among the bush Negroes), Haiti, Cuba, and the Sea Islands off the coast of Georgia and Carolina in the United States. Again, firm retentions are frequently found in religious cult practices. Stylistic features of the music and dance of the cults—as well as other components of the ritual—are unmistakably African.

Among the several areas where groups of Africans were able to isolate themselves is Palenque, Colombia. Dr. Charles Wright, director of the Afro-American Museum in Detroit, provides the following information about this village, as told to him by Professor Delia Zapata Olivella, director of Folkloric Dances of Colombia. Palenque has a patois drawn from various African languages and from Spanish. Here many rituals have been retained, including the absorbing ritual of death. The Palenqueros place great emphasis upon death, for they feel that it is the only certainty of their lives! There is a dirge named "Velorio" in which the dancing women move as a body in circles. They sing in the Lumbalu language, and they weep for the deceased. Others clap their hands, while one person praises the dead in song to the steady tempo of a small drum, called *llamador* because of its petite size. The *pechiche,* a larger drum, is also played to accompany the dirge with variations or improvisations around the smaller instrument. One person also sings in praise of this drum.

According to Professor Zapata Olivella, only in the village of Palenque have such concentrated Africanisms been found in Colombia; the majority of folkloric rhythms in that country are syncretized with European, or European and Amerindian, elements.

Dutch Guiana (Surinam) is an area where a large group of Africans, mainly Asantes, managed to penetrate the dense forest in order to regain their freedom. The habits of the Surinam bush people, who were able to maintain the Akan culture, are distinctly different from those of the town dwellers, who are of more mixed ancestry. However, both groups exhibit numerous survivals in both material and nonmaterial culture. Drums and other percussive instruments, with unaltered manner of performance, are utilized for religious purposes and for secular, but otherwise ritualistic, use. Songs and dances for the deities and ancestors and also folk (tale) tunes have continued to exist with little if any modification, according to Dr. M. Kolinski, writing in *Columbia University Contributions to Anthropology*.

Among the dance songs of the Djukas (bush people) is a type called *Susa,* which is used for competitions. On page 579 of the above volume, the author describes this pantomimic dance, in which two men fight with weapons, leaping toward each other, "the left foot of the one dancer parallel to the right foot of the other, changing until the song is broken [until] the one whose foot is on the outside is said to have 'killed' his opponent."

The town people reveal their African heritage in many of their songs or folktales. For instance, here is a war song which refers to Osei Tutu, an important *Asantehene.* Below is Dr. Kolinski's translation of this song, as it appears in the *Columbia University Contributions to Anthropology:*

> *I will play the Agida* [drum] *today,*
> *I will play the Agida today—O!*
> Kopsi *will receive the evil magic,*
> *That the cock may crow—O!*
> *Oh, I will drum on the Agida today,*
> *I will change into the Agida today—O!*
> Kopsi *will remove the evil magic,*
> *That the cock will crow—O!*

The *Agida* is associated with Dahomey and has survived in several places in the New World. In Haiti there is a special drumstick that is used in *Arada* (sacred) rites in conjunction with the *Arada* drum. (Harold Courlander, *The Drum and the Hoe*. Also see Janheinz Jahn, *Muntu*.) The songs also include references to the practice of voodoo—an African mode of sympathetic magic.

The ancestors of most people in the West Indies were African. In that area two groups of slaves, in the Antilles, are known to have violently escaped from bondage. These are the Maroons of Jamaica and a group that became known as the Black Caribs, who surrounded themselves with defenses on the island of Saint Vincent.

Off the coast of the states of Georgia and Carolina are a group of islands where much more of the traditional African culture has been preserved than on the mainland. This is due to the fact that Afro-Americans are the only people to have remained on the islands after a great exodus to Europe. Also, the blacks had had little contact with the plantation owners previous to their departure. The language spoken is Gullah, and most Africanisms in it are to be found in vocabulary rather than syntax. This is the only area of the United States where several recognizable types of African carving are known to survive. Distinctive music and dance forms still exist, and others, even when syncretized with European forms, always have a distinctively African manner of rhythmic complexity.

There is a dance called the buzzard lope, in which a scarf is laid on the ground. The "vulture dancer" cavorts in front of it while others sing, clap, and play percussive instruments. The scarf designates the dead, who are determined to go to heaven despite the fact that they are intimidated on their upward journey by the greedy vulture. Significantly, the Gullah also display the antiphonal-responsorial manner of singing that is the most distinctive style of African-derived vocal music in the Americas.

On the United States mainland the call and response technique is reflected in the work songs or field holler and its closely aligned type of prison song, as well as the gospel, ring shout, dance games, some narrations of legends, and jazz.

It has often been said that there is little, if any, formal structure in the black dances from North America, but this simply is not true. To reiterate, where there is a musical form, there exists a corresponding dance form. Writing in the *American Forum,* Robert Farris Thompson has noted in his "An Aesthetic of the Cool: West African Dance" the antiphonal and responsorial form of dancing whereby the "men 'interrupt' the movement of their women in a call-and-response manner, for they begin a new step or flourish considerably before their partners have finished the execution of their basic movements." I have noted that among typically mainland blacks, the women also may interrupt the basic movements of their partners. In fact, it is a point of virtuosity when the men and women successfully improvise their steps in succession, the soloist concluding each phrase with a figure from the basic movement in its proper sequence in time. My description from the mainland is one characteristic of the jazz dance as well as the more decidedly Afro-Latin dances.

Although jazz has descended from the blues and ragtime, many elements of the work song, spiritual, and ring shout are incorporated into it. Again, as the antiphonal-responsorial features are displayed in the music, so also in the dance. Partners are usually embraced in ballroom jazz (though not necessarily in the jam session, at which one may dance alone), but in the measures of the antiphon are to be found the space for great stylistic improvisation. It is not difficult for a good dancer to either "base"—that is, to execute the basic movement when the musician begins the riff (extended period of improvisation)—or even to improvise himself, in contrast or complement to the musician. An example of the definite antiphonal-responsorial style in African instrumental music is found in the *Damba* music of the Dagomba of northern Ghana. The drums are of two kinds: the hourglass

55

squeeze drum (*lunga*) and the rounded wooden drum with two flat sides (*gongon*), which is slung around the neck. The soloist plays the *lunga,* and both the *lunga* and the *gongon* are played in the chorus. The soloist of the talking *lunga* leads off in praises of the chief and ancestors, and the chorus responds in unison. I have described the *Damba* music in greater detail in *Journal of the Society for Ethnomusicology,* in my article "Drummers in Dagbon: The Role of the Drummer in the Damba Festival."

The improvisatory style of the jazz group, the concept of playing what one "feels," is evident in Afro-Cuban music, too. Indeed, jazz and Afro-Cuban style have influenced each other. Cuban drumming, which has incorporated many African styles including that of the Yoruba, Ibo, Ibibio, Fon, and some Congolese tribes, has retained many undeniably tribal rhythmic patterns, instruments, and manners of performance. The Afro-Cuban style spread north to the United States and was immediately seized upon and further developed (that is, improvised upon, also with the addition of as many other African rhythmic and spatial components as could be employed), both musically and choreographically. In this manner, Cubans were responsible for re-enculturating mainland North Americans with some more directly African retentions. As a result of this, United States blacks became ever more conscious of their African derivation.

As Cuban musicians moved to the United States, especially to New York, they began to sit in on the sets or jam sessions of jazz artists. It is obvious that they lent Latin rhythms and instruments to the jazz music, and yet again, more direct Africanisms. These Cubans incorporated syncopation, more improvisation, and the jazz riff into their own popular music and dance.

The jazz ensemble functions in a similar manner to the African drumming group. Each instrumentalist in the African percussive group plays a separate rhythmic pattern, which differs from that played on the other instruments. (As implied in my description of the *Damba* music, there are notable exceptions to the normal variety of the ensemble.) The master drummer has set patterns to play, if he is drumming proverbs, but he also may improvise. A great deal of variety is lent to the performance by rhythmic complexity, that is, polyrhythm and polymeter; by the difference in timbre of the instruments, which is due to the method of producing sound (that is, by a vibrating membrane, as on a drum, or a vibrating body, as on a gourd rattle); and by the characteristic quality of sound produced by each instrument and the spatial patterns or dance created by the drummers.

The jazz ensemble has retained its great emphasis upon rhythm. Jazz, however, has employed the rhythmic element of syncopation to such a degree that this element, along with spontaneity, has become synonymous with the concept of jazz and has greatly influenced Western music. While syncopation was not unknown in the West, it has been more consciously utilized by recent composers, who acknowledge the influence of jazz.

In the jazz ensemble the underlying ostinato accompaniment, which is most frequently in the bass or percussive parts (which may be harmonic as well as rhythmic), has a melodic line superimposed upon it which may be improvisatory after the theme has been stated. Long or short ostinato motives are also played by the more melodic instruments, and the improvisations by alternating musicians fit into the chord progressions harmonically. Each member of the jazz ensemble may play independently, the better to insure a "free" performance; the result is cohesive.

During the period of slavery in the United States the use of African instruments was discouraged, and European instruments gained ascendancy. Since the complete distribution of aerophones, chordophones, idiophones, and membranophones was (and still is) well known in Africa, the shift to European instruments was not a radical one. However, many improvised instruments, such as the washtub bass, sprang up to compensate for the loss. The banjo, also, was used in early jazz (ragtime), but has been discarded. New Orleans jazz musicians, the originators of jazz, danced as well as played their music and walked in procession from place to place upon ritual occasions—as is common in Africa.

Early Forms of Music and Dance in the United States

In addition to jazz, which is a relatively late form, there are several other, and often earlier, types of music and dance in the United States. Probably the oldest is the slave song, or spiritual, which developed on the southern plantations. Most songs of this type are religiously oriented, but some, such as "Musieu Banjo" or "Charleston Gals," are secular. In the religious songs there is but little allusion to the African way of life, and more to Christian concepts of salvation and the afterlife, for the slaves responded to some Protestant missionary teachings. They did not, however, transform their melodic scales or their rhythmic modes. Again, as in Africa, we find that the indigenous people sing the music of a foreign group only to its nearest approximation of their own scale—a process which may almost transform the intervallic structure. It is not difficult to understand that the slaves, when receiving a Protestant hymn to sing, would only approximate it, and when left to themselves would incorporate a familiar singing style throughout. The style might include nasality, extensive improvisation, and a lapse into an antiphonal-responsorial pattern and rhythmic complexity due to the addition of their characteristic manner of hand-clapping and foot-stamping. It is not inconceivable that some of the very old songs, which are quite African in style, could have been well-known melodies from the motherland, in which only the text was changed.

The elements that may induce spiritual possession (by one or several deities in African religions or by Christ in Christianity) are included in the religious "shout," which is sung in marked rhythm and to which a marked style of dancing is applied by means of shuffling and stamping the feet (but not crossing one foot over the other, which was forbidden by the missionaries), clapping the hands, swinging the arms, bouncing the torso, shifting weight from the hips, and a posture that is sometimes bent forward (which produces overbreathing and in some cases consequent dizziness) and sometimes prancing.

The songs are sung with deep conviction; but the constant repetition of melody and text by the chorus (which includes the antiphonal response), along with a very marked rhythmic style of dance, lends itself to the onset of possession—a phenomenon which is quite common in Africa. (This is not to imply that spiritual possession is peculiar to Africa, but the stylistic features which the form of worship exhibits are distinctly African.) Whereas in Africa the talking drums and singing chorus are usually responsible for calling the deity, in the Protestant religious music of the United States and West Indies the fervor with which the chorus or soloist sings or the minister preaches, as well as a heavy percussive quality in the service (made by drums, rattles, tambourines, clapping, and stamping), may bring the spirit "down" to the worshippers.

In areas of the New World such as Brazil, Haiti, Trinidad, or Cuba where cult practices have been retained, even though the separate identity of the cults frequently has become indistinct, the movements, rhythms, musical instruments, and song texts or ritual language of possession are identical to African counterparts.

The intensity produced by the repetitive movement and musical patterns and the nuances which build up to a dynamic climax are, of course, at their peak when a devotee becomes possessed. Frequently the possession is visualized by jerking, twitching, twisting, or bobbing motions of the head, limbs, and/or torso. But once the worshipper has become fully entranced, his style of movement differs. For after this initial phase has passed, his ecstatic behavior may change into mime—usually into emphatic dance movements, which portray the particular deity who has "descended" upon his devotee.

59

The Distribution of African-Derived Music and Dance in the Americas

Brief mention should be made of the distribution of African-derived music and dance in the Americas. Writing in the *Journal of the Society for Ethnomusicology*, Paulo de Carvalho Neto describes "The *Candombe,* A Dramatic Dance from Afro-Uruguayan Folklore." Among other types, there is in Uruguay the dramatic dance and folklore which is part of a play that supports a mixture of dances and dramatic poetry. According to this author, "The Candombe . . . or dramatic dance of the lubola masquerade . . . is a (collective) dramatic dance with its *dramatis personae,* which develops various choreographic styles, learned by (Negro) folkloric transmission throughout the years. Moreover, in it there survive suggestive mimetic dialogues."

In addition to cultistic forms, Brazil has produced dance types which derive from religious sources, such as the *Samba,* which originated in the richly Africanized area of Bahia. As depicted in the October 1968 Afro-Brazilian exhibition at the National Museum in Accra, Ghana, there is another dance which originated as a type of duel, in which only the legs are used and sharp blades are held between the toes. This dance is called *Capoeira* in Brazil, but is known as the *Calinda* (or variations of that word) in Haiti, Trinidad, Martinique, Guadeloupe, and Puerto Rico, according to Harold Courlander. The dance is related to a type which is found among the Ewe of Togo, maintains Courlander. And the description of the *Susa* in Surinam suggests that it also belongs to the same category as the *Calinda.*

African-derived drums, basketry rattles, double iron gongs, a notched stick, and a musical gourd bow (monochord), which have a wide distribution over Africa, are used for the *Capoeira.* The gourd bow is also found in Uganda, along with a seed shell rattle to be played on the bow (Margaret Trowell and K. P. Wachsmann, *Tribal Crafts of Uganda*). It is also played in the Congo, and I have observed it among the Dagomba of Ghana, where it is called *jinjelin.*

60

In Argentina dance styles have been produced—the *Chacharara, Cadomba, Milongo, Malamba, Gato,* and *Semba*—which have also retained the African rhythmic structure. In Dutch Surinam there is an abundance of both religious and secular music. Dr. M. Kolinski, in the work cited previously, indicates that many song texts, for example, actually reflect historical situations which occurred in Africa, such as the war campaigns of a famous Asante ruler, Osei Tutu (d. 1712).

Guatemala has so incorporated the *marimba* (African xylophone) that it has become the national instrument. Many Guatemalans believe that the *marimba* is indigenous. Similarly, the *Fandango,* the national dance of Spain, actually originated from Cuba. Cuba has contributed as many, if not more, African-derived secular types of music and dance as any other country in the Americas, among the most famous being the *Rhumba, Conga, Tango,* and *Mambo.* African percussive instruments have been preserved (the gourd rattle has popularly been painted bright colors), and drummers in the back hills are especially noted for their virtuosity on these instruments. Of course, derivative types of drums have developed for the popular dances; such is the *Conga* drum, a double drum which is generally played between the knees and with both hands instead of sticks. It is interesting that the *Conga* drum has found its way into Africa and often is used for recreational music.

Features of the Yoruban Shango cult of Nigeria still exist in Trinidad, and the inhabitants of the island are well known as being the originators of steel-drum bands and the *Calypso.* The *Calypso,* in which social commentary is sung out in very bold terms, reached the shores of West Africa and was disseminated by West Indian sailors. It became very popular and influenced the *Highlife,* which is the latest and most widely diffused style of popular music in West Africa. Even today, much *Highlife* employs those peculiar *Calypso* rhythms and provocative themes. The allusive and stimulating themes which the Trinidadians employ are, however, Africanisms, and so also are the bases of their rhythms.

Haiti is well known for its survivals in the realm of cult music and festivals and in secular music such as work songs, folktales, political songs, and songs of allusion. Courlander, in *The Drum and the Hoe,* provides the following translation of both a ritual and a dance song. It concerns a snake god from Dahomey named Damballa:

> *We thread our way [like a snake],*
> *Damballa Wedo is a snake, oh!*

According to Courlander, "The 'threading' is a description of conventionalized dance movements suggesting the crawling of a snake."

Haiti also has many African musical instruments, among which are talking drums and other drums for ritual purposes, gongs, rattles, and hardwood sticks which are clapped together, stamping tubes and stamping sticks, horns and trumpets, earth bows, the *sansa,* and improvised instruments such as a scraper, which is related to the washtub bass of the United States.

This has been but a general view of the music and dance of the Americas which has been influenced by African cultures. There are innumerable studies yet to be made of the relationships between the art forms which are found on these continents. Study has been made difficult because of the inevitable syncretism, the lack of scholarly research until quite recently, and the outmoded concept, still prevalent in some areas, that African music is not worthy of study and international recognition, and that the dances, however intricate, are merely exhibitions of frenzy and lust.

This description would be incomplete without brief mention of other strong survivals, such as the Jamaican cultistic practices or spider song-stories; or the many styles of music in the United States, such as the blues and gospel; or dance types such as the black-bottom, the turkey trot (one-step), and the Charleston.

There are many songs and dances, musical dance styles,

and instruments which are identical or quite similar in several areas of the Americas. This is attributable to the interaction of participants both during the era of slavery and its aftermath, as well as to the fact that separate African ethnic groups established their art forms in a variety of locations in the New World.

SOURCES

COURLANDER, HAROLD, *The Drum and the Hoe*. Berkeley and Los Angeles, University of California Press, 1960.

DE CARVALHO NETO, PAULO, "The *Candombe,* A Dramatic Dance from Afro-Uruguayan Folklore," *Journal of the Society for Ethnomusicology,* vol. 5, 1962.

HERSKOVITS, MELVILLE J. and Frances S., *Suriname Folklore,* with transcriptions of songs and musicological analysis by M. Kolinski. *Columbia University Contributions to Anthropology,* vol. 27, 1936.

JAHN, JANHEINZ, *Muntu*. London, Faber and Faber, Ltd., 1961.

KINNEY, ESI SYLVIA, "Drummers in Dagbon: The Role of the Drummer in the Damba Festival," *Journal of the Society for Ethnomusicology,* vol. 14, 1970.

Notes from an Afro-Brazilian exhibition at the National Museum in Accra, Ghana, October 1968.

THOMPSON, ROBERT FARRIS, "An Aesthetic of the Cool: West African Dance," *American Forum,* vol. 17, 1967.

TROWELL, MARGARET, and Wachsmann, K. P. *Tribal Crafts of Uganda*. London, Oxford University Press, 1953.

WRIGHT, CHARLES, director of the Afro-American Museum, Detroit, interviews with Professor Delia Zapata Olivella, director of Folkloric Dances of Colombia, in Colombia, July 1967.

5

JULIUS M. WAIGUCHU

Black Heritage: of Genetics, Environment, and Continuity

Introduction

This essay presents two general arguments: one, that in spite of some five hundred years of cultural and physical genocide, the African peoples in the diaspora have retained the fundamental native cultural traits with which they were endowed by the creator and mother Africa; and, two, that throughout their history there have existed among the African peoples in the motherland and in the diaspora periods of cultural communion that tended to reinforce the survival and the continued growth of what Sterling Stuckey has termed an "amalgam of Africanisms." These two arguments are necessarily interdependent in that they represent the case of a human unit interacting with its environmental setting so that the resultant situation is a product of their interaction.

The term "Africanism" has also been used by Melville Herskovits to mean the survival of the indigenous African cultural traits among peoples of African descent living in the diaspora. Lerone Bennett, Jr., seems to have borrowed the same usage from Herskovits, in his *Before the Mayflower.* We shall adopt the same usage for the purposes of this essay. The word "survival" here is important, because we are talking about what has survived and the possible explanations for such a survival. The essence of my argument, then, is that the survival of African cultural traits among the peoples of African descent is a function of two aspects; one is the genetic process, and the other is the acquired or transmitted cultural traits. It is further argued that an Africanism cannot be adequately explained by either genetics or the transmissive process alone, because it is the result of the interplay of the biological unit and the spatial setting. The point has been succinctly put by René Dubos in his book *So Human an Animal,* when he observes that

> external environment constantly affects the composition of the body fluids, in part by introducing certain substances directly into the system, in part by affecting hormone secretion and other metabolic activities. Such changes in the body fluids alter the intercellular medium which in turn affects the activity of the genetic apparatus. In this manner, the individual's experiences determine the extent to which the genetic endowment is converted into the functional attributes that make the person become what he is and behave as he does.

The Bases of Culture

Culture is formed by traits acquired through parental example and/or other factors of environment and by those traits inherited genetically from within, according to Siegfried Mandel in *Dictionary of Science*. The familial role in cultural transmission is considered an integral part of what we have called environmental factors. Following Mandel, the term "genetics" is here defined as the study of the transmission of individual characteristics from one generation to another. It is a branch of biology that deals with heredity. Culture is understood to be the totality of all the attributes which make up a way of life of a people at a given period in history. In relating culture to genetics, there are at least two important considerations that must be made. First, there exists a universal relationship between the two insofar as the same relationship is common among all races and their respective cultures. Secondly, for genetics to be a contributing factor in the survival of Africanisms, it must be established that the black man is genetically different from the white man. Such a difference may be the reason why an Africanism could and/or would survive the devastating onslaughts black people have had to endure, so that it could be transmitted as an Africanism to the succeeding generations. Put differently, this is to say that if an Africanism possesses at least a partial genetic basis, it would seem logical that such an Africanism cannot be destroyed totally as long as its genetic basis exists, and that if it possesses no such genetic base, it cannot be transmitted as an Africanism.

In regard to the universality of the relationship between genetics and culture, René Dubos, in the work referred to previously, argues that "biological evolution always takes place through the spontaneous production of genetic mutants which are then selected by environmental forces." The selective mechanisms, he goes on to say, are very complicated, since they involve continuous processes of feedback between the organism, its environment, and its accumulated way of life. Elsewhere Dubos supports his position by advancing the idea that heredity does not determine fixed characteristics and traits (such as two legs, two eyes, one head), but only controls the developmental process (growth of these features

66

and others). In other words, the fixed characteristics and traits are really constituent parts of anatomical genetics. But the path followed by the developmental process is conditioned by both genetic and environmental variables. For instance, if it can be said that environmental factors do not change a four-chambered heart into a one- or three-chambered heart, the same cannot be said of the changes that produce mental maturity, or, even less important, suntanning.

A different view is provided by Leslie White, who, in his *Science of Culture*, downgrades man's genetic makeup as an insignificant factor in both cultural formation and development. To him, genetically transferred biological differences —such as color, hair, eyes, the size of the lips, and the shape of the head—are superficial, but such features as the brain, bone, muscles, glands, and sense organs are the fundamental biological features. First of all, the inference here that skin color is necessarily less fundamental biologically than, say, the bone, or that the shape of the head is less fundamental biologically than the glands, and so forth, is perfect nonsense. To proceed from such differentiation of superficial and fundamental features to the argument that man is a biological constant who does not vary with cultural evolution is certainly not quite the case. Note, first, that we are not talking about man ever having four legs or half a head. Neither are we talking about his brain ever enlarging or shrinking. We are saying that being "biological" is not the same as being immutable. We are also saying that growing old is definitely "biological." Perhaps White's point is that the shapes of the various human organs do not change, and this is conceded; but the sizes and the metabolisms of human organs change in the process of growing. This, it might be added, is perhaps the point that Dubos makes when he says that "men do not behave as passive objects when they become established in a given environment." Changes in environment lead to other changes in the organism's habits, which in turn modify certain characteristics of such an organism. Dubos thinks that this is so because "continued residence in a particular environment tends to favour the selection of mutants adapted to it. Eventually, such mutations are incorporated into the genetic structure of the species involved." In this connection, it should perhaps be added that living organisms possess great ability "to learn from experience and to transmit this learning to their progeny [through] certain peculiar characteristics of their genetic equipment," as the same author states.

It is hoped that the preceding statement, although not exhaustive, will sufficiently indicate that culture, as a way of life of a people, is at least partially determined by the genetic mechanisms of the people in question. What remains to be shown, though, is that such genetic mechanisms differ in the black and white races. It is in such a difference that we may be able to find at least a partial explanation of the survival of African cultural attributes. The absence of any genetic difference between the two races can only mean one of two things: either that Africanisms do not exist, or that whatever exists is common to all human beings, as argued above, and that as such it has no justification as a basis for an Africanism.

Posing the question, Are Africans genetically different from Europeans?, as Leonard Doob has done in *The African World: A Survey of Social Research,* is fraught with dangers of misunderstanding especially in the light of the past history of black and white peoples. Let me justify both the question and the answer before I respond.

First of all, whatever differences may be found to exist between the African and the European peoples need not be looked at in terms of the inferior-superior dichotomy so common among some scholars. Secondly, those who oppose or disagree with the inferior-superior categorization of the differences between white and black people also tend to gloss over a lot of ground with nothing more than condemnation and denunciation. Thirdly, it is not that I do not appreciate the potential menace and the outrageously damnable inferences stemming from this kind of scholarship, but the fact is that some of the differences brought forth in some of these studies are for real, whether one likes it or not. Fourthly, I point out that to be different is not to be inferior or superior. To be different is not to be unsuitable for comparison, and to be

68

comparable is not to be equal or unequal. You can compare a goat to a sheep according to various criteria such as physical features, lips, and brains, but it would seem idiotic to assert from such comparison that the goat is superior to the sheep; it would be equally idiotic to assert that the two are not different. Regardless of their inner and external features, both can be and are tamed and/or raised to live together (and harmoniously, too) without having to ask the sheep to become the goat. Because the differences between black and white people have been made to serve bad uses, it does not at all mean that such differences cannot and should not be looked at from another perspective.

Now, to answer Doob's question, I wish to begin by citing those studies that have indicated differences of the types suggested above.

As already inferred, many white social scientists, especially anthropologists and psychologists, have designed and conducted studies that are clearly geared to placing the black man in an unfavorable posture: for instance, Margaret Mead's "Research on Primitive Children," François Raveau's "An Outline of the Role of Color in Adaptation Phenomena," J. L. M. Dawson's *Cultural and Physiological Influences upon Spatial-Perceptual Processes in West Africa,* and the entire gamut that describes non-European peoples as primitive and/or equates non-European adults with "civilized" European children. Among those studies that try to prove that Africans and their descendants are inferior to Europeans and their descendants are S. Biesheuvel's *African Intelligence: A Study of African Ability* and his *Race, Culture, and Personality,* C. R. Dent's *An Investigation of Certain Aspects of Bantu Intelligence,* and Leonard Doob's "On the Nature of Uncivilized and Civilized People." The list is, of course, inexhaustible. The studies cited, and many others, have approached black-white differences from at least three perspectives—namely, the genetic, the perceptual, and that of intelligence-aptitude. In his article in *The African World* Leonard Doob has made brief summaries of many studies done in each of these areas. To the question posed earlier as to whether Africans and

Europeans are genetically different, Doob's summaries indicate an affirmative answer that such differences do exist—but with important exceptions. For instance, the point is made that behavior is explained by both genetic and cultural factors, a point stressed in the present argument. What I consider important here is that these studies, however varied, have not dismissed the genetic factor as Leslie White has done.

Another question posed and answered by Doob on the basis of the many studies conducted in the field is: Do Africans and Europeans perceive the external world differently? Again, on the basis of his summaries of the various studies, the answer is in the affirmative, with important exceptions. In all cases concession has been made to the undetermined influence of cultural factors. The third and final question has to do with intelligence and aptitude: Are Africans basically less intelligent than Europeans? And the answer is, to quote from Doob's summaries: "Without question, the mean intelligence of samples of Africans, as measured by a conventional European intelligence test, is always below that of the corresponding European norm. . . ." Doob cites some criticisms of both the content and format of the tests to suggest that the validity of these studies may not be conclusive.

It is hoped that the preceding comments, inadequate as they may be, sufficiently indicate that there exists a genetic explanation of the differences between the black and white races. And, as said earlier, the damage done by many of these studies in the field of race relations is here appreciated. The damage, to be sure, has not been confined to race relations alone; it is also found in the quality of academic objectivity as it relates to black people. It also seems to me that white people's perception of reality and of themselves has been blurred by such distortions as are found in some of these studies. But bad use of any data, or distortion of a fact, does not and should not preclude some other, different use. I believe many of the differences between black and white people cited in these studies are genuine—genuine in the sense that they stem from the genetic constitution of a people and are thereafter manifested in the transmissive process. It is not enough for a people to possess certain biological attributes, for, as such, the attributes would be rather insignificant. It is necessary, in addition, for such biological attributes to interact with the spatial-environmental setting to provide a context within which we, as biological units, derive particular meanings. This is the reason why, to quote Dubos again, "the individual's experiences determine the extent to which the genetic endowment is converted into the functional attributes that make the person become what he is and behave as he does." It is the total sum of those genetic and cultural characteristics and traits peculiarly pertaining to the black race that we call Africanisms. (There is certainly no gainsaying that corresponding characteristics and traits pertaining to the white race exist; but our concern is with the former.) The relationship between the genetic and spatial aspects of any cultural manifestation is too intricately complicated to have full justice done to it in such a short paper as this.

Manifestations of Africanisms

Having thus far explored the relationships between genetics and culture, we now turn our attention to some of the aspects of an Africanism (which, as defined earlier, is itself a cultural manifestation produced by the interactions between the genetic unit and the spatial setting). We shall begin with Edward Blyden's point in *African Life and Customs* that black people live in close communion with nature, which is to say that their way of life is not compartmentalized. Dubos is of the same opinion. The implication here is that communion with nature is intended to suggest the genetic makeup of an African interacting with his environment. Such communion may be expressed or manifested in a variety of ways, among which are religious experience and practice and artistic, musical, and choreographic expressions and gestures. It needs to be added here that this argument does not preclude the existence of corresponding communion with nature and/or its expression in some particular manner by any other racial group, but it is argued that the similarity between, say, the African form of communion and the European one may be likened to the earlier example of a sheep and a goat.

Or, when Robert Park and Ernest Burgess say, even if pejoratively, that black temperament consists of certain distinctive characteristics "determined by physical organization and biologically transmitted" (*Introduction to the Science of Sociology*), they are, in effect, acknowledging a cultural manifestation produced by those peculiarly African genetic qualities interacting with the environmental setting. The uniqueness of a people is in the way they interact with the various stimuli of their particular environment. It is, therefore, not quite so presumptuous to say with Kwame Nkrumah that there exists a great difference "in mental orientation between the Africans and the Europeans," if that is understood to mean that such an orientation comes about as a result of the different ways in which black and white people respond to the physical realities of their environment. Even in sensory communication, it has been found that blind persons are able to recognize immediately the races of the people they meet with little or no mistake, and that they tend to act friendly or unfriendly depending on what races they find the other parties to be, as reported by Roger Bastide in "Color, Racism, and Christianity." Again, the point is that the possibility that such ability to distinguish different races (which is by no means a monopoly of black people) is genetically rooted and cannot be ruled out.

Being an African or of an African descent is independent of one's likes and dislikes. It is genetically determined. To identify or not to identify with the African heritage does not necessarily make one more or less part of the African heritage. Not identifying with one's heritage may, however, involve a certain amount of self-hatred, indulgence in fantasies of all sorts, and alienation from one's self. One is born African and/or of African heritage, and there can be no shedding away or acquiring Africanisms. Nathan Hare's *The Black Anglo-Saxons* is very instructive with respect to certain people of African descent who attempt to escape from their true identity. No such escapes should fool anybody as to the true identity of such individuals. They cannot abolish their racial heritage because they do not like it, as Hare points out. It may be conceded, however, that white people's efforts to Europeanize black people constitute a physical and mental reality that the black person must reckon with in day-to-day activities. It is to this reality that we find what V. O. Awosika has described as the black man's "intuitive adjustment." To this extent, then, one could say that the process of adjustment represents a constituency of contemporary black cultural manifestation, because it represents the black man's interaction with, and reaction to, his spatial setting.

Or, to put it differently, such a cultural manifestation could be viewed as an invention of black people necessitated by the desire to survive. It is an invention because the black man has had to circumvent the white man's atrocities by building up around his cultural impositions "his own ways of surviving, submitting, and resisting." Indeed, when the history of black people is properly read in the proper perspective, it will become clear that it is the history of an unusual people —unusual because no other people, throughout the entire history of mankind, have taken what black people have taken and survived. Black people have not only survived, but in fact have continued to increase both their numbers and their cultural contributions to the rest of the world. In those instances when the black man's Africanism was beaten out of the daily operational realities (that is, the black man was compelled to live in a manner contrary to his nature or to imitate some other person's mode of life), it went into hibernation, so to speak. In other words, when black people's day-to-day pattern of living appears similar to that of the white people, it is because the reality of the environment has demanded such adjustment.

Notwithstanding such adjustment, the differences between black and white people would seem to be here to stay. Note, for instance, the influence of color on general behavior. Ultimately, the cultural forms of black and white people have always been different. History is very clear on this point that the color of one's skin, particularly that of the African as

73

opposed to the European peoples, is a very important factor. Black and white cultural systems have never merged, even in the Americas. When race-relations experts say that "we are all human beings," or "we are all children of God," or "we are all Americans," they are basically correct, but what they leave unsaid is that we are also basically different—whether human beings or children of God or Americans or whatnot, we are different races and peoples, and no amount of evasion will ever erase the difference. The fact that European culture was imposed on the African peoples forcibly does not mean that the black man became white, and the chances are a million to one against his becoming European.

It is sometimes argued that the impositions of slavery on black people have succeeded in acculturating the blacks; but while it cannot be denied that such impositions have left their mark on contemporary black culture, it must be noted that throughout the history of Afro-European contact, there exists no time or place that one can cite as having witnessed any form of cultural communion between the black and the white races. Franklin Frazier seems to suggest, in *Race and Culture Contacts in the Modern World,* that meaningful cultural communion is only possible if the processes of both acculturation and assimilation have taken place in total. It is perhaps possible to argue that black Americans are acculturated to a good extent, but it is not possible to argue that they have been assimilated. Again, this is a commonplace observation. And, even if one conceded that such cultural communion ever took place, it should additionally be pointed out that the communion would still be subject to certain biological and spatial limitations such as we have mentioned in the preceding pages. The bits of acculturation and pretensions that one sees paraded around by the black bourgeoisie may perhaps be the nearest thing to a black-white cultural communion. The thing about the black middle class is that they are like the missionary who goes to Africa and lives with the African natives, pretending that he is one of them, but when he comes back to the United States, he does not live or mix with black people unless it be in the local bank or in the supermarket. The point is that such a missionary's general attitudes toward Africans while he is in Africa are a put-on job necessitated by the reality of living in Africa and among Africans. Once he is back home, he acts himself. This analogy could be usefully employed in depicting the dilemma of the black middle class in America. It may also throw some light on the comradeship between the black bourgeoisie and the liberal establishment.

What has happened in societies like that of the United States is that there is a tendency to speak of the "American culture," meaning or at least implying that there has evolved, since 1619, a culture that is uniquely American. What this kind of argument leaves unsaid is that first, the American culture is definitely European, and even more than that, it is an Anglo-Saxon culture which definitely does not incorporate the African or the Indian culture. What white social scientists have done in legitimizing the "American culture" is to saturate the academic marketplace with theories and learned-sounding pronouncements about "the melting pot" and "the pluralistic society," leaving out completely the fact that the pot never melted in the case of the Africans in America or the native Indian whose culture is actually the American culture.

To go back to the surviving Africanisms among the African peoples in the diaspora, it may be added that Blyden's notion of close communion with nature and its symbolization by an undifferentiated pattern of life is manifested in the African religious understanding and practice, which, according to John Mbiti, in *African Religions and Philosophy,* permeates all departments of life so fully that it is not always easy or possible to isolate it. Mbiti goes on to add that:

> In traditional [African] religions there are no creeds to be recited; instead, the creeds are written in the heart of the individual, and each one is himself a living creed of his own religion. Where the individual is, there is his religion, for he is a religious being. It is this that makes Africans so religious; religion is in their whole system of being. . . . Religion in African societies is written not

75

on paper but in people's hearts, minds, oral history, rituals and religious personages like the priests, rainmakers, officiating elders and even kings. Everybody is a religious carrier. . . . So then, belief and action in African traditional society cannot be separated; they belong to a single whole.

Now, with this kind of a general pattern and outlook on life, how has the black man used his natural gifts and insights to survive the genocidal atrocities of the white man? Sterling Stuckey, in a paper presented at the Institute in Afro-American Studies held at Brooklyn College, June 1969, had some interesting comments in this regard, saying that black people

> were able to fashion a life style and a set of values, an ethos, which prevented them from being imprisoned altogether by the values which the larger society sought to impose. This ethos was an amalgam of Africanisms . . . which helped slaves . . . feel their way along the course of American slavery, enabling them to endure. . . . The values expressed in folk lore acted like a wellspring to which slaves, trapped in the wasteland of American slavery, could return to in times of doubt, to be refreshed. In short, I shall contend that the process of dehumanization was not nearly as pervasive as [some] would have us believe, that a very large number of slaves, guided by this ethos, by this life style and system of values, were able to maintain their essential humanity.

Stuckey's point is elsewhere emphasized by Casely Hayford, who is quoted by Edward Blyden as arguing that even when and where the African has been compelled to convert to an alien religious worship, such as Christianity, "he remains forever afterwards only a Christian worshipper in form, if he cannot openly revolt . . . while at heart he remains true to the faith of his fathers."

Stuckey has also presented an insightful exploration of the role of the African-American spiritual music and folklore. He seems to be arguing that such music is not just another type of music, and that black people do convey some general and some particular information regarding the state of the African life under bondage. He cites Frederick Douglass as say-ing that "I have often sung to drown my sorrow but seldom to express happiness. Crying for joy and singing for joy were alike uncommon to me while in the jaws of slavery." Stuckey also quotes Sterling Brown as saying that the meaning of these songs is "the best expression of the slave's deepest thoughts and yearnings," and that spirituals speak convinc-ingly against the myths of the contented slaves.

The point here is that black people, while seemingly artic-ulating an eschatological cause, never forget their situation here on earth, in America and in Newark, New Jersey! That their religious worship is intricately intertwined with their daily struggles and joys! To substantiate this view, several lines from several spirituals have been cited. Among these lines are the following: "Lord help me from sinking," and "Don't know what my mother wants to stay here for, this old world ain't been no friend to her." From another song, these lines are cited: "I have been rebuked, I have been scorned, done had a hard time sure as you're born." And in the same instance: "When I get to heaven, gwine be at ease, me and my God gonna do as we please, gonna chatter with the Father, argue with the Son, tell 'em 'bout the world I just come from." Spirituals with similar message are many. It is hoped, however, that the few lines cited above do serve the point. And the point is that the black man, though not unaware of the world hereafter, never loses sight of his status on earth. This is an indication of his instincts or natural aptitude for living in close communion with nature regard-less of the hostility of the terrain. Also clearly implied in the lines cited above is that typically African characteristic of informality—chatting with "my God," arguing with the Son. It might be added that the kind of informality referred to here is a cultural manifestation stemming from the undif-ferentiated indigenous African way of life, so that chatting and arguing with God become as expressive of the real life and its unspeakable hardships as are the sad hymns, the mournful blues, the prayerful peals, or the squeals of human misery and pain.

Perhaps a better illustration of this aspect of black life is the black minister that you all know about—the minister who preaches as he sings, sings as he gestures, gestures as he shouts. Through all of these doings, he draws his audience so that they, too, become involved, with lots of "Yes, sir!", "Teach, teach!", and similar responses. Many of the sermons you hear are not about the world to come, and even when they are about the world to come, the status of life here and now is very much present. Such, then, is at least one side of black people's close communion with their nature. Even among the straightest black bourgeoisie (that is, black people who ape Judeo-Christian behavior, belief, and values), these qualities are present to some extent. At least it is easier for even the straightest black to reproduce that kind of a thing than for a Tom Jones or Janis Joplin to sing black or gesture black, try as they may. It is, to be sure, a matter of biocultural heritage. A recent piece by Albert Goldman from *The New York Times* is an interesting commentary:

> The roots of soul music—a fusion of gospel, blues and jazz—are black, but its most extensive audience is white . . . the kids [white] who were once content merely to listen and dance to the sounds of Ray Charles and Little Richard have moved on to adopt a whole new identity of black gesture and language—of black shouts and black lips, black steps and black hips. . . . There is something providential about the occurrence of this music miscegenation just at the moment when the races seem most dangerously sundered. Driven apart in every other area of national life by goads of hate and fear, black and white are attaining within the hot embrace of soul music a harmony never dreamed of in earlier days. Yet one wonders if this identification is more than thin skin deep. What are the kids [white] doing? Are they trying to pass? Are they color blind? Do they expect to attain a state of black grace?

Although Albert Goldman does attempt to answer his questions a little later on in the article, it is somewhat instructive to note that, though probably unaware of the fact, he does delineate some aspects of what we have here described as an Africanism—for example, the fusion of gospel, blues, and jazz, plus the "black shouts" and "lips," "steps" and "hips," and so on. Such a fusion, whether Goldman says so or not, is clearly implied in what we have described as an undifferentiated way of life, or that characteristic informality mentioned previously.

Historical and Cultural Continuity

Another area of interest here was postulated earlier, when it was contended that there has always existed some form of cultural communion among the African peoples both in the diaspora and Africa. This is to say that there existed periodic contacts, trickling as they may have been, between the African peoples on both sides of the Atlantic. In these early times, the seventeenth century, the African population in the New World was comparatively small, say, a little over a quarter of a million black people in the United States by the end of the seventeenth century, about half a million by 1710, and over four million by the mid-1800's, according to Lerone Bennett. This black population was comprised of free, indentured, and bonded Africans. The point here is that during these early days, there was little (as far as I am able to ascertain) made of the fact that some of the people in the new communities of the United States were black. This is not, of course, to say that there were no difficulties, or that the bonded or indentured blacks did not resent the kind of treatment they received. But compared to what was to follow, these early years were comparatively calm. Maybe some insights could be derived from the fact that the number of black people was small, and that some of them had come to America during the seventeenth century on their own to live or to work here (see Lorenzo J. Greene, *The Negro in Colonial New England*), which may be grounds to assume that the atrocities committed against black people were not so extensive and intensive as they later became.

By the middle of the eighteenth century the African popu-

79

lation in the United States had increased and the problems facing black men had multiplied sufficiently to make some people talk about sending black people back to their home to work among their own kind as either missionary workers or traders. In fact, by 1740 the Anglican Church had already drawn some plans to this effect, and by 1773 there were black Americans working in Africa as missionaries. Of these black Americans, some, like Newport Gardner, were very enthusiastic about the idea of returning to Africa. In the meantime, free Africans in some northern states not only began speaking out and referring to themselves as Africans or African descendants, but also started forming free African communities in America. Thus, Richard Allen, while describing his founding of the African Methodist Episcopal Church in December 1784, referred to his neighbors and colleagues as "my African brethren." On April 12, 1787, the Free African Society of Philadelphia was formed to perform certain religious and secular functions among the African people. The articles of the Free African Society specifically refer to "We, the free Africans and their descendants of the city of Philadelphia." Paul Cuffe, a shipbuilder and trader from Boston, described himself in the following terms: "And, as I am of the African race, I feel myself interested for them and if I am favoured with talent, I think I am willing that they should be benefitted thereby." The African Institution of Boston wrote to a Philadelphia group on August 3, 1812, that "we ought most cheerfully to sacrifice ease and many other privileges and comforts, for the purpose of diffusing light, and civilization and knowledge in Africa. There are several men in this place who calculate to go on to Africa with you whenever there is an opening. . . ."

Further evidence that self-conscious black Americans have always regarded themselves as either Africans or descendants of Africa is expressed by the Reverend David Nickens, a free African preacher and leader from Massachusetts. As quoted in *Black Nationalism,* he expressed strong pan-Africanist sentiments and great distaste for discrimination against the African peoples. He challenged the white people to:

look through the dark vista of past ages, and read in the history of Hannibal and others, who were Africans, the strength of intellect, the soundness of judgement, the military skill, which existed in ancient Africa. Africa was the garden and nursery where learning budded and education sprang. . . . If our ancestors were instructed and became great on the burning shores of Africa, why not their descendants . . . even on the continent of America? It is not essential that three millions of the sable sons and daughters of Africa must be sent to Liberia. . . .

Of great interest also is the work of Dr. Martin Robinson Delaney and Robert Campbell of the 1859–1860 Niger Valley Exploring Party, as described in their book *Search for a Place*. The treaty they signed with the African kings describes them as "Commissioners from the African Race of the United States and the Canadas in America," and wherever they attached their signatures, they did so "on behalf of the African race in America"; in fact, Delaney states the policy of the Exploring Party to be:

> and I hazard nothing in promulgating it; nay, without this design and feeling, there would be a great deficiency of self-respect, pride of race, and love of country, and we might never expect to challenge the respect of nations. . . . Africa for the African race, and black men to rule them. By black men I mean, men of African descent who claim an identity with the race.

It is to be hoped that these instances constitute sufficient ground for postulating that the African peoples in the New World and in Africa have always maintained some form of contact. It is also sufficiently shown that an African consciousness has always existed among the Africans in the diaspora. Both the content and the method of contact have varied from time to time and from generation to generation. After the Civil War black people were more or less preoccupied (or, at least it seemed so) with their situation in America, attempting to consolidate what seemed to be power but what was essentially a hoax. But it was not long before a new surge of pan-African activities started in the Caribbean and then in the States and Europe. The essence of pan-Africanism is unification, wherever possible, and cooperation of the African peoples, wherever they may be; it emphasizes the racial bonds, the experience, and the problems of the African peoples. Like previous expressions of Africanisms, pan-Africanism has had its champions and disciples: Silvester Williams called the First Pan-African Congress in London in 1900, and W. E. B. Du Bois predicted that the problem of the twentieth century would be the problem of color line.

Du Bois is among the giants of pan-Africanism. Perhaps more than anyone else, he is to be credited with the growth of the movement. He looked at the situation of black folks from a pan-Africanist perspective. He wanted Africans and peoples of African descent to be free wherever they might be, and with that freedom to move to Africa if they chose to, not to be repatriated against their will or interests. Some others of prominent standing in the pan-African movement were George Padmore, C. R. James, Kwame Nkrumah, Jomo Kenyatta, and Diagne Blaise. Not generally included among the intellectual pan-Africanists is Marcus Garvey. Perhaps this omission is the greatest letdown of the rank and file of black people by the intellectuals who are supposed to write and articulate these things. The point is that Garvey's contribution to the awakening and pride of the African peoples is unmatched in the entire history of black people. This is yet another instance of black intellectuals' inability to see the realities of their race. It is probably so because most black intellectuals are still very much in the man's bag and do not see too far beyond that pathological preoccupation with academic purity and objectivity.

The importance of the preceding comments on cultural transmission is that such contacts, whether by the black missionaries or by free Africans coming to live or work in the New World, or whether through various cultural and/or political congresses, served as the meeting ground for the various components of African culture that have evolved through time and place. A second method of cultural communion among black folks is in the written material which may have circulated among them throughout the world. The danger here is that black intellectuals *per se* are actually culturally deprived; now, it is not that they are devoid of the kind of Africanisms referred to earlier, but rather that at the point of biophysical interaction in a European kind of setting, they tend generally to respond in a mixed manner—mixed in that it attempts to incorporate the white man's conceptualization and practice into its operation. Thus, the net outcome is necessarily far removed from the original conceptualization and practice of black culture. To say that the black intellectual is culturally deprived is not to denigrate him, for he really is deprived. He is educated in a nonblack frame of reference; his education is white middle class oriented; he conceptualizes reality in the white frame of mind because that is the objectivity he has been taught and the one he feels compelled to reproduce in order to be accredited by the man. Most black intellectuals, writes E. Franklin Frazier in an article in *Apropos of Africa,* "simply repeat the propaganda which is put out by people who have large economic and political interests to protect." And as Frazier goes on to imply, black intellectuals and artists (our only cultural link, through their writings or artistic works) have been and continue to be for "sale." These two groups, perhaps the only two we could have relied on for meaningful, continued cultural communion among the African peoples, have bloodied their hands, like the slatees (the African slave captors), by availing themselves to the man for purchase.

Our dilemma is that what little contact we have maintained through history and what little cultural exchange we have maintained has been through a handful of black intellectuals. To this extent, then, they have served the African communities usefully. Ideally, that is what black intellectuals should be doing, but as has already been said, many of them spend their entire lives dancing at the man's intellectual court.

A third and the last method of cultural transmission mentioned here is that of acquiring cultural traits from the parents and peer groups. When in slavery or in the ghetto, black kids get what they can and what is available of their heritage from their parents. This is the old way, and it still works. As is commonly known, we are all somehow influenced by the prevailing fashions and attitudes of our contemporary peers. To this extent, then, black culture is passed on from generation to generation in just this fashion.

In conclusion, it should be emphasized that the black race, like any other race, possesses certain basic cultural traits that are genetically inherent in it. These genetically determined traits interact with environmental factors to produce the cultural manifestation we have described as Africanisms. These Africanisms have survived the most vicious atrocities and savageries ever committed against any group of humankind. Their survival has assured cultural survival and continuity among all the African peoples. The African peoples have strived, against terrible odds, to communicate and exchange their joys and sorrows and achievements throughout their history. It takes an unusual people to survive and be creative under similar circumstances.

SOURCES

AWOSIKA, V. O., *An African Meditation*. New York, Exposition Press, 1967.

BASTIDE, ROGER, "Color, Racism, and Christianity," in John Hope Franklin, ed., *Color and Race*. Boston, Beacon Press, 1968.

BENNETT, LERONE, JR., *Before the Mayflower*. Baltimore, Penguin Books, 1966.

BIESHEUVEL, S., *African Intelligence: A Study of African Ability*. Johannesburg, South Africa, African Institute of Race Relations, 1943.

_____ *Race, Culture, and Personality*. Johannesburg, South Africa, African Institute of Race Relations, 1959.

BILLINGSLEY, ANDREW, *Black Families in White America*. Englewood Cliffs, N.J., Prentice-Hall, Inc., 1968.

BLYDEN, EDWARD W., *African Life and Customs*. London, African Publication Society, 1908.

BRACEY, JOHN H., JR.; Meier, August; and Rudwick, Elliott M., *Black Nationalism in America*. Indianapolis and New York, The Bobbs-Merrill Company, 1970.

CICALA, GEORGE A., *Animal Drives*. Princeton, N.J., D. Van Nostrand Company, 1965.

CROWDER, MICHAEL, *West Africa Under Colonial Rule*. Evanston, Ill., Northwestern University Press, 1968.

DAVIS, DAVID B., *The Problem of Slavery in Western Culture*. Ithaca, N.Y., Cornell University Press, 1966.

DAWSON, J. L. M., *Cultural and Physiological Influences Upon Spatial-Perceptual Processes in West Africa*. London, Oxford University Press, 1963.

DE COY, ROBERT, *The Nigger Bible*. Los Angeles, Holloway House Publishing Company, 1967.

DELANEY, MARTIN R., and Campbell, Robert, *Search for a Place: Black Separatism and Africa*. Ann Arbor, University of Michigan Press, 1969.

DENT, C. R., *An Investigation of Certain Aspects of Bantu Intelligence*. Pretoria, South Africa, Government Printer, 1949.

DOOB, LEONARD, "On the Nature of Uncivilized and Civilized People," *Journal of Nervous and Mental Diseases*, no. 126.

———"The Use of Different Test Items in Non-Literate Societies," *Public Opinion Quarterly*, vol. 21, 1957-58.

DU BOIS, W. E. B., *The World and Africa*. New York, International Publishers, 1965.

DUBOS, RENE, *So Human an Animal*. New York, Charles Scribner's Sons, 1968.

FORRESTER, ANN, Paper presented at the Institute in Afro-American Studies, Brooklyn College, June 1969.

FRANKLIN, JOHN HOPE, ed., *Color and Race*. Boston, Beacon Press, 1968.

FRAZIER, E. FRANKLIN, *Race and Culture Contacts in the Modern World*. Boston, Beacon Press, 1957.

GOLDMAN, ALBERT, column in *The New York Times*, Dec. 14, 1969.

GREENE, LORENZO JOHNSTON, *The Negro in Colonial New England*. New York, Atheneum Publishers, 1969.

HARE, NATHAN, *The Black Anglo-Saxons*, New York, Marzani and Munsell, Inc., 1965.

HERSKOVITS, MELVILLE J. and Frances S., *Dahomean Narrative: A*

Cross-Cultural Analysis. Evanston, Ill., Northwestern University Press, 1958.

HILL, ADELAIDE CROMWELL, and Kilson, Martin, *Apropos of Africa*. London, Frank Cass and Company, Ltd., 1969.

JACQUES-GARVEY, AMY, ed., *Philosophy and Opinions of Marcus Garvey*. New York, The Humanities Press, 1963.

JONES, LEROI, *Home*. New York, William Morrow and Company, Inc., 1966.

LYSTAD, ROBERT A., ed., *The African World: A Survey of Social Research*, New York, Frederick A. Praeger, Inc., 1965.

MANDEL, SIEGFRIED, *Dictionary of Science*, Dell Publishing Company, 1969.

MBITI, JOHN, *African Religions and Philosophy*. New York, Frederick A. Praeger, Inc., 1969.

MEAD, MARGARET, "Research on Primitive Children" in L. Carmichael, ed., *Manual of Child Psychology*. New York, John Wiley & Sons, Inc., 1946.

PARK, ROBERT, and Burgess, Ernest, *Introduction to the Science of Sociology*, Chicago, University of Chicago Press, 1924.

PRICE-WILLIAMS, D. R., *Cross-Cultural Studies*. Baltimore, Penguin Books, Inc., 1969.

RAVEAU, FRANCOIS, "An Outline of the Role of Color in Adaptation Phenomena," in J. H. Franklin, ed., *Color and Race*. Boston, Beacon Press, 1968.

STUCKEY, STERLING, Paper presented at the Institute in Afro-American Studies, Brooklyn College, June 1969.

THOMPSON, V. B., *Africa and Unity*. New York, Humanities Press, 1970.

WHITE, LESLIE, *The Science of Culture*. New York, Grove Press, Inc., 1949.

6

COLIN A. PALMER

The Slave Trade

The institution of Negro slavery attained its greatest proportions in the New World. As an unfree laborer, the African found his way into the cotton and tobacco plantations
of North America, the textile factories and silver mines of
Mexico and Peru, the cane fields and sugar mills of Brazil
and of the French and British Caribbean, the households of
countless numbers of people in all of these areas—indeed into

every form of economic activity performed in the New World. The forced migration of the Africans to the Americas represented one of the greatest and widest dispersals of peoples throughout man's experience. Beginning in the early sixteenth century and continuing until the nineteenth century, this traffic in human merchandise assumed massive proportions as the demand for slaves increased.

The study of slavery and the slave trade has long commanded the attention of historians. Their objectives have generally been twofold. In the first place, such scholars have attempted to unearth the facts regarding the "peculiar institution" as a part of the general quest for truth. Secondly, historians have sought to understand contemporary problems by digging into the experiences of the past. For, to a very high degree, the question of Negro slavery and its aftermath still poses serious problems to societal integration in certain countries. The issue of race and race relations is the most crucial that the United States faces today. Other countries such as Guyana and Trinidad, which possess the seeds of potential racial turmoil, owe their status directly to Negro slavery and the voluntary immigration of East Indians after the abolition of slavery.

Although the study of the slave trade and slavery has evoked such great interest, it is often difficult to reconstruct meaningfully the slaves' experience in this hemisphere. Overwhelmingly illiterate, slaves left few records of the trauma of their experience. In the absence of numerous slave accounts, therefore, the historian has to rely extensively on the evidence left by masters, missionaries, or travelers, who, by virtue of their status, could not be expected to reflect in depth the nature of the slaves' story. In spite of this problem, studies of slavery, in order to be worthwhile, must be written essentially from the standpoint of the slave. A dedicated attempt must be made to recapture the totality of the slaves' experience.

In this essay, our attention will be focused on the machinery of the slave trade from Africa to the New World, particularly in North America. I shall discuss the organization of the trade during its legal and its illegal existence. Special attention will be paid to the Middle Passage, to the international competition which this trade generated, and to the efforts to suppress this infamous practice.

European Origins of New World Slavery

The Spaniards, who were the first Europeans to establish colonies in the New World, were not unfamiliar with the institution of slavery. Since the Roman occupation slaves had been a feature of Spanish society. Such slaves, drawn from a variety of peoples, were generally captives taken in war or people convicted for religious offenses. Slavery took on a new lease of life in Spain during the Moslem invasion in the eighth century, and as late as 1600 there were Moorish and Jewish slaves in that country.

As a separate group, Negro slaves did not become an important part of Spanish society until the late fifteenth century. The Portuguese discoveries on the African coast in the mid-fifteenth century initiated the trade in slaves between Africa and Europe. Historians recognize the year 1441 as that which marked the first direct involvement of the Portuguese in the African slave trade. In that year some Portuguese sailors captured a dozen Africans near Cape Blanc and took them back to Lisbon as slaves. In later years, in response to the demands of the Spaniards, the Portuguese began to supply them with the slaves they required. By the turn of the sixteenth century Lisbon and Seville had emerged as the two most important trading centers for African slaves in Europe.

Negro slaves played an important role in Spanish life and customs. In the absence of large-scale agricultural enterprises, such slaves were used principally as household workers, stevedores, nursemaids, and porters. Others found their way into the galleys and royal mines, perhaps the most physically demanding of the jobs the slaves had to perform. Faced with the problem of ensuring the security of the realm, the authorities introduced restrictive measures from time to time for the control of the slave population. On the other hand, the slaves possessed certain rights, as outlined by the legal code *Las Siete Partidas*. Drawing its inspiration from Roman and canon law, this code contained clauses which delineated the status of slaves and provided protective measures for them. The consensus among historians is that slavery was a relatively mild institution in Spain.

In view of the existence of Negro slavery in Spain, it is not surprising that Spaniards in the New World would look to Africa as a source of labor once the need arose. The discovery and colonization of the Indies gave a new dimension and added momentum to the slave trade. The Iberian colonists had brought to the New World new diseases to which the Indians were not immune. The result was a series of epidemics which substantially reduced the Indian population. In less than a century, for example, the Indians of the Caribbean islands had all but disappeared. In Mexico the decline was equally phenomenal. W. W. Borah and S. F. Cook, in their demographic study, *The Aboriginal Population of Central Mexico on the Eve of the Spanish Conquest,* estimate that the population of Central Mexico declined from about 25 million at the time of the Conquest in 1519 to slightly more than a million by 1605. With this drastic decline of the Indian population, it was obvious to the Spaniards, who balked at the indignity of manual labor, that an alternative labor supply would have to be found. Black Africa was exploited to fill this need.

The Slave Trade with the Americas

It is generally believed that the first black man came to the Americas during the second voyage of Christopher Columbus in 1493. Negro slavery as an institution, however, was not introduced into the New World until 1501. In that year, in granting their approval of this proceeding, the Spanish sovereigns Ferdinand and Isabella cautioned Nicolás de Ovando, the newly appointed governor of Hispaniola, not to "give permission to come there, Moors or Jews nor heretics, nor reconcilables, nor persons newly converted to our faith, except if they are Negro slaves or other slaves who were born in the power of Christians, our subjects and natives." Once formal permission had been granted for the introduction of Negro slavery in the New World, it would take centuries to reverse this decision. In the meantime, millions of Africans would be brought to this hemisphere to work in an economic system in which they had no stake.

There is no agreement among historians regarding the number of slaves that came to the New World. Most of the statistics cited in the books are nothing more than intelligent guesses. Consequently, there is a great disparity in the size of these estimates, which range generally from 15 million to as many as 50 million. The most systematic accounting of the slave trade is that recently done by Philip Curtin in *The Atlantic Slave Trade: A Census*. Curtin estimates that only about 9,391,000 slaves arrived in the Americas throughout the duration of the trade. The majority of these went to tropical areas—to the Caribbean islands and to Brazil. North America received only a small proportion of this influx of Africans, probably less than 5 percent of the total. Curtin calculates that about 345,000 slaves came to this country prior to the abolition of the traffic in 1808 and that approximately 54,000 entered illegally between 1808 and 1861, making a total of 399,000 slaves. Although these estimates are the most reliable that we possess, nevertheless they should be used with caution.

The business of supplying these African slaves to the American markets proved extremely attractive to the European traders. As already mentioned, the slave trade in the early days rested in the hands of the Portuguese, and they sought to impose a monopoly on this trade. They erected several forts along the western coast of Africa to consolidate their control. In the sixteenth century, however, with the colonization of the Americas and the demand for slaves in those colonies, other Europeans began to cast jealous eyes at the Portuguese monopoly. In order to participate in the unholy trade and to break the monopoly, the English pirate John Hawkins made his first voyage to the African coast in

1562—a mission which he repeated in 1564 and in 1567. His example was followed by other traders in later years. The intense competition which this trade generated brought in the French, the Dutch, the Danes, the Prussians, and the Swedes. As the trade progressed, these nations granted national monopolies to groups of their own merchants. In this way, for example, the Dutch West India Company was created in 1621, and the Company of Royal Adventurers of England, later reorganized as the Royal African Company, was established in 1663.

In the eighteenth century England established a clear supremacy over the other nations in the African slave trade. In addition to supplying slaves to her own colonies, she gained control of the *Asiento,* which was a contract to supply the Spanish colonies with all the slaves they needed. The transportation of slaves to the North American colonies, however, was not the exclusive preserve of the English traders. Many colonists, especially the merchants and shipowners of the New England states, found slave trading a profitable venture. By the eighteenth century Boston, Salem, and Newport had carved out prominent places for themselves. Other slaving ports included Portsmouth, Providence, and Bristol.

The extent of the profits derived from the slave trade is largely unknown, but most authorities agree that it was a lucrative enterprise. Eric Williams, in *Capitalism and Slavery,* asserts that profits of 100 percent on a slave cargo were not unknown in Liverpool. He cites the example of Bristol in the 1730s, where "it was estimated that on a fortunate voyage the profit on a cargo of about 270 slaves reached £7,000 or £8,000, exclusive of the returns from ivory. In the same year, the net return from an 'indifferent' cargo which arrived in poor condition was over £5,700." Similar success stories were reported for the North American traders. The profits from the slave trade had an impact much greater than the enrichment of a few individual traders. Daniel Mannix and Malcolm Cowley, in their *Black Cargoes,* conclude that "the slave trade in New England, as in Lancashire and the English Midlands, provided much of the capital that helped to create the Industrial Revolution."

The men who participated in this lucrative trade were blind to the horrors that it created. They looked on indifferently as several African societies were ripped apart by its ravages. In this rape of Africa the foreign traders had the support of some African chiefs who often warred with their neighbors for the sole purpose of obtaining captives for the slave market. These African middlemen exchanged their captives for cheap European manufactured goods, gunpowder, molasses, and alcohol. The following quotation, cited by Mannix and Cowley in *Black Cargoes,* describes quite vividly how the greed of the African trade corrupted its participants.

> Whenever the king of Barsally wants goods or brandy, he sends a Messenger to our Govenor at James Fort, to desire he would send a sloop there with a Cargo; this News being not at all unwelcome, the Govenor sends accordingly. Against the arrival of said Sloop, the king [plunders] some of his enemy towns, seizing the people and selling them for such Commodities as he is in want of, which commonly is brandy, or rum, Gunpowder, Ball, Guns, Pistols and Cutlasses. . . . In case he is not at war with any neighboring king, he falls on one of his own towns, which are numerous, and uses them in the very same Manner. . . . It is [owing to] that insatiable thirst of his after Brandy that his Subject's freedom and families are in so precarious a Situation. . . . He often goes with some of his Troops by a Town in the Daytime and returns in the Night and sets fire to three parts of it, placing guards at the Fourth to seize the People that run out of the fire, then ties their Arms behind them . . . sells them.

The slave trade extended its tentacles into numerous parts of black Africa. But the oft-repeated story of slaves trekking thousands of miles through the jungle to the waiting ships on the coast is an exaggeration. In general, most slaves came from within a few hundred miles of the coast. The majority of these slaves that reached the Americas hailed from ports along the western coast of Africa, generally between Senegal and Angola. The major slaving ports included Elmina, Lagos, Whydah, Old Calabar, Luanda, Cabinda, and Benguela. In addition, particularly in the nineteenth century, many slaves came from East Africa, especially from Mozambique.

The hapless African, who was a victim of this traffic, experienced the most brutal kind of degradation from the moment he was captured. The slave looked on helplessly as the African agent and the foreign trader haggled over his price and as the surgeons examined him to see whether he was made of the kind of mettle demanded by the hard labor overseas. The doctor's examination having been concluded, the cruel branding process followed, in which, according to John Barbot, a trader who is quoted by Basil Davidson in *The African Slave Trade,*

> each of the others, which have passed as good, is marked on the breast with a red hot iron, imprinting the mark of the French, English or Dutch companies, so that each nation may distinguish their own, and to prevent their being chang'd by the natives for worse, as they are apt enough to do. In this particular, care is taken that the women, as tenderest, be not burnt too hard.

The Middle Passage

The journey of a slave ship from an African port to the New World lasted between six and ten weeks. Known as the Middle Passage, this journey was the second leg of a voyage which generally originated at one of the European ports. The third and final leg of this triangular trade was the return journey from the American ports back to Europe; during this journey the ship was laden with tropical products. The Middle Passage was the graveyard of numerous slaves and crews. Conditions aboard the ships were intolerably bad. The hands and feet of the male slaves were shackled, and the great mass of humans was wedged into quarters much too small to accommodate them. John Newton, a slave trader, wrote from personal experiences in *Thoughts upon the African Slave Trade* that

> the cargo of a vessel of a hundred tons or a little more is calculated to purchase from 220 to 250 slaves. Their lodging rooms below the deck which are three (for the

men, the boys and the women) besides a place for the sick, are sometimes more than five feet high and sometimes less; and this height is divided toward the middle, for the slaves lie in two rows, one above the other, on each side of the ship close to each other like books upon a shelf. I have known them so close that the shelf would not easily contain one more. The poor creatures, thus cramped, are likewise in irons for the most part which makes it difficult for them to turn or move or attempt to lie down without hurting themselves or each other. Every morning, perhaps, more instances than one are found of the living and the dead fastened together.

These tightly packed and unsanitary slavers facilitated the spread of epidemic diseases. Smallpox, measles, dysentery, and a form of blindness known as opthalmia often proved to be the scourge of the slave cargo. In addition, some slaves committed suicide, resorted to hunger strikes, or even "willed" themselves to death by a process known as "fixed melancholy." This was a kind of psychically induced ailment, probably a result of the state of shock in which the slave found himself. Isaac Wilson, a surgeon in the Royal Navy, wrote, in a passage quoted by Mannix and Cowley in *Black Cargoes*, that

> no one who had it was ever cured, whereas those who had it not and yet were ill, recovered. The symptoms are a lowness of spirits and despondency. Hence, they refuse food. This only increases their symptoms. The stomach afterwards got weak. Hence, the belly ached, fluxes ensued, and they were carried off.

Although the traders expected the onslaught of several diseases during the Middle Passage, the provisions made for the care of the sick were appalling. In 1788 Alexander Falconbridge, an English surgeon, observed in *An Account of the Slave Trade on the Coast of Africa* that

> the place allotted for the sick Negroes is under the half deck, where they lie on the bare planks. By this means, those who are emaciated frequently have their skin, and even their flesh, entirely rubbed off, by the motion of the ship, from the prominent parts of the shoulders, elbows

and hips, so as to render the bones in those parts quite bare. And some of them, by constantly lying in the blood and mucus that had flowed from those afflicted with the flux [dysentery], and which, as before observed, is generally so violent as to prevent their being kept clean, have their flesh much sooner rubbed off, than those who have only to contend with the mere friction of the ship.

It is not possible to arrive at any conclusive figures regarding the mortality rate during the Middle Passage. Most historians, however, have tended to put it somewhere between 13 and 33 percent. Philip Curtin points out in his *Atlantic Slave Trade* that "mortality rates varied greatly according to the route, the length of the voyage, the original disease environment of the slaves themselves, the care they received, and the chance occurrence of epidemics." Some of the available records suggest that probably because of the construction of faster ships and the improved methods of sanitation aboard them the mortality rate declined during the eighteenth and nineteenth centuries.

It is debatable whether the survivors of the Middle Passage should be termed fortunate or unfortunate. For the fate that awaited them in some parts of the Americas was often an extension of the horrors they had already endured. In preparation for the brisk business that usually greeted the arrival of a slaver in an American port, the slaves would be released from their chains and given better and larger meals a few days prior to actual docking. On their arrival, the slaves were shaved and oiled and generally made ready for the hordes of prospective buyers. Often these wretched human beings were paraded through the public square so as to expose them to the anxious eyes of the waiting purchasers. Thereafter, the bargaining for each slave took place, while the terrified Africans often believed they were being bought in order to be eaten. The purchase of the slave by the master meant that the road to slavery was irrevocably completed.

The Domestic Trade

The road to the master had, of course, two aspects—the one international, the other domestic. The domestic trade involved the sale of the slaves within the territory by individuals unconnected with the external trade, and it began after the slaves had arrived from Africa and had been sold to their master. Any resale of such slaves could be considered part of the domestic trade. Native-born slaves who were sold also formed a part of this internal trade.

The domestic slave trade was particularly brisk in North America. If Curtin's estimates that only 399,000 Africans came to North America are correct, then the reproductive rate of the slave population must have been very high, since at the time of the Emancipation the slave population stood at approximately 4.5 million. In strong contrast to the other slaveowning areas of the New World, North America replenished its slaves principally by internal reproduction. This internal breeding produced a brisk traffic, especially after the international trade became illegal in 1808. Virginia played a prominent role in the domestic trade: between 1830 and 1860 it sold almost 300,000 slaves to other states. During the same period North Carolina sold approximately 100,000 slaves; South Carolina, 170,000; and Maryland, approximately 75,000. This thirty-year period coincided with an increase in the price of slaves. The average price of a prime field hand in Georgia, for example, rose from $700 in 1828 to $1,050 in 1851 and to $1,800 in 1860.

Legal Abolition of the Slave Trade

Although the plantation system had come to depend very heavily on slave labor, a few colonists questioned quite early the morality of enslaving other human beings. These voices were not very influential in the early days, but nevertheless they were not stilled. The Quakers were the most vocal and the most persistent members of the public that voiced their opposition to the slave traffic. In 1688 the group at Germantown publicly condemned it. During the eighteenth century the Society of Friends continued its opposition, but had only a limited degree of success. In 1761, for example, Pennsylvania, in response to Quaker pressure, imposed a duty of £10 on each slave it imported—a measure which effectively killed the slave trade within its borders.

The Declaration of Independence and the Revolutionary War accelerated the movement for the abolition of the slave trade. It became obvious to some of the "founding fathers," though they were slaveowners themselves, that the existence of the slave trade and slavery contradicted the ideals of the Declaration of Independence. These moral doubts, however, were not sufficiently compelling to warrant their inclusion in that particular document. Thomas Jefferson had included in the first draft of the Declaration of Independence a strong indictment of England's involvement in the trade. This was nothing more than sheer hypocrisy, since the colonists themselves were active participants in that trade. Jefferson's condemnatory words proved too unpalatable to some northern delegates, but particularly so to those from South Carolina and Georgia. In order to placate its opponents, the offending passage was removed from the final draft.

It is clear, nevertheless, that the Declaration of Independence helped to create an environment favorable to the end of the trade. Yet this is not the only explanation for the statutes forbidding it that appeared in the last quarter of the eighteenth century. Many people feared that the presence of too many restless African slaves would pose a severe threat to public order. Consequently, they were willing to support measures to end the trade from Africa. The fear of the slave population increased tremendously after the famous rebellion in Haiti in 1791. In that year half a million slaves rose up to destroy the sugar plantations and murder their masters. From that time onward the Haitian Revolution became the bogey of all the slaveowners in the hemisphere. In this atmosphere of intense insecurity, Georgia became, in 1798, the last state to declare the slave trade illegal.

The Illegal Phase

Although the states had made the slave trade illegal, and some citizens worried over the presence of too many slaves, many continued the traffic. In fact, the demand for slaves increased after Eli Whitney invented the cotton gin in 1793.

This invention made it possible for one person to separate far more cotton seeds from the staple in one day than had previously been the case. The boost given to cotton production by the new invention was reflected in the increased acreage given over to cotton and in the export figures from the South. In 1792 the export figures for cotton stood at 138,000 pounds; in 1795 they jumped to 6,276,000 pounds; and in 1800 they rocketed to 17,890,000 pounds.

The increasing profitability of cotton production and the consequent demand for more labor led to an open violation of the laws forbidding the slave trade. Many New England traders welcomed this opportunity to enrich themselves. On their part, the southern planters looked favorably on any activity which allowed them to obtain more slaves. South Carolina even legislated to reopen the trade in 1803. By 1807, however, Congress acted to end this inhuman traffic by making the international slave trade illegal as of January 1, 1808. However, it was one thing to pass such a law and quite another to see that it was enforced.

Legislation by the federal government did not effectively end the trade. The United States continued to receive African slaves. Georgia and Louisiana became the two principal centers of this traffic. The British government, which had abolished the slave traffic to its colonies in 1808 also, dedicated itself to a complete suppression of this trade to the other European colonies in the New World as well as to the United States. Although this determination stemmed essentially from humanitarian motives, the British also wanted to deprive their New World competitors of any economic advantages which could accrue to them through the continued availability of cheap slave labor. To this end, England persuaded the other maritime powers of Europe to sign treaties providing for the mutual right to board a suspected slaver of another nation and to search it. Such ships, if found to possess slaves, could be seized. By the mid-1830s Portugal, Spain, the Netherlands, France, and Denmark had all signed this treaty with England.

The United States was the only maritime nation that

stoutly rejected such a treaty. Acting on their own volition, the British at first boarded a number of American slavers after 1812, but desisted in the face of an outraged Congress and an inflamed public. In 1818 the British formally proposed a mutual right-to-search treaty to the United States, but the measure was stillborn. The British repeated their proposal to the Americans during the course of the next two decades, but their efforts were to no avail.

The refusal of the United States to sign the treaty meant that any slaver that hoisted the stars and stripes was immune to search by the British navy. As a result, United States citizens as well as foreigners who transported slaves mainly to Cuba and Brazil, all flew the American flag to avoid being hounded, thus frustrating British efforts to end the trade. Without a doubt, the United States was one of the greatest stumbling blocks to the suppression of the illegal slave trade in the nineteenth century. As the governor of Liberia, Thomas Buchanan, expressed it, "The chief obstacle to the success of the very active measures pursued by the British government for the suppression of the slave trade is the American flag. Never was the proud banner of freedom so extensively used by those pirates upon liberty and freedom."

On its part, the United States pursued a series of halfhearted measures to suppress the illegal trade. In 1819 Congress allowed the use of armed cruisers to patrol the coasts of West Africa as well as those of the United States to intercept slavers. The squadron had a short existence, since it was withdrawn in 1823. In 1820 participation in the slave trade was declared to be piracy and punishable by death. This law remained unenforced until Lincoln's presidency. In 1842 the United States and Britain agreed to undertake joint cruising off the African coast, but despite this concession the United States still looked unfavorably on any right-of-search treaty.

The American squadron was less than vigilant in its efforts to terminate the slave trade. In fact, the United States navy did not even see the suppression of this trade as its primary responsibility off the African coast. In 1843 the secretary of the navy, Abel P. Upshur, advised Commodore Perry, the first commander of the squadron, that "the rights of our citizens engaged in lawful commerce are under the protection of our flag, and it is the chief duty of our naval power to see that these rights are not improperly abridged or invaded." With this kind of injunction from such a high authority, it is not surprising that the various commanders of the squadron showed no active desire to apprehend the traders.

During the eighteen years that it remained off the African coast, the American squadron captured 24 ships and released 4,945 Africans. In strong contrast to this inertia, the British squadron in the same period captured 595 slavers and freed 45,612 captives. The American ships were invariably unseaworthy, too slow, or too cumbersome—factors which did not contribute anything to the success of their mission. In 1862, when the federal government withdrew the ships in order to use them in the blockade of the Confederate States, this charade came to an end.

The year 1862 marked the end of American participation in the illegal slave trade. In June of that year the United States finally agreed to sign the right-of-search treaty that Britain had requested all along. The treaty provided for the creation of nationally mixed courts in New York and Sierra Leone, and on the Cape of Good Hope, to try accused slavers. As was to be expected, this gave a tremendous boost to the international efforts to end the trade. The American flag no longer provided the slavers a sanctuary. By 1867, therefore, the British withdrew their squadron from the African coast—an event which showed that for all practical purposes the trade in humans across the Atlantic had come to an end.

The slave trade with the New World had endured for almost four centuries. It represented one of the most despicable episodes in man's history. Its continuation was fostered by the need for an exploited labor force in the various economic enterprises in the Americas. The fight to terminate this trade was a frustratingly slow process, since men's consciences were often numbed by greed. This numbness, unfortunately, is still a fact of life today.

SOURCES

BOOTH, ALAN R., "The United States African Squadron, 1843-1861," in J. Butler, ed., *Boston University Papers in African History*, vol. 1. Brookline, Mass., Boston University Press, 1964.

BORAH, W. W., and Cook, S. F., *The Aboriginal Population of Central Mexico on the Eve of the Spanish Conquest,* Ibero Americana Series, 45. Berkeley, University of California Press, 1963.

CURTIN, PHILIP D., *The Atlantic Slave Trade: A Census,* Madison, University of Wisconsin Press, 1969.

DAVIDSON, BASIL, *The African Slave Trade.* Boston, Little, Brown and Company, 1961.

DU BOIS, W. E. B., *The Suppression of the African Slave Trade to the United States of America, 1638-1870.* New York, Russell and Russell Publications, 1896.

FALCONBRIDGE, ALEXANDER, *An Account of the Slave Trade on the Coast of Africa.* London, J. Phillips, 1788.

MANNIX, DANIEL P., and Cowley, Malcolm, *Black Cargoes: A History of the Atlantic Slave, 1518-1865.* New York, Viking Press, 1962.

MEIER, AUGUST, and Rudwick, Elliott M. *From Plantation to Ghetto: An Interpretive History of American Negroes.* New York, Hill and Wang, Inc., 1966.

NEWTON, JOHN, *The Journal of a Slave Trader, 1750-1754, and Thoughts upon the African Slave Trade,* Bernard Martin and M. Spurrel, eds. London, Epworth Press, 1962.

ROTBERG, ROBERT, *A Political History of Tropical Africa.* New York, Harcourt, Brace & World, Inc., 1965.

SOULSBY, H. G., *The Right of Search and the Slave Trade in Anglo-American Relations, 1814-1862.* Baltimore, Johns Hopkins University Press, 1933.

STAMPP, KENNETH, *The Peculiar Institution: Slavery in the Antebellum South.* New York, Alfred A. Knopf, Inc., 1956.

WILLIAMS, ERIC, *Capitalism and Slavery.* Chapel Hill, University of North Carolina Press, 1944.

Why Study History?

Americans at large and, indeed, American scholars, have from time to time shown themselves unwilling to look beyond what seems to be the surface of many questions and to deal with the basic issues, the real problems. Rather, they deal with the outward expressions. In talking about automobiles, Ralph Nader suggests that the problems connected with our highways are due not only to the drivers, but to the machine itself. Historians have only recently begun to deal with the issue of race relations in this country and with the traditions of black Americans in the Nader fashion. They, like other Americans, have for the most part looked at the outer expressions, and they have held the black American responsible for what was happening to him, rather than looking underneath to see the underlying causes in American society. There is a story that developed during the heyday of the civil rights movement which perhaps makes this somewhat clearer. A man is driving through Mississippi, and, as often happens when one has been driving for long hours, he dozes at the wheel. When he awakens a second later, he realizes that he's bearing down on two black men who are walking toward him on the road. He swerves but is too close to stop, and he strikes the men with such force that one is knocked off the road a few yards. The other is thrown into the air and crashes through the windshield. Now since the driver is a white man of reasonable good will, he is in a state of shock when the Mississippi state police arrive and inquire as to what happened. When he explains, the state police assure him, "Don't worry about a thing: we'll charge one of the boys with breaking and entering, and the other with leaving the scene of an accident." This story suggests to some degree the way certain historians have treated matters related to black Americans in this country.

If one is alive and breathing in 1970, it should be clear to him that there are major differences between blacks and whites. There are differences in income, education, employment, crime, health, and indeed in attitude. The median income in this country for blacks is below that of whites in

all occupations, even when blacks and whites are performing the same job. Lifetime earnings of nonwhites who have
not finished college are about 60 percent of those made by
whites who have not finished college. The lifetime earnings
of nonwhites who finish college are only about 50 percent
of those made by whites with similar educational background.
Whites average several more years of education than blacks,
and the unemployment of blacks has consistently, since the
1950s, been about double that of whites. The question
is, Why do these differences occur? How do you explain
them? Is it sufficient to say, "Blacks simply don't work hard,"
or "Blacks don't work toward an education"? Perhaps, but
I am saying that even when education is the same and when
the same duties are performed, there are differences in income. In addition, whites live longer than blacks. Infant mortality among blacks is significantly higher than it is among
whites.

It is such questions that one faces when people ask, "What
is the relevance of history? Why study history?" Much of
the opposition to history expressed by so-called militant blacks
is due to the feeling that there is nothing in history as it has
been written by whites which serves to promote the cause of
human dignity.

The feeling is that one could throw out what we call "history" and in its place institute something else that would
leave us none the worse off. Some suggest discarding history completely. Others say that it must serve a propaganda
purpose, that it always has been used in this way and will
continue to be so used. There is certainly something to support this position in light of the historian's treatment of
black Americans.

But there is much of importance in history, as I see it. I
should like to offer my definition of history to provide a
framework for what follows—in order to suggest how and why
I think history serves an important purpose, and how it
might help us to deal with some of the questions growing
out of the differences between blacks and whites in this country and the related problems that we face in our social life.

I suggest that history is an attempt to systematically and analytically study selected points in time and space to the end that we better understand ourselves and the society in which we live. History aims to study these points in time and space with the hope that we can better understand who we are, what our society is, and how we fit into it. I am not in accord with those who say that there is some intrinsic value in the study of history and in ideas originating long ago, and that as one gets into these ideas one senses something of real merit. I believe the value of history comes to us only if we can use it in some way to better understand ourselves, our world, and our society. This kind of understanding enables us to approach some of the problems we face. Now obviously there is a danger if this is taken so narrowly as to mean that we must absorb only what serves our interests at this moment. The dangers of this narrow view we have seen in a number of totalitarian operations in the very recent past. But if we consider understanding ourselves and our society in a realistically broad sense, this meaning can stand up under severe examination. With this background and this framework, I turn my attention to the topic of American Negro slavery.

Early Concern with Legal and Moral Questions

The materials on the subject of slavery are, of course, great in quantity. There are official government documents of all kinds—local, state, and federal. There are religious tracts, there are plantation records, there are slave narratives, there are diaries of slaveowners, a wide range of biographies, and a number of novels which can quite properly be considered resource material. The early writers who drew on this material seem not to have concerned themselves with the contemporary questions which are so obvious to us today, but rather with some philosophical questions that had to do with the legality and the morality of slavery. They were asking themselves whether slavery was a legal institution and whether it was moral—this at the very time that black men were being physically destroyed, and blacks and whites in the country were being psychologically damaged. Throughout the nineteenth century—indeed, continuing after the end of slavery to the middle of the twentieth century—the kinds of questions with which historians dealt when they approached slavery had to do with morality or legality. I suggest that these are very narrow questions. Thomas R. R. Cobb, in his book *An Inquiry into the Laws of Negro Slavery in the United States of America,* published in 1858, and John C. Hurd, in *The Laws of Freedom and Bondage in the United States,* published in the same year, took opposing views but were both concerned with the legal approach. Cobb was a Georgia jurist who insisted that slavery was indeed legal, that all the laws of mankind—common law as well as the laws of the United States—supported it. Hurd contended that there was not in basic law any legal support for this institution. Other writers of the time followed one or another of these approaches. One guesses that the well-established legal profession in the mid-nineteenth century and the not so well established historical profession in America are responsible for this early legal approach to the question of slavery.

The moral issue faced the same kind of debate. Along with others, writers like William E. Channing, in *Emancipation,* published in 1840, and Lydia Child, in *An Appeal in Favor of that Class of Americans Called Africans,* published in 1833, questioned the morality of slavery on religious and humanitarian grounds. They set aside the legal question to ask if it was right for people to treat other people in such fashion. This is a perfectly good question but, again, a very narrow question.

As history began to develop as a discipline, the early historians continued to follow much the same patterns as the writers whose concerns were limited to the morality and legality of slavery. James Ford Rhodes, an early American historian who wrote at a time when long titles were the rule, in his *History of the United States from the Compromise of 1850 to the Final Restoration of Home Rule in the South in 1877*, denounced slavery as an evil for both the master and the slave. His approach was contradicted by the man whose work came to dominate the approach to slavery for almost half a century and who set the pattern for historians until the time of the Second World War. This was Ulrich B. Phillips. Phillips' *American Negro Slavery*, published in 1918, followed a number of articles he had published between 1900 and 1918, all picturing slavery as a benign institution more beneficial to blacks than it was to whites. Indeed, Mr. Phillips saw whites as suffering through a great deal in giving the semblances of civilization to the savage blacks who had been brought from Africa to this country. It is very interesting that his book appeared just at the end of the progressive period of American history, following which we find among historians attitudes about slavery that are perhaps the most conservative that the country has ever seen. Phillips helped to set the stage for this development, and he played the leading role. His was the dominant approach to slavery until the 1950s, when a number of books challenged his stance. One has no doubt that this challenge resulted in part from the influences of the Second World War and the exaggerated racism of Nazi Germany. Had earlier writers been able to look more closely at the United States, they might have more quickly been moved to this new approach.

In 1944 the sociologist Gunnar Myrdal produced *An American Dilemma*. Historians soon took up the efforts to answer the kinds of questions with which he dealt. Kenneth Stampp, author of *The Peculiar Institution: Slavery in the Antebellum South*, published in 1956, is one of these. Stanley M. Elkins, author of *Slavery: A Problem in American Institutional and Intellectual Life*, published in 1959, is another. David B. Davis' *The Problem of Slavery in Western Culture*, published in 1966, and Winthrop Jordan's *White Over Black: American Attitudes Toward the Negro, 1550–1812*, published in 1968, are also examples of books which reflect this focus, which begin to look at the more serious questions. Examine the title of the Elkins book. He is no longer asking, "Is the institution of slavery moral or immoral?" or "Does it have

legal standing?" He is asking, "What have been the problems for American institutional and intellectual life caused
by slavery?" This is the kind of probing question which may
help us to get at some of our basic concerns in respect to
people in this country today. If we really want to know why
blacks and whites are different, we must explain, somehow,
the effect of slavery, segregation, and discrimination on our
personalities and our physical and intellectual life. This
kind of examination may help us to serve what seems to me
to be the purpose of history. Thus, in spite of the vast quantities of literature that have been written about slavery, it
is only in the very recent past, within the last quarter of a
century, that historians have begun to ask the kinds of
questions that may help us deal with some of the problems
we have always had.

We know a great deal about the nature of slavery, and
can answer some of the questions that historians are beginning to ask. But there is still a great deal that we do not
know about slavery, and about its effects on our personalities and our intellects. These are the topics that I will explore very briefly, hoping more to raise questions than to
provide definitive answers. While there are some things
which are generally accepted by historians concerning the
nature of slavery, I feel far less comfortable in suggesting
to you that I have the "correct" answer—historians seldom
do—for questions related to the evolution of the slave institutions or their effect on our lives. Let us take some of the
issues and discuss them separately.

The Evolution of Slavery

In considering the evolution of slavery, there are some
facts which can be established. We know that there was no
antecedent in Great Britain that can be pointed out as the
model for the slavery which developed in this country.
Slaves could be found in Britain, and, indeed, that country
was seriously implicated in the slave trade. The Royal Adven-
ture into Africa, which was established in the 1660s, and the

Royal African Company, chartered in 1672, were the leading institutions involved in transporting slaves to North America. They established for Britain a monopoly on this trade. Through these business ventures, which were aided by her navy, Britain dominated the slave trade. It continued under British direction, the British government supporting it until about 1807; slavery in the British Empire continued until about 1833. Nevertheless, there is not a pattern of slavery in Britain that gives us a model of what happened in this country. British law simply did not provide for slavery. Three legal maxims, which were well established by the beginning of the eighteenth century, said that (1) England's air was "too pure" for slaves to breathe in; (2) a slave was free the moment he set foot on English soil; (3) once free for an hour, a person was free forever. For those persons who appeared on British soil as slaves, freedom was to come automatically. There still were occasional examples of slavery in England, but the idea was well established that slavery could not exist on that island, that a man was free forever if he once became free, and that there was no such thing as returning a man to slavery. The decision on a famous case in 1772, the Somerset case, expressed these maxims. The statements handed down by the court included the following: "The state of slavery is of such a nature that it is incapable of being introduced on any reason whether moral or political but only by positive law. It is so onerous that nothing can suffer to support it but positive law." The British were saying that one man could not hold another as a slave simply because of the absence of laws prohibiting slavery. The very fact that no law was passed to establish slavery was the point. Unless there existed a positive law to this effect, the institution was too evil to exist.

Such an attitude does not provide any assistance in understanding what the British colonists were to do in North America. The first Africans appeared in the North American British colonies in 1619. They came as indentured servants. Exactly what happened to this group—the degree to which each one worked off his indenture and moved into society— is little known. What happened to the Africans who came immediately after this first group is also not known with certainty. One of the very difficult and crucial periods to understand is that following the first arrival of Africans. What happened later in the relations between blacks and whites undoubtedly was influenced by this period, but we know very little about it. We do know that the initial growth of the number of Africans in the colonies was rather slow, and then there was a period of rapid growth. Take the two colonies of Virginia and Maryland as examples—two leading colonies in terms of the number of slaves in the early colonial period. Virginia in 1650 had only 300 Africans among the servants; in 1670 there were 2,000 Africans out of a total servant population of 8,000—not a very large increase in twenty years. Apparently Virginians preferred white servants to black servants at this point. By 1708 the number of Africans had increased to 12,000; thirty-five years later it was 43,000; and in the middle of the eighteenth century it had swelled to 120,000 out of a total population of 292,000. Thus, after a very meager beginning—300 Africans in 1650, three decades after the first had appeared; and only 2,000 in 1670, providing a quarter of the servant population at that time—a century later African slaves formed almost half of the population.

In Maryland the pattern was much the same. In 1708 blacks and whites were about equal in the population, but in 1765 there were 90,000 blacks and 40,000 whites—more than twice as many blacks as whites. Incidentally, one of the assumptions that seem to be unthinkingly accepted is that there has been a continuous increase in the proportion of black Americans in the population. The fact is that there has been a general decline in the proportion of black Americans in this country over the period of its independent history, due to the heavy immigration of whites from Europe in the nineteenth and twentieth centuries. At the first census in 1790 somewhere between 20 and 25 percent of the entire population was of African ancestry. Today the figure is approximately 11 percent, this representing a slight increase over the last century. Yet in Maryland, in 1765, the white population numbered less than half the black population.

That there were differences in the treatment of black and

white servants we know from court records. Decisions tell of the punishment of runaway black and white indentured servants, with the white servant having his time increased by three to five years and the black servant being assigned to servitude for life. There are some cases of black indentured servants being given no additional period of time—apparently these persons already being servants for life. Thus, a change in attitudes toward, and treatment of, black and white servants had taken place. It is, however, difficult to pinpoint just when and where.

There are some theories advanced for the cause of the unequal treatment. It is probable that the voluntary migration of most white indentured servants was one factor. If white servants had been enslaved, others would have simply ceased coming. But black servants did not come of their own accord. They were forced to migrate, and thus there was no feeling that the supply had to be ensured by protecting their rights. It is probable that a preference for white servants existed, but that the inability to get sufficient numbers to serve what was America's number-one need—and that was labor—caused colonists to turn more and more to the use of black servants, and to impress them into service for life. The increase in the flow of black servants after 1710 can perhaps be explained by the absence of legal obstacles to enslaving Africans. British common law spoke against enslaving Englishmen, and the rights of Englishmen were protected by British law. Likewise, there were governments of other countries which would have been concerned if colonials of French, Spanish, or Portuguese origin had been enslaved. But there were no governments recognized by the British or by the American colonists that were able to protect the rights of Africans, and of course this allowed officials to do what they would with these people.

It is probable, too, that the fact that Africans were not Christian when they arrived had its influence. Some of the early apologies for slavery describe it as serving to bring heathens to Christianity. Indeed, during the early colonial period of American history there were a number of apologies for slavery. Quite often they were couched in terms of the Christianizing of heathens or the bringing of savage people to a civilized society. But we must also realize that there was great profit in the slave trade and in slavery, and this undoubtedly was the chief influence on most white people involved with slavery.

The change that produced servitude for life is not the final change in the evolution of slavery. This evolution developed along lines peculiar to its American nature. In 1661 in Virginia, the law assumed that Negro servants would serve for life, Negro *servants* thus having evolved to Negro *slaves* between 1619 and 1661. In 1669 in Virginia, the law defined slaves as property. It provided that "if a slave resist his master and should chance to die his death should not be considered a felony but the master acquitted since it can't be assumed that malice would induce any man to destroy his own estate." The implication was clear here that the slave was a part of the property of the master, and that a slaveowner would not be found guilty of murder because nobody would destroy his own property out of malice.

There was, however, some ambivalence in the minds of colonists as to what kind of property slaves were. Some wanted to describe slaves as real estate, rather than as personal property, because a man who got into financial difficulty and was bordering on bankruptcy might have his personal property taken away. Slaves were a capital investment, an important means of profit; their loss would be a severe economic liability. Nevertheless, there was also an effort to describe the slaves as chattel—personal property—property that one could use like clothing or trinkets. By 1726 the law provided for slaves to pass from person to person as chattel, as personal property. The law was more explicit in 1740 when it said slaves were "chattel, personal in the hands of their owners and possessors to all intent, construction, and purposes whatsoever."

By 1740, then, evolution had brought blacks in North America from their indentured servitude of 1619 to the point where they were not only servants for life, but were property.

They were not human beings, possessed of certain rights; not real estate, protected by laws that apply to land—but personal property, chattel, that could be used or misused as the master saw fit.

A further indication of what had happened can be seen in the action of the Maryland Assembly in 1664. A bit of that record says:

> be it enacted that all Negroes and all other slaves already within the province and all Negroes and all slaves hereafter to be imported into the province, shall serve for life, and all children born to any Negro or any other slave shall serve as their fathers were for the term of their life. And insofar as much divers freeborn English women, forgetfull of their free condition and to the disgrace to our nation marry Negro slaves. . . . Be it further enacted . . . that whatsoever freeborn women shall marry any slaves from and after the last day of this Assembly shall serve the master of such slave during the life of her husband. And that all the issue of such freeborn women so married shall be slaves as their fathers were. And be it further enacted that all the issues of English or other freeborn women that have already married Negroes shall serve the master of their parents until they be thirty years of age. . . .

This is quite an effective way of doing away with miscegenation. It suggests that there was no *natural* division among blacks and whites, and that those who observed advantages in separation of the races were worried. One guesses that the law was moving to institutionalize the local opposition to mixing of the races, ratifying formally what the local colonists had taken objection to.

Religion and Slavery

One can not talk about the evolution of slavery without talking about religion, so closely was religion interwoven with law in colonial society. An early justification for slavery, or a rationalization for it, was that slaves were being brought to

Christianity. In one of his books, *Life and Labor in the Old South,* U. B. Phillips sets forth this point of view when he says of slaves, "They were heathens who by transportation to some Christian Land might attain eternal bliss at the mere price of lifetime labor."

One can see the problem that arose for people who at first defended slavery as being a way to bring heathens to Christianity: what happened when the slave was born a Christian? This had to be dealt with, and the Virginia law moved to do so in 1667. The law specified that "baptism does not alter the person as to his bondage or freedom in order that masters free from this doubt may endeavor the propagation of the Christian faith." In Maryland a 1671 law said, "Any Christianized slave is at all times hereafter to remain in servitude and bondage for all intentions and purposes as he was and subject unto before becoming Christian or receiving of the sacraments of baptism." The very existence of these laws says clearly that this question was indeed in the mind of Virginians and Marylanders. What did one do when the African one had acquired as a heathen and converted to Christianity gave birth to children who knew only Christianity? Indeed, some owners were unwilling to convert their Africans, because to convert them to Christianity suggested that owners were supposed to consider them as brothers. But the law stepped in to provide support for the owners.

This position with regard to Christianity represented part of a movement which gained much greater strength in the nineteenth century. Then not only did Christianity serve to justify slavery, but it condoned it as a positive good—a matter to be mentioned a bit later. Let me simply say here that the biblical justifications of slavery which occurred in the nineteenth century were not widely expressed in the eighteenth century.

It is very difficult to explain how Englishmen, with their concepts of the rights of Englishmen and the rights of human beings, could accept such ideas. And make no mistake about it—Americans of English descent always knew blacks were human. They forced themselves at various times to rationalize this in one way or another, but this was never a serious issue. Englishmen, coming from that part of the world which perhaps was the most advanced at the time in its concern for the rights of men, in the United States developed a system by which human beings who came as servants, fitting into a pattern of servitude that had existed for a long time, became servants for life and finally personal property to be handled in any way the owner saw fit. The facts that we know are not sufficiently obvious to explain this evolution. It raises questions to which many sociologists and historians must turn their attention.

There are some additional points to be made on this matter. The evolution of the slave system was not accepted by all people involved. Revolts took place among slaves. You might wish to examine Herbert Aptheker's *American Negro Slave Revolts* (1943), one of the books that breaks with the traditional idea that slaves enjoyed their situation, that Africans looked forward to traveling abroad, and what better way than a free trip on one of His Majesty's slave ships? More recently other works have examined this issue. Aptheker tends to define the term "revolt" in very broad fashion, but this does not destroy the value of his work, which points out clearly the opposition of slaves to the slave system. There is evidence to suggest that people being captured often sought suicide rather than slavery. We also know that some white Americans were opposed to slavery for a variety of reasons. Some said it was detrimental to whites in this country; others thought it was morally wrong, based on religious standards. One such person was Benjamin Rush, M.D., graduate of Princeton University, signer of the Declaration of Independence, and organizer of the Philadelphia College of Physicians. In a radical statement for the years just before the American Revolution he wrote:

> Ye men of SENSE AND VIRTUE-Ye ADVOCATES for American Liberty, rouse up and espose the cause of Humanity and general Liberty. Bear a testimony against a vice which degrades human nature. . . . Remember that national crimes require national punishment and without declar-

ing what punishment awaits this evil . . . it cannot pass
with impunity, unless God shall cease to be just and
merciful.

The Further Protection of Slavery
Through Law and Custom

It should further be said that the slave interest grew and
prospered and the evolution of the institution did not end as
it reached the point of declaring blacks to be chattel. Indeed,
during the eighteenth and well into the nineteenth century
the slave interest increased its influence. Let me suggest
some things that illustrate this. In spite of the fact that the
Northwest Ordinance of 1787 outlawed slavery in the Northwest Territory, in the same year the Constitution condoned
slavery—the three-fifths clause clearly recognizing its existence, although not using the term. The slave trade continued
until 1808. Citizens of the states (according to the Constitution) were entitled to all the privileges and immunities of
the citizens of all the states, which might be interpreted to
mean that a man could carry his property wherever he
wanted. In addition, states formed in the Old Southwest—
Alabama and Mississippi, for example—wrote in their constitutions laws which provided that legislatures could not take
action to prevent the importation of slaves into the states, nor
could they move to free slaves without the owners' permission,
and there were a whole series of laws in all the southern states,
and in the vast majority of northern states, limiting and
restricting the rights of free blacks.

Where law did not provide restrictions, tradition did.
Alexis de Tocqueville, in his *Democracy in America,* related
a conversation with a Quaker friend in Philadelphia. He
asked his friend to explain how it was that in the Quaker
stronghold of liberalism blacks were not allowed to vote. His
friend answered that Tocqueville did Philadelphia an injustice. There was no law which would prevent such action.
Blacks were free to vote like anyone else. Tocqueville said
that he had observed people at the polls that morning but

did not see any blacks in line. The friend replied that he was quite right. Black people had the right to vote, but they declined to do so. Tocqueville asked why. His friend replied that in spite of their desire to vote they declined to do so because they knew that white people would not react favorably. Tocqueville's point was that the majority makes the law providing for the right to vote, but it also breaks the law by making clear that blacks should not vote. Not only were laws being made to protect slavery, but traditions moved to protect it also. Where the law did not do it, the majority of the people often acted through tradition to protect the institution of slavery and the idea of white superiority.

To summarize, while much is yet to be known about the evolution of slavery, there are some generalizations that can be made: (1) The first Africans who arrived did not come as slaves, as we later see slaves in America. (2) Within half a century after the arrival of the first Africans, Americans had moved to define very clearly that key element which makes a person a slave—the length of servitude. Throughout the colonies, servitude for life had come to be applied. (3) Within a century after the arrival of the first Africans, the definition of slaves as chattels had been firmly established. So it is that somewhere within a century after 1619 Americans had developed the institution that we know, and this institution continued in strength and virility for quite some time.

The Nature of Slavery and the Plantation

There are great quantities of documentation and considerable agreement among people who study slavery about the nature of the system as it operated in the United States.

We can say that the experience of the typical slave was a plantation experience: even though the typical slaveowner was not a plantation owner, the vast majority of the slaves were on plantations. Drawing on the census of 1850 we see that approximately 569,000 agricultural units existed in the southern area where slavery prevailed. Not more than 100,000, or 18 percent, were large enough to be called plantations. According to the same census, there were 285,000 slaveowners, half of which held less than five slaves. One out of ten held as many as twenty slaves. The total number of slaves in 1850 was 3,638,000, more than half of these existing on plantations holding twenty or more. This would suggest that 10 percent of the owners owned more than 50 percent of the slaves. The other slaves were scattered among small holdings, where they worked side by side with owners, or they were city slaves, about whom I shall not say much here. I refer you to the book by Richard Wade, *Slavery in the Cities,* as one of the good sources on this aspect of the topic.

The plantation itself was largely a self-sufficient unit. The few manufactured goods it needed were brought from England or New England. It produced most of its own foodstuffs, and usually one or two staple crops. The major crops were corn, produced not for sale, but for food and feed; tobacco, which served to get the plantation system started; cotton, not of much importance in the country until after the American Revolution; rice, grown in Georgia and South Carolina on the Sea Islands and in the coastal region; indigo, which was often produced along with rice because the climate allowed for the growing of two crops and made more profitable use of slaves and land; and sugar, grown mainly in Mississippi and Louisiana.

The work of the slaves on the plantation included cultivation of the fields, care and harvesting of the crops, clearing land for new plantations or extending the land under cultivation, and the manufacture of simple articles, as well as housework. Two systems of control were used in the handling of slaves, the task system and the gang system. They almost explain themselves. Under the task system each slave was assigned a certain task, after which, theoretically, he was finished. The gang system provided drivers who set a pace that the slaves were to follow. The driver was sometimes the slaveowner himself, if he happened to have a small number of slaves, or he might be one of the slaves, who was rewarded with some small benefits such as better clothes, additional food, and certain liberties within the plantation if he did his job well. The aim of the owner, of course, was to get the greatest possible use out of his slaves without incapacitating them; slaves were his most valuable property, since labor was in short supply. Land, however, was very cheap and so readily available that there was very little desire to use it properly. So badly was it misused, that the records are full of stories of entire plantations moving westward after the land had worn out.

Such a system suggests problems existing within it, and the problems for the slaves were very real. The example of cotton culture can be used to suggest, in general terms, their year-round routine. Cotton, grown in large plantations, was by Civil War days, symbolically as well as economically, the most important crop in the South. On a plantation the early months of each year were spent picking seeds from and baling cotton that had been grown the year before. Time was also spent preparing buildings, splitting rails for fences, cutting wood, clearing land, and doing other tasks that could be done in winter. When the spring came, the field had to be plowed and prepared. Corn was planted in March and cotton in April, and their cultivation went on all during the summer. The picking began in September. This went right into the next year, and the cycle began again.

The sugar plantations are considered by most writers to be the places where the greatest mistreatment of slaves took place, the nature of the work being more demanding than that on a cotton plantation. Indigo and rice were grown together, and when one crop was finished the other crop was put in, making full use of the labor and the land. The treatment of slaves on the various plantations differed to some degree according to the crop, but more importantly, according to the owner and the overseer. There is no real dispute about the statement that violence and terror were standard procedures in getting work done. Evidence of this comes from the slaves, slave managers, and owners in their writings about the time. There seems to be no real disagreement. Let me quote from the narrative of Solomon Northup, a slave for some years before escaping to freedom. This excerpt from Milton Meltzer's *In Their Own Words: A History of the American Negro* gives Northup's view of the fear, violence, and the threat of violence on a cotton plantation:

> The day's work over in the field, the baskets are "toted," or in other words, carried to the gin-house, where the cotton is weighed. No matter how fatigued and weary he may be—no matter how much he longs for sleep and rest—a slave never approaches the gin-house with his basket of cotton but with fear. If it falls short in weight—if he has not performed the full task appointed him, he knows that he must suffer. And if he has exceeded it by ten or twenty pounds, in all probability his master will measure the next day's task accordingly.
>
> So, whether he has too little or too much, his approach to the gin-house is always with fear and trembling. Most frequently they have too little, and therefore it is they are not anxious to leave the field. After weighing, follow the whippings; and then the baskets are carried to the cotton house, and their contents stored away like hay, all hands being sent in to tramp it down. . . .
>
> This done, the labor of the day is not yet ended, by any means. Each one must then attend to his respective chores. One feeds the mules, another the swine—another cuts the wood, and so forth; besides, the packing is all done by candle light. Finally, at a late hour, they reach the quarters, sleepy and overcome with the long day's toil. Then a fire must be kindled in the cabin, the corn ground in a small hand-mill, and supper, and dinner for the next day in the field, prepared. All that is allowed them is corn and bacon, which is given out at the corn-crib and smoke-house every Sunday morning. Each one receives, as his weekly allowance, three and a half pounds of bacon, and corn enough to make a peck of meal. That is all—no tea, coffee, sugar, and with the exception of a very scanty sprinkling now and then, no salt. . . .

The softest couches in the world are not to be found in the log mansion of the slave. The one [bed] whereon I reclined, year after year, was a plank twelve inches wide and ten feet long. My pillow was a stick of wood. The bedding was a coarse blanket, and not a rag or shred beside. Moss might be used, were it not that it directly breeds a swarm of fleas. . . .

An hour before day light the horn is blown. Then the slaves arouse, prepare their breakfast, fill a gourd with water, in another deposit their dinner of cold bacon and corn cake, and hurry to the field again. It is an offence invariably followed by a flogging, to be found at the quarters after daybreak. Then the fears and labors of another day begin; and until its close there is no such thing as rest. He fears he will be caught lagging through the day; he fears to approach the gin-house with his basket-load of cotton at night; he fears, when he lies down, that he will oversleep himself in the morning. Such is a true, faithful, unexaggerated picture and description of the slave's daily life, during the time of cotton-picking, on the shores of Bayou Boeuf.

Other evidence would suggest that this statement is probably true. References about violence and its use also come from slaveowners, as reported by Kenneth Stampp in his book *The Peculiar Institution*. He reports an Arkansas slaveowner as saying, "It is like casting pearls before swine to try to persuade a Negro to work. He must be made to work and should always be given to understand that if he fails to perform his duties he will be punished for it." Stampp reports a Virginian as saying, "Slaves will not labor at all except to avoid punishment." Another slaveowner is recorded as saying, "Punishment does not tend to make Negroes revengeful as it did members of other races, rather it tended to win his attachment and promote the happiness and well being of the man." Mary B. Chestnut, the wife of a plantation owner in Montgomery, Alabama, wrote in 1861, "I wonder if it be a sin to think slavery a curse on any land. Men and women are punished when their masters are brutes not when they do wrong. God forgive us, but ours is a monstrous sys-

tem, a wrong and an iniquity." So there seems to be no doubt
about the brutality of slavery, so far as the sources are concerned. Slave masters say they use it because they have to;
and one goes so far as to say that it is also good for the slaves
—it makes them happy and content.

The Concept of Racial Inferiority

Slavery was more than a system of labor. It was also a
system of social control aimed at establishing in the minds
of blacks and whites the idea that blacks were inferior. There
is no question about this. If one examines the laws which
continued in existence until the end of slavery, as well as the
laws put into existence by southern states after the Civil
War and the ways of treating blacks in the northern states
(not so much legal as traditional), then it is clear that the
system was aimed at establishing the inferiority of blacks
to whites. The Slave Codes, which were fairly uniform
throughout most of the South, specified, among other things,
that slaves could not own property unless it was sanctioned
by the master; slaves could make no contracts; and marriage
among slaves did not have the force of law. Slaves could not
possess guns, nor could they have drums or horns, which
might be used to convey signals; they were not to be allowed
out after curfew; and they were not to travel singly without
a permit or in groups without a white escort. Slaves could not
assemble at night unless a white person was present. Slaves
could not strike a white person, even in self-defense. Rape
of a female slave was not a crime, but it was a crime to teach
slaves to read and write.

Incidentally, on this matter of reading and writing—having come to believe that Christianity would serve to maintain control over the slaves, the southern white was caught
in the position of wanting to teach them Christianity without teaching them letters. The result was a process of "Christianity without letters." The idea was to teach the slaves
orally what the Bible called for them to do—to obey the master was the point getting greatest stress—without giving them

the ability to read or write. In the biography of Frederick Douglass, one discovers how he managed to learn to read and write in opposition to the will of his owner and the owner's wife: he bribed poor white boys with food from the house in which he worked. Other slave narratives report similar kinds of experiences.

The patterns of laws that are described here are clearly reflected in the religion of many whites. The biblical defenses and justifications for slavery provide a clear indication of what the thinking was like. The Reverend Josiah Priest, writing in *Biblical Defense of Slavery* in 1852, said the following:

> The fact of the inferiority and consequent subordination of the black race to the whites, being in accordance with the Supreme rules of the universe, is not like a mathematical problem, susceptible to absolute demonstration.

He goes on to say that you have to believe this, you have to accept it—accept it as truth. Amor Patriae, in his little book *The Blasphemy of Abolitionism Exposed: Servitude and the Rights of the South Vindicated; A Biblical Argument* concludes as follows:

> Now, Honorable Sir, I have cited all the passages of scripture in both the Old and New Testament of any importance, that touch directly upon the subject under consideration. Enough, at any rate, one would think, to satisfy the most skeptical, that slavery is a DIVINE INSTITUTION. . . God would never have authorized slavery if he had not intended it as a blessing to mankind. If it does not so result it is the fault of man, not of the institution.

Interpretations of the Uniqueness of American Slavery

Why did slavery in the United States develop as it did? The fact is that historians are not in agreement on this. It is one of those questions which are roundly debated, but for which there is at present no definitive answer. Slavery had long existed in Europe and Africa. From ancient times it had existed. In most cultures slaves were people who were unfortunate enough to be captured in war. There was no concept of the inferiority of the slave as a person. The Romans, for example, quite often considered captured Greeks as being equal or superior in some things and sought Greek slaves as teachers. The Spartans in ancient Greece held a people called helots as slaves and came closest to paralleling the attitudes of Americans. Their system included certain aspects of serfdom in that the helots were bound to the land. By and large, however, it is hard to find in early slavery or in slavery outside of the United States anything quite like the system which developed in this country. Slavery was abusive in all places; the mistreatment of slaves (as in the mines and on the plantations of ancient Rome) was universal, so that the brutalization of people is not what sets American slavery apart. The real difference appears in the attitudes resulting from slavery, which in this country have been more long-lasting and more severe than was the case elsewhere. Once a slave was freed in Rome, he might move on to a rather important position in life. Some did. One was considered unfortunate if he was a slave, but it did not carry with it the peculiar stigma which Americans associated with slavery.

Some people have pointed to the large number of blacks in America—principally in the South—as the best explanation of why slavery in this country developed in such a peculiar way. They say that it was the fear of large numbers of blacks and the consequent possibility of slave revolts which explain the American system. This is hard to accept fully when one finds that in Brazil—where the proportion of blacks to whites in the population was even larger, and where slave revolts were much more common—the system of slavery that developed did not have such long-lasting effects and never established patterns of prejudice and racism to the same extent. Brazil does have some problems that relate to color and former condition of servitude, but it does not have the kind of racial problems characteristic of America. Also, it's odd to examine this fear of slave revolts and consider the consistent

America to which we must look. I find it a little difficult to accept the idea that within certain people there were natural evil tendencies which made them move in certain directions. I suggest that one has to look elsewhere for an explanation. Stanley Elkins, author of *Slavery: A Problem in American Institutional and Intellectual Life,* holds that the peculiar nature of American slavery arose out of the absolute dependence of the plantation slave on the master. He makes the comparison with Jews in Nazi concentration camps, in which some of the inmates came to identify themselves with the guards who abused them. However, to refer to Brazil once again: masters there had the same sort of control, and the same kind of brutalization went on, but the psychological effect was different.

I want to suggest for consideration a different kind of approach. I suggest that instead of mistreating black men because they hated them, whites may have come to hate black men because they mistreated them. If we are going to understand what happened in the development of slavery, perhaps we ought to examine other things that were happening in the North American colonies and in the early United States at the same time that slavery was evolving into the peculiar institution it became. We have to remember that Europeans came to this country hoping for certain benefits, among them religious freedom and economic gain, and that these people brought with them, or soon developed, considerable concern for such things as the rights of man. Quite early they expressed interest in liberty, equality, and salvation through direct contact with God. The religious, social, and economic benefits which attracted the early colonists to the country and which were the concerns of early people in the independent United States were denied to those men who happened to be black.

What happens when we examine this contradiction more closely? Maryland, for example, the colony which passed the Toleration Act in 1649, passed in 1664 the law concerning slavery which set blacks and whites apart. Eighteenth-century America, which produced the Declaration of Independence ("We hold these truths to be self-evident, that all men are created equal"), also produced a law in Massachusetts which limited relations between blacks and whites and a law in Connecticut which made it impossible for blacks to own land. Earlier I mentioned the constitutions of Alabama and Mississippi and their positions on slavery in the early nineteenth century, a few decades after the Declaration of Independence. The Constitution of the United States provided for rule by the majority, with respect for the rights of the minority, but also provided for slavery and supported the continuation of the slave trade. The Bill of Rights (1789) and the Fugitive Slave Law (1793) belonged to the same period. It is most unlikely that concern for these contradictions in the minds of Americans could have done anything other than cause conflicts. On the one hand Americans were proclaiming liberty, equality, and the rights of man, and on the other they were saying they wanted a system which controlled black men and allowed whites to have blacks do their bidding in all things whatsoever.

It appears, then, that the colonists, and later the Americans, were caught between two extreme positions: the acceptance of all human beings as entitled to all those rights they professed to believe in, and the definition of these rights in a very narrow, selfish sense that excluded people who were different in appearance. In this conflict lies a clue for examination of the peculiar nature of the American system. To resolve the conflict whites rationalized that slaves were not entitled to things others were entitled to because they were somehow subhuman. Through conscious and unconscious actions, they came to believe their rationalizations of the situation and to set them forth as eternal truths.

I suggest that it is not *in spite of* the Declaration of Independence and concern with the rights of man that slavery developed in such a peculiar way; rather, it is *because* of the Declaration of Independence and the beliefs in liberty and equality that American slavery developed the way it did. If an American was to believe in lofty ideals, he could not believe in them comfortably and deny them to certain men. So the only solution was to believe in these high ideals and at the same time believe that black people who were enslaved and mistreated were not men. Thus no conflict existed. I do not suggest that this is a final explanation. But it does seem to me that we will never get at the answer to this question of racism in America unless we see slavery as developing side by side with ideals which were diametrically opposed to it—a contradiction which led white people to rationalize in such a way as to allow themselves to believe both in their ideals and in slavery.

SOURCES

APTHEKER, HERBERT, *American Negro Slave Revolts*. New York, International Publishers, 1943.

CHANNING, WILLIAM ELLERY, *Emancipation*. Boston, E. P. Peabody, 1840.

CHILD, LYDIA, *An Appeal in Favor of that Class of Americans Called Africans*. Boston, Allen and Ticknor, 1833.

COBB, THOMAS R. R., *An Inquiry into the Laws of Negro Slavery in the United States of America*. Philadelphia, T. & J. Johnson and Company, 1858.

DAVIS, DAVID B., *The Problem of Slavery in Western Culture*. Ithaca, N.Y., Cornell University Press, 1966.

DEGLER, CARL, *Out of Our Past: The Forces that Shaped Modern America*. New York, Harper & Brothers, 1959.

ELKINS, STANLEY M., *Slavery: A Problem in American Institutional and Intellectual Life*. Chicago, University of Chicago Press, 1959.

HURD, JOHN C., *The Laws of Freedom and Bondage in the United States*. Boston, Little, Brown and Company, 1858.

JORDAN, WINTHROP, *White Over Black: American Attitudes Toward the Negro, 1550-1812*. Chapel Hill, N.C., published for the Institute of Early American History and Culture at Williamsburg by the University of North Carolina Press, 1968.

MYRDAL, GUNNAR, *An American Dilemma*. New York, Harper & Brothers, 1944.

NORTHUP, SOLOMON, "Picking Cotton," in Milton Meltzer, ed., *In*

Their Own Words: A History of the American Negro, vol. 1. New York, Thomas Y. Crowell Company, 1964.

PATRIAE, AMOR, *The Blasphemy of Abolitionism Exposed: Servitude and the Rights of the South Vindicated; A Biblical Argument*. New York, 1850 (no publisher given) .

PHILLIPS, ULRICH B., *American Negro Slavery*, 1918. Reprinted: New York, D. Appleton and Company, 1940.

_____ *Life and Labor in the Old South*. Boston, Little, Brown and Company, 1929.

PRIEST, JOSIAH, *Biblical Defence of Slavery and Origins, Fortunes, and History of the Negro Race*. Glasgow, Ky., Rev. W. S. Brown, pub., 1852.

RHODES, JAMES FORD, *History of the United States from the Compromise of 1850 to the Final Restoration of Home Rule in the South in 1877*. New York, The Macmillan Company, 1906.

STAMPP, KENNETH, *The Peculiar Institution: Slavery in the Antebellum South*. New York, Alfred A. Knopf, Inc., 1956.

TOCQUEVILLE, ALEXIS, DE, *Democracy in America*, 2 vols., 1835, 1840. Reprinted: New York, Alfred A. Knopf, Inc. 1945.

A family in Africa, before slavery. Ardjoumani, king of Bondoukou, sits between his sons.

130a

White America prospers from the marketing of slaves, while the black man proclaims that he is not a commodity. *Below,* a diagram shows how to pack human cargo; *opposite page,* slaves are put up for sale, 1835, in New Orleans. *Above,* a drawing that headed an 1835 broadside published by the American Anti-Slavery Office, New York.

(The Schomburg Collection, New York Public Library)

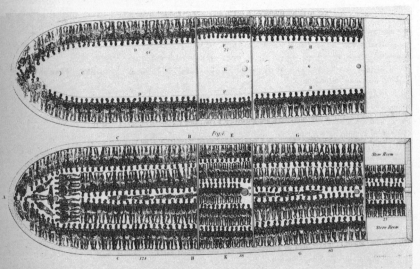

BY
HEWLETT & BRIGHT.

SALE OF

VALUABLE
SLAVES,

(On account of departure)

The Owner of the following named and valuable Slaves, being on the eve of departure for Europe, will cause the same to be offered for sale, at the NEW EXCHANGE, corner of St. Louis and Chartres streets, on *Saturday,* May 16, at Twelve o'Clock, *viz.*

1. **SARAH,** a mulatress, aged 45 years, a good cook and accustomed to house work in general, is an excellent and faithful nurse for sick persons, and in every respect a first rate character.

2. **DENNIS,** her son, a mulatto, aged 24 years, a first rate cook and steward for a vessel, having been in that capacity for many years on board one of the Mobile packets; is strictly honest, temperate, and a first rate subject.

3. **CHOLE,** a mulatress, aged 36 years, she is, without exception, one of the most competent servants in the country, a first rate washer and ironer, does up lace, a good cook, and for a bachelor who wishes a house-keeper she would be invaluable; she is also a good ladies' maid, having travelled to the North in that capacity.

4. **FANNY,** her daughter, a mulatress, aged 16 years, speaks French and English, is a superior hair-dresser, (pupil of Guillac,) a good seamstress and ladies' maid, is smart, intelligent, and a first rate character.

5. **DANDRIDGE,** a mulatoo, aged 26 years, a first rate dining-room servant, a good painter and rough carpenter, and has but few equals for honesty and sobriety.

6. **NANCY,** his wife, aged about 24 years, a confidential house servant, good seamstress, mantuamaker and tailoress, a good cook, washer and ironer, etc.

7. **MARY ANN,** her child, a creole, aged 7 years, speaks French and English, is smart, active and intelligent.

8. **FANNY or FRANCES,** a mulatress, aged 22 years, is a first rate washer and ironer, good cook and house servant, and has an excellent character.

9. **EMMA,** an orphan, aged 10 or 11 years, speaks French and English, has been in the country 7 years, has been accustomed to waiting on table, sewing etc.; is intelligent and active.

10. **FRANK,** a mulatto, aged about 32 years speaks French and English, is a first rate hostler and coachman, understands perfectly well the management of horses, and is, in every respect, a first rate character, with the exception that he will occasionally drink, though not an habitual drunkard.

☞ All the above named Slaves are acclimated and excellent subjects; they were purchased by their present vendor many years ago, and will, therefore, be severally warranted against all vices and maladies prescribed by law, save and except FRANK, who is fully guaranteed in every other respect but the one above mentioned.

TERMS:—One-half Cash, and the other half in notes at Six months, drawn and endorsed to the satisfaction of the Vendor, with special mortgage on the Slaves until final payment. The Acts of Sale to be passed before WILLIAM BOSWELL, *Notary Public,* at the expense of the Purchaser.

New-Orleans, May 13, 1835.

130c

During the Civil War, black soldiers fought for freedom. *Above*, a regiment is in battle. *Below*, troops liberate slaves in North Carolina. (The Schomburg Collection, New York Public Library)

8

ANN J. LANE

The Civil War,
Reconstruction, and
the Afro-American

I do not believe that history is lies that historians agree upon. That is, I do not believe this statement is accurate in general, but it is in many ways a vivid description of the way in which the Civil War and Reconstruction period in United States history has been presented through the years. What is still the prevailing notion of Reconstruction, for example?

Bernard A. Weisberger, in his famous article "The Dark

and Bloody Ground of Reconstruction Historiography" describes it this way:

> "Vindictives" and "Radicals" in Congress shouldered aside Johnson and the Supreme Court and imposed "Carpetbag" and "Scalawag" and "Negro" governments on the South by the bayonet. These new governments debauched and plundered a proud but helpless people until finally, desperately harried whites responded with their own campaigns of violence and persuasion. These respectable folk at last took advantage of mounting Northern disgust with "carpetbag crimes" to restore "home rule" unopposed.

Such distorted notions still dominate elementary and high school textbooks, as well as movies, and popular literature. They even appear in some college texts. Weisberger points to Thomas A. Bailey's popular one-volume text, published in 1956:

> The Radicals would "Republicanize" the South by making the freedman an unwitting tool of their own schemes, and ride into power on his lash-scarred back. The gun-supported reconstruction of the South, begun so brutally in 1867 . . . under the stern eye of bayonet-bearing Union soldiers, resulted in Southern legislatures which sometimes resembled the comic opera.

Just as Americans have been unwilling to examine critically the real story of Reconstruction, so we have also been unable to come to terms with the larger problems of our history. Reconstruction confronts us with all the aspects of American life we go to such lengths to avoid confronting: violence and its manipulations, class conflict, black-white antagonism. That these elements dominated the Civil War and Reconstruction period is what makes our understanding of that past so crucial to any analysis of the present.

What, then, really did happen during the Civil War? More specifically, what happened to the black in this period? What was the role of the slave and then the freedman? What did they do, and what was done to them? Since this period of history is not one in which I have done any original work, much of the subsequent analysis is built upon *Black Reconstruction in America,* written by W. E. B. Du Bois. Although this monumental work was published in 1935, it is, in my opinion, still the best book written on the subject.

The Role of Slaves
and Free Blacks in the Civil War

Until black historians such as W. E. B. Du Bois, Carter Woodson, and others began writing, the prevailing notion was—and to many still is—that the slave during the Civil War provided an element of strength to the Confederacy, was consistently submissive, and passively supported the slave system. As James M. McPherson points out in his introduction to *The Negro's Civil War,* in a biography of Ulysses S. Grant, written in 1928, W. E. Woodward stated that

> the American negroes are the only people in the history of the world . . . that ever became free without any effort of their own. . . . They twanged banjoes around the railroad stations, sang melodious spirituals, and believed that some Yankee would soon come along and give them forty acres of land and a mule.

"In spite of information to the contrary, the belief still persists among many that the slave was the passive, docile, uncomprehending recipient of freedom in 1865 and that the four and one-half million blacks in the United States played no important or effective role" in the Civil War, says McPherson. In fact, free blacks and emancipated slaves played a vital part in the war. Negroes were not merely passive recipients of its benefits, such as they were. Their writers and political activists provided an important part of the leadership in the struggle for emancipation and equal rights.

In the North numbers of free blacks immediately offered their services in the army, and initially they were refused, often with insult and indignity. The larger story, however, concerns the South, for that was where the war was carried on, and in that section there were 3,980,000 black slaves and 260,000 free blacks.

In the South the story repeated itself over and over: as the Union army moved into slave territory, the slave joined. Despite all efforts to dissuade him, and in the face of threats to return him and refusals to keep him, wherever the Union army marched, appeared the fugitive slaves.

The Course of the War Transforms the Northern Position on Slavery

The North initially ignored the black. The war was viewed as a white man's war to save the Union, not to free the slave. The South expected all her white men, most of whom did not own slaves, to defend the slaveholders' property. Everyone expected a short war. The North expected a quick victory. The South expected to secede peacefully and then, once outside the Union, impose terms as her condition for returning. Thus, both North and South began the war ignoring the black. Yet the slave soon became the center of the struggle.

Probably not even 10 percent of the northern white population would have fought a war to free the slaves, says Du Bois. He points to a refrain popular at the time:

> *To the flag we are pledged, all its foes we abhor,*
> *And we ain't for the nigger, but we are for the war.*

The North disclaimed any plans to interfere with slavery. Lincoln's Inaugural Address said so. So did the Republican party platform. So did Congress in the early Crittenden Resolution. The assumption was that slavery was a domestic institution, and domestic institutions were under state control.

But having repeatedly declared the object of the war to be the preservation of the Union, and not a fight that would in any way involve slavery, the Union army found itself faced with a stampede of fugitive slaves. What was to be done with them? The location of the war in a slaveholding region and the mass exodus of slaves to the approaching Union army forced upon the northern government certain practical problems. Confronted with fugitive slaves in Virginia early in the war, General Benjamin Butler refused to give up three of them. He described them as contraband of war, declared that he needed workmen, that slaves were being used by the enemy for construction, and that the Fugitive Slave Act did not apply to a foreign country, which Virginia claimed to be. Three months later, in August 1861, General John C. Frémont proclaimed martial law in Missouri and announced confiscation of all slaves, whom he then declared free. Lincoln repudiated Frémont's order and demanded he modify his proclamation to conform to existing law. In the meantime, the Frémont effort had wide repercussions. There were reports that whole companies of white volunteers threw down their arms and disbanded. Lincoln soon after again overruled an antislavery act, this one by General David Hunter, who announced that he was freeing "persons in Georgia, Florida and South Carolina, heretofore held as slaves."

While the pressure from abolitionist-oriented generals and abolitionists, black and white, continued to be exerted upon an increasingly embarrassed president, Congress was nibbling away at slavery in its own way.

The Confiscation Act of August 6, 1861, provided that when slaves were engaged in hostile military service, all claims by their owners to their services were forfeited. The Second Confiscation Act of July 17, 1862, went further. Anyone who committed treason, that is, supported the rebellion, was to be punished by having his slaves freed. The Militia Act in the following months freed all slave soldiers and their families who belonged to enemy owners. Later in the war freedom was extended to soldiers who had formerly been slaves of loyal owners.

In March 1862 Congress prohibited the use of military authority to return fugitive slaves who fled to the Union side. In July 1862 Congress proclaimed that escaped slaves could not be sent back to their owners, unless those owners were loyal to the Union.

In March 1862 slavery was abolished in the District of Columbia, with compensation. Three months later emancipation was declared in the territories, without compensation.

Congress initially did as much, on paper, as Lincoln's Emancipation Proclamation was to do later. Lincoln's early plan was for compensated emancipation. He tried to convince Delaware to pass an emancipation bill offering $400 a slave. Delaware refused. He then called a conference of the Union slave states: Maryland, Delaware, Virginia, Kentucky, and Missouri. He tried to convince them to emancipate their slaves by arguing that eighty-seven days of financing the Civil War would provide enough money to compensate all the slaveowners in these loyal states. But his efforts failed.

If the North went into the war unwilling to touch the question of slavery and yet was forced to move in the direction of abolition almost immediately, it was a result of the "swarming of slaves, the quiet but persistent determination of increasing numbers no longer to work on Confederate plantations," says Du Bois. The rising tide of fugitive slaves coincided with the sudden recognition that it was, indeed, going to be a real war, and a long war, "and the North found itself actually freeing slaves before it had the slightest intention of doing so, indeed when it had every intention not to," Du Bois goes on. He says:

> Another step was logical and inevitable. The man who handled a spade for the Northern armies, the man who fed them and as spies brought in information, could also handle a gun and shoot. Later his services as soldier were not only permitted but were demanded to replace the tired and rebellious white men of the North. But as a soldier, the Negro must be free.

And what was happening in the rest of the South? That, too, is part of black history. "The white South preened itself on the absence of slave violence. For every slave who escaped to the Union army there were ten left on the untouched and inaccessible plantations," says Du Bois. And further: "The slaves showed no disposition to strike the one terrible blow which brought black men freedom in Haiti. . . . There was an easier way involving freedom with less risk." According to another distinguished black historian, Benjamin Quarles, those slaves who had an opportunity to break their bonds promptly did so. Others bided their time. Still, the services of slaves to the Confederacy were of marked importance. In Quarles' words, the black "was the stomach of the Confederacy." A somewhat astonishing part of the story, if a small one, were the mulatto volunteers in New Orleans who offered to fight with the Confederacy.

In general, then, after the first year of the war, when South and North recognized that it was to be a long and bloody and expensive war, the whole relation of the North to the black and the black to the North changed. The free blacks in the North, together with many white abolitionists, had long been pressing the government and the community at large to make it a war against slavery. "Slowly an economic dispute and a political test of strength took on the aspects of a great moral crusade," as one historian phrases it.

The Negro Becomes the Key to the Civil War; The Raising of Black Troops

The Negro became the key to the Civil War. Lincoln, with his remarkable insight and flexibility, began to see that this was true. He then began to talk about compensated emancipation coupled with plans for colonization, for he was unable to envisage free blacks living in large numbers in the United States. Lincoln had come to realize the truth—not simply that slaves ought to be free, but that thousands were already free. He recognized that the North would have to declare publicly that it was fighting for emancipation, or it would lose the necessary support of the rest of the world. He recognized that either the slave would fight in the army or there would not be enough white men to fight in the army.

So in August 1862 Lincoln discussed the Emancipation Proclamation, and on September 22 he issued it. After January 1, 1863, it declared all slaves in areas in rebellion against the United States "shall be then, thenceforward, and forever free."

The North had been reluctant to pay the price of abolition to maintain the Union, but it ultimately was forced to. The North was not abolitionist. It was overwhelmingly hostile to blacks. While northerners in general probably opposed slavery, they were unwilling to do much about it so long as slavery did not interfere with northern life. Only a small minority wanted to fight for genuine equality and emancipation. Its position through the war gained in prestige, and it was to provide much of the leadership during Reconstruction.

To the world, Lincoln, on January 1, 1863, declared 4 million slaves "thenceforward and forever free." The truth was less than this. The Emancipation Proclamation applied only to slaves of those states or parts of states still in rebellion. Hundreds of thousands of such slaves were already free by their own action and that of the Union armies. To the majority of slaves still within the Confederacy, the Proclamation would apply only if they followed the fugitives. As Secretary of State William H. Seward sarcastically described the Emancipation Proclamation: "We show our sympathy with slavery by emancipating slaves where we cannot reach them and holding them in bondage where we can set them free."

The Emancipation Proclamation had two major motives. It was designed to make easier the replacement of unwilling northern white soldiers with black soldiers. And it sought to provide a new push toward northern victory from the mighty impact of a great moral ideal in the North and in Europe.

Shortly before he issued the Proclamation, Lincoln made his position clear.

> My paramount object in this struggle is to save the Union and is not either to save or to destroy slavery. If I could save the Union without freeing any slaves, I would do it; and if I could save it by freeing

all the slaves, I would do that also. What I do about slavery and the colored race, I do because I believe it would help to save the Union.

Lincoln justified his act as a war measure. But although he characterized it as an act warranted by the Constitution as a military necessity, what was important was its dramatization in the popular mind. After the Emancipation Proclamation the war took on a new look.

After the Proclamation, for instance, sentiment for permitting black troops increased. The War Department gave official sanction to their recruitment in the winter of 1862. This was indeed a rapid development. At first this was to be a white man's war, because the North did not want to affront the South and because the war was going to be short; besides, if blacks fought in the war, how could it help but turn into a war for abolition? And for this the North would not fight. Yet scarcely a year after hostilities had started, the blacks were fighting, although they were unrecognized as soldiers. In two years they were free and joining the army.

Du Bois again quotes a popular refrain to reflect the changing opinion as the war was prolonged.

> *Some say it is a burnin' shame*
> *To make the nagyurs fight,*
> *An' that the thrade o' being kilt*
> *Belongs but to the white;*
>
> *But as for me 'pon me sowl*
> *So liberal are we here*
> *I'll let Sambo be murthered in place o' meself*
> *On every day in the year.*

Five days after the Emancipation Proclamation, the secretary of war authorized the governor of Massachusetts to raise two black regiments for three years of service. These were the celebrated Fifty-fourth and Fifty-fifth Massachusetts regiments—the first regularly authorized black regiments in the war. The regiments were supposed to pass through New York on the way to battle, but the chief of police in the city warned that the men would be subject to great insult, so the troops went by sea to South Carolina.

It would not have been American not to maintain some discrimination. First, the matter of pay. Soldiers received $13 per month, but black soldiers received $10, with an additional deduction per month of $3 for clothing. The Fifty-fourth Massachusetts Regiment refused to accept any pay for an entire year until the payment was equalized. Not only in pay, but in matters of rank, food, medical care, assignment, and duty the black soldier was discriminated against.

By the end of the war some 200,000 Negro soldiers (120,000 from the South, 80,000 from the North) had fought in 450 battles in the Union army. Probably 500,000 freedmen had come within the Union lines. Black labor raised thousands of bales of cotton, earned hundreds of thousands of dollars, and accomplished millions of man-hours of work on Union installations during the war. Negroes worked for the federal army as laborers, teamsters, cooks, carpenters, nurses, spies, fortifications builders, and guides, in addition to playing their key role as soldiers. Colonel Thomas Wentworth Higginson, commander of one of the Negro regiments (there were no black commissioned officers leading black troops) commented:

> No officer in the regiment now doubts that the key to the successful prosecution of this war lies in the unlimited employment of black troops. . . . Instead of leaving their homes and families to fight they are fighting for their homes and families. . . . It would have been madness to attempt, with the bravest white troops what I have successfully accomplished with the black ones.

When Lincoln was criticized for permitting the authorization of black troops, his answer was one of expediency.

> The slightest knowledge of arithmetic will prove to any man that the rebel armies cannot be destroyed by Democratic strategy. It would sacrifice all the white men of the North to do it. There are now in the services of the

U.S. near 200,000 able-bodied colored men, most of them under arms, defending and acquiring Union territory. . . . Abandon all the posts now garrisoned by black men; take 200,000 men from our side and put them in the battlefield or cornfield against us, and we would be compelled to abandon the war in three weeks. . . . My enemies pretend I am now carrying on this war for the sole purpose of abolition. So long as I am President it shall be carried on for the sole purpose of restoring the Union. But no human power can subdue this rebellion without the use of the emancipation policy.

Anti-Negro sentiment in the North, always prevalent, erupted in several serious race riots. Draft laws passed for the first time in 1863 meant that the war could no longer be carried on by volunteers. It meant that men were going to be compelled to fight, and it meant further that these would be poor men who could not afford to buy an exemption, such as was permitted in the draft act. The new draft resulted in widespread disaffection throughout the nation. In New York the general riot, which was at first directed to the military establishment and the police, soon turned against the black community. Blacks were the cause of the war and hence the cause of the draft. They were, or would soon be, bidding for the same jobs. Thereupon, hundreds of white New Yorkers attacked "all the blacks they could lay their hands on," as one historian phrases it. The property loss was estimated at $1,200,000, and it was estimated that hundreds were killed in four days of rioting. There were also riots in many other cities. They were not all specifically race riots, but they did show the North that unless white soldiers were replaced with black soldiers, the war would be in jeopardy.

The Confederates, in the meantime, denounced vigorously the arming of Negroes. Said Jefferson Davis: "A restitution of the Union has been rendered forever impossible by the adoption of a measure which . . . neither admits of retraction nor can coexist with union."

Shortly after, Davis proclaimed that slave soldiers, and by

141

that he meant all black soldiers, slave or free, and federal commissioned officers serving with them, if captured, would be turned over to the appropriate state in the South to be dealt with by the law of that state—that is, put to death for insurrection. In April 1863 the Confederate Congress provided that white officers commanding Negro soldiers would be viewed as inciting servile insurrection and would be put to death. To counter this legislation, Lincoln issued a statement that for every Union soldier killed in violation of the laws of war, a rebel soldier would be executed.

The dilemma that the South itself faced in relation to black troops grew more severe. Blacks made good soldiers —that the northern experience proved. The prospect of freedom led many slaves into the federal army. "That stream might be diverted to the southern army, if the lure of freedom were offered by the Confederacy. But this would be an astonishing end for a war fought in defense of slavery," writes Du Bois.

During the first year of the war Negroes, slave and free, were used as laborers by the Confederacy. Finally, in March 1865, the Confederate States of America announced to the world the destruction of its own society when, in what was soon to be proved a futile gesture, it passed a law calling for the enlistment of slaves into the army as soldiers. While the enactment was ambiguous as to emancipation, it was generally acknowledged that freedom was inseparable from, was a necessary concomitant of, the arming of slaves. But the measure came too late to be acted upon; Lee surrendered the following month.

Although the abolitionists struggled relentlessly to make the war for the Union also a war for emancipation, and although their contribution was enormous, they alone did not secure freedom for the slaves. This freedom was the logical result of attempting to wage a war in the midst of 4 million black slaves while at the same time trying to ignore their interests. The slaves had extraordinary leverage. They not only could offer their services in a variety of ways, but at the same time they prevented the South from using them.

The End of the War; Lincoln's Plans

As the Civil War "staggered toward its end," there came the slow recognition that although emancipation had freed 4 million slaves, it left to be considered 4 million vulnerable people. In general, the South was left in utter ruin; it was, in the words of John Hope Franklin, "a howling waste." The problem facing the nation was how to put the pieces back together again.

The white South faced, not just military defeat, but a total humiliation. She had not been fighting for specific objectives, but for her very sovereignty, her life as a distinct society. The loss of the war meant the end of all her dreams. Not only was the economy smashed, but the antebellum class structure was totally disrupted with the liberation of the slaves and the loss of the power of the planters.

The picture of the North imposing a vindictive, military reconstruction falls far short of what might have followed such a long and bloody civil war. There was never a question of large reparations, mass deportations, or even imprisonment and execution of vanquished leaders. Except for Major Henry Wirz, the commander of the prison camp Andersonville, who was hanged, there were no executions. Only a few political leaders were imprisoned, and of these, only the Confederate president, Jefferson Davis, was not released promptly. The great devastation and suffering in the South were caused by defeat in war and not by Reconstruction policies. In fact, the North made only three general demands of the defeated section: that it renounce secession, destroy the institution of slavery, and repudiate the Confederate debt.

Although Lincoln had no uniform plan or even well articulated general principle of Reconstruction, he did have an interim plan for the secessionist states that fell into federal hands during the war. Under this plan only the very high ranking military and civil officers of the Confederacy and state governments were excluded from politics. There was a general amnesty and restoration of all property, except slaves, to those who took an oath of allegiance to the United States government. And when 10 percent of the number that had voted in a state in 1860 took an oath of fidelity to the Constitution, a new state government could be formed, a state constitution could be written, and representatives could be elected to Congress. There was a good deal of opposition in Congress to Lincoln's generous reconstruction policy, but the issue was unsettled when he was assassinated.

Andrew Johnson probably attempted to carry out what he thought was Lincoln's policy—that is, his position emphasized the preservation and quick restoration of the Union and viewed Reconstruction as an executive, not legislative, function. However, Johnson lacked Lincoln's political adroitness, his flexibility, his experience. He was rigid, inept, and stubborn. Johnson conceived of Reconstruction as essentially a problem of the loyalty of southerners as individuals rather than as a relationship of Confederate states and institutions to the Union, and he therefore relied heavily on the pardoning power as an important instrument of reform.

Johnson at once recognized Lincoln's "ten percent governments" (Louisiana, Arkansas, Tennessee, Virginia), appointed military governors in the rest of the defeated states, and began activities to bring the states quickly back into the Union. The southerners had only three requirements to meet other than the oath of allegiance: repudiation of the ordinance of secession, abolition of slavery, and repudiation of the war-incurred debt. When these conditions were met, a state would be completely free from federal control and could resume self-government.

The South's Response to Defeat

How did the South respond? Conventions called under Johnson's provisional governors revealed that region's spirit of defeat. Few states complied with Johnson's program for repudiation of the acts of secession—that is, a declaration that they had been null and void when passed. Some states only barely managed to repeal the acts of secession. Mississippi refused to ratify the Thirteenth Amendment, which abolished slavery. Mississippi and South Carolina refused to repudiate the Confederate debt. Not a single southern state even gave casual consideration to the possibility of limited black suffrage.

The arrogance of the southern response was also reflected in the choice of elected officials. To Congress by December 1865 the South had sent the vice-president of the Confederacy, Alexander Stephens, as well as four Confederate generals, five Confederate colonels, six Confederate cabinet officers, and fifty-eight Confederate congressmen. And furthermore, the South, no longer bound by the three-fifths clause, used her entire black population for determining representation. (In the three-fifths compromise the writers of the Constitution had agreed that each five slaves should be counted as three persons for purposes of taxation and congressional representation.) By the fall of 1865 the former Confederate states were safely in the hands of former Confederate leaders.

Then came the disgraceful Black Codes, which forecast the future attitudes of the white South to the Negro. The Codes confirmed the North's worst fears, and increasingly northerners came to view Johnson's Reconstruction as an undoing of Appomatox. The violence directed at the black community reflected the determination of the former Confederates to maintain white supremacy. This was Reconstruction, Confederate style.

The Black Codes legally placed the freedman in an inferior caste. They did make the necessary adjustments of legally recognizing marriages among blacks, and of granting blacks the right to sue and be sued, bear evidence in court, make contracts, and own property. But the labor and social regulations were a virtual return to slavery. The Codes were an affront to emancipation. The Negro's access to land was limited, his rights to work curtailed, his rights to self-defense denied. His employment was virtually reduced to contract labor, with penal servitude as a punishment for leaving his job. "Making every allowance for the excitement and turmoil of war, the mentality of a defeated people and the admitted variations in the Codes from state to state, the Black Codes were infamous pieces of legislation," writes one analyst.

Radical Reconstruction

Congress refused to accept Confederate Reconstruction. How to check the president's course of action and take the program of Reconstruction into its own hands became its prime concern. First Congress refused to seat Confederate congressmen. Then it proposed the Fourteenth Amendment and insisted that all southern states ratify it before admission to the Union. All the southern states rejected the Fourteenth Amendment. (Note, though, that most northern states did not permit black suffrage either.)

Congress then set forth its own plan for Reconstruction, and although Johnson was outraged by the usurpation of his authority, there was little he could do. Even the moderates joined with the radicals to provide the two-thirds vote needed to override his vetoes.

Congressional Reconstruction divided the South into five military districts, each under a general who was to use the armed forces, if necessary, to maintain martial law. He was to supervise the election of a new constitutional convention, all adult males being permitted to vote. For the first time, nearly one million Negroes were franchised. Those excluded by the Fourteenth Amendment—that is, those who had held high office in the Confederate government—could neither vote nor hold office. New state governments had to ratify the Fourteenth Amendment before returning to the Union. When registration was complete in the South, there were 660,000 qualified whites and 703,000 qualified blacks.

The three issues with which Radical Reconstruction is usually associated—Negro suffrage, exclusion of the southern states from the Union for a time, and enmity to Johnson—were attitudes shared in varying degrees by all Republicans in the Johnson Administration. Radical Reconstruction should be viewed "as a reaction against a series of provocations rather than as a plot to subdue the South," as one historian observes.

What were the governments like during this brief period of so-called Radical Reconstruction? First, radical governments were never dominated by blacks. They did not even hold state offices in proportion to their number in the general population. There was no black governor; there were three black lieutenant-governors. There were only two black senators and fifteen black congressmen. In terms of the quality of their leadership, much of it was impressive; none of it was below the standard of comparable white leadership.

As for the charges of corruption in radical governments, postwar corruption was a national, not a specifically southern, disgrace, and in fact it was on a smaller scale in the South, where the rewards were not as high.

Taxes were heavily increased, and states were left with huge debts after Radical Reconstruction, but this can be largely explained in terms of immense increases in the cost of running governments. Recovering from the devastation of the war required great outlays of money. The entire structure of social and educational welfare, unknown in the South until Reconstruction, was expensive. In a close examination of Radical Reconstruction in one state, South Carolina, W. E. B. Du Bois makes the following observations: During this period was enacted one of the most liberal suffrage provisions of all southern states; women's rights were enlarged (for example, the first divorce law in the state's history was passed); a free common school system was established; the judiciary was reformed; imprisonment for debt was abolished; property qualifications for voting and office holding were abolished. An indication of the value of the radical constitution was its retention for eighteen years by the conservatives, when they resumed power.

Such was Radical Reconstruction. It began to fall apart almost as soon as it was instituted. Political pressure exerted by former Confederates, economic sanctions, and unbelievable violence brought it crashing down. There is a widespread misconception that Radical Reconstruction lasted a long time—a decade—and did not end until the election of

Rutherford B. Hayes in 1877. Actually, all that remained by 1876 was for the nation to take cognizance of the reality that Reconstruction was a shambles. The South was again back in the Union, with a leadership strikingly like that of the South that had seceded.

The Return of White Supremacy

The story of these years has been told by C. Vann Woodward: the return of white supremacy, the establishment of a new political coalition which saw the Democratic redeemers resume power, disfranchisement of the black, and, finally, the willingness of the North to accept these changes.

The descriptions of the terror are horrifying. In this period the Ku Klux Klan, the Knights of the White Camelia, and other secret organizations roamed the South shooting, flogging, terrorizing blacks and sympathetic whites, burning homes and public buildings, attacking Reconstruction officials, pillaging, and looting. A government report on the KKK in 1871 said that in nine counties in South Carolina in a six-month period the Klan murdered 35 people, whipped 262, and shot, mutilated, burned out, or otherwise outraged 101. The Negro secretary of state in Florida reported 153 murders in Jackson County in the same period. "The cry of the bewildered freeman rose, but it was drowned by the Rebel yell," says one historian of this period.

Forces Involved in the North's Capitulation

Why did it happen the way it did? Why did the North, in general, and the federal government, in particular, after struggling through four bloody years and ultimately emancipating the slaves, then relinquish all reponsibility when the white South refused to acquiesce?

We must begin with the recognition that the nation as a whole, not just the South, did not believe in black equality. During the enthusiasm of the war these feelings were overlooked, but they remained close to the surface, easily revived.

There were two different forces, each with a different vision of the future, that emerged from the North. One had a belief in universal democracy, which was expressed by abolitionists like Wendell Phillips, Charles Sumner, Thaddeus Stevens, and Frederick Douglass. These abolitionists represented a liberal movement among a few who accepted the American creed of free enterprise but saw the danger of slavery in moral terms. They began the struggle against slavery in the 1830s. For these people—and they were always a handful—the object of the Civil War was the abolition of slavery and then the protection of the emancipated slave by turning him into a free citizen and voter. At the time of the Civil War it became clear to Sumner and Stevens, but not even to most of the other abolitionists, "that freedom in order to have meaning required economic protection in addition to political rights, and further, that these rights, economic and political, could only be protected against the natural hatred of the Southern white by some sort of federal control," according to Du Bois.

Sumner faced the problem when he asked: "Can emancipation be carried out without using the lands of the slave-masters? Without their [the blacks] votes we cannot establish stable governments in the Rebel states. Their votes are as necessary as were their muskets. . . . Without them, the old enemy will reappear."

And Wendell Phillips proclaimed, "No class is safe, no freedom is real, no emancipation is effected which does not place in the hands of the man himself the power to protect his own rights." Such was the thinking of the first force affecting change during Reconstruction.

The thinking of the second force was entirely different, but it is frequently confused with the abolitionist ideal because the two visions often were found in the same person, and because writers of history frequently have not distinguished between the two. The second force was connected with the development of large-scale industry in the United States and of a new industrial philosophy. With the end of the Civil War came vast economic development and agricultural expansion based, in part, upon the expectations of a reconstructed southern market. To people with this perspective freedom was

149

the legal abolition of slavery and the establishment of a marketplace for black labor.

But then the South persisted in its prewar conception of the role of the Negro. It sought to reestablish slavery without any conception of, or concern with, the needs of modern industry. While the South was suspended and the abolitionists were working with the moderates to crystallize opinion and a program, industry in the North was surging ahead with furious intensity Freeing the nation from "the strangling hands of the oligarchy in the South" meant that the whole "fabric of the country was changing by the prospects of a glorious and prosperous future"—again in the words of Du Bois.

Coalition between Abolitionists and Emerging Business Interests

Those who represented this new vision of industrial expansion in the post–Civil War period were in control of the government, but only insecurely. The Republican party, which represented these interests, was in truth a minority party, and if northern and southern Democrats had been able to unite with the disaffected West, the Republicans might have been swept out of power, asserts Du Bois. At this point, he claims, the Republican party made its appeals on high moral ground. "Thus a movement which began primarily and sincerely to abolish slavery and insure the Negroes' rights, became coupled with a struggle of capitalism to retain control of the government."

The first and most exciting product of the union between industrial expansionists and abolitionists was the Freedman's Bureau, a government agency which openly directed its efforts in behalf of the free black and the poor white. "It was the most extraordinary and far-reaching institution of social uplift America ever attempted," says one historian. The Freedman's Bureau began systematic teaching of the illiterate, black and white; it established day and night schools, industrial schools, Sunday schools, and colleges. Nearly all the major black universities and colleges were founded or substantially aided by the Bureau. It provided plans to care for the sick. It provided assistance to protect the freedman from violence and injustice. To the newly freed slave it helped to impart—however imperfectly—a conception of civil and political rights. It offered itself to the country as a reasoned and thought-out plan for protecting those who needed protection —the poor. It met intense opposition and was finally emasculated and then abolished by those in the North who did not wish to finance or support such a precedent and by those in the South who passed the Black Codes.

In the meantime, the South's arrogant and unyielding response made the North realize that if the South was returning the same people to Congress with increased political power, it probably retained the earlier notions about running the country and the same hostility to a program aimed at industrial expansion: the tariff, homestead legislation, railroad subsidies, banking legislation.

At the same moment the abolitionists were coming to terms with their program: freedom for blacks, civil rights, economic opportunity, education, the right to vote. They began to realize increasingly the need for an economic foundation to maintain the gains of the war.

For a short moment in history the paths of two widely and utterly dissimilar visions coincided. The business element, while not willing to follow the abolitionist program to the extreme of confiscating and redistributing property, was less willing to turn the South back to the prewar southerner, and so was willing to accept part of the radical program and reconstruct the South on the basis of black suffrage. In this way Radical Reconstruction was born.

Commitment to Blacks Ends; Conclusion

Then why did it end so abruptly? For much the same reason. In the ensuing struggle for new wealth old party designations disintegrated and the coalition collapsed.

To win the Civil War the United States freed the slave and armed him. But most Americans were willing to use the black to defend their interests and were quite willing to desert him when those interests were protected.

To achieve the full range of rights the abolitionists demanded—and these were necessary for black equality—would have required a total revamping of southern society, and it would have called into focus a variety of precedents that might have had meaning for the North as well as the South. If the North had taken land from the rich to give to the free black in the South, would not this have been potentially dangerous? Northern power was not especially interested in freedom for the black. It was interested in destroying slavery because slavery impeded the work of nation building. For a while during the Civil War the nation builders and the abolitionists merged. After the war the coalition continued for a while. But when it became clear that the white South would not put up with it, the North, except for a handful of abolitionists, was perfectly willing to relinquish its commitment to the black in order to maintain its real commitment, which was to capitalism.

SOURCES

BASLER, ROY P., et al., eds., *The Collected Works of Abraham Lincoln,* 9 vols., New Brunswick, Rutgers University Press, 1953-55.

CRUDEN, ROBERT, *The Negro in Reconstruction.* Englewood Cliffs, N.J., Prentice-Hall, Inc., 1969.

DU BOIS, W. E. B., *Black Reconstruction in America,* 1935. Reprinted, Atheneum Publishers, New York, 1962.

FRANKLIN, JOHN HOPE, *Reconstruction After the Civil War.* Chicago, The University of Chicago Press, 1961.

HIGGINSON, THOMAS WENTWORTH, *Army Life in a Black Regiment,* 1869. Reprinted: Boston, Beacon Press, 1962.

RANDALL, J. G., and Donald, David, *The Civil War and Reconstruction,* 2nd ed. Boston, D. C. Heath and Company, 1961.

WOODWARD, W. E., *Meet General Grant.* New York, The Literary Guild of America, 1928.

9

W. M. PHILLIPS, JR.

Survival
Techniques
of Black Americans

I propose to explore the issue of survival techniques of black folk from the bases of understanding, intuition, and experience. It is my opinion, as a sociologist, that neither the radical nor the traditional framework of my discipline has provided usable knowledge about this matter. Some questions will be raised and mainly left unanswered.

The Context: American Society

Two general ideas are essential for understanding the survival of black folk in the United States. First, American society is, and has been, essentially pluralistic. That is, it exhibits two features: racial and ethnic groups characterized by distinctive social and cultural styles of life, and an ordered way of living made up of relatively distinct social institutions, such as the political, moral, economic, educational, familial, and legal systems. Second, American society historically has featured a persistent pattern of conflict relations between subordinate and dominant racial and ethnic groups, as revealed by the studies of G. E. Simpson and J. M. Yinger, and Allen D. Grimshaw. Accordingly, the existence and survival of black folk is only to be understood as occurring within such a scenario. That is, white America to black folk is, and has been, a hostile environment, a setting whose salient atfribute is its exploitation of their vulnerability and their powerlessness.

One feature appears to distinguish most of the techniques of survival black folk have developed in American society. This is their involuntary character. These survival techniques all seem to have the distinguishing character of being responses to force, coercion, oppression, and bestiality. I am saying simply that the survival techniques of black folk appear to have the mark of devices created by people who have to deal with an enemy. Additionally, a bit of reflection tends to give the impression that in dealing with the enemy—whether the society, the state, or the individual—these people perceived their choices as being extremely limited. Their freedom to decide was apparently defined as minimal; thus they had a meager range of alternatives, when compared to other groups in the society, for coping with the immense and overwhelming forces and life situations over which their control was so cruelly limited.

In brief, the ideological, structural, and processual character of American society has been such as to provide black folk with few voluntary options. By "ideological" I refer to the paradox, in a so-called pluralistically organized society, of a virtual consensus on the doctrine that blacks are categorically inferior to white citizens. By "structural" I mean the abundantly documented knowledge that American institutional, class, and reward systems are organized and function such that differentiated outcomes can be predicted with extreme accuracy for black and white Americans. By the "processual" character of American society is meant the persistent occurrence of patterns of conflict and even more deadly interactions which inform black and white group relationships. The involuntary character of many of the survival techniques of black folk is primarily a consequence of these conditions.

Collective Solidarity: Shadow and Substance

Survival techniques of black folk take many forms, and they can be looked at from different perspectives. A primeval form of survival in a supposedly open society with multiple racial and ethnic groups is the cultivation of group identity and solidarity. Historically, in the United States, each ethnic group organized its members voluntarily along cultural, religious, and ethnic lines into political and economic blocs to tend to their own interests. Principles of ethnic solidarity were used deliberately to enhance survival and improve social position. Black folk, however, had no such choice. They were compelled to manifest the shadow rather than the substance of collective solidarity. The substance of collective solidarity in a racial group in the American tradition denotes the power to approximately satisfy essential group interests even within the cauldron of a multigroup mix. Black folk were forced into the position of a self-conscious outgroup; and out of the inevitable social isolation of such a status they had to create cultural, institutional, and psychological patterns of coping and survival. This imposed, artificial, and powerless pseudo-solidarity carried with it individual and group injury, insult, and humiliation.

Let me cite a homely example. It is painfully clear to students of the question that a large part of the higher delinquency rate of black youth is due to employment discrimination against black adult males. This discrimination has the double effect of destroying hope and belief among black youth and of making the black family appear to be essentially female-centered. Clearly "the society" has "decided" that reducing the destruction of black youth is not worth the cost of having to reduce employment discrimination. Few black individuals would deny this "knowledge"; studies are unnecessary. And most feel the sting of powerlessness, of individual and collective injury, insult, and humiliation resulting from such insightful knowledge.

The failure to achieve collective solidarity had the effect of preventing the creation of collective mechanisms of social consciousness to complement the inevitable group self-consciousness. The paradox is critical; black folk were *together,* but incapable of effective social action toward collective ends according to the doctrine, and within the ideals of, American democracy. Thus, the design and implementation of collective defenses against the enemy in the form of cultural, political, economic, and psychic instrumentalities of power were delayed. Only now is there evidence of serious attempts to create and use group or community solidarity of blacks to define and deal with the existential truth (the primacy of black control of the fate and destiny of black folk) of their survival in American society. As Julius Lester has preached in *Look Out, Whitey,* the concept of black power, in all its complexity, is simply a call for black folk to use group or community solidarity strategically for survival; to organize themselves as other groups of Americans do to capture power as a first step in really determining their fates in the United States.

Survival Under Slavery:
Development of a Counter-Culture

The official societal policy toward black folk under the reign of the "peculiar institution" was to reduce them to a state of total dependency. I know not how to put it less bluntly. All imaginable techniques of dehumanization and bestiality were used routinely to reach and maintain this end. It is to be stressed that black folk under slavery could only define slavery as a hostile environment; they had, collectively and individually, few, if any, voluntary options. Nevertheless, many of the transactions and incidents historically ascribed to black slaves may be interpreted as survival techniques. The trick is to see what actions slaves engaged in that violated their state of dependency. In the economic or productive sphere they could resist by covert, and sometimes even overt, acts of sabotage and subversion (the evidence describing work-control techniques devised and used by slaves is abundant and unequivocal—for example, suicide, self-mutilation, infanticide, tool and equipment abuse, livestock misuse, slowdowns, running away, and revolt). Proscribed activities such as assembly, "mental instruction," marriage and familial relations, religious activity, and escape or freedom were deliberately sought after and obtained by some. In the realm of the artistic and the aesthetic—such as in metaphoric language, music, dance, humor, folklore, and gossip—a complete stream of rebellion, dissent, and humanity is recorded as examples of survival devices and mechanisms. (The study of survival techniques as revealed within the artistic and aesthetic streams of black culture has not been begun seriously or systematically. Moreover, it is not a major interest of this paper. Suffice it to urge exploration of the work of Sterling Brown, B. A. Botkin, and Arna Bontemps, and of *Black Folktales* by Julius Lester.)

Now the records even reveal systematic revolts, insurrections, and guerrilla activity by black slaves during this infamous period of our history. The accumulated weight of these largely intuitive, desperate, and yet essentially human acts of defiance is the foundation of what today is called black culture. These survival devices and techniques constitute what may be called the beginning of the creation of a black counter-culture—one to take the place of the deliberate and ruthless stripping away of the several African heritages, and one to insure some measure of success in coping with the violent and destructive forces the slaves faced. A concrete example seen even today of a survival technique handed down from the slavery era is, according to Addison Gayle, Jr., in his essay "Dreams of a Native Son," the minstrel's mask—the metaphorical language, the wide, timid smile, and the "tom" or "mose" mannerisms of some black folk.

By the term counter-culture I mean the creation of an ethos, with associated patterns of behavior, around which the reorganization and development of the black community in the United States evolves. This ethos has as a key axiom the belief by black folk that dealings with white folk entail grave risk and that they can be deadly. They have learned and know empirically that in both the long and short run violence, shame, brutality, and dehumanization can usually be expected from dealing with American whites. A kind of cynical detachment, disenchantment, and innocent unbelief about the intentions, the actions, and the consequences of the working of the essentially white social world tends to be a prominent characteristic of the masses of black folk. They, and theirs, have been had too many times. A counter-culture, based in large part upon the above impulses, becomes a design, a shield, a complex developmental process inherent in the lives of black folk.

Mobility as a Survival Technique

The freedom to move, roam, and migrate is one of the major survival techniques to which black folk had recourse after the slavery era. It is being used today. For example, take the matter of the demand for domestic servants in the suburbs and cities of the urban North. Are you aware of the heavy traffic of young black females from the South to the North? The criminal absence of educational and employment opportunities these young people face at home; their desperate need to escape the heavy sanctions of the small community when pregnancy and birth occur without a husband; the elaborate network of newspaper advertisements and traveling recruiters to entice them to the faraway, glorified, domestic service market; the long train ride and cattlelike accommodations for a few nights while the urban affluent paw and select; the heavy financial debt to the employment agency and future employers; the enforced isolation of "living-in," heavy and dirty work, and low pay; the seeking out of other black folk and eventually the decision to escape by perhaps going on welfare. This exploitative system, made use of as an escape and survival device by young black females, is functionally connected with the major institutional structures of our society. That is, this abuse of young black American women serves the need of those cultural arrangements in American society dependent upon masculine superiority; the criminal prostitution of our entire public educational system to miseducation and to the reinforcement and maintenance of existing stratification boundaries; the insatiable hunger for "dirty work" hands in our labor force; our need for objects to satisfy our obscene "moral" urges to make condescending and philanthropic gestures; and even the patching up of, or making do with, our sordid marriage and familial systems. What I wish to emphasize, however, is the use of the right to move about as a means of survival, and the cumulative inheritance of this process by black folk today from their postslavery experiences.

The use of mobility as a survival technique has taken many forms. Students of plantation tenancy in the South described the apparent restlessness of black sharecroppers or tenants in moving from farm to farm—year in and year out—within the same county or general area. A direct quotation from Charles S. Johnson's *Shadow of the Plantation* may give you the flavor of the matter.

> I am working myself to death, mighty near; been working hard. I am trying to get straight. I made a bale and a half last year, but never got nothing out of it. I stayed in that little house over there and paid $60 and never got nothing last year, I worked and dug and never got a thing, and when I told him I wasn't making nothing he said, "Well, you are making money for me, ain't you?!" And I said, "Well, I can quit." I moved from there, and he didn't know it. Folks went up there looking for Dick Richards and Dick Richards done moved.

For several decades after the Civil War, organized attempts were made to resettle rural, southern blacks in the

Midwest and the West. An early pioneer in these endeavors was the legendary "Pop" Singleton, who attempted with some success to settle black folk of the rural South in the state of Kansas. An accelerating movement of black folk was continually underway from rural areas to urban places, and from 1915 to the present there has been a massive resettlement of black folk in the urban centers of the nation. This precipitate fleeing from oppression to perceived hope, freedom, and opportunity can only be interpreted as a survival technique.

Mobility played a survival role within the interpersonal web of relations of the black family. T-Bone Walker expresses it well in a Blues whose words I will share with you.

> I've got bad news for you baby,
> And I hope you understand [Repeat];
> I've got another woman, why don't you
>   find you another man.

> I can't stand your ways,
> Just can't stay here no more [Repeat];
> Going for good, pretty mama,
> Don't you know, Little Girl, don't you know.

> I could never please you baby,
> From now on I won't even try [Repeat];
> If you see me no more, woman,
> Please don't wonder why.

> I'm leaving you Baby,
> Now I've got to go [Repeat];
> Yeah, I'm going for good, pretty mama,
> Little Girl, don't you know, don't you know.

The literally unattainable expectations placed upon the black male role culminated in the pattern of the absent husband and father. For sheer sanity and survival, he left. The consequences of this for the structure and function of the black family are only now being seriously and objectively studied by such scholars as Andrew Billingsley. The conclusion is being advanced formally that, in reality, the black family is a survival structure—a strong, resilient social institution characterized by an amazing degree of strength and stability. How else, it is argued by Alphonso Pinkney in an article in *The Black Scholar,* could it have survived the brutality of slavery and the degradation of institutionalized oppression to the extent that it has?

Organized Religion as a Mechanism of Survival

Organized religion has been one of the more powerful survival techniques available to black folk. The black church—from Voodoo to the Lost and Found Children of Islam—provided a haven of refuge from a hostile white world; it afforded, according to E. Franklin Frazier in *The Negro Church in America,* a structured social life in which black folk could give expression to their deepest anguish, agony, and desperation and at the same time achieve status and perform satisfying roles to give meaning to their existence. The pattern of autocratic leadership and tyranny found in black churches was, in a quaint way, the sole means of sanity for black males effectively barred from participation in the political life and the play of power in their communities. This pattern of authority and use of power may be found even today in some aspects of the organizational life of the black community. Even if, in fact, it did sometimes block effective mass participation in so-called democratic processes and was often allied with the white rather than the black community, the black church can be legitimately defined as performing a survival function for black folk.

The Contemporary Response

In contemporary society, made turbulent by ceaseless and accelerating change, some mention must be made of survival techniques favored by black folk now. In my opinion, the most significant are grounded in the surfacing and the general acceptance of two long-held truths among black folk.

These are that preparation must be made for an anticipated acceleration of the massive use of illegal force by white folk upon black folk, and that we cannot risk relying or depending upon white folk to aid black folk toward liberation, in any important way. The response to this development is the creation of an organized, radical, and revolutionary ethos in some segments of the communities of black America. The phenomenon of the Black Panther party serves as the outstanding example of this type of survival technique. Drama, as created and produced by brothers Imamu Baraka and Ed Bullins, among others, is another significant example of a response to this development.

Several features of these radical and revolutionary responses deserve mention. For instance, among all adherents of these developments the following elements appear: a calculated emphasis upon the character of the black male and female roles (the political significance of the traditional roles of the black wife and mother for the continued exploitation, oppression, and degradation of the black community is being deliberately examined); a massive appeal to children and the young; an obsession with the collective, group, or black community rather than the individual interest; the cultivation of positive identity to enhance self-respect, pride, and collective solidarity; the clear political interpretation of all dimensions of black existence in the United States; and the rejection of a "talented tenth"—an elite mode of black leadership and action—for a movement appealing directly and pointedly to the black masses for support and commitment. Most of the survival strategies and tactics of the black world dating from the attempts of late nineteenth century labor organizations and the Niagara Movement of 1906, and up to the onset of deliberate action by black students in the late 1950s, have been essentially replaced.

Costs of the Past: Questions for the Future

Socialization to an oppressive system paid off in untold costs to the black psyche and, equally unfortunate, to that of all Americans. Self-hatred, shame, negative self-esteem, suppressed aggression and rage, dependency, and subserviency are often, according to Alvin F. Poussaint, the learned survival characteristics of the black individual generated out of traditional black-white interaction. These survival mechanisms manifest themselves in such conduct as refusal to have aspirations or shying away from competition; denial of the possession of ability, intelligence, and talent; the tendency to react submissively or to avoid the display of aggressiveness; an overwhelming feeling of insecurity, helplessness, and powerlessness; the adoption of protest or liberation movements founded upon philosophies of passive resistance and nonviolence; a trained incapacity for that assertiveness which is the quintessential quality of the entrepreneurial spirit; the adoption of the emotional attitude of compliance, docility, or even "being cool"; the channeling of aggression into the pseudo-legitimate paths of sports, music, or dancing; and a vulnerability to such deviations as alcoholism, drug addiction, and compulsive gambling. Note well my statement earlier that such consequences are costly not only to black folk, but to all Americans.

I conclude, as promised, by raising questions. First, are we mad to even try to discuss calmly such a topic as the survival of black Americans in the United States? Would it not be considered absurd to ask such a question about Americans of western European descent, of Jewish descent, of Asiatic descent, of southern European descent, and of Latin and South American descent? What are we about? Second, when we raise the question of survival, are we referring to the survival of the black world or community, or of the black individual? We must be able to discriminate between the doctrinal myth of individualism and the fact of collective or group reality in American society. I suggest that this distinction must be made before the question can be properly addressed. Third, from what inferno are black folk to survive? What are the forms, limits, and dynamics of tyranny, oppression, and viciousness? In order to appreciate the fates of black folk in the United States and to devise plans for social action, ought we not to study the 1968 Czech resistance movement for its near perfect use of nonviolence as a survival technique, the experiences of the German Jew under Nazi totalitarianism, the infamous way of life of the Republics of South Africa and Rhodesia, the tragedy of Vietnam, the liberation of Algeria, and our own brother, the American Indian? Finally, given the reality of American society possessing a pluralistic ideology and structure, operating by the dynamics of conflict, and showing an undeniable genius in resisting change or thwarting all reasonable efforts to erase racism—what viable alternatives, and with what priorities, do black folk in the United States have?

SOURCES

BILLINGSLEY, ANDREW, *Black Families in White America*. Englewood Cliffs, N.J., Prentice-Hall, Inc., 1968.

FRAZIER, E. FRANKLIN, *The Negro Church in America*. New York, Schocken Books, 1963.

GAYLE, ADDISON, JR., "Dreams of a Native Son," *Liberator,* vol. 10, no. 2, Feb. 1970.

GRIMSHAW, ALLEN D., *Racial Violence in the United States*. Chicago, Aldine Publishing Company, 1969.

JOHNSON, CHARLES S., *Shadow of the Plantation*. Chicago, The University of Chicago Press, Phoenix Books, 1934.

LESTER, JULIUS, *Look Out, Whitey*. New York, Grove Press, Inc., 1968.

PINKNEY, ALPHONSO, "The Assimilation of Afro-Americans," *The Black Scholar,* vol. 1, December 1969.

POUSSAINT, ALVIN F., "The Psychology of a Minority Group with Implications for Social Action," in Charles U. Daly, ed., *Urban Violence*. Chicago, The University of Chicago Center for Policy Study, 1969.

SIMPSON, G. E., and Yinger, J. M., *Racial and Cultural Minorities*. New York, Harper & Brothers, 1953.

WALKER, T-BONE, "Little Girl, Don't You Know," on disk *Stormy Monday Blues*. Bluesway, #BLS-6008, no date.

HERBERT APTHEKER

Afro-American Superiority: A Neglected Theme in the Literature

Social, political, economic, and physical resistance to the condition of special oppression permeates the history of the Afro-American people. Similarly, intellectual resistance permeates the written record created by this people. Indeed, that record, in all its forms—petitions, poems, songs, folktales, formal histories, stories, novels, plays, autobiographies, writings in periodicals—in largest part is made up of the rejection of, and arguments against, the idea of the innate inferiority of African-derived peoples.

These peoples have had their moments of doubt; "at times," wrote W. E. B. Du Bois, in his "Of Spiritual Strivings," these "seemed about to make them ashamed of themselves"; moments, indeed, of despair, again articulated by Du Bois, as in his "Of the Training of Black Men": "Suppose, after all, the World is right and we are less than men?" But these waverings did not last long; from Margaret Walker to Frederick Douglass to W. E. B. Du Bois, from Claude McKay to Countee Cullen to Langston Hughes to Richard Wright to Alice Childress to James Baldwin to Eldridge Cleaver the opposite note has dominated—a note rejecting as a lie with transparent purposes the notion of racism in general and black inferiority in particular.

Dominant analysis and commentary have emphasized the opposite. From Bruno Bettelheim to Harvey Cox one reads of "self-fulfilling prophecies," according to which—to quote Cox, in his book *The Secular City*—when a people "are given no other identity images than those served up to them by the white majority, [they] tend to enact the expectation, which in turn reinforces the prejudice." This would seem to assume that black people have been incapable of providing their own image of themselves—an assumption which reflects an ignorance that can only be called staggering.

One finds now, from Senator James O. Eastland to Stanley Elkins, agreement as to the essential reality of Sambo; explanations differ, but the end result is—Sambo's reality. One finds now not simply a mayor of Los Angeles and other distinguished American statesmen describing the Afro-American as animal-like; no, now that the crucial testing time has come, one finds so liberal a writer as Harriet Van Horne in so liberal a paper as the *New York Post* (January 29, 1969) writing an article entitled "A Liberal Dilemma" and concluding that the trouble is that "America did dehumanize the Negro," and so now this dehumanized one "is turning, he is rending and we shall have to bear it." Poor things, how they suffer!

Along with this deluge concerning Sambo and dehumanization go lamentations about self-hatred and a "crippled" folk who are "culturally deprived," etc., etc. Of this flood, one example will suffice. Thomas A. Johnson, of *The New York Times*, in his introduction to the 1969 report submitted by the Civil Violence Research Center of Case Western Reserve University to Milton Eisenhower's National Commission on the Causes and Prevention of Violence, writes of "generations of black people being crippled" and goes on to affirm: "Self-hatred among American blacks has been supplanted to a great extent by self-love. And this within a few short years."

As has been noted, the inner doubts do occur—and it would be miraculous if they did not—but the central fact is that the literature as a whole damns as a falsehood concepts of inferiority. This conclusion—which is shouted by the evidence —is neglected in the texts and the conventional wisdom. Furthermore, a consistent theme in the literature not only rejects the concept of black inferiority, but also projects the idea of black superiority—meaning this, generally, in terms of ethical or moral superiority, but carrying over also in terms of standards of beauty, aesthetic sense, and modes and values of life. The idea does ring frequently with a kind of national pride or consciousness, but it is not racial; that is, it does not affirm, and often explicitly denies, anything smacking of the biological or genetic, and so, in that sense, too, it is the negation of racism.

At times, something approaching an awareness of this affirmative quality in the literature of the Afro-American people appears in the comments of white writers. When it does, however, it is put in tentative terms, and it is affirmed as something quite new or rather startling. For example, V. F. Calverton, in his introduction to the 1929 Modern Library edition of *Anthology of American Negro Literature,* wrote:

> The admission of inferiority which was implicit in so much of the earlier verse, the supplicatory note which ran like a lugubrious echo through so many of its stanzas, has been supplanted by an attitude of superiority and independence on the part of Countee Cullen, Langston Hughes and Gwendolyn Bennett.

167

It would be interesting to discover some of the "admissions of inferiority" and the evidence of supplication in the earlier verse; Mr. Calverton supplied none. Perhaps it would be in the work of Phillis Wheatley, whose 1784 poem entitled "Liberty and Peace" opens: "Lo! Freedom comes." Perhaps it would be in the poetry of George Moses Horton, who, writing in 1829 "On Liberty and Slavery," opened:

> *Alas! and am I born for this,*
> *To wear this slavish chain?*

Or perhaps it is supplied by James M. Whitfield, who, in his poem "America," published in 1853, opened with these lines:

> *America, it is to thee,*
> *Thou boasted land of liberty,—*
> *It is to thee I raise my song,*
> *Thou land of blood, and crime, and wrong.*

Or perhaps it is stated by Frances E. W. Harper, whose poem "Bury Me in a Free Land," published in 1854, commenced:

> *Make me a grave where 'er you will,*
> *In a lowly plain, or a lofty hill;*
> *Make it among earth's humblest graves,*
> *But not in a land where men are slaves.*

In all these one clearly has enough "admissions of inferiority" and suppliatory notes to satisfy anyone!

Again, Harvey Swados, in an essay which appeared in Herbert Hill's 1966 anthology *Anger and Beyond*, announced:

> It is already apparent that we are going to witness a substantial movement of new Negroes, liberated from ignorance, self-underestimation and self-depreciation, into the fields of poetry, drama and fiction.

168

Here Mr. Swados has not only forgotten—if he ever knew —the people forgotten by Calverton in 1929; he has neglected the people that Calverton did have the good sense to observe in the 1920's—that is, Cullen, Hughes, and Bennett—not to mention, then and thereafter, Jessie Fauset, Jean Toomer, Rudolph Fisher, Claude McKay, Sterling Brown, James Weldon Johnson, Arna Bontemps, Chester Himes, William Attaway, Frank Horne, Margaret Walker, and Theodore Ward, let alone Richard Wright and W. E. B. Du Bois!

The dominant note in historical writing, too, when dealing with the Afro-American people, is to emphasize ideas of self-depreciation and to convey the notion that self-pride is something quite new. The former appears, for example, in much of the writing of Eugene Genovese and is central to William Styron's nightmare published as *The Confessions of Nat Turner;* and since professional historians—including Genovese, Martin Duberman, and C. Vann Woodward—have spoken highly of the authenticity of the latter monstrosity, one is uncertain in just what genre it belongs. As to the note of discovering something new, an example is Edmund Cronon's useful biography *Black Moses: The Story of Marcus Garvey and the Universal Negro Improvement Association.* We are told there:

> . . . the racial doctrines of Marcus Garvey were infusing in Negroes everywhere a strong sense of pride in being black. For the first time in the long bitter centuries since their ancestors had left Africa in chains, masses of Negroes in the United States and elsewhere in the New World were glorying in their color.

It is as dangerous for a historian to write "for the first time" as it is to write "never." In this case, for example, one wonders what Mr. Cronon would do with the following poem by Du Bois—published a generation before Marcus Garvey touched the United States:

> *I am the Smoke King.*
> *I am black,*

I am darkening with song
I am hearkening to wrong:
I will be black as blackness can,
The blacker the mantle the mightier the man.

Du Bois' classic—or, one of his classics—was called, of course, *The Souls of Black Folk,* and that appeared in 1903. Its whole point was to express "a strong sense of pride in being black"; indeed, its very title had a note of irony in it, for it appeared when divines who were white were publishing books with titles such as *The Mystery Solved: The Negro A Beast,* and here a black man was writing one long prose poem exalting the souls of these animals!

What is the point of W. J. Simmons' *Men of Mark: Eminent, Progressive and Rising,* except to express this "sense of pride" and to strive to further it? And that book, of course, came from a black minister who was then president of the State University in Louisville, Kentucky; it was published back in 1887. Here, for example, is the preface: "I wish the book to show to the world—to our oppressors and even to our friends—that the Negro race is still alive, and must possess more intellectual vigor than any other section of the human family. . . ."

Carter G. Woodson's preface to the fourth edition of his *The Negro in Our History,* published forty years after Simmons' book, did not claim for the black more intellectual vigor than the white, but it certainly affirmed that he had no less than any other people and that whites suffered from a serious "handicap." Thus:

> In the proportion as Americans and Europeans become removed from such nonsense as the Nordic myth and race superiority, they will increase their interest in the history of other peoples who have accomplished just as much good as they have. So long handicapped by this heresy, however, they still lack the sense of humor to see the joke in thinking that one race has been divinely appointed to do all the great things on this earth and to enjoy most of its blessings.

An examination of the short stories and novels produced by Afro-Americans will show that a fundamental theme is the moral superiority of the black as compared with the white. This is the heart, for example, of one of the earliest short stories from a black person's pen—Frederick Douglass' "The Heroic Slave," first published in 1853, and dealing with the uprising of slaves in 1841 aboard the domestic slave-trader *Creole,* led by Madison Washington, "the heroic slave." Thereafter, the examples are endless; thus, one has Du Bois' short story "Of the Coming of John," which forms chapter thirteen of his *Souls of Black Folk.* In that story two Johns are depicted, one white and the other black; no reader can for a moment doubt which of the two is ethically the inferior and which the superior. By the way, in Walter White's novel *Fire in the Flint,* published a generation later, the chapter in which the hero, Bob Harper, avenges the rape of his sister and is then lynched is essentially the same story and with the same point. White, in fact, hammers home the point of ethical superiority and inferiority by showing the white mob tearing apart the hero's body, for souvenirs, and then writing: "The show ended. The crowd dispersed. Home to breakfast."

This note of moral superiority begins with the beginnings of Afro-American prose; it infuses, for example, David Walker's *Appeal to the Colored Citizens of the World,* which shook the slaveholders to their boots when it appeared in 1829. Furthermore, one finds, even before the Civil War, a quite explicit affirmation of the superiority of the black as compared with the white in aesthetic or physical terms. A notable example is afforded by Dr. John S. Rock of Massachusetts—a remarkable and singularly neglected figure. Dr. Rock was an important abolitionist, a physician, and the first Afro-American attorney admitted to the bar of the United States Supreme Court. Here are a few lines from a speech he delivered in Boston in 1858 (the full text is published in the first volume of my *Documentary History of the Negro People in the United States*):

> When I contrast the fine, tough muscular system, the

beautiful, rich color, the full broad features, and the gracefully frizzled hair of the Negro, with the delicate physical organization, wan color, sharp features and long hair of the Caucasian, I am inclined to believe that when the white man was created, nature was pretty well exhausted—but, determined to keep up appearances, she pinched up his features, and did the best she could under the circumstances.

One may well compare this with the marvelously witty and ironic essay that Du Bois published in Mencken's magazine *The Smart Set,* in April 1923, entitled "The Superior Race." It was written in the form of a Socratic dialogue between Du Bois and his "white friend."

This "white friend" is, understandably, somewhat startled to find Du Bois saying that "in faces I hate straight features; needles and razors may be sharp—but beautiful, never." While Du Bois consoles his friend that all such matters are simply "personal opinions" and "matters of taste," he inexorably goes on to express his own tastes: he chooses, he says, "intricately curly hair, black eyes, full and luscious features, and that air of humility and wonder that streams from moonlight." Du Bois continues pitilessly: "Add to this, voices that caress instead of rasp, glances that appeal rather than repel, and a sinuous litheness of movement to replace Anglo-Saxon stalking—there you have my ideal."

When one speaks of the white world and its reality, Du Bois asks:

> Is this superiority? It is madness. We are the supermen who sit idly by and laugh and look at civilization. We, who frankly want the bodies of our mates and conjure no blush to our bronze cheeks when we want it. We, who exalt the Lynched above the Lyncher and the Worker above the Owner and the Crucified above Imperial Rome.

Du Bois ends by telling his "friend": "Can you not see that I am laughing at you?" Do you not understand that the world of human beings is not "simply a great layer cake with superimposed slices of inferior and superior races, interlaid with mud?"

But he adds, and here Du Bois is deadly serious:

> All that I have really been trying to say is that a certain group that I know and to which I belong, as contrasted with the group you know and to which you belong, and in which you fanatically and glorifyingly believe, bears in its bosom just now the spiritual hope of this land because of the persons who compose it and not by divine command.

Compare this specific thought—and even language—with that of James Baldwin in *The Fire Next Time:* "The tendency really has been, insofar as this was possible, to dismiss white people as the slightly mad victims of their own brainwashing."

Du Bois' novel *Dark Princess,* published in 1928, is in essence a fictionalized version of his 1923 essay. Added in that book is Du Bois' growing belief in the potency of the oppressed as such; he has the hero, Matthew Towns, say in a conversation with Asians and Africans: "We come out of the depths—the blood and mud of battle. And from just such depths, I take it, came most of the worthwhile things in this world." This suggests another dimension to the whole discussion of superiority and inferiority—namely the Christian-Marxist concept of the "saving grace" or the "liberating potential" of the oppressed, exploited, and despised of this world. Within the limits of this essay, one can only call attention to the relationship; another essay—or, better, a book —would be needed (and merited) to trace out its full implications.

Du Bois' contemporary, John Galsworthy—whose work Du Bois knew, and with whom he briefly corresponded—was putting similar thoughts in novels produced in the same period. Thus, in *The Freelands* (first published in 1915), two of the Freeland brothers, Felix and Stanley, discuss the aristocratic Mallorings. Stanley thinks "they really *are superior.*" "That," Felix replies, "I emphatically question." Felix continues to detail the mode of existence of the Mallorings and those who labor for them and then asks: "Which of those two lives demands more of the virtues on which human life is founded . . . which of the two men who have lived these two lives has most right to the word 'superior'?" Stanley's reply is the classical one: "Felix, you're talking flat revolution."

Related to the ideas dramatized in this novel are the concepts of "The Intellectual Pre-Eminence of Jews"—to use the words of an essay by Thorstein Veblen, first published in 1919—and of *The Natural Superiority of Women*, to use the title of Ashley Montagu's book issued in 1953. Both writers based their concepts on the salutary effects—upon character and/or intellect—of oppression and, especially, resistance to oppression. As reported in *The New York Times* of April 1, 1969, C. P. Snow offered the opinion that the apparent intellectual superiority of Jews might well be explained genetically rather than in Veblen's terms. Far be it from me to display excessive modesty, but I must say I would have had greater confidence in Lord Snow's stimulating suggestion had it not been offered in a speech before the Hebrew Union College and Jewish Institute of Religion in New York City!

Another related theme is the insistence, that also runs through the literature of Afro-American people, upon the corrosive and debilitating impact that the existence of oppression exercises upon the brains and souls of the oppressors. This theme was, of course, basic to the arguments of the abolitionists—white and black; it appeared also in the worries of certain southern whites about slavery: for example, see the comments on this subject by Thomas Jefferson. Jean-Paul Sartre, having in mind South Africa, was quoted in the March 1968 *Tri-Continental Information Center Bulletin* as making the following relevant remark: ". . . the very principle of racism leads the whites to render themselves very inferior to those whom they oppress. For them, as for the blacks, it is hell, with this difference, that it is a hell which they have chosen."

As for Afro-American literature itself, space allows the

presentation of only a few examples. Here, for instance, is Kelly Miller, a distinguished educator and leader during the early part of the twentieth century, who published in pamphlet form in 1905 an *Open Letter to Thomas Dixon, Jr.* (Dixon was the notorious racist and glorifier of the KKK: the film *Birth of a Nation* was based upon his novel *The Klansman.*) Said Miller:

> Those who become innoculated with the virus of race hatred are more unfortunate than the victims of it. . . . Race hatred is the most malignant poison that can afflict the mind. It freezes up the fount of inspiration and chills the higher faculties of the soul.

Du Bois' writings are filled with these concepts. Thus, in his poem "The Burden of Black Women," published in *The Crisis* in November 1914, he denounced the "white world" with scorching lines:

> *Valiant spoilers of women*
> *And conquerors of unarmed men;*
> *Shameless breeders of bastards*
> *Drunk with the greed of gold,*
> *Baiting their blood-stained books*
> *With cant for the souls of the simple, . . .*

Back in 1910, in his essay "Souls of White Folk," published in *The Independent* (August), Du Bois had published two paragraphs whose prophetic quality is astonishing, even coming from a man whose capacity in this respect was almost incredible:

> I sit and see the souls of the white folk daily shriveling and dying in the fierce flame of this new fanaticism [i.e., racism]. Whither has gone America's proud moral leadership of the world? Where is the generous thought, the sweet applause, the soul's wide freedom with which we once were wont to greet the up-struggling of human kind? How natural it has become that our ambassador to the world, fresh from the laurels of Brownsville, [the reference is to Theodore Roosevelt] should greet old

Egypt's fight for freedom with a blow between the eyes!
Onward we reel. Peace? Ten thousand dollars for peace
and two hundred millions for war. How can there be
peace for those who are white and hate "niggers"? Democracy? Absurd! Dream of infants! Let Disfranchisement
and Privilege and a Solid South rule this great republic.
The rights of women? Do they not bring the highest
titles in the market? Does free America want to enfran-
chise any more dagoes and hybrids?

In his essay "On Being Black," first published in *The New
Republic* (February 18, 1920) and reissued in his book *Dark-
water,* later that year, Du Bois noted that since he was able
to view the white world "from unusual points of vantage,"
this gave him an advantage, and he saw the whites "crouch-
ing as they clutch at rags of facts and fancies to hide their
nakedness. . . ."

In his address at the 1926 Annual Convention of the National Association for the Advancement of Colored People,
held in Chicago (published in *The Crisis,* October), Du Bois'
theme was the emptiness and rottenness of the dominant
white world's values, and the possibility and opportunity of
the black population—especially, he added, "the Youth that
is here today"—to yet rescue the nation by the very act of
transforming its values.

That essentially the same theme dominates expressions coming from black militants today demonstrates that this militancy represents the continuity of the fundamental character
of Afro-American reality and feeling throughout that people's existence.

The poets of the so-called Harlem Renaissance period in
the 1920s often conveyed a sense of black superiority. Thus,
Countee Cullen:

> *My love is dark as yours is fair*
> *Yet lovelier I hold her*
> *Than listless maids with pallid hair,*
> *And blood that's thin and colder*

Langston Hughes, in the same period:

> *We should have a land of trees*
> *Bowed down with chattering parrots*
> *Brilliant as the day*
> *And not this land where birds are grey:*

And Gwendolyn Bennett, also in the 1920s:

> *I love you for your brownness*
> *And the rounded darkness of your breast;*
> *I love you for the breaking sadness in your voice*
> *And shadows where your way-ward eye-lids rest.*

The obverse—that is, comment upon the debilitating effect of being the exploiter—appears in the literature of the same period. Who can forget, for instance, the four-line epitaph that Cullen penned, "For a Lady I Know"?

> *She even thinks that up in heaven*
> *Her class lies late and snores*
> *While poor black cherubs rise at seven*
> *To do celestial chores.*

And in the novels from black writers of the 1920s, in addition to Du Bois, the same note is pervasive. Once more, a single example—from Claude McKay's *Banjo*, published in 1929; a main character, a black man named Goosey, is talking:

> You don't know why the white man put all his dirty jokes on to the race. It's because the white man is dirty in his heart and got to have dirt. But he covers it up in his race to show himself superior and put it on to us.

Might not one, reading this and not knowing its source, think that it was LeRoi Jones, for instance, writing in the present period, and not McKay forty years earlier? Or, to quote from James Baldwin's *The Fire Next Time:*

It is so simple a fact and one that is so hard, apparently, to grasp: *Whoever debases others is debasing himself.* That is not a mystical statement but a most realistic one, which is proved by the eyes of an Alabama sheriff—and I would not like to see Negroes ever arrive at so wretched a condition.

In a way, the whole thesis is in one of those remarkable paragraphs that Langston Hughes managed to utter through Simple's mouth:

I just want to know how come Adam and Eve was white. If they had started out black, this world might not be in the fix it is today. Eve might not of paid that serpent no attention. I never did know a Negro yet that liked a snake.

Read or reread James Weldon Johnson, Pauli Murray, Alain Locke, Alice Childress, John O. Killens, Arna Bontemps, Margaret Walker, Melvin Tolson, and see if one does not find quite the opposite of Harvey Swados' "self-underestimation and self-depreciation." No, this literary Sambo is quite as fictional as the historical Sambo—insofar as black artists have created literature. Both are constructs of racism, and neither in fact represents the reality of the history nor the literature of the Afro-American people.

I close with the great speech of Dr. Martin Luther King, Jr., when in December 1955, in Birmingham, he called upon the black community to express their determination to resist and to resist and to resist again—with the results the world knows:

. . . when the history books are written in future generations, the historians will have to pause and say, "There lived a great people—a black people—who injected new meaning into the veins of civilization." This is our challenge and our overwhelming responsibility.

For us who work in history—whatever our color—this stands large among *our* challenges and responsibilities.

SOURCES

APTHEKER, HERBERT, ed., *A Documentary History of the Negro People in the United States*, 2 vols. New York, Citadel Press, 1951.

BALDWIN, JAMES, *The Fire Next Time.* New York, Dial Press, 1963.

CRONON, EDMUND D., *Black Moses: The Story of Marcus Garvey and the Universal Negro Improvement Association.* Madison, University of Wisconsin Press, 1955.

COX, HARVEY, *The Secular City.* New York, The Macmillan Company, 1965.

DU BOIS, W. E. B., *The Souls of Black Folk,* 1903. Reprinted: New York, Blue Heron Press, 1953 (the 1953 edition contains significant changes).

GALSWORTHY, JOHN, *The Freelands,* 1915. Reprinted: London, William Heinemann, Ltd., 1936.

HUGHES, LANGSTON, *Simple Speaks His Mind.* New York, Simon & Schuster, 1950.

JOHNSON, THOMAS A., introduction to Masotti, Louis H., and Corsi, Jerome R., *Shoot-Out in Cleveland: Black Militants and the Police, July 23, 1968.* New York, Bantam-New York Times, 1969.

KING, MARTIN LUTHER, JR., *Stride Towards Freedom.* New York, Harper & Brothers, 1958.

SWADOS, HARVEY, "The Writer in Contemporary American Society," in Herbert Hill, ed., *Anger and Beyond: The Negro Writer in the United States.* New York, Harper & Row, Publishers, 1966.

Tri-Continental Information Center Bulletin, vol. 2, no. 3, March 1968. New York City.

RALPH DAVID ABERNATHY

The Nonviolent Movement: The Past, the Present, and the Future

It is often stated, and I contend it is a true fact, that today we live in one of the most critical periods in the history of our nation, and I would venture to include even the world. This position is held by many scholars, including clergymen, world historians, students of history, and the vast majority of the concerned peoples of the world.

Men and women of all nations are demanding their human

rights. Young people are rising up, asserting their power in many and varied forms, calling for an end to the injustices and inequities of the wealthy, affluent, and even the struggling and undeveloped societies of the world. No one can truthfully and honestly deny the fact that we are in the midst of a revolution. For an accurate definition of the revolution, I leave that to others; I wish here and now only to describe it.

First, I wish to make it crystal clear that the revolution does not necessarily have to be violent. And yet I must admit, even as a nonviolent leader, that fears and frustrations have been so deeply entrenched in millions of my poor brothers and sisters, that they believe the violence against the oppressed must be likewise inflicted upon the oppressors.

There is violence in the land. The violence that is present, and of which I speak, takes on various forms. It is inflicted mainly upon poor and black people. There is the violence of an unjust war perpetuated upon a tiny nation of brown people 10,000 miles away from the United States mainland. There is also the violence of racism, which manifests itself in many forms. The violence is seen in the practice of denying decent human survival to the masses, only to give large sums of unnecessary resources to the classes. The violence of racism is seen in police brutality; exploitation of the ghetto, the plantation, the colony, or whatever you choose to call that area where poor and black people struggle to live or exist. Violence is evident in an unjust educational system, which pollutes the mind because it is not honest and truthful; in unemployment, underemployment, poor housing, inadequate medical and dental care, and the many other forms of repression and oppression imposed by the power structure upon the black and poor people. This violence is seen so clearly in our country, the United States of America—the wealthiest and most prosperous of all nations—a nation that preaches one thing and practices another. This is the most destructive form of violence.

It is violent for any nation to exist under the creed that it is "a government of the people, by the people, and for the people" and after almost two centuries not even have a modicum of representative government. The violence of "Billions for the Moon and Pennies for the Poor" is more cruel than physical violence. This has been experienced by the poor and black people of America. We are witnesses, living and dying witnesses. As a result, there is a revolution in the land.

However, I must hasten to add that it would be tragic indeed for poor people to imitate the worst of "The American System"—that is, violence. I am confident that the poor and black people, as well as all people of good will, must find new, creative, and constructive ways of dealing with the forces of evil which resort to the various forms of violence. I submit that the violent forces must be met with "soul force." The oppressed do not have the weapons, tools, or positions to carry on a violent revolution. This, in addition to the immorality of violence, would render our revolution most ineffective. We must not be cowards, nor must we passively permit "the system" to continue to heap violence upon us and our children and families. We have an abundant supply of soul force, which must be used if the human race is to survive.

The Past

In order to understand the revolution which is presently taking place in our nation, we need only to take a look into the history of "the Movement."

It all began in Montgomery, Alabama, on December 1, 1955. Montgomery is commonly known as "the cradle of the Confederacy." But now it is also quite appropriately called "the cradle of freedom" by millions in the Movement.

It was in Montgomery that Mrs. Rosa Parks ignited a spark which began the modern-day revolution. She did this when she would no longer cooperate with the system of segregation on the city buses and refused to obey a white bus driver and give up her seat so that a white man might sit down on the late evening of that first day in December.

I was in Montgomery at the time, serving as the pastor of the First Baptist Church. It became my duty and responsibility to call together the community leaders on the night following Mrs. Parks' arrest. It was in that meeting that we planned a boycott of the city buses that began on Monday, December 5, 1955, and lasted for 381 days. This boycott did not end until the segregation ended on the buses.

This historic beginning ended with the first concrete victory for justice in more than half a century, to be exact, since Reconstruction. Our victory is well known to all, but lest it be forgotten, let me repeat it for the record and especially for the youth and those of unborn generations.

The triumphant crusade was the desegregation of all intracity travel on public conveyances in the United States. This was the first victory of the present modern-day revolution, even though the 1956 Supreme Court ruling which sealed it postdates the 1954 school desegregation decision. I take this position simply because the 1954 decision came about mainly through court action, and even today, after fifteen years, school desegregation has not been fully achieved.

The Montgomery victory did several things. First, it gave black people a sense of their own worth, dignity, and "somebodyness." Second, it stood blacks erect on their own feet and emancipated them from the crippling shackles of fear. And third, it gave the black race its first national leader in more than forty years. Ever since the death of Booker T. Washington, black people had claimed no national leader. But the Montgomery bus boycott brought forth a new spokesman—Martin Luther King, Jr.

Martin Luther King, Jr., was my dearest friend and closest associate all the way from Montgomery to Memphis. This covered a span of nearly fourteen years. We were often called by the people, and even at times by the press, "the civil rights twins."

M. L. K. and I were perennial jail mates, for nineteen times we were jailed together in our struggles to gain freedom for all men. I was pastoring the oldest black church in Montgomery, First Baptist, when Dr. King came to that capital city to pastor the Dexter Avenue Baptist Church, a daughter church of First Baptist.

I remember very clearly our first meeting in Montgomery. My lawn was the first place he set foot on, in the early spring of 1955. It was all accidental, or it may be more accurate to say that it happened by chance.

Martin (as I always called him in private, except when I referred to him in more intimate circles as Michael) was generous enough to give an automobile ride to the former pastor of the Dexter Avenue church, now the late Reverend Dr. Vernon Johns. Dr. Johns had made his way from his home in Virginia as far as Atlanta, en route to Dillard University at New Orleans, where he was to conduct religious-emphasis-week services.

He was a dear friend, my idol, and one of the greatest preachers produced by black or white America. Dr. Johns, whom history someday will record as Montgomery's "John the Baptist," had informed me of the approaching engagement in New Orleans and his desire to stop over in Montgomery and preach for me at the First Church.

Our friendship had begun, blossomed, and grown to full maturity during those days of segregation and discrimination, when the black community was chained in apathy, complacency, and fear. He had been my "Paul" and I had been his "Timothy" for at least the prior three years while we ministered to the congregations of the mother and daughter churches.

But on that beautiful spring day, that Saturday of destiny, Dr. Johns needed a lift to my city, church, and home. Dr. King, the young man who would stand in Dr. Johns' former pulpit the next morning and who would soon become his successor, had the vehicle ("The Way") and Dr. Johns had the courage ("The Will"). So, in his usual tradition of asking for what he wanted, Dr. Johns gave young King a phone call from a booth in the segregated bus station. Within a few hours the journey from Atlanta to Montgomery had been completed, and we were all seated and eating the "soul" dinner which Mrs. Abernathy had prepared especially to the liking of the Giant Old Prophet, Vernon Johns. He was very pleased to share his food with the young man who had shared his car with him.

I was happy to share these moments with our old friend and with this young man who would become my colleague and my best friend. There would be no Paul-Timothy relationship between us, but there would be a friendship equal to that of David and Jonathan.

Dr. King preached at the assigned place the next morning and warmed the hearts of that congregation, which soon extended the invitation to him to be its pastor.

Prior to December 2, 1955, the beginning of the Movement, Dr. King, Mrs. King, Mrs. Abernathy, and I spent countless hours in fellowship and misery discussing the problems of segregation, discrimination, injustice, and inequality in our city, the state of Alabama, and the nation. We discussed philosophy, theology, sociology, and the techniques of social change. Because of segregation, these nightly discussions always took place at dinner in our homes, usually on a rotating basis, and they lasted often far after the midnight hour. Our wives always served food superior to that of any restaurant in town. This added to the rich fellowship and enhanced greatly our creative dialogue.

We had no specific programs or plans for the cure of the ills of our society. All we knew was that "the system" was evil, unjust, and wrong, and that something had to be done about it. We thought, however, that things could wait—at least until I could receive a Bachelor of Divinity degree (B.D.) from Colgate-Rochester Divinity School and Martin could put into action the most dynamic social Gospel and action program ever in the history of his first church, Dexter Avenue Baptist. He felt that his extensive training for the Christian ministry demanded that of him, and I felt that my academic training had to be buttressed with a theological degree, since I had resigned my position as a college professor to become the pastor of a prominent Christian church.

But things did not wait. December 1 came on schedule for Mrs. Parks and the other oppressed blacks who had not participated in our discussions. They knew nothing of our desire to wait for action. They were tired of waiting. Destiny soon placed Martin's pulpit in the wilderness of America's "Egypt land," and my classrooms in theology became the streets of an unjust society and the jail cells of a nation, sick and even dying from the cancerous disease of racism, poverty, and war.

The impact of Martin Luther King, Jr., on the life of the nation soon became apparent as he was proclaimed the moral leader of America. Others looked upon him as a bright star of hope in a dark and dismal sky. For the old black men and women who had waited so long and patiently, chanting, "Come by here, my Lord, come by here; somebody needs you, Lord; somebody is dying, Lord; come by here, my Lord," he was a deliverer, a Messiah, sent from Heaven. Dr. King became the inspiration of the young and restless. He was faith with work; he was prayer in action. He took religion outside the sacred walls of the sanctuaries, cathedrals, and synagogues. This was unique. This was different. This was welcomed. Through him, "the word had become flesh" again and was dwelling in our midst. Let me repeat, the black man was hungering and thirsting for a new leader, having been without a national leader since the days of Booker T. Washington. Even with Washington, there were many who questioned his theory and philosophy, but he was an undisputable national black leader. This is not to say that during the span of years between the leadership of Washington and King we did not have black scholars, educators and some business and professional leaders who had achieved the ranks of local, regional, and even national spokesmen. The NAACP was on the case; the Urban League was doing its things—a good thing. Marcus Garvey, A. Philip Randolph, Walter White, Mordecai Johnson, Roy Wilkins, Benjamin Mays, William Holmes Borders, Thurgood Marshall, A. T. Walden, Grand Master Dobbs, Andrew Jackson Stokes, Peter James Bryant, A. D. Williams, C. T. Walker of the National Baptist Convention, Inc., Emory Jackson, J. E. Pierce, Martin Luther King, Sr., Bishops William A. Fountain, W. J. Walls, W. W. Wright, Jr., C. Ward Nichols, Vernon Johns, Mary McCloud Bethune, Charallette Hawkins Brown, Howard Thurman, and countless numbers of others were championing the cause of black people and speaking out fearlessly for the rights of all men, black and white, rich and poor. Many would not bow, or compromise their position. Consequently, they were persecuted, and they, along with their families, suffered many acts of intimidation and reprisal.

Many others, too many to catalog, had found their way to the gallows, having become the victims of lynching mobs, because of their stand for the rights of their people. But in spite of their dedication, brilliance, profundity, and action, none of these personalities had been proclaimed by the people as "the voice of Black America," and neither had Black America chosen any of them unanimously (that is, almost unanimously), as THE LEADER.

I write these words not to discredit these persons, for they are all my heroes in one way or another. But honesty impels me to point out a fact of history. I guess there is truth to the old saying that the hour and the man must meet at the right time. Maybe the persons listed above and many others made their greatest contribution by creating the hour and unknowingly producing the man: Martin Luther King, Jr. Naturally, I believe very firmly that there was also an additional factor—the hand of God moving in the affairs of men. History does repeat itself. So I believe that what happened in Israel for the Hebrew people many centuries ago happened now to the black man. "I have heard the groans of my people . . . Go down, Moses, way down in Egypt land and tell Ole Pharaoh to let my people go." Like Moses, Martin accepted the God-given challenge.

The attributes and skills of Martin Luther King, Jr., were many. He was richly endowed with the gifts of a great orator, with special appeal to black people. There was music in his baritone, melodious voice. The courage, strength, and brilliance which came from this man of average physical stature were most fascinating indeed.

Although a product of middle-class society, Martin had an unusual compassion for the poor of all races. He was well educated, but he never looked down on the uneducated. If he possessed an attitude in the area of education at all, it was an adamant disdain for pseudo-educated Americans. He would often say to me, when we were trapped in some falsely sophisticated gathering, "Ralph, I am bored to death. Man, get me out of this place." In private, he would often take to battle some professor of philosophy who might be trying to impress a group with what he knew. Dr. King's tenacity would come forth, and he just might prove to the group that the professor knew no philosophy at all. This was not his usual behavior. He only felt that training in any field should be used to ultimately lift one's fellow man.

Dr. King was a man of the people. He loved all people, but most especially the poor and ordinary people. He loved to speak to large crowds of people who were full of "soul," and who were so uninhibited that they would sincerely respond when moved by his oratory. His photographic memory, coupled with his ability to use uncommon words wisely, made him a success on any platform. He could charm any audience, and his utterances were readily accepted, even though in many cases they were not understood. "I don't know what that boy is saying, but whatever it is, it sure sounds good to me" was often heard on or near the platforms across America.

People were moved. People listened, and they tried to understand when "my buddy"—as I have often called Martin —would say something like this:

"If I had the wisdom of a Plato; the courage of an Aristotle; the eloquence of a Demosthenes; the vision of a Socrates, I would still be unequal to the task of addressing you this evening." Or: "Let freedom ring—let it ring from every mountainside . . . Let it ring from the snowcapped Rockies of Colorado . . . Let it ring from the prodigious slopes of the Alleghenies of Pennsylvania . . . Let freedom ring from the lofty peaks of the East and West. Let freedom ring from every mountainside . . . Let it ring from every molehill in Mississippi . . . Let it ring even from Look-Out Mountain in Tennessee to Stone Mountain in Georgia . . . from every mountainside, let freedom ring."

This sounded good. It was sweet to hear, for it was like "music in a sinner's ear." It gave the black man hope, for never before had he heard such beautiful, rhythmic words flowing in the courts of the Pharaohs to the Pharaoh, and never before in our times had a people backed up a leader and made it possible for him to utter such phrases any and everywhere. These words by Martin—but even more important, his vast followings—troubled the power structure. The news media had exposed a "black King," and they could not rescind this exposure.

The Ground Crew

Aside from Dr. King's ability to articulate the hopes, longings, and aspirations of an oppressed people through love and nonviolence, his next greatest asset, in my estimation, was to attract and hold an efficient, dedicated, and fearless staff. He also had a concerned group of friends, some of whom were white. They were mostly Jewish, and a few were wealthy or had influence with friends of wealth. Martin made it clear that the role of the whites in our struggle was to be a supportive one, and not one of leadership. This amassing of support proved quite helpful to him in crystallizing his own thinking, and to the Movement in terms of fundraising, program, and strategy.

Finding a staff was no problem, since direct action against the system was being organized for the first time in this generation. This alone attracted men and women of all levels, and our nonviolent resistance philosophy was much more militant than the other schools of thought that pervaded the black community at that time.

There were only three other schools of thought in 1956. The first was, "Wait on the Lord and He will fix it by and by." The second was, "Justice can only be achieved through the courts." Yet this was a long drawn out process, with very few black lawyers and, with only one or two exceptions, no white lawyers who were willing to take civil rights cases. There were also the problems of funds necessary for court battles and of the attitude in the Deep South of many judges, who would permit the defense counselors to use words such as "nigger" and "boy." Other forms of intimidations and reprisals made it difficult not only to secure lawyers, but to find plaintiffs to challenge the unjust system. The third school of thought stated that education is the only tool by which social change is brought about and that this lengthy process was the black man's way out. I suppose the adherents of this school of thought had been inspired by Booker T. Washington, or maybe by W. E. B. Du Bois or some other prominent educator.

With Martin Luther King, Jr.'s., program of action, many joined his staff seeking no salary. The black church had never been involved in social action, so members who were weary with a gospel of long white robes, golden slippers, streets of gold, and sweet milk and honey in Heaven joined in the demonstrations and brought their pastors along. They wanted these things, and even more, right down here on Earth. The white church had never courageously taken a firm stand on our Judeo-Christian principles. Therefore, our marches and demonstrations gave priests, pastors, and rabbis an opportunity to back up their paper resolutions with limited direct action.

So the man and the hour had met. His genius rested in his ability to use the hour wisely. This he did with excellence. He knew very well that the first victory of the present revolution—the Montgomery bus boycott, which came about through nonviolence—could become a pattern for attacking the unjust system of segregation all across the South, and that it would have great appeal to the black community, which was predominantly religious, and gain support for the cause from northern blacks and liberal whites.

Soon after the Montgomery bus boycott was over, Dr. King led in organizing a South-wide movement. On January 10, 1957, a meeting was convened in Atlanta. I was present as one of the organizers in Atlanta and had shared in giving birth to the whole idea. I participated in drawing up the purpose and working papers, but my stay at this two-day meeting was interrupted when I was awakened at 2:00 A.M. to receive a long-distance telephone call from my wife, Juanita. She informed me that our home had been blown nearly to pieces by a bomb; that there were no lights any longer in the house. Even though she was pregnant with our second child, Donzaleigh, Mrs. Abernathy thought—but in the absence of lights could not be certain—that she had escaped injury, and she felt the same about the baby, Juandalynn, who was crying in her bed in the same unlighted room. My wife informed me that she felt that the ruins surrounding her in our bedroom were minor compared to the damages done to the rest of the house.

The front of the house had been ripped completely off, and there were many voices outside, but she could not be sure if they were a mob or if they were our friends. The policemen were there, also, and their orders were that no one was to enter the house. They did this under the pretense that it was for their own safety, since there might be other explosions in the building. Other more serious dangers, according to them, might be live electric wires or burst gas lines, which might ignite the remains of this frame church parsonage, which had been our home for the previous five years.

It was unsafe for anyone to enter, according to the policemen, yet they were making no attempts to get my wife and baby out of there. "Get back, you. I said get the Hell away from here, you black S. O. B." This I could hear faintly in the far distance, 175 miles away, as I stood trembling while holding the telephone in the bedroom of the Reverend and Mrs. Martin Luther King, Sr. My courageous wife prodded me to hear by saying, "Just listen," and pointed her receiver in the direction of the unfriendly voice. But this policeman was talking to our neighbor, whose home was separated from ours by only one house situated on a small lot. He was bellowing these insults to a lady who represented woman's power. Even though she was an educator and one of the few black administrators in the Montgomery school system, with an office downtown in the Board of Education building, she was not a slave to the system, and she was not afraid. She is a practicing Christian, and her Christianity came forth as I heard her say, "Man, you had better get out of the way. Don't you know that lives are at stake—there is an expectant mother in there and also a baby in a crib. *Get out of my way. If you don't care about them, I want you to know that we do. If you don't try to save them, then I will."*

Then I heard her calling, "Juanita, Juanita, where are you? Are you all right, and what about Juandalynn?"

Mrs. Abernathy, now feeling better, replied to the inquiry, "Oh, here I am, Mrs. Norris. I am right here in the middle bedroom. I am all right and so is the baby, I believe." I assured my wife that I would call back shortly and let her know of my time of arrival. I hung up the phone, thus freeing her to talk with Mrs. Arthur Mae Norris, our dear friend, whose love had moved her to risk her life for her friends.

Fortunately, the explosion missed the gas line—by one inch, according to both city and state investigators. Therefore, there was no fire. But when I called back one hour later, at 3:00 A.M., to inform my wife that Dr. King and I would be on the 6:00 A.M. flight to Montgomery to check out her physical condition as well as that of our baby, this call was interrupted with cries of, "Oh, God! No! Another one!"

After a pause, Mrs. Abernathy informed me that the policemen had told the people in the house and the thousands outside that my church, First Baptist, had just been bombed. The church was more than a mile away, being located in the industrial section of downtown Montgomery. They were correct; the church had been bombed.

When I arrived a few hours later, not only were my home and the surrounding area and streets roped off, but so was the church. This century-old house of God, which had been a refuge during the darker days for black men who were forced to flee from angry white lynching mobs; this grand old church, which was built by blacks on slave wages according to a program whereby each member was assessed by the pastor, the Reverend Dr. Andrew Jackson Stokes, to bring a brick each Sunday; this fortress, which had stood proudly as an irresistible force in the Confederate capital under the motto "Towering O'er the Wrecks of Time," housing at intervals the only college for blacks in the city, the Montgomery Improvement Association, and the NAACP, and sheltering the

Freedom Riders and 2,000 persons at a mass rally while President Kennedy's federal marshals tried in vain to subdue the angry mob that Governor Patterson's National Guard had "protected" from the peaceful protestors who were confined all night in the church; this institution of truth, which the white church had given birth to for black people during the dark days of slavery, but whose creed had always been, "Whosoever will—black or white—let him come"—this church stood that morning for the first time in its history with its doors closed and signs reading "condemned" plastered on its weather-worn exterior walls.

The foundation of handsome, proud, stately, and towering First Baptist had been shaken. She stood battered, and appeared to me to be engulfed in shame. The old church still stood tall on the hill at the corner of Columbus and Ripley streets, even amidst the ruins which surrounded it. Much of the unwholesome surroundings were not new, for they were filth and shanties, the products of poverty. These I had found there when I became the church's youngest and seventh pastor in November 1951. They were not new to me. I was accustomed to them, and in many ways I had adjusted to them. But the rubbish of the bombing was new.

The shroud of defeat that seemingly covered this towering church edifice covered my soul. It appeared to me that the forces of evil had finally succeeded in causing Dr. Stokes' church banner, "The Triumph of Truth, Love, and Justice," to trail in the dust. For me, this was unbelievable; even worse, it was unbearable.

Policemen ordered me not to enter the church building, for it was unsafe. But I committed civil disobedience, willing to die if necessary in the ruins of those hallowed walls or on the ground made sacred by the sweat, blood, and tears of so many in the development of my people. That church had meant so much to me personally. When I could bear it no longer, when there was nothing but love in my heart, even for the person or persons who had committed these ungodly acts, I whispered a prayer at the altar and gave in to the pleas of my associates and left. I paused outside and read the words and letters of my proposed sermon for that coming Sunday, which were on the bulletin board: FATHER FORGIVE THEM, FOR THEY KNOW NOT WHAT THEY DO. I then returned to the remains of 1327 South Hall Street, where my deacon, Dr. Moses Jones, came to treat me. I was sick.

The Movement had suffered violence before. It had been inflicted upon us many times. There had been some bombings, but none so severe as these. Thursday, the day of my return to the city, was an awful day in my life, and I felt that Friday was just as dark, if not darker, than Jesus' Good Friday.

The officers of the church brought in contractors who boarded up windows where beautiful stained glass once stood and placed temporary supporting beams against the sagging walls. They secured permission from the city building officials to use the basement for the Sunday services. Upon my request, they removed all the "condemned" signs after making sure that no one could enter the main sanctuary. To see First Baptist condemned was more than I could endure.

Two of our members, Margaret and Frank Brown, gave my wife and me new quarters in their lovely home. This turned out to be our home, also, for the next six months. We were able to return to our house just prior to the birth of our second child, Donzaleigh, on August 5.

Saturday, after the bombings, I carried my burden alone. For no one could understand what First Baptist meant to me and the black people of Montgomery. In addition to being the mother church, it is the largest and most stately of all of Montgomery's black churches (many would say it is the finest and most beautiful in the city). Its doors had always been opened to those who would bring about justice and equality. It was in that church that both the Alabama and National Baptist conventions, the largest black organizations in Alabama and the United States, respectively, were organized soon after the close of slavery.

The bombing of the parsonage was all right, for it was a modest frame home for the pastor and his family, and Juanita and I were prepared to make the sacrifice. But the

194

church? I just didn't know. It meant so much to so many people. So many of the parents of members, and even a few of the present members, had brought a brick a Sunday to help build this church. In this church the young had been blessed, baptized in the pool, and then joined in holy wedlock at the altar. In this church so many mothers and fathers, relatives, and friends of the members had accepted a new life in Christ and had received teachings and instructions which shaped and molded their personalities. In this church countless members had worshipped God, had toiled and labored, and had finally been laid to rest. In that holy place so many burdens had been lifted, and thousands had received the faith to "hold on." It was the church of our forefathers; it was the church of many members and friends' grandparents; it was their parents' church; it was their church; and I wondered if they fully realized that it was God's church. So many great preachers, freedom fighters, and statesmen had proclaimed the Gospel and declared the truth there; and even though I was only the seventh pastor in its history, which predated the Emancipation Proclamation, I felt that I was the least of the seven.

Never before had that church called a pastor at age twenty-six. So I tried to carry my burden all alone during those dark and dreadful days. This is not to say that my friends, fellow church members, associates, and above all, my darling wife did not equally share my grief. I am only saying that I tried to conceal my true feelings. I tried to keep the problem, which I felt so deeply, to myself. The load was heavy, but it was lifted in the basement of the old church on Sunday morning.

At the close of my sermon Mrs. Susie Beasley, one of the oldest surviving members in the church at that time, and one of those who brought a brick each Sunday in an effort to build it, began to speak. She was the mother of five or six school principals, administrators, and teachers, many of whom were scattered across the state and all of whom were in my congregation. She made a moving and profound statement. Among her eloquent and unforgettable words, which I

still recall, were these: "Brother Pastor, you are troubled
this morning. There must never be any fear in your heart,
for you are God's prophet and a leader of His people. *This
is God's church.* He is the head of it and you are the overseer
of the flock."

With an unusual pride, found only in one who was a member of one of the first families of Montgomery and a disciple
of Dr. Stokes, the old soldier braced herself, lifted her chest
high, and stood on her toes like a bantam hen, throwing her
voice to the ceiling and into every corner. She continued,
*"This building cannot hold First Church, for this church is
in the hearts of men.* They may destroy these stones, but
they cannot destroy this church. Let them burn it down, if
they choose, but be assured, Brother Pastor, that just as we
built this one, we will build another one. So lead on, Pastor
Abernathy. I say lead on until black men are free. Lead on,
Pastor, until there is no segregation and discrimination in
this city or in this land. My grandchildren are looking to you;
unborn generations are depending on you; the saints who
have passed on, especially Dr. Stokes, have invested in you.
God has richly endowed you."

Then, in a voice just above a whisper, Mrs. Beasley closed,
"Don't let me down; don't let black people down, and above
all, don't let yourself down and God down."

As tears met under her chin, her voice swelled to full force
again and trembled flute-like. Everyone knew now that the
powerful Susie Beasley meant business as she warned me,
"Don't let Satan win this victory. Lift your head high and
lead us on. Know that you have a God who never fails and
a congregation who is with you all the way."

She had achieved her purpose, and she knew it. So in a
sweetly mellow and motherly voice, Sister Beasley said,
"Therefore, I wish to offer a motion that we give the Pastor
a rising vote of confidence, reaffirming our faith in his leadership, reassuring him and his little wife of our love, and let-
ting the forces of evil know that nothing will turn us around."

I do not know who seconded the motion, for there were so
many. My eyes were so full of tears that I could not see

clearly. Neither can I recall if the chairman of the Board of Deacons, Mr. A. L. Autry, placed the motion before the congregation. All I know is that visitors as well as members, young people and children, all stood on their feet, and the organist finally caught up with the spontaneous singing of "Where He Leads Me I Will Follow."

I fumbled through a benediction and the worship was over —and so were my worries about First Baptist Church. We left as the church organist (who, incidentally, was the wife of one of Mrs. Beasley's sons) played a postlude on the piano, Handel's "Hallelujah Chorus." I left feeling good and humming, "And He Shall Reign Forever and Ever. . . ." We immediately launched a financial drive, and soon had the $56,000 necessary to restore the parsonage and the church to their former status.

The two-day meeting in Atlanta had, meanwhile, led to the creation of a new force—the Southern Christian Leadership Conference. SCLC completed its organization two months later in New Orleans. Dr. King was elected our president, and I was elected secretary-treasurer.

Dr. King had the unusual ability to milk a staff dry of ideas, and back then we did not face the problem of headline seekers. He would announce the collective thinking of our group as the program, and we marched from one victory to another. The most outstanding of Dr. King's accomplishments, in addition to integrating transportation, was the passage of the Civil Rights Act of 1964 and the Voting Rights Act of 1965. But the accomplishments of this man cannot be limited to items, dates, places, and things. The fact that a revolution was started is the important thing.

Before Montgomery little or nothing was happening in the black community. Now much is happening in many, many ways. Today we have many organizations on the move. Black people are proud of their heritage, and many feel that nonviolence has outlived its usefulness. We have many voices, leaders, and organizations. This I do not condemn. Rather, I encourage it. I believe it is healthy. Certainly, no one single person can be given the credit for creating this present climate. But the brightest star on the horizon, the moving spirit behind it all, the individual who played the leading role which made this present phase of the drama possible, the person whom the people brought to match the hour was Martin Luther King, Jr.

When I think of him, the following words by Ralph Ellison often enter my mind:

> Sometimes—yes, sometimes—the good Lord . . . I say the good Lord . . . accepts His own perfection, and closes His eyes, and goes ahead, and takes His own good time, and He makes Himself a man. Yes! And sometimes that man gets hold of the idea of what he's supposed to do in this world, and he gets an idea of what it is possible for him to do. And that man lets that idea guide him as he grows, and struggles, and stumbles, and sorrows . . . until finally he comes into his own God-given shape, and achieves his own individual and lonely place in this world. It don't happen often. Oh, no! But when it does, then even the stones will cry out in witness to his vision, and the hills and towers will echo his words and deeds, and his example will live in the breasts of men forever. . . . So you look at him awhile, and be thankful—that the Lord let such a man touch our lives, even if it were only for a little while.

The society could not break him, so it killed him. It would be most difficult for Dr. King if he were alive now in this critical period. He played his role amazingly well. His stay was brief, but it was most effective. Few personalities have accomplished in a life of seventy years what this modern-day Moses achieved in his short thirty-nine years. His work continues, and his spirit is still with us.

Some of his final words to me were, "Ralph, we live in a sick nation, a nation that refuses to respond adequately to the nonviolent demands of the black and poor people. We are in a period of violence and maybe we will just have to let violence run its course." He knew very well that nonviolence was the only way for human survival. He had said this over and over again from platform to platform. He never gave up on nonviolence, but we were in agreement that some people and some nations only learn the hard way.

So the bells tolled as Martin Luther King, Jr., had become the victim of the violence he abhorred and denounced. Like Lincoln, he now belongs to the ages—but the Movement must keep moving.

The Present

During the present period, we are in a different stage of the revolution. No longer are we seeking civil rights, but now we are demanding human rights. The enemy is no longer a group of separate states of the old Confederacy, or a few symbolic personalities in the South. The Jim Clarks and the Eugene (Bull) Connors have been removed from their roles of dramatizing the evils of our society. Few Lester Maddoxes and George Wallaces are around. In fact, we have a sophisticated, skillful opposition, whose intent is more destructive, but whose tactics are more divisive and deceiving.

Actually, the enemy was never limited to the South, nor were its racist practices America's only forms of injustice. The white South has merely been a tool of the more sophisticated sections of the country. I identify the real enemy as our own federal government, which consistently fails to live up to its creed and be true to the principles on which it was founded.

It was the lack of representative government which led to the establishing of this nation. It also gave birth at the very same time to the writing of the Declaration of Independence: "We hold these truths to be self-evident, that *all Men* are created equal, that they are endowed by their Creator with certain inalienable Rights, that among these are Life, Liberty, and the Pursuit of Happiness [italics mine]."

Taxation without representation sparked the American Revolution and brought into being a government that is supposed to be of the people, by the people, and for the people. It is the task of representative government to destroy the three great evils of the United States of America: racism, poverty, and war.

The Poor People's Campaign

In an effort to achieve a decent society and preserve the nation in the process, we in SCLC launched the Poor People's Campaign in the spring of 1968. The Kerner Commission confirmed the fact that ours is a racist society. We must all be honest and make this confession, for racism does pervade our land. It manifests itself in the other two great evils: poverty and war. That is why SCLC is concentrating mainly on a program to make life better for poor people in a nation that spends billions for the moon and only pennies for the poor. The Poor People's Campaign is presently in Chapter Three.

In the first chapter of the campaign we mobilized not only the poor black people, but the poor Mexican-Americans, the American Indians, the Puerto Ricans, and the poor whites of Appalachia, and we went to Washington. "The Time to Act Is Now!" was our slogan.

Dr. King eloquently said, "Poor people's lives are disrupted and dislocated every day. We want to put a stop to this. Poverty, racism, and discrimination cause families to be kept apart, men to become desperate, women to live in fear, and children to starve."

Unfortunately, our place of abode during the campaign, Resurrection City, became the symbol of our activities, and the vast majority of Americans are still unaware of our achievements. The accomplishments of the Poor People's Campaign are many, but the greatest victory of Chapter One is the fact that we exposed poverty in the richest and most affluent nation in the world.

Prior to our trek to Washington, very little was being said about poverty. President Kennedy had spoken on the issue, and some authors were writing about the two Americas— rich America and poor America. However, the average American knew very little about the seriousness of this issue, and the nation was not fully aware of the misery which one-fifth of our population faced while isolated on a lonely island of poverty in the midst of an ocean of plenty. It therefore became our task to dramatize poverty and to call it to the attention of the nation.

The drama was so effective that not only did the president and his cabinet move into action, but also Congress. I would be the first to admit that the action taken by both the executive and legislative branches of the government was much too limited and slow, but we set something in motion and we faced the issues of the new period courageously with a plan, a program. The demands we made must never be overlooked, and our actions must be recorded by astute writers and politicians as the greatest accomplishments for black and poor people since the Emancipation Proclamation.

By focusing attention on the evil of poverty, and by exposing it through the Poor People's Campaign, we caused editors of the major magazines, newspapers, and periodicals to write about poverty. Television documentaries on hunger and poverty were made. Even some senators from the South decided that they would take a look to see if hunger existed in their states. Naturally, they found it there, and I am reasonably certain that they knew it existed all the time.

The first chapter of the Poor People's Campaign ended with my being jailed, along with hundreds of my followers, as we tried to take the campaign against hunger from the Department of Agriculture and Secretary Orville Freeman to the Capitol, where the elected officials and representatives of the people held forth. I served twenty days in the District of Columbia jail for this "crime." Resurrection City was destroyed by the police, and its mayor—my most courageous staff member, Hosea Williams—and those left in the city to take care of the housekeeping chores were also dragged off to jail.

This did not end our impact. It is reported that the Associated Press *Year Book* of 1968 gave the second largest amount of space, out of all the many features covered that year, to the Poor People's Campaign.

There are those who still feel that the Poor People's Campaign was a failure. I guess they came to this conclusion simply because they were untouched by this gigantic and dynamic movement.

In Chapter One of the campaign I tried to carry out the plans of Dr. King, even though these plans had been in his mind and very little had been put on paper. After my release from jail in Washington, D.C., I began plans for the second chapter of the campaign. I drew up these plans and decided that the most effective method would be to concentrate on solving the problem at the state and local levels. We did not abandon the idea of bringing pressure on Washington, but we reserved the right to determine when and how.

I secured the services of another staff member, the Reverend Walter Fauntroy, then the vice-mayor of Washington, D.C., to serve as coordinator of the second chapter. Our Committee of 100 moved into Washington on schedule in the spring of 1969; there we stated our demands to President Nixon and some of his cabinet officials, leaders of both the Democratic and Republican parties, and certain congressmen. Our demands were so simplified that even an elementary scholar could understand what the poor people wanted. These demands were:

(1) That hunger be wiped out in America now. All persons with incomes of less than $3,000 per year should be provided with free food stamps. A minimum of $2.5 billion additional monies for fiscal 1970 should be immediately appropriated in order to insure an adequate diet to every needy person.

(2) That an adequate federal standard of welfare be immediately implemented, and that legislation be enacted to guarantee an annual income above the poverty level for every poor person. We also demand immediate repeal of the "freeze" on AFDC (Aid for Dependent Children) recipients and we demand the mandatory adoption by states of welfare assistance to unemployed fathers.

(3) That a comprehensive jobs bill be adopted to provide 3 million new jobs in the private and public

sectors for the unemployed. We also strongly demand that the federal government effectively enforce Executive Order 11246 and stop spending billions of federal tax dollars annually to foster racial segregation and discrimination through federal contracts.

(4) That every poor child be provided with a quality education. That Title I [of the Elementary and Secondary Education Act, providing federal funds for educationally disadvantaged pupils] and other education funds be appropriated on an equal basis to white and black, rich and poor. That the Department of Health, Education, and Welfare insure that local school districts comply with Title VI [of the 1964 Civil Rights Act, outlawing de jure segregation] by completely ending the dual school system by the fall of 1969.

(5) That the Vietnam war be ended promptly and that rising military expenditures be drastically cut back so that desperately needed funds can be shifted to the crying domestic needs that are tearing this nation apart. We also demand that the projected ABM expenditures be abandoned and that the military draft be changed so as not to discriminate against the poor.

(6) That Title VII of the Civil Rights Act of 1964 and the National Labor Relations Act be expanded to cover employment by state and local governments and private nonprofit institutions, and that the rights of public employees and farm workers be protected by collective bargaining.

(7) That the full appropriations originally authorized be provided for the Housing and Urban Development Act of 1968. That a housing trust fund be established that would guarantee a continuous supply of decent housing for the poor and the prompt and orderly reconstruction of our cities and rural areas. That fair-housing laws be vigorously implemented to provide true housing choice for the poor and for Americans now deprived of such choice because of skin color or race.

(8) That a national health program for the poor be implemented.

(9) That eighteen-year-olds be granted the right to vote.

(10) That increases in public-assistance benefits and social-security benefits be based on the cost-of-living index. And that fundamental tax-reform measures be enacted to redistribute the burden the poor and the nonpoor carry under the present discriminatory tax system.

After presenting our demands in Washington, we then moved to the local scene. Involvement in local activities took us to Charleston, South Carolina, where we won a marvelous victory for the nonprofessional hospital workers of that city. The final result was a raise for all state workers, including the state troopers who had accosted and jailed us during the demonstrations.

Another clear-cut victory of Chapter Two is seen in our political accomplishments in Greene County, Alabama, under the competent direction of Hosea Williams. We took over control of the Greene County Board of Commissioners and the Board of Education. A majority of qualified black persons were elected to these two significant departments of government in this Alabama Black Belt county.

The Charleston victory gave impetus to the winning of many other victories for nonprofessional hospital workers (organized in several cities) through Local 1199 of New York City. Many of these victories were won without our having to begin an action campaign. Hospitals responded all across the country. Cities which did not want a repeat of the events in Charleston gave creative leadership which led to settlements. The combination of "soul power" and union power proved to be a winning combination, and it brought victory to thousands of poor hospital workers.

All of these victories were undergirded by struggles. Much suffering and great sacrifices were involved. Twice during the summer of 1969 I was jailed in Charleston and fasted to dramatize the plight of poor workers. This greatly strengthened the Charleston strategy of daily marches, jail-ins, and boycotts, and gave courage to the people to follow the leadership.

Today we have come a long, long way for an oppressed and despised people, but we still have a long, long way to go. Total victory for black and poor people is not even in sight, and no one knows what the end will bring. Through our powerful coalition of representatives of the poor, we have moved Congress to begin to pass meaningful legislation against hunger and poverty. We have focused attention on the evils of war and have consistently played a leading role in the movement to end the war in Southeast Asia. To achieve these goals, I have had to travel extensively, taking the message of peace and human rights throughout the world, including Africa, Asia, South America, Europe, and all over the United States and other parts of North America.

I sought the counsel of Pope Paul VI in my visit with him at the Vatican, and the help of other leaders of the great religions of the world as Mrs. Abernathy and I journeyed around the world on a peace mission. My platform has not always been in the great cathedrals, synagogues, and churches of America; often it has been in the remote areas of Mississippi, Alabama, Georgia, Louisiana, and South Carolina, and in the forgotten ghettos of Chicago, New York, Detroit, Baltimore, and Washington, D.C. I have always said, and I still proclaim, that "wherever injustice is, I have business there." My pulpit is wherever suffering and misery are.

My most depressing and yet rewarding experience was on a recent visit to Brazil, where I toured the unbelievably poverty-stricken area of that country and met possibly the world's foremost nonviolent leader, Archbishop Helder Camara, who has courageously stood up against "the system" despite terrorism, assassinations of his followers, and other acts of intimidation.

The nonviolent efforts of the Southern Christian Leadership Conference have not always borne fruit with the desired speed and rapidity, but we are still on the case, for our efforts have succeeded abundantly.

It was the decentralization of the Poor People's Campaign to the local level which brought about the successful defeat of Judge Clement Haynsworth and G. Harrold Carswell as nominees to the United States Supreme Court. The opposing senators were responding to pressure from their constituencies at the local level. It is this very same pressure that has caused senators and congressmen to project strategy to end the war in Vietnam, and has even moved the president to adopt a program of the Poor People's Campaign—a guaranteed annual income—as his program. The adoption of this idea is a gigantic step for the Nixon Administration, even though we must admit that the proposed figures are grossly inadequate.

Now a wave of repression engulfs our land. The murdering of Black Panthers, the killing of students on the campuses of our colleges and universities, and the shooting and slaughtering of citizens in the streets must be stopped. This is not a police state. We live in a free country where there should be civilian control. Consequently, our work is with concerned groups of people of all racial, ethnic, political, and religious persuasions. But we must move even farther into the deep waters of adversity and nonconventionalism. We have worked and cooperated on a limited scale with groups whose methods and philosophy differed from ours, but whose goals are the same as ours: "To build the beloved society."

Time demands of us a togetherness we have never known before. We can have unity without having unanimity. The white community has never possessed one philosophy, and that should not be expected of the black community.

The Future

Now we have many voices, and we have many leaders and many philosophies. I hold firmly to the fact that all of this is healthy for the black man, for today no one single voice can speak for all of us. But if we are to be victorious, there must be only one goal—to make America be America to all of its citizens.

To achieve this, black Baptists must work with Black Panthers; black believers must work with black nonbelievers; and those who have studied at Morehouse must work with those who have no house.

There are many program areas in which we must work. The key to democracy is representative government, in which the people—not the politicians—make the decisions. During the 1960s SCLC worked toward "People's Government" by securing the right of black people to vote and enforcement of the Fifteenth Amendment, and by building for a new politics in the nation. In the South alone, since 1965 more than one million black voters have registered, and nearly five hundred black candidates—including judges, mayors, legislators, sheriffs, aldermen, city and county commissioners, and school board members—have been elected to office. The challenge to SCLC in the 1970s is to complete the job of achieving representative government. We will join with the forces of the black and poor communities, the peace movement, the student and youth movement, and others concerned about representative government. We will define political issues, organize voter-registration and political-education campaigns, and make the politicians come to the people for the people's decisions. SCLC's "Politics '70," according to which we are working in selected communities in the South and North, is the first step in this decade's movement for People's Government.

Students and young people have always provided, with massive participation, much of the courage and commitment in the freedom movement. SCLC helped organize and support SNCC, and over the years has recruited thousands of youthful workers in the struggle. Today SCLC staff members are assigned to consult with students and young people on the tactics and strategy of movements against racism, repression, war, and poverty. Young volunteers remain the active backbone of our mass direct-action campaigns and our full-time programs.

Thousands of local community leaders and Movement participants have received training from SCLC. Our Citizenship Education workshops began in 1962 and are held for "grass roots" adults, as well as youth, for the development of community organization and movements. A full-time education and training staff is also engaged in defining the educational crisis in America and helping to develop new solutions to that crisis, in urban ghetto schools, in the rural South, and on college campuses.

People who support the movements and programs of SCLC

can more closely identify with the organization either by becoming individual members or by affiliating their local groups with the national organization. SCLC affiliates and chapters may adopt SCLC programs with the advice and help of our staff.

Several special continuing services are available from SCLC. A nationwide radio program, "Martin Luther King Speaks," is broadcast each Sunday on ninety stations across the country. The official SCLC journal, *Soul Force,* and other materials such as posters, brochures, and speeches are printed by SCLC. Audiovisual materials include photographs and the motion pictures *King: A Filmed Record . . . Montgomery to Memphis; I Have a Dream;* and *I Am Somebody,* the story of Resurrection City, U.S.A. All of these are valuable organizing and information tools.

SCLC's Operation Breadbasket began in 1962 as a ministers' movement to gain new and better jobs for black people. Since then it has become a comprehensive program of economic development in the urban black community. Operation Breadbasket has now expanded to major cities across the country. As developed in recent years in Chicago, the program organizes for control of jobs, expanding marketing opportunities for local businesses, and improving services within the black community. In amassing economic power, SCLC's Operation Breadbasket seeks to gain political power for the community, affecting all other aspects of community life.

The programs listed above are only a few of the activities of our Movement. All of these and many other programs must be carried out to the fullest extent if we are to achieve our goals.

SCLC's most potent weapon has been, and still is, mass direct action. Massive direct action movements, the distinctive feature of SCLC's strategy, are designed to dramatize issues and to mobilize the power of people to achieve specific goals. The Montgomery bus boycott raised fundamental questions of human dignity, and also forced the desegregation of the city's buses. The Birmingham Movement of 1963, with its mass jail-ins and economic boycotts, attacked the basic evil of racism, affirmed civil rights, won economic benefits in Birmingham, and led directly to the Civil Rights Act of 1964.

The Selma Movement of 1965 went to the root of democracy and compelled passage by Congress of the Voting Rights Act. The Poor People's Campaign revealed to the world the widespread poverty in its richest nation and finally set in motion serious efforts to combat hunger, disease, poor housing, unemployment, and economic oppression.

In 1969 the Charleston hospital strike could not have ended in a historic victory for poorly paid workers without the combination of union power and the "soul power" movement of daily mass demonstrations, jail-ins, and a strong economic boycott.

The March Against Repression, organized in Georgia by SCLC in May 1970, protested the Vietnam-Cambodia war and the killings and repression at home, and launched SCLC's "Politics '70" for political power and representative government.

This is the key that will unlock the door to a future in America for black people. I will never abandon my belief in nonviolence or my love for my fellow man. I will never give up on America, for America is my home. I will never become a part of "the system," but I will always seek to destroy the corruption and evil of that system. I will move in the faith that there are brighter days ahead.

12

EMILY ALMAN

Desegregation at Rutgers University

In 1963, nine years after the Supreme Court decision on desegregation of the school systems, a small group of faculty
members undertook a campaign to implement the decision at
Rutgers University. It had taken nine years of civil rights
agitation—countless sit-ins, demonstrations, mass rallies—to
raise the level of consciousness of northern white liberals
and radicals to the realization that a problem existed in the

schools and universities of the North. It would take another five years for them to understand that token integration is in fact nonintegration, and de facto segregation is in fact segregation. It would take many more years of a concerted campaign and the tidal waves of societal change to convince the university community at large that a problem did indeed exist.

Here I will focus on the process of change which began at Douglass College, the women's college at Rutgers, in 1963, and which continues to affect the lives of students, faculty, and administration to this moment. I will deal with structural change in the university, with ideological change and perceptual change as I have experienced them and attempted to understand them during the past nine years. I will deal with policies, ideologies, confusion, and contradictions. I speak as a participant rather than as a participant-observer, since the latter position calls for some degree of detachment from the arena, and I cannot boast a scholarly detachment. I was deeply involved and have remained deeply involved in the history of change and have shared with others its faults, its confusions, its victories, and its defeats. I will address myself to three general periods of change, starting with the status quo of 1963, a situation of token integration. I will move to a period of incipient change which may be called the "correcting the imbalance" or "desegregation" period and then into the present period characterized by black separatism, uneasy black-white alliances, and nascent integration. For each of these periods I will try to analyze the ideological basis for change, the method of implementation utilized, and, when possible, the life experiences of the involved students.

In speaking of these changes at Douglass College, I address myself to the problems of the university and of the larger community. For if our short history of change, in this one small segment of American society called Douglass College, is of any significance at all, it is because it reflects the currents and confusions in larger society, because it is a microcosm of that society.

211

The "Correcting the Imbalance" Period

The initial period of change, that of "correcting the imbalance," reflected the perceptions of concerned northerners —radicals, liberals, and at times socially aware conservatives. These northerners tended to view the Supreme Court desegregation order as applying mainly to the southern caste system of separate but equal education which had been established some fifty years before, and had been upheld by previous Supreme Court rulings. The 1954 Supreme Court decision was hailed as a victory and viewed as an affirmation of the correctness of northern educational policy. The northern school system envisioned itself as offering equal education to all regardless of race, color, or creed. Northern blacks and white liberals and radicals had congratulated themselves on having resisted the corrupting influences of southern racism, on having fought for and achieved the reduction of institutional barriers to the integration of blacks into the school system. They had battled together against segregation, formal quotas, gentlemen's agreements. They had forced the removal of race designation on applications of admission and the removal of identifying snapshots. They had achieved the integration of dormitories and eating places. They had fought hard and, they felt, successfully for integration victories. They had lost numerous battles and some wars. The fraternity system remained a bastion of segregation. Some schools insisted on placing black students with black roommates, and black attendance at institutions of higher education in the United States represented less than one percent of the total student body.

In 1963 all of these conditions existed at Rutgers University. The fraternities discriminated against blacks at the College of Arts and Sciences (as Rutgers College, the men's undergraduate campus, was then called); black students were automatically roomed with black students; and the total number of them at Douglass College, a community of 3,000 women, was less than 20 students in all four classes combined!

Yet there remained a sense of moral superiority to the

South. Both black and white northerners accepted the essential rightness of the northern position and a superior moral stance vis-à-vis southern institutions. Thus, the incipient phase of social change was actually perceived as being mildly corrective. Its participants viewed the existing reality as a distortion of an ideal which could be corrected with intelligent awareness brought to bear on the matter. There was to be no really serious problem. With some minor modifications, justice would prevail.

The Ad Hoc Committee on Human Rights

This attitude was reflected at Rutgers in the first meeting of an Ad Hoc Committee on Human Rights held on December 11, 1963. The meeting ratified the position of those who sponsored this initial step, and that position was that such a committee

> is necessary to give full expression to the special interests of the faculty in seeing to it that all members of the Rutgers family enjoy equality within the boundaries of the campus, and to insure that Rutgers sets the pace for the community, and is true to the best in our tradition. As an outgrowth of discussion between those of us whose names are signed below, we have reached the conclusion that there is work that can be done by a faculty group to improve the situation of Negro students at Rutgers, and enhance the positive role of the University in the racial problems of the general community. We believe that a faculty committee should concern itself with educational opportunities for Negroes and with community problems which affect the educational environment. It should also exist to facilitate the contribution of the expert knowledge of individual faculty members to the solution of community problems.

The Ad Hoc Committee created subcommittees to deal with precollege preparation, recruitment of minority students, social life within the university, recruitment of black personnel and black graduate students, and community relations. Mild as the goals of this group may seem in the world at this time, its very formation created serious controversy within the university community. The committee was accused of maligning the university, raising false issues, attacking the university administration and the admissions department. I quote for you a letter written by a member in defense of the Ad Hoc Committee on Human Rights and published in the school newspaper, *Targum:*

> We know that the Director of Admissions and other University authorities have at all times worked hard to increase the number of Negro students at Rutgers; they are very much aware of the need to do so. We are, therefore, not asking or pressing for more admissions and most certainly we are not combatting Rutgers' admissions techniques, which we in fact agree with. What we do recognize is that the Admissions Office can only operate within a given framework determined both by the number of Negro high school graduates qualified for college and by the kind of on and off campus atmosphere the prospective student will encounter after admission. What our group wishes to do is to improve both of these crucial aspects of the situation. We hope to increase both the number of qualified Negro and other minority group high school students, and this will take much devoted work by both students and faculty, and to create an atmosphere which induces a larger fraction of these to apply.

Key to this initial statement was the assertion that "most certainly we are not combatting Rutgers' admissions techniques, which we in fact agree with." Agreement with admissions policy was, in fact, consistent with the mechanical approach to equalitarianism which was prevalent and continued to pervade our thinking. For, given a large number of people (applicants to the university), a small number of "resources" (places in the university), and any ideology of equalitarianism, there are only a limited number of distribution mechanisms considered "fair" within this society. Under the mantle of fairness, it is usually suggested that (1) people's needs should be met on a first-come-first-served basis (obviously we don't do that at this school—the day one's application comes in has nothing to do with who gets in); (2) people should be chosen by lottery (we haven't quite reached that yet, but it might be one of the viable alternatives); and (3) people should be placed on a continuum and selected accordingly. In the educational system it is fairly traditional to start on top of the continuum and count downward—stopping cold at the point at which the institution has run out of resources. We then convince ourselves that this is the group that it is "fair" for us to educate.

This philosophy, certainly, was the one that had guided Rutgers University and most other universities for the last thirty years. A philosophy consistent with the values of the larger society, it was also consistent with the faculty's own life experiences, since faculty members had always been among the chosen. They had been the top of the class in their youth. They had been in that section of the continuum that gained entrance into colleges, that made it through colleges, that made it into graduate schools, that made it through graduate schools, and that ultimately was judged the most worthy to teach. In a highly competitive society, in which the fruits of victory are always distributed on a first place, second place, third place basis, the idea of an elitist continuum was ideologically acceptable.

It was consistent, as I said, for this early group of faculty on the human rights committee to disavow any effort at subverting (and that's what it seemed like) the university's admissions procedures. Given this ideology, there was very little for them to be doing, other than passing some pious resolutions about the need for better primary and secondary schools and creating little havens of acceptance for the few black students who managed to gain entrance into the university.

To accomplish even this modest goal, the question of recruitment became crucial. Rutgers University was virtually an all-white university. Its two major branches, the College of Arts and Sciences and Douglass College, with a total enrollment of 9,000 students, had less than 75 black students enrolled in all of its classes in the years 1964–65. Many of us assumed quite naively that there were black students in other parts of the university until phone calls to the Newark campus, the Camden campus, University College (the evening branch), and the graduate schools of law, social work, and education established the embarrassing fact that the Rutgers University student body was less than one percent black.

Identifying Black Students

At that time, one problem we encountered was difficulty in identifying black students. Rutgers University did not have any official indication of race or color on applications. A "guessing game" took place every fall as to how many incoming freshmen were black—yet there appeared to be an unofficial system of race identification. For years a freshman who was black would find that he or she had been placed in a dormitory room with another black student. (Douglass College NAACP membership demonstrated against segregated rooms in 1962, and in the following year, for the first time, black students were assigned to rooms with white roommates.) This question of identification was important, because a perplexing problem for many well-meaning, decent people, black and white, was the inability to stomach the idea that, having spent thirty years getting racial identifications removed from official records, they were now preparing to reverse themselves. They were now asking that race, color, and even national origin be indicated on all official records in order to guarantee a more equitable number of minority students. Yet there appeared to be no alternative. The fact is that the only way concerned students had known how many blacks were being admitted was to organize an informal count. When school opened in the fall, black students would search out faces of incoming freshmen and try to identify their fellows by skin color. The method was far from accurate, since summer tans, sallow Latin complexions, and people of Puerto Rican, Indian, and Caribbean descent were mixed into the preliminary estimates. In time, discreet questions reduced the count to a more or less accurate figure.

When the Ad Hoc Committee on Human Rights tried to find out how many black students had been on campus for the past twenty years, they were told that no official figures existed. The committee studied pictures in the college year-books and came up with the only available figures which can be used for comparative purposes. Obviously, problems of identification from yearbook pictures are many, and the following figures are subject to correction, but they do provide an estimate of the extent of the problem since 1940. I'll start with that year, and where we have information, indi-cate how many black students were graduated from Douglass and Rutgers colleges. Remember that Rutgers has almost two and a half times as many students as Douglass, and that we are talking about a student body of 9,000 here.

Douglass				**Rutgers**			
1940	1	1952	0–1	1940	1	1952	0
1941	0	1953	3–5	1941	0	1953	5
1942	?	1954	0	1942	?	1954	3
1943	0	1955	3	1943	3	1955	3
1944	2	1956	0	1944	0	1956	1
1945	1	1957	1	1945	0	1957	3
1946	?	1958	4	1946	0	1958	2
1947	0	1959	2–5	1947	1	1959	6
1948	3–4	1960	4	1948	0	1960	4
1949	1	1961	3	1949	0	1961	6
1950	?	1962	3–4	1950	0	1962	8
1951	0	1963	7	1951	2	1963	3

In November 1963 the Rutgers and Douglass faculty took note of this condition in issuing the following statement:

> . . . from our discussion, the following areas of imme-diate concern have emerged: the relative scarcity of black students at the undergraduate and graduate levels, the relative scarcity of Negroes among faculty and other university personnel; questions have also been raised about the social life of Negro undergraduates, enforcement of university policy against discrimination in off-campus

student housing, the absence of Negroes on University construction projects, and policies which apparently permit the purchase of supplies from discriminating businesses. In addition, a number of projects related to the University's roles in the community have been discussed.

Rutgers Policies
Continue to Be Questioned

At the same time, community leaders in the state of New Jersey, black and white students in the Rutgers-Douglass NAACP, and visiting students from Asia and Africa began to question the token integration at Rutgers University. For example, the executive committee of the Rutgers-Douglass NAACP, at a special meeting with the president of the university, discussed with him the implications of policies which resulted in the continued exclusion of blacks from the faculty and the student body. Among other matters, they questioned him about recruitment of black faculty. He responded that from his point of view race was not an important factor, and he had never discriminated knowingly; that he was prepared to hire the most highly qualified faculty from the most prestigious universities whatever their race. He indicated his concern with education in this state and noted that he was meeting with elementary school educators in an effort to improve the quality of grade school education in the ghetto communities, to the end that these children would some day be eligible for Rutgers University!

The student committee rejected this concept of gradualist improvement. They felt that the basic attitudes of the university community would have to be changed before black faculty and students would be welcomed into the university. Drawing attention to the social acceptance accorded the African president of the International Students' Association by highly placed university officials—such as invitations to private dinners—black students pointed out that the president of the campus NAACP was virtually ignored. The students were not fighting for the right to dine with the university president, but rejected the differential treatment accorded to international students and American blacks.

Statewide NAACP Conference at Rutgers

The Rutgers-Douglass NAACP organized a statewide conference on civil rights in 1964, at which time the problem of being a black student in a white university community was explored. Spelled out, this experience included the culture shock of finding oneself alone in a sea of white faces, some of which were openly hostile, some of which were determinedly neutral, and some of which were deceptively friendly. The experience might consist of five-day-a-week integration and two-day-a-week segregation; of never being invited into the white "friend's" house; of meeting a "friendly" white classmate in town and being snubbed; of being constantly mistaken by white students for another black student; of being invited to International Day as a visiting dignitary by a classmate after having been on campus for three years; of having a classmate's mother turn to one in an elevator and call out the desired floor number; or of being taken for a maid; of having white boys burst into the living room of a dormitory in search of "girls" for a party and ignore the presence of black girls; of working with faculty who were patronizing, hostile, or defensive; of encountering campus police who were suspicious, or administrators who were insensitive, indifferent, or hostile. It was crystal clear, in the light of these observations, that black students would not recommend Douglass College to their friends or their younger sisters, and would not one day send their daughters to the college. The Rutgers men voiced parallel sentiments. The major conclusion of this conference with regard to Rutgers University was that the problems with which it was concerned would not be solved until there were sufficient numbers of black students to effect a change.

Black students were needed, and their recruitment would have to be undertaken in a deliberate way. Logically, the admissions officials would have to be involved first. The year 1964–65 was devoted to planning conferences and meetings with these and other university personnel, at which ideological positions were explored and developed. With the cooperation of a subcommittee on student recruitment appointed by the provost of the university and chaired by the director of admissions, George Kramer, a new concept of "fairness" in admissions procedure was developed. Briefly it posited that (1) black students were not mentally inferior to white students; (2) black students were not entering the university system in representative numbers; and (3) these facts suggested that barriers did exist in the normal upward flow of black students. The formulation was deliberately simplistic. It generated a search for barriers and mechanisms to overcome them.

The Five High School Committee

The Five High School Committee was such a mechanism. A voluntary effort, it consisted of faculty, administration, and students, and of representatives of five "integrated" high schools which were invited into the program. Its role was, through cooperation of the university with secondary schools, to discover and remove the roadblocks to black students' upward mobility. The university admissions office undertook the sponsorship of the program. It undertook the task of contacting secondary school personnel and enlisting them in an intensified recruitment effort. At the same time, Dr. Allen Robbins worked with the faculty at the College of Arts and Sciences to modify entrance requirements for black students, and I worked with the Douglass faculty to the same end. Initially the response was encouraging, as the faculty and administration of both colleges, against some vocal opposition, acknowledged a social responsibility for offering "equal opportunity" to black students.

The urgency of the situation did not, however, become apparent until there was heightened pressure from the outside community. When the country was in turmoil, when the black community was aroused, when black students became organized, one could get past the secretarial stalls. When there was silence in the community, the telephone calls made by the Five High School Committee chairman remained unanswered. As that person, I usually knew what kind of year was in store when I came back to campus in the fall by my first calls to various sections of the university; I knew whether or not there was going to be interest that year in recruiting black students. A call would go something like this: "Hello, this is the chairman of the Five High School Committee." "Who? I never heard of the Five High School Committee!" Those were the years I knew we were in trouble. The one year that we really made progress was signaled by my finding messages in my letter box from many parts of the university upon my return to campus—messages which asked for information about, and expressed willingness to cooperate with, recruiting efforts. The year was 1967. It had been a long, hot, troubled summer.

The Five High School Committee called its first conference on September 23, 1965, with invited representatives from five high schools: East Orange, Plainfield, Trenton, Montclair, and Princeton. The choice of these non-ghetto schools was deliberate. It was thought that the initial steps taken to alter racial imbalance should not neglect class differences within the black community, and that the initial recruitment of black students should concentrate on bringing in young people whose class positions were similar to those of their white counterparts. It was also believed that these students would have been exposed to white culture patterns and would therefore be less likely to be threatened by participation in a predominantly white world. This first conference was attended by approximately fifty people.

Five barriers to recruitment which we delineated were (1) the financial barrier: a key reason black students were not at Rutgers University was because most of them lacked the financial resources to come; (2) the parental attitude: many parents were unprepared for the idea of sending their children to college; (3) the secondary school: the high school advising policies were identified by black university students as promoting a defeatist attitude among black students—"You'll never make it," "You can't make it," "Rutgers isn't for you," "Douglass isn't for you," were recurrent themes in high school advising offices; (4) the college itself: its admission policies, its lack of supporting services for the less academically prepared student, its ruthless elitist attitude, were all barriers; and finally (5) the student school life: the limited number of black students, combined with a segregationist social and dating policy resulted in loneliness for black students. The black men at Rutgers felt that there were not enough girls at Douglass who were black. The girls at Douglass felt that there were not enough other girls there for the needed companionship. Furthermore, the students spoke of their sense of alienation in attending a school with an all-white faculty and administration, and in studying a curriculum which made no mention of black history, black accomplishment, or black problems.

Initially each of these five barriers which we identified seemed equally important. In time, however, numbers 4 (the college) and 5 (social life) proved to be the most resistant to change. The barrier identified as parental attitudes was almost, although not entirely, illusionary. The financial problems were handled by a state and national scholarship program. The secondary school as a barrier diminished in importance as the program of recruitment reached into all the high schools in the state and the demand for college admission grew.

The Five High School Committee organizing meeting was the beginning of a process of social change at Rutgers University which would, over the next five years, see the creation of a University Equal Opportunities program affecting every segment, every college, every department, the students, the faculty, the administration, the board of governors, the state legislature, and the electorate of the state of New Jersey. Within five years the numbers of black students would rise into the hundreds, an open-registration program would go into effect in the three host communities of the university, and special summer programs would be developed. A new college would be built with a positive orientation to the problems of the urban community and with special emphasis on the world of blacks and Puerto Ricans. Ernest Lynton, a founding member of the human rights committee and a participant in the Five High School Committee, would be chosen to head that college.

The change would be the result of deliberate efforts on the part of faculty, administration, and students. It would also be the result of a new period of black activism which reached into the foundations of the entire American social system and changed irrevocably certain definitions and power relationships.

Educating the Elite

The problems delineated within the first meeting of the Five High School Committee (which later became a Ten and then a Fifteen High School Committee) would remain as a central core to the conflicts, confrontations, blueprints, and discussions of the succeeding years. The issues discussed were central to our times, and they remain such to this day. Two major generalizations surfaced at this conference. One was that Rutgers University and Douglass College were often insensitive to the needs of *all* students, and this created severe problems for the more vulnerable ones—for example, the black students. Therefore, anything done to improve the education of black students would maximize the opportunity for all students.

Secondly, it was recognized that the business of Rutgers had been to educate the elite of the state through the use of elite faculty and staff; that this had precluded the entrance of black students in the past and would continue to discriminate against them in the future. Therefore, Rutgers would either have to change its orientations, its goals, and its structures, or it would be necessary to create a series of preferential accommodations for the admission and education of black students. Resistance to both of these propositions was high

223

and continues to trouble some people to this day. Efforts made to ameliorate some of the hardships faced by students who come from poor school systems or varied cultural backgrounds are still met by cries such as, "You are trying to lower our standards, to destroy our commitment to excellence."

Faculty, students, parents, alumni, community leaders, and even state legislators continue to express concern that Rutgers University will become a second-rate institution if it modifies any of its requirements for admission or for graduation. Overlooked in the heated discussions surrounding the question has been the fact that many of these criteria developed during a gradual escalation of expectations, as the university admitted smaller and smaller proportions of the state's college-bound young; it has also been overlooked that some of the criteria were developed twenty and thirty years ago, frequently reflecting vested academic interests rather than sound educational philosophy. Such considerations are ignored to this day.

The admission of black students on a preferential basis has also been difficult for large numbers of the New Jersey community to accept. The idea of quotas of any kind was repugnant to people who prided themselves on having accepted students as individuals irrespective of race or religion or ethnic identity. It also violated their sense of fairness to have a black with lower college entrance board scores and class standing admitted to the university in preference to a white student. Interestingly, none of those who protested this preferential treatment were bothered by certain time-honored admissions practices that had offered preferential treatment to other students, based both on geographical distribution and on the university's needs for skills.

For example, Rutgers University had long admitted students with lower board scores from the rural communities of the state, while bypassing more highly scoring industrially based students. Since rural schools were known to provide a poorer primary and secondary education than many of those in industrial communities, it was considered reasonable to provide preferential treatment for graduates of these rural communities. In effect, the principle of geographic quotas had been utilized for many years, and it was accepted by the very people who rejected the principle of racial and ethnic representation.

In addition, the university had, like so many others, offered preferential treatment to students who possessed special skills, who could kick a football farther and higher than their fellow students, or who were tall enough and athletic enough to tip a ball into a basket that loomed high above the heads of others. Those who could run fast or swim fast or hit a baseball were also favored above their brothers with higher academic scores.

Again, the very people who attacked and continue to attack the idea of preferential treatment for black and Puerto Rican students defend vehemently the university's right to discriminate in favor of athletes.

De Facto Segregation Attacked

Resistance to the preferential treatment concept, and the dialogue which this resistance engendered, made it apparent that the university's problem was not merely one of imbalance, which well-meaning people could restore, but was truly a de facto segregation which the white community as a whole accepted and supported. It became clear that the university's civil rights forces would have to overcome this pattern of de facto segregation in order to create an integrated university community.

The first half of the sixties saw the height of civil rights agitation for integration within the nation, the aim being the development of an interrelated society of blacks and whites working in a recognized mutuality. The ideal came close to the psychoanalytical definition of integration offered in Webster's dictionary: "The organization of various traits or tendencies into one harmonious personality." This was the ideal of black-white relations held by whites in 1964–65. Despite the obviously racist resistance black students encountered within our community, all efforts were made to achieve this goal. In a hardheaded way, black students and white activists had cast their lot with this ideal, believing they could accomplish desegregation and integration in one giant step. This goal proved illusionary. We found we were able to manage one half of the goal, desegregation. The goal of integration remains unachieved, its validity questioned by many.

The phase of "correcting the imbalance" and chipping away at de facto segregation had begun in 1963 and lasted through 1965. Describing her strained relationships with white students at the beginning of this period, a black woman student gave the following example. Students in dormitories rotate the responsibility for answering the telephone. The person "on duty" is expected to answer all calls, and others are quick to call her to task if she does not fulfill her responsibility. "In my case," the black student said, "they do not knock on my door if I neglect to answer. I hear them whispering outside of it, but none of them will just rap on the door and say, 'It's your turn.' Sometimes I just won't answer to see if they'll get up the courage to treat me like anyone else."

At the end of the "correcting the imbalance" period, we had admitted fifty young men into Rutgers and thirty women into Douglass. We had appointed Dr. Sabra Meservey as adviser for the students and had insured special counseling. We had created a ten-day summer preparatory program which would acquaint students with study at college. The school year which followed came the closest to the integration ideal that we were ever to come. Our program of recruitment of black students had included poor white students as well. Our emphasis was on "sensitivity to students' motivations and abilities" as additional criteria for admission, rather than on naked preferential treatment. The black student recruits opted to be treated "like anybody else." And a black student who didn't answer the phone could count on her fellow students to rap on the door.

Yet, all was not well. Overt racism, subtle insult, parental prejudice, were all part of the experience of our students.

Young black men were invited to join fraternities and told they could not dance with white women. Black women students continued to feel rejected and ignored when they entered into the social, dating world of their white fellow students. The university was still "white"—its faculty was white; its administration was white; its secretarial staff, library staff, hospital staff were white. The young were getting impatient.

This period was, above all, marred by the nature of the grudging cooperation given it by significant segments of the university community. As concession after concession was wrung from them, as black students entered this community, the resisters to change carried out a continued rearguard action against the students and those who worked with them. An alliance for change had been entered into by the university administration and a number of faculty and students. But individual college administrators, faculty members, clerical staff members, and students remained resistant. It was obvious that the changes which had come about would be short-lived if a continued and continuing pressure was not exerted.

Yet the needed pressure could not be sustained as initial enthusiasm for change began to fade and initial enthusiasts moved on to other schools. Many of the faculty members who were involved in the desegregation effort were non-tenured junior faculty. Their "devotion to the cause" cost them time and energies needed to overcome the "publish or perish" barrier to promotion, and in many cases it created a number of personal enemies among the established college elite whose recommendation for promotion was required. The calculated risk to their careers had been understood and accepted. But there was an inherent danger to the program in the continued attrition of the most active civil rights workers (in point of fact, barely one third of the original members of the Five High School Committee are presently employed at the university).

This attrition contributed to the feeling that in time the gradual tide of preferential admission would recede and the university could be expected to drift back to a de facto segregation.

Black students and newly recruited black faculty and administrators, as well as certain white members of the university, tried to insure against this possibility by building change into the very structure of the university. Nonetheless, it must be admitted that their success was modest up to the time that the black communities of the United States, in the second half of the sixties, erupted into massive rebellion against the status quo. Civil disorders took place in major cities, including Newark, New Jersey.

Black Demands

Like many other universities, in 1968–69 Rutgers experienced coordinated student demonstrations at most of its branches. Federal, state, and local communities began to respond to black demands, and as this happened, activists began to escalate both their promises and their demands. Programs of change already underway were discounted and discredited. New programs and new monies were committed to the effort; hundreds and then thousands of young black men and women were invited, encouraged, and cajoled to enter the universities.

Schools prided themselves on, and administrators boasted of, the high "risk" they were willing to take in making these admissions. The percentage of failures which resulted from this first flurry of enthusiasm was high at some schools (though not so at Rutgers), as embittered youngsters, black and Puerto Rican, found themselves spun out through a revolving door. Yet enough students remained to ensure a base for black militancy. A lifeline had been thrown into the hopelessness of ghetto existence. The young seized it, pulled themselves into a position of relative power, and then turned around and demanded further entry for their younger sisters and brothers.

The Separatist Phase

The desegregation stage was not ended at Rutgers, as

black students rejected the concept of integration into the white university community and organized themselves into a unified pressure group for transforming the place into an institution "relevant" to their needs. Reflecting the ideological concepts of black power and black pride which were developing among large segments of the black community and being echoed in the Puerto Rican community, the young people organized a campaign to wrest power—rather than concessions—from the university. The struggle was bitter. The action was led by blacks, with activist whites left uninformed as to plans, timetables, or demands. Friendships between black and white students and faculty faltered, communications broke down, and deep resentments and enmities arose as the white community reacted to black demands and black rejection of white alliances. "Our" black students declared their independence of all whites, and this included innovators as well as the resisters to change. The faculty member who was sometimes called the "white mother" of all the black students found herself politely but firmly ejected from their inner councils and asked to leave their confrontation meeting with the college administrators.

Organized into a power-seeking faction and threatening reprisals from the black community at large, black students at Douglass demanded—where heretofore they had petitioned for—changes in the curriculum, admission procedures, and recruitment patterns of students and faculty. They demanded their right to be represented on all school committees and at all councils. They rejected the right of any white people to represent them, including those elected by the total student body. Joining together, they demanded of each other a total discipline and a total commitment to the black experience.

Within a week's time, friendships and associations which had taken years to establish were broken. Separatism became the order of the day. Black students were urged to act together, walk together, meet, study, talk, and eat together. Those who defied the discipline were educated, pressured, threatened, and cajoled. The white community reacted by increasing its social distance from the black community, while

ceding to it some areas of power. White activists generally found themselves discredited—repudiated by blacks on
the one hand and treated with ill-concealed hostility by conservative whites on the other. Their role as liaison between
black and white was no longer functional. In this the college
mirrored the development of black separatism and black militancy that characterized the movement throughout the country. The civil rights movement had become the black liberation movement.

The black community had opted to deal directly with the
resister to change. The years 1968–69 and 1969–70 saw the
fruition of this policy. Only the most stalwart white members of the university community have remained in contact
with the black students. But administrators treat them with
respect. Two years of hostilities have resulted in a large
measure of distrust and overt hatred between white resisters
to change and black activists. Most black students gather together in enclaves, live, sleep, eat, and study together, rejecting those who would do otherwise. The white students tend
to seek as much physical distance and social distance as they
can achieve. White students will not rap on a black student's
door and say, "Hey, it's your turn to answer the phone."

The Present

The school has a black culture, a black student body, a
black studies program, a black student recruiter, an African and Afro-American House, a black dean.

The school also has an Equal Opportunity Board, on which
black and white members of the community sit. They meet,
they address themselves to the problems of black and other
minority group students in the college. With the initiative
of black students focused on consolidating their own gains,
the Equal Opportunity Board has begun to seriously look
into the need for recruitment of Puerto Rican students.
Black students are beginning to share their experience with
the three Puerto Ricans who now form not one percent of the
Douglass student body, but one-hundredth of one percent.

The shortest time in any period of change is "the present." What of the future? Where will it go? What are the possibilities? What are the harbingers of change? In 1970 the Douglass special six-week summer school program was organized and administered by two young black Douglass alumnae, assisted by five black and Puerto Rican student counselors. It accommodated sixty-five students, the majority of whom were eligible for special state assistance under the New Jersey Equal Opportunity Fund program. According to current eligibility guidelines, assistance is offered only to students who fulfill two criteria: they must be very poor, and they must have done very poorly in high school. If they are only a little bit poor but have done comparatively well in high school, they are not eligible for financial support. If they are only a little bit poor and have done very poorly in high school, they are not eligible for financial support. If they are very poor but have done comparatively well in high school, they are not eligible for financial support. In any case, the summer program was short of funds; enthusiasm for social change had waned. By cutting out of the university budget a \$350,000 Equal Opportunity allocation, the state legislature had all but destroyed the opportunity for any students not covered by the state E.O.F. program described above. The implication of this is that there is comparatively little likelihood that the potentially most promising students will gain admission into the college and be able to go on into graduate school.

The incoming black freshmen enter a school in which black-white relationships reflect the national dilemmas. They join older sisters, some of whom are separatists or revolutionaries, and most of whom are committed to the development of black pride. They will be living with students who have spent the summer in black ghettos and in traveling and studying in Africa. They will find black administrators committed to the development of Afro-American studies. They will meet white students and faculty who are themselves going through a period of turmoil and change, whose views range from overt racism to a revolutionary commitment to changing the power structure. And they will be joined by Puerto Ricans committed to Puerto Rican power and women committed to women's liberation—and men and women organizing peace activities.

The college has, in fact, become a society in which the winds of social change have all but engulfed its entire population in a turbulent search for tomorrow. Within that search, the black student and the white student, the black faculty and the white faculty, the black administrator and the white administrator, will struggle for meaningful relationships within the context of an educational commitment.

SOURCES

Statement of purpose of the unofficial Faculty Committee on Human Rights, November 14, 1963.

S. Cliadakis, report of yearbook survey, based on *Quair* (Douglass College Yearbook) and *Scarlet Letter* (Rutgers Arts and Sciences Yearbook); statistical list of Negroes graduated from both institutions through 1963. November 1963.

Memorandum to Executive Committee of University Committee on Human Rights, with appended draft describing purposes of University Committee and listing members of its executive committee, from Paul Tillett, chairman. February 27, 1964.

Program, Five Secondary Schools Conference held at Rutgers University, September 23, 1965.

"Opportunity Rutgers," description of plan for recruiting disadvantaged pupils in Plainfield High School. December 3, 1965.

Memorandum from East Orange High School—Rutgers Faculty Committee describing guidelines for development of recruiting plans for disadvantaged students. Undated.

Letter to guidance directors on work-study programs available at Douglass College, from Janice Harvey, director of admissions, Douglass College. January 1966.

Memorandum from Emily Alman and Allen Robbins to Dr. Mason Gross, president; Dr. Malcolm Talbott, vice-president; and Dr. George A. Kramer, dean of admissions, on funding and planning necessary to implement recruitment of disadvantaged students. May 2, 1966.

News release, from Rutgers News Service, on beginning of pilot educational opportunity program for disadvantaged high school girls. May 23, 1966.

Estimated Number of Negro Graduates of the Undergraduate Colleges of Rutgers, The State University, for the Past Fifteen Years. November 9, 1967.

Letter to Janice Harvey, director of admissions, from Dorothy Redden, coordinator of Special Academic Advising Program. April 15, 1968.

Committee of Concern, Douglass College Committee on Equal Opportunity, fact sheet. 1968.

Release to Douglass College Community describing faculty actions at March 11, 1969, meeting, based on recommendations resulting from the March 3 and 4, 1969, meetings of the six Special Committees on the Needs of Black Students. March 12, 1969.

African and Afro-American Studies Program rationale, and description of program. September 16, 1969.

13

RONALD S. COPELAND

Community Origins
of the Black Power
Movement

I will attempt to chronicle the development of the Black
Power movement in the United States, viewing it from the
perspective of one who lived it and experienced it in a New
Jersey community.

To understand the emergence of the black revolt, we begin
with the integration movement that started in the South in
1955. I would say that the real thrust of the integration move-

ment began that December, when Mrs. Rosa Parks refused to take her traditional seat in the back of the bus in Montgomery, Alabama. In those days black people felt that they were being denied their constitutional rights because of the Jim Crow, or separatism, that existed so blatantly in the South. The Reverend Martin Luther King, Jr., incensed by the arrest of Mrs. Parks, started what eventually became a national movement. This, the early phase of the Black Power struggle—the nonviolent, passive-resistance phase—centered around the constitutionality as well as the moral aspects of denying blacks their rights to equality in public accommodations and schooling, and, in general, their rights to first-class citizenship. The strategy was to expose and focus attention on these social ills through the use of mass demonstrations, in the form of sit-ins, lie-ins, picket lines, freedom rides, and mass marches.

By the late 1950s the struggle that was initiated by black people for black people had become significantly controlled by white America. However, equally as important is the fact that middle-class persons, both black and white, were then playing the major role.

Let us examine the participants in the so-called black revolt, or the Negro revolt as it was called in those days. It included such organizations as the Student Nonviolent Coordinating Committee (SNCC), the National Association for the Advancement of Colored People (NAACP), the Congress of Racial Equality (CORE), and the Southern Christian Leadership Conference (SCLC), which were called in the late fifties and early sixties "the big four."

Both CORE and SNCC were composed predominantly of college students or the upwardly mobile class. They included many of the youngsters who had left their ghetto communities and were striving to make it in America by the traditional method that had been taught to them; and that was that you had to have a good education in order to get a decent job and to make a decent living. The NAACP and SCLC were predominantly black middle class—but black *working* middle class and white middle class. I would define the black working middle class as being composed of those black non-professionals who normally have steady jobs (though under-paid) and who more often than not align themselves with the establishment sense of values. This is not an indictment of the black working middle class by any stretch of the imagination. To make such an indictment, I would have to indict myself, because I considered myself as part of that class in the late 1950s and early 1960s.

Then what does my statement mean? It means that the members of this class accepted the concept of integration, in which blacks were fighting to achieve equality by sitting next to Mr. Charlie in the toilet or Mr. Charlie at the lunch counter, or by being accepted at any place of public accommodation. While I am not opposed to this concept, it should be something that is guaranteed to all Americans just by virtue of the fact that they are indeed American citizens. However, the aim of integration did not reach the imagination or deal with the plight of the *average* working class black man who formed the masses of blacks in this country. Thus, the result was, particularly in the North, that there was not a great deal of involvement on the part of the bulk of black Americans during this phase of the struggle.

Integration Attempts on a Local Scene

This brings me to the era when I first became involved in the black revolt. When I moved to the state of New Jersey, I came into a small township composed of about 19,000 people, and found there a group of liberal whites and a group of middle-class blacks struggling to eliminate a de facto segregated school within the local system. Without going into the long history of this case, the struggle manifested itself in demonstrations, negotiations, and one meeting after the other. The school board, being representative of the traditional educational system that we have in our country, repelled these efforts, saying that youngsters should go to the school closest to where they lived. There was a unique thing about the fight that took place in Franklin Township (now renamed Somerset), which was that a group of white parents there were charging the Board of Education with denying their youngsters an adequate education by not permitting them to go to school with blacks. They charged that their children were not having a rounded education because they could not learn anything about the culture of black people. That struggle moved on and was eventually won by the interracial group known as the Parents' League for Educational Advancement (PLEA), after its members led a court suit against the Board of Education to end de facto segregation.

Absence of Working-class Blacks in Local Efforts

One of the things that I noted during the PLEA activities was that there were few, if any, working-class blacks involved in them. Certainly there were a handful here and there who would get involved for a short period of time, but there was not the long, sustained effort characteristic of the black and white middle class. So I, and a group of others, sat down to examine what had gone wrong with our effort. After all, we were trying to achieve something for black people, and yet we could not get black people involved.

We came to the conclusion that the question of education was not what would move the masses of the working-class blacks. So we decided that a new organization should be formed to attack the other questions that we believed were plaguing the black community, and we did just that, creating the Community Action League (CAL). In trying to involve the working class we found that they just did not identify with us because of our efforts during the school integration movement. That movement had been considered very middle class. Nevertheless, in forming CAL we were attempting to reach the working class black community, and we had a reasonable degree of success. One of the issues we took up was the unfair policy that existed in the low income, predominantly black housing project in the township. Here

we got a fair amount of involvement from the people concerned. However, once the issue was resolved, the tenants of
that project went right back into what we considered to be
apathy. We also made an effort to get into the political scene
with black candidates and to align ourselves with one of the
two parties—the Republicans, who, at that time and place,
were the more positive. Still, there was no significant
amount of movement that came out of the working-class community.

Again being puzzled, we sat down once more and went
through what we considered a "workshop" for our own
internal growth. We again examined what we were doing
wrong. We concluded that we had not succeeded in generating enough enthusiasm among all the people, and that the
Community Action League was at a disadvantage in being
a small, unheard-of organization. A decision was made to
bring in a nationally known organization to help us alleviate some of the problems that we considered important in
Franklin Township. A few of us got together and visited the
New York regional office of CORE, spoke with James Farmer,
who then headed that organization, obtained all the data necessary on how to get a chapter started, and then organized
one. Thus, the Somerset County CORE was born. But we
made the same silly mistake again; we only involved the
black middle class and the white middle class! We finally
realized, as once again we were unable to attract the masses
of blacks, that their major problem was one of economics.
This was their major concern, and until they could free themselves from their daily plight of just not having enough
money, they would not get involved in the overall community struggle.

Deciding to focus on the question of economics, of obtaining better jobs for black people, we looked for a point of
attack. At that time there was a bank that had been in
existence in the township for sixty years and that had never
hired a black person. We said to ourselves that here was an
issue with which all black people could identify: blatant discrimination in hiring policies. We did then, indeed, attack

the bank through boycotts, picket lines, press releases, and the same tactics that were used throughout the days of CORE's most noted activity. I remember vividly the largest picket line we had, one cold February morning. We had approximately sixty persons on the line. It struck me there and then, as I looked around and asked myself who was on that line, that they were the same middle-class blacks and whites —not one person from the ranks of the people that we swore we were helping.

The Black Power Concept Emerges

To look at the national scene again, or more specifically, the northern scene, let me describe what happened at the 1966 CORE national conference, held in Baltimore. We found that what we were experiencing in our small community was, by and large, being experienced throughout the North. Blacks in the ghetto were not being moved by the issues raised by the NAACP, CORE, or SNCC. It was then, at this convention, that CORE decided it would change its direction. This was the real turning point for community action in the North; it was certainly the turning point for us. I recall some of the conversation that took place around this new concept. The basic thought was that black people did not just need integration, they did not just need equality, but they did need power. It was recognized that one of the things that the black community suffered from most was the feeling of powerlessness: no power to control its own destiny, no economic power, no political power, and extremely little sense of unity. This was the conference at which the concept of Black Power was born for CORE. Just prior to that Stokely Carmichael, a veteran of SNCC's southern campaigns, had taken part in a march in Mississippi, and it was then that he had used the phrase.

Many of you may recall the storm that the concept of Black Power caused in America. I remember very vividly that at the national conference I attended there were a number of whites, including several priests, nuns, and minis-

ters, who were not the least bit upset about the concept of
Black Power. They felt it was the best thing for black people.
When I returned from that conference and opened *The New
York Times* to read what we had been talking about, I thought
I had been to a different meeting. Black Power meant riots,
it meant we were going to burn down the country, it meant
we were going to kill all whites. It was almost impossible to
believe that the newspaper was describing the same conference I had left the previous day. But then we came to understand that we could not leave it to the news media to explain what we in the movement were talking about. Reports
were written by the same people who had distorted our history and who had made the country see things to the advantage of white people rather than black people.

What did we actually mean when we referred to the concept of Black Power? In those days it meant three things:
(1) We wanted to establish an economic base within the black
community. How were we to do this? Through a collective
effort of black people we would pool our financial resources
and purchase many of the tenements, many of the stores
that existed in the black community. (2) Through collective efforts we would stop the exploitation of our people and
have the money remain in the ghetto; previously it had been
taken out of it and into the suburbs. This is how we hoped to
establish a black economic base. (3) Black Power also
meant a new political awareness. Not just political consciousness, but electoral politics, in which we would seek out
and elect those blacks who could best represent us in the
state legislatures, Congress, the local councils, or other bodies. That was the political power we were talking about
building in the black community.

But before all this could occur, something else also had to
occur. Black people would have to gain a new sense of unity
and awareness. They would have to begin to truly love their
brothers; as you can see, this thought was at the origin of
the broader nationalist movement that is so prominent today. In using the term Black Power we were aware that the
very word "black" had been synonymous with something evil

in the past. Black people had been programmed to view and think of the world as being nonblack, antiblack, or the opposite of black. Their world view was dominated by the Euro-American determinants. The sociological, political, cultural, and physiological conditioning that resulted in this world view appeared to be the same for both the working class and middle class black people. While the content of black experience within the class system differed in some ways, it was similar in that all classes tended to think and behave in a manner that degraded blackness. It was believed that black people came from a strange, uncivilized, "dark" continent; that black history only began in 1865; that slavery had acted as a civilizing experience.

We felt strongly that we had to come back to our respective communities and advocate the beauty of blackness, the rich cultural heritage inherent in being Afro-American. Once we could teach the masses to stop viewing themselves as ugly, we could begin to develop the needed sense of solidarity. And we began to force this ideology down our people's throats. I say "force" it because most of the people were still more concerned with where their next meal was coming from, and they didn't understand what we were talking about. The youth, however, did; they began to grasp the concept of black identity and to move on that basis. By and large the adult community could not understand what we were talking about, because they did indeed believe that as blacks they were inferior, and they hated themselves. As a youngster growing up in Harlem I often heard the phrase "a nigger ain't shit," and that's what I believed until I became an adult. So black people, in hating themselves, did not have the incentive or motivation to lift themselves up out of "the mud," as we call it. They did not have the incentive to lift themselves up out of the conditions under which they were forced to live. They had been taught the white concept of beauty: thin lips, straight hair, light skin. So who would want to identify with something black? Rather escape from it! This concept of beauty attached to whiteness was so deeply rooted that it was a monster to attack. This is why the emphasis would have to be on the children in the schools. We would have to start there because of the difficulty in reaching adults with the concepts of black beauty and black identity. As you know, these concepts are now flourishing and growing. However, they should not be confused with the liberation struggle as being the end to the problems of blacks in America. The concepts are important for providing the proper motivation so that people will struggle to break the chains of oppression.

After the CORE convention we returned to our small community in Franklin Township, as Harlem CORE returned to Harlem, Chicago CORE returned to Chicago, and all the delegates of other chapters returned to their hometowns. All of us began to advocate this new direction that CORE had taken, and it spread to other organizations. Small community groups began to spring up; cooperative efforts began. In the Harlem where I was born and raised, blacks did butt out some of the merchants who had been there for years. Blacks did begin to buy up some of the tenements in the ghetto areas.

Some Afterthoughts

To go a little beyond the question of the development of Black Power, I want to raise some issues that I see today. I have seen on Seventh Avenue and Lenox Avenue in Harlem black merchants as well as black landlords. Unfortunately, I have also seen exploitation of blacks by blacks. I see virtually no change in the conditions of the people who live in the black ghettos across our nation. Here, in the year 1970, I see no changes in the material conditions and no changes in the control over their destiny of the masses of people in northern and southern ghettos. I, for one, am not willing to be exploited by black people any more than I am by white people. This brings me to a new premise, as part of my process of growth. That is, is it truly a question of black versus white, or is it indeed a question of one class of people against another class of people?

The black man's entry into political life: *Left,* Frederick Douglass, runaway slave who became a leading abolitionist and statesman. *Below,* a Currier & Ives print of the first black senator, Hiram R. Revels of Mississippi, (at left) and early black members of the House of Representatives, who served during Reconstruction. (The Schomburg Collection, New York Public Library)

Teaching children violence.

242b

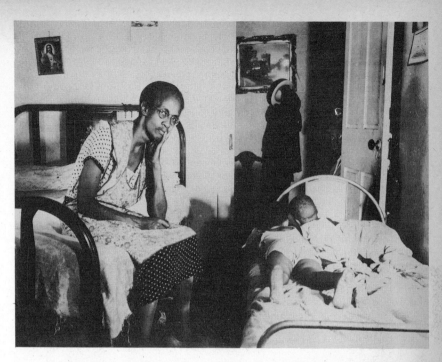

Survival in the city: a view from the inside and outside.
(The Schomburg Collection, New York Public Library)

Black people are making their presence felt, on campus and in the neighborhood. *Above,* Dr. Cecelia H. Drewry conducts the Rutgers-Douglass Black Arts Group. *Below,* economic boycotts continue, as in this early example of action by Harlem residents.

(Douglass College Alumnae Bulletin; The Schomburg Collection, New York Public Library)

Men who shaped and recorded black history in the twentieth century: *Above,* Herbert Aptheker (at left) takes leave of W. E. B. Du Bois, departing for Ghana, 1961. *Below,* the Reverends Ralph Jackson, Martin Luther King, Jr., and Ralph David Abernathy march in behalf of striking garbage collectors, Memphis, March 1968.

(International Publishers Co., Inc.; Wide World Photos)

Voices that speak to the black masses: *Right,* Black Panther party National Chairman Bobby Seale, shown to the left of Minister of Defense Huey P. Newton. *Below,* Malcolm X, speaking at a Muslim rally, New York, 1963.
(Wide World Photos)

14

ALPHONSO PINKNEY

Contemporary Black Nationalism

The beginning of the second half of the twentieth century marked a crucial juncture in the history of black people in the United States. It was around this time that the oppression of the black man in America was first recognized as a social problem worthy of consideration. This concern resulted, in large part, from changing world conditions, especially the political independence of former European colonies in Africa and Asia. Since colonialized peoples throughout the world were demanding freedom and self-determination, it would not be long, it was felt, before the millions of black people in America's internal colony would demand that their status be altered.

In the 1930s and 1940s several judicial decisions and administrative rulings favorable to black people foreshadowed the *Brown* v. *Board of Education* decision of the Supreme Court in 1954. This decision was hailed by black leaders and white liberals as proof that the stated American ideals of freedom and equality were intended to apply to all citizens—black and white. When southern whites (both leaders and the rank and file) publicly declared their intention to preserve racial separation, and thereby white supremacy, the general feeling was that opposition to the decision was to be expected but that it would be short-lived, and segregated public education would cease "with all deliberate speed." The importance attached to this decision stemmed, in part, from the feeling of many blacks that racially integrated schools would ultimately lead to integration in other aspects of American life, thereby accelerating the process of assimilation.

Since segregation in public education had been declared unconstitutional, leaders of civil rights organizations attacked other forms of racial segregation and discrimination, especially in the South. Integration was viewed in each of the major civil rights organizations as the logical means through which black people would achieve equality with their white counterparts. The civil rights movement, from its beginnings in 1955 to its decline in 1965, championed the cause of racial integration, frequently to the point of viewing this projected ideal state of race relations as an end in itself, rather than a means to an end. When the likelihood or desirability of integration was questioned, leaders of the major civil rights organizations were quick to issue statements in support of this principle. While black nationalists were still to be found in the United States, they were few in number and were completely overshadowed by the integrationists.

By the mid–nineteen sixties, it was evident to many black

people that the methods and goals of the civil rights movement were such that they would not liberate black people from the oppression under which they lived in the United States. It was at this time that two of the major civil rights organizations, the Congress of Racial Equality and the Student Nonviolent Coordinating Committee, which later became the Student National Coordinating Committee, adopted positions in support of black nationalism by embracing the philosophy of Black Power.

But black nationalism was not a new phenomenon. It had had a long history in the United States, dating back to the eighteenth century. And while Marcus Garvey's Universal Negro Improvement Association, an early twentieth century nationalist organization which championed black pride and black solidarity, achieved the largest grass roots membership of any black nationalist organization in the history of the United States, it is the decade of the 1960s in which various expressions of black nationalism have had their greatest impact on the black community. Perhaps more than any other individual, the late Malcolm X is responsible for the current rise of black nationalism. It is with these expressions of contemporary black nationalism that this paper is concerned.

Expressions of Black Nationalism

Membership in organizations which embrace an ideology that may be broadly defined as nationalist is but one manifestation of black nationalism. At any point in time an organization's influence is likely to extend far beyond its membership. At the present time expressions of black nationalism may be observed throughout the United States in a variety of forms. Few individuals and families in the black community have escaped the influence of contemporary black nationalism. And some measure of the scope of this phenomenon is reflected in the proliferation of national and local black nationalist groups, organizations, and caucuses. They are found among college and high school students; in police departments; in the armed forces; among athletes, poets, and playwrights; and in virtually all professional organizations which have black members. On the individual level, black nationalism is manifested in styles of dress, standards of physical beauty, name changes, music, the dance, food habits, and many other aspects of culture.

Many educational institutions that are expressly black nationalist—in addition to special departments and institutes at regular colleges and universities—have sprung up in recent years. They include the Center for Black Education in Washington, D.C.; Malcolm X Liberation University in Durham, North Carolina; Nairobi College in Palo Alto, California; the Topographical Institute in Chicago, Illinois; the Institute of the Black World in Atlanta, Georgia; the University of Islam in Chicago; and many others, ranging from kindergarten to college level. Furthermore, the movement for community control of the various institutions in the black community represents a nationalist attempt on the part of black people toward decolonization.

Organizations and groups which may be described as nationalist cover a wide spectrum of ideology and practices, ranging anywhere from those which are primarily religious or economic to those in which well-defined black nationalist ideology encompasses all aspects of the lives of their members. Fundamental to all contemporary black nationalist ideology, regardless of organization, are three characteristics: black solidarity (or black consciousness), pride in cultural heritage, and self-determination. At the present time there is a proliferation of groups and organizations in the black community which although different in many ways, embrace this ideology.

Black Community Development and Defense (BCD), an outgrowth of LeRoi Jones's Spirit House Movers, was founded in Newark, New Jersey, in January 1968. It is dedicated to the creation of a new value system for the black community, and utilizes the methods developed by Maulana Ron Karenga's US Organization in Los Angeles, which inspired its creation. Jones sees the struggle for liberation among blacks in the United States as "the freeing of one nation (culture) from the domination of another." It is a move away from "death and degeneracy." The establishment of a new value system for blacks is essential because, "If you internalize the white boy's system, you will come to his same conclusions about the world." The new black value system is based on seven principles: unity, self-determination, collective work and responsibility, cooperative economics, purpose, creativity, and faith.

At BCD the creation of the new system of values is manifested by African dress, the speaking of Swahili, the absence of Christian names, and the insistence on courtesy, promptness, and sharing. Participants do not drink alcoholic beverages, smoke, use narcotics, or eat pork. In addition, BCD has joined with several other groups in Newark in an effort to vote blacks into all the elective offices in that city.

The leaders of BCD oppose alliances with white groups, even those which are revolutionary in their ideology. Jones feels that among whites who claim to be revolutionaries, their whiteness takes precedence over their revolutionary zeal.

Similarly, the members of BCD reject the notion of armed struggle at the present time because black people are too powerless and lacking in unity. They see the building of a united black community, with a new system of values, as an essential prerequisite for black liberation.

The **Black Panther party,** founded in Oakland, California, in 1966, has established itself as a leading black nationalist organization in the United States. The platform and program of the Black Panther party are put forth each week in its national newspaper, *The Black Panther*. The platform of the party consists of ten points. These are: (1) the freedom of black people to determine the destiny of their community; (2) full employment; (3) an end to white robbery in the black community; (4) decent housing; (5) a system of education in the black community which meets the needs of black people; (6) the exemption of all black men from military service; (7) the end of police brutality and murder in the black community; (8) the release of all black people from jails and prisons; (9) the trial of black people accused of crimes by juries of black people; (10) land, bread, housing, education, clothing, justice, and peace.

Clearly, most of the points of this platform pertain to

changes which are essentially reformist. However, since its founding, the Black Panther party has adopted a revolutionary Marxist-Leninist ideology. It advocates the arming of black people as essential for liberation. The liberation of the black community, it maintains, can only be achieved through armed self-defense and armed struggle. Its position on armaments comes from the writings of Chairman Mao Tse-tung of the People's Republic of China. Members of the Black Panther party see black liberation as part of the worldwide nonwhite struggle against the forces of colonialism and imperialism, led by the government of the United States.

Within the United States the Black Panther party has effected alliances with both nonwhite and white radical and revolutionary groups such as the Peace and Freedom party, the Students for a Democratic Society, the Young Lords, the Young Patriots, and the White Panther party. It is the position of the Black Panther party that in order for black people in the United States to liberate themselves, they must align themselves with other groups struggling to overcome the forces of American oppression, both internally and internationally.

The *Republic of New Africa (RNA)*, was founded on March 31, 1968, when some 200 black people from across the country gathered in Detroit, Michigan, and signed a "Declaration of Independence," proclaiming black people in the United States "forever free and independent of the jurisdiction of the United States." The aims of RNA include the following: (1) to free black people from oppression; (2) to support and wage the world social revolution until all people everywhere are free; (3) to build a new society that is better than what we now know and as perfect as it can be made; (4) to end the exploitation of man by man; (5) to assure justice for all; (6) to place the major means of production and trade in the hands of the state.

The leaders of RNA have proclaimed their organization "the government of the non-self-governing blacks held captive within the United States." They have demanded that the territory which now comprises the United States be partitioned into two separate states, one for blacks and one for whites. In negotiations with the United States Department of State they have demanded that Alabama, Georgia, Louisiana, Mississippi, and South Carolina be set aside as the territory for the new republic, and that the United States government provide this new state with $400 billion in reparations.

Anticipating the difficulties involved in negotiations with the government of the United States, officials of RNA have urged black people to migrate to Mississippi, the state with the highest percentage of blacks, and peacefully take over the electoral offices of that state. In case of resistance, armed force would be used. The military forces would be made up of urban guerrillas who would be ready to strike simultaneously throughout the United States, should the need arise. They maintain that a significant number of blacks sympathetic to their position are already armed and engaged in a holding action. All blacks who are unarmed are urged to purchase guns for self-defense.

Inasmuch as the president of the Republic of New Africa was in exile in the People's Republic of China at the time of his election, the leaders of RNA feel that as a last resort military assistance, including nuclear weapons, could be secured from China. Additional support would come from other Third World nations.

The *Revolutionary Action Movement (RAM)* was organized in 1963 by a group of black people who advocated militant self-defense as a means of dealing with white racism. It was envisioned as a "third force" somewhere between the Student Nonviolent Coordinating Committee and the Nation of Islam. In 1964 a manifesto was issued setting forth the objectives and program of the organization. The objectives include: (1) instilling in black people a sense of pride, dignity, unity, and solidarity in struggle; (2) bringing about a new image of manhood and womanhood among black people; (3) freeing black people from colonial and imperialist bondage everywhere, taking whatever steps may be necessary to achieve this goal; (4) inculcating a sense of purpose in black people.

Members of RAM feel that in order for black people to

gain control over their lives, they must seize power through revolution. In this regard RAM envisions its program as the vanguard of the impending black revolution. Like RNA, RAM sees all the nonwhite people of the world as enslaved by the same force, namely white capitalism. Hence, revolutionary nationalism becomes internationalism. The government of the United States is seen as the enemy of freedom and self-determination throughout the world.

Again like RNA, RAM demands that the United States be partitioned into two separate states, one for blacks and one for whites. The black nation to result from this partition would consist of the nine states of Mississippi, Louisiana, Alabama, Georgia, Florida, Texas, Virginia, South Carolina, and North Carolina. This land rightfully belongs to black people, RAM maintains, because black slave labor cultivated it for centuries. In addition to this territory, the leaders of RAM demand an unspecified sum as a form of reparations for racial crimes committed against black people in the past.

Finally, RAM feels that black people must arm themselves for the inevitable revolution. Its definition of revolution is " . . . one group's determination to take power away from another."

The *US Organization,* founded in the mid–nineteen sixties by Maulana Ron Karenga, is based mainly in Los Angeles. Since its inception it has become one of the leading cultural nationalist groups in the United States. In the words of the founder, "US is a cultural organization dedicated to the creation, recreation, and circulation of Afro-American culture." In the strict sense of the term, US is not a political organization.

Karenga feels that blacks can live interdependently with whites, once they have achieved sufficient power, but in order to do this they must develop a separate, autonomous culture. Culture, he feels, gives "identity, purpose, and direction." In order to create this culture, blacks must "Think Black, Talk Black, Act Black, Buy Black, Vote Black, and Live Black." In general, blacks must create a cultural nation, utilizing whatever of their own they have created in the

United States and whatever Africanisms have managed to survive. It is only after the black cultural nation has been achieved that black people can seriously consider revolution.

In order to wage a violent political revolution, Karenga feels, it must be preceded by a cultural revolution, for it is the cultural revolution which gives direction to violent revolution. During the process of nation-building, "To play revolution is to get put down." Acts of violence, in this process, are as inadequate as acts of nonviolence.

There are many more nationalist groups and organizations, such as the Congress of Racial Equality (CORE), which supports a program of black control of the black community —that is, black community self-determination. The Dodge Revolutionary Union Movement (DRUM) of Detroit was organized by black members of the United Automobile Workers union to oppose the racist oppression of both the union and management. The organizers of DRUM have expressed solidarity with oppressed workers throughout the world. Floyd B. McKissick Enterprises is a corporation organized to promote "black business development with social commitment to black communities." It proposes to develop chain restaurants and shopping centers, dramatic productions, and a publishing company, all in the black community.

The Nation of Islam (Black Muslims) was founded in the 1930s but achieved national and international prominence in the 1960s. It is a nationalist organization which advocates both partition of the United States into two separate nation-states and the payment of reparations to the descendants of former slaves. Until separation can be effected, the Muslims concentrate on economic development in the black community. The National Black Economic Development Conference, founded in 1969, set forth its objectives in the "Black Manifesto." In this manifesto a demand of $500 million—later raised to $3 billion—from white Christian churches and Jewish synagogues was put forth. This money—reparations to black people—would be used for such projects as a southern land bank, black publishing houses and television stations, and a black university.

The Organization of Afro-American Unity (OAAU), founded by the late Malcolm X in 1964, was patterned after the Organization of African Unity. The purpose of the organization is the unifying of all people of African descent throughout the world.

Finally, the Student National Coordinating Committee (SNCC) has moved to a position of revolutionary nationalism. To this end, SNCC has formed alliances with other Marxist-Leninist groups in the United States.

Cultural Nationalism versus Revolutionary Nationalism

The various contemporary black nationalist groups in the United States represent a wide range of ideologies and programs. While there are many similarities in all of these groups, there are fundamental differences which militate against effective cooperation. Perhaps the greatest division in the organized black nationalist movement at the present time is that between cultural nationalism and revolutionary nationalism. While the two designations are frequently confusing, there exist clear-cut differences between these two varieties of black nationalism, and, according to Nathan Hare, writing in the November 1969 issue of *The Black Scholar,* this division formed the basis of the major debate at the First Pan-African Cultural Festival in Algiers in July 1969. The debate centered on the positions of Stokely Carmichael, representing cultural nationalism (Pan-Africanism, in this case) and Eldridge Cleaver, representing revolutionary nationalism.

Most of the major nationalist groups discussed above can be placed into these two categories. The Black Community Development and Defense organization, and the US Organization are clearly cultural nationalist groups. The Black Panther party, the Republic of New Africa, and the Revolutionary Action Movement, on the other hand, are revolutionary nationalist groups. The major points of disagreement between these two branches of nationalism may be discerned from the stated positions of the groups they represent and from the speeches and writings of their spokesmen. The major spokesmen for the cultural nationalist position are LeRoi Jones, Maulana Ron Karenga, and Harold Cruse. The revolutionary nationalist position is best represented by such spokesmen as Eldridge Cleaver, Robert F. Williams, H. Rap Brown, Huey P. Newton, and Bobby Seale.

Both cultural nationalists and revolutionary nationalists stress black solidarity, pride in cultural heritage, and self-determination for black people. But it is on other aspects of ideology that the split between the two is most pronounced. In general terms, for the cultural nationalists culture itself becomes the major ideology. Perhaps the clearest statement on the ideological use of culture is contained in Harold Cruse's *The Crisis of the Negro Intellectual,* and in his *Rebellion or Revolution.*

LeRoi Jones insists that blacks can only liberate themselves by the adoption of a unified, cohesive black culture which is completely divorced from that of the white man. "It is white culture that rules us with guns," he maintains in an essay in Floyd Barbour's *The Black Power Revolt.* "Our freedom will be in bringing Black Culture to Power. We Cannot Do This Unless We Are Cultured. That is, Consciously Black." Furthermore, writing in *The New York Times,* he criticizes the revolutionary nationalists as "mis-guided dudes" who have "turned left on black people," with a confused mixture of Marxism-Leninism and integration. He dismisses them as "violent integrationists."

In his *The Quotable Karenga,* Maulana Ron Karenga has written: "We must free ourselves culturally before we succeed politically. . . . Culture provides the basis for revolution and recovery." Harold Cruse, writing about cultural nationalism in *Rebellion or Revolution,* has said:

> We maintain that this new concept affords the intellectual means, the conceptual framework, the theoretical link that ties together all of the disparate, conflicting and contending trends within the Negro movement as a whole in order to transform the movement from a mere rebellion into a revolutionary movement that can "shape actions to ideas, to fit the world into a theoretic frame."

The revolutionary nationalists, on the other hand, embrace the socialist ideology of Marxism-Leninism, and stress class over race. A statement prepared by the national office of the Black Panther party for a special supplement in the *Guardian* begins as follows:

> The Black Panther Party stands for revolutionary solidarity with all people fighting against the forces of imperialism, capitalism, racism, and fascism. Our solidarity is extended to those people who are fighting these evils at home and abroad. . . . We will take our stand against these evils with a solidarity derived from a proletarian internationalism born of socialist idealism.

H. Rap Brown in his *Die Nigger Die!* has written: ". . . We cannot end racism, capitalism, colonialism and imperialism until the reins of state power are in the hands of those people who understand that the wealth, the total wealth of any country, and of the world, belongs equally to all people." In his widely publicized "Open Letter to Stokely Carmichael," Eldridge Cleaver defended the ideological position of the Black Panther party because, ". . . if you look around the world you will see that the only countries which have liberated themselves and managed to withstand the tide of counterrevolution are precisely those countries which have strong Marxist-Leninist parties."

The most crucial difference between the cultural nationalists and the revolutionary nationalists, then, is on the question of ideology. The former see Marxism-Leninism as alien to the black struggle, and for them culture itself becomes the ideology. The latter see world revolution as a prerequisite to cultural revolution.

A second major point of disagreement, and one which is an outgrowth of the ideological split, centers on the question of alliances and coalitions with white revolutionary groups. The cultural nationalists reject such relationships, while the revolutionary nationalists support them. LeRoi Jones has written, again in *The New York Times:*

> We "support" the white revolution of dope and nakedness because it weakens the hand that holds the chain

that binds Black people. But we must not confuse the cry of young white boys to be in charge of the pseudo-destruction of America (with a leisure made possible by the same colonialism) with our own necessity. Just because the slavemaster has long hair and smokes bush does nothing to change the fact that he is and will be the slavemaster until we, yes, free ourselves.

Karenga also rejects coalitions with whites at the present time. "We can live with whites interdependently once we have black power," he has written.

Eldridge Cleaver, on the other hand, strongly supports coalitions with white revolutionary groups. He sees them as a force with which the Black Panther party can operate as an equal partner. When questioned by an interviewer for *Playboy* magazine about the possible retreat of white revolutionaries in the event of large-scale violence, he replied:

You have to realize how deep the radicalization of young whites can become as the agents of repression against both them and us intensify their efforts. It's inevitable that the police, in order to suppress black militants, will also have to destroy the base of their support in the white community. . . . They cannot, let us say, put black people in concentration camps and allow whites who are just as passionately involved in the liberation struggle to run around loose.

And in his "Open Letter to Stokely Carmichael" he wrote:

One thing . . . we know, that seems to escape you, is that there is not going to be any revolution or black liberation in the United States as long as revolutionary blacks, whites, Mexicans, Puerto Ricans, Indians, Chinese and Eskimos are unwilling or unable to unite into some functional machinery that can cope with the situation.

In the August 1969 issue of *Ebony* magazine, Huey N. Newton has written:

Today in some white communities people are suffering from the same repression that we in the black community suffer. The same forces are there—the police, the National Guard and sometimes even the Regular Army. This will continue to happen time and again in the coming years, thus forming a basis for unity between the peoples of both the black and white communities. Not only are we coming together in unity in this country, we are all part of the international brotherhood of oppressed people.

A third major area of disagreement between these two camps concerns the use of revolutionary violence at the present time. The cultural nationalists maintain that the United States is not yet ready for armed revolutionary struggle, while the revolutionary nationalists maintain that the country is already in a state of guerrilla warfare. Karenga has written: "Violence in itself without consideration for time is as inadequate as nonviolence."

LeRoi Jones considers the revolutionary nationalists to be misguided. In his *New York Times* article he says that they think when they say, "Pick Up The Gun that the devil will wither up and die, or just by picking up the literal gun, without training, using the same sick value system of the degenerate slavemaster, the same dope, the same liquor, the same dying hippy mentality, that they will liberate all the slave peoples of the world. NO."

After the death of Martin Luther King, Jr., Cleaver wrote in the pages of *Ramparts* magazine: "The violent phase of the black liberation struggle is here, and it will spread. From that shot, from that blood, America will be painted red. Dead bodies will litter the streets. . . ." Some revolutionary nationalists advocate a form of guerrilla warfare because, as Cleaver said in the *Playboy* magazine interview: "This government does not have unlimited forces of repression; it can't hold the whole world down—not at home *and* abroad. Finally, in his *Die Nigger Die!* H. Rap Brown has written: "Violence is a necessary part of revolutionary struggle. Nonviolence as it is advocated by negroes is merely a preparation for genocide. . . . The very fact that white folks fear guns shows the value of being armed. Power, indeed, must come from the barrel of a gun."

From the foregoing quotes one is able to see that the major differences between the cultural nationalists and the revolutionary nationalists stem from different ideological emphases, disagreement on the desirability of alliances and coalitions with white groups, and diverse views on the appropriateness of the use of revolutionary violence at the present time. They pose fundamental questions, which have been debated through the years. Spokesmen for both of these camps make their points convincingly, and are confident that their approaches will ultimately lead to the liberation of black people in the United States.

Unlike earlier nationalist movements and leaders, especially the American Colonization Society and the Universal Negro Improvement Association, contemporary black nationalist groups and individuals reject emigration and concentrate on black liberation within the United States. Most of the spokesmen appear to be convinced that this goal can be achieved without the establishment of a separate nation-state within what is now the United States, but several demand partition. All of them agree, however, that some form of black autonomy (separation) is an essential first step in the movement for black liberation.

The questions raised by divergent positions of the cultural nationalists and the revolutionary nationalists have been widely discussed in recent years. Similarly, these points have stimulated discussion among black students at colleges and universities, and among others in the black community, throughout the country. It is not the purpose here to attempt an evaluation of these positions in detail, or to predict which holds the greatest promise for black liberation, the stated goal of both of these branches of the black liberation movement. Rather, the purpose is to describe the major differences and similarities in the positions of the cultural nationalists and revolutionary nationalists. Spokesmen for each of the camps are in agreement on a number of crucial points, but the differences which separate them are real and understandable.

Members of the radical left in the United States have never developed a strategy (theory) for black liberation based on the reality of the experience of black people in the United States. They have tended to rely on theories of revolution which have been developed in czarist Russia, in China, or in countries which have successfully accomplished anti-colonial political revolutions (e.g., Algeria). The conditions present in contemporary America are hardly such that these ideologies can be successfully implemented here at the present time. On the other hand, nation-building within the black community seems hardly sufficient for complete black liberation. While it might lead to greater political awareness among blacks, and thereby promote greater solidarity, this is only a first step in the process of liberation. It is an essential first step, however.

The role of white participation in the black movement has emerged as one of the most controversial issues in recent years. All of the contemporary black nationalist groups refuse membership to whites, but differences between cultural nationalists and revolutionary nationalists center on the formation of alliances and coalitions with white groups. Phil Hutchins, the past national director of SNCC, has recently suggested in his column in the *Guardian* that since the most radical of young white people have had little contact with individual blacks and black groups, coalitions should be formed in which black organizations send some of their representatives to take over leadership positions in white organizations. He justifies this position because, "Without black direction and participation whites cannot be trusted to fight racism," which is their major function.

Karenga at the symposium on Afro-American studies at Yale University suggested that proper roles for white people sympathetic to black aspirations are nonintervention in the black community, financial and technical aid to the black colony, and the creation of a "civilizing movement" among whites. While black people will no doubt ultimately need the support of whites and other nonwhites sympathetic to their goals, black solidarity is crucial in the beginning phase of the movement. In most cases this will probably mean the exclusion of white people.

The question of the use of revolutionary violence depends

upon one's perception of the nature of the black movement in the United States, and whether one sees the country as ripe for revolution. This question is frequently confused with that of the possession of weapons for self-defense. Both the cultural nationalists and the revolutionary nationalists support the possession of armaments for self-defense in the black community. The seventh point in the platform of the Black Panther party reads as follows:

> We want an immediate end to POLICE BRUTALITY and MURDER of black people. We believe we can end police brutality in our black community by organizing black self-defense groups that are dedicated to defending our black community from racist police oppression and brutality. The Second Amendment to the Constitution of the United States gives a right to bear arms. We therefore believe that all black people should arm themselves for self-defense.

The well-coordinated series of search-and-destroy missions which have resulted in death for dozens of members of the Black Panther party by the police justifies the inclusion of this point in their platform. At the same time, to exonerate the police on grounds of justifiable homicide is to transfer the guilt from the aggressor to the victim. Like the Black Panthers, members of the Republic of New Africa and the Revolutionary Action Movement have been the victims of police harassment and violence. While some revolutionary nationalist leaders call for armed struggle, it is unlikely that such a position is widely shared in the black community, and the advocacy of armed self-defense is frequently distorted to imply that blacks are being urged to engage in guerrilla warfare.

Conclusions

Within the last few years black nationalism in the United States has had a greater impact on race relations than almost any comparable movement in history. This movement has seriously challenged many of the most fundamental assumptions of American life, ranging from the racism endemic to the educational system to the imperialist character of relations with other countries. Black students at colleges and universities, through demanding the inclusion of black studies into curricula which already include heavy doses of such areas of study as Celtic poetry and Croatian literature, have forced educational institutions to alter their distorted portrayal of black culture and history. Black nationalists have taken the lead in opposing many of the more grotesque features of American foreign policy. As a young Detroit black nationalist wrote to his draft board in rejecting its demand that he report for a preinduction physical examination in 1965:

> . . . when the call is made to free South Africa; when the call is made to liberate Latin America from United Fruit Co., Kaiser and Alcoa Aluminum Co., and from Standard Oil; . . . When the call is made to free the black delta areas of Mississippi, Alabama, South Carolina; when the call is made to FREE 12TH STREET HERE IN DETROIT!: when these calls are made, send for me, for these shall be Historic Struggles in which it shall be an honor to serve.

Few areas of American society have not been challenged by the black nationalists. Because of their explication of the injustices of the society, they have stimulated others to challenge heretofore accepted American values and practices. Liberation movements have sprung up among American Indians, Mexican-Americans, and Puerto Ricans; among homosexuals, and among women. These groups have all borrowed tactics and rhetoric from the black nationalists.

Within the black community, black nationalism has served to create what is probably the greatest mass base for radical social change in the society. This is especially true for secondary school pupils and college and university students—a significant segment of the population—for the type and quality of education are crucial aspects of the liberation process. The resistance of school officials to community control of education in the black community may be seen as attempts on the part of the colonial power to maintain its status.

Within the black nationalist movement a division exists between the cultural nationalists and the revolutionary nationalists. Such a division is to be expected in a movement attempting to arrive at solutions to the many problems which black people face in the United States. The ultimate goal of the two camps is the same, but the points of difference center on methods of achieving the goal. It is impossible at the present time to say whether the program of one branch of the movement is more likely to yield the desired result—the liberation of black people—than that of the other. It seems clear, however, that if the status of black people is to be significantly altered in the United States—and domestic tranquility depends upon such an alteration—a fundamental change in American institutions and practices is necessary. The major social institutions in the South developed through the oppression of black people, and with the "reconciliation" after the Civil War, their oppression became fundamental to the national society.

Both cultural nationalists and revolutionary nationalists reject the values underlying the structure of American society and thereby call for fundamental social change. The revolutionary nationalists insist that complete social change is necessary for any significant alteration in the status of black people. The cultural nationalists, on the other hand, focus their efforts on nation-building within the black community in an attempt to inculcate a new system of values in black people. Because the low status of black people in the society has been permitted to exist unattended for centuries, the problem has intensified. Therefore, short of a master plan designed to guarantee success, numerous approaches are no doubt warranted.

SOURCES

BARBOUR, FLOYD B., ed., *The Black Power Revolt*. Boston, Porter Sargent, Inc., 1968.

The Black Panther, newspaper, published weekly by the Minister of Information, the Black Panther party.

BRACEY, JOHN H., JR.; Meier, August; and Rudwick, Elliott M., eds., *Black Nationalism in America*. Indianapolis and New York, The Bobbs-Merrill Company, 1970.

BROWN, H. RAP, *Die Nigger Die!* New York, Dial Press, 1969.

CLEAVER, ELDRIDGE, "Open Letter to Stokely Carmichael," *Ramparts*, September 1969.

_____ *see* Robert Scheer, ed.

CRUSE, HAROLD, *The Crisis of the Negro Intellectual*. New York, William Morrow and Company, Inc., 1967.

_____ *Rebellion or Revolution?* New York, William Morrow and Company, Inc., 1968.

ESSIEN-UDOM, E. U., *Black Nationalism*. Chicago, The University of Chicago Press, 1962.

HARE, NATHAN, "Algiers 1969: A Report on the Pan-African Cultural Festival," *The Black Scholar*, November 1969.

HUTCHINS, PHIL, "Second Coming," *Guardian*, January 17—March 14, 1970.

JONES, LEROI, "A Black Value System," *The Black Scholar*, November 1969.

_____ "To Survive 'the Reign of the Beasts,'" *The New York Times*, November 16, 1969.

KARENGA, MAULANA RON, *The Quotable Karenga*. Los Angeles, US Organization, 1967.

LINCOLN, C. ERIC, *The Black Muslims In America*. Boston, Beacon Press, 1961.

LLORENS, DAVID, "Ameer (LeRoi Jones) Baraka," *Ebony*, August 1969.

MARINE, GENE, *The Black Panthers*. New York, New American Library, 1969.

MUHAMMAD, ELIJAH, *Message to the Blackman in America*. Chicago, Muhammad Mosque of Islam No. 2, 1965.

NEWTON, HUEY P., "The Black Panthers," *Ebony*, August 1969.

ROBINSON, ARMSTEAD L., et al., eds., *Black Studies in the University*. New York, Bantam Books, Inc., 1969.

SCHEER, ROBERT, ed., *Eldridge Cleaver: Post-Prison Speeches and Writings*. New Haven, Yale University Press, 1969.

SEALE, BOBBY, *Seize the Time: The Story of the Black Panther Party and Huey P. Newton*. New York, Random House, Inc., 1970.

SHERRILL, ROBERT, "Birth of a Black Nation," *Esquire*, January 1969.

15

THEODORE TAYLOR

Race and Class in the Urban Ghetto: An Interpretation

Most white people, when addressing themselves to the black man, accept rather unconsciously the notion that blacks are all alike—all with common education (usually poor), all of common mentality, all having common goals and objectives. They attempt to say that the mere fact that blacks are the same color and historically of the same blood line in and of itself identifies them as a distinct, monolithic unit of people in the United States. So we hear such phrases as: "What do black people want?" "What do colored folks want?" "Who is the Negro leader?" I am attempting to refute the notion that blacks are a distinct unit of people. In doing so, I think it is necessary to go back and look at the development of cities in the United States.

All cities owe their development to concentrations of industrial growth. When we talk about Pittsburgh, we have to talk about steel; Detroit, the auto industry; Chicago, packing-houses; Pennsylvania, coal mines. People migrate to these cities to enter into their economic production. They do not go there generally for the scenery. Now, one of the very interesting phenomena about the migration of black people to city ghettos is that they generally come from specific areas of the South to certain cities; for example, most of the people in the Trenton, New Jersey, area come from Virginia and North Carolina. And if one wants to take the time to make an analysis of the backgrounds of blacks in various cities, he will find that they do not all come from the southern part of the United States. Throughout the entire eastern region there are blacks who can trace their history without going anywhere near a slave camp. There are blacks whose ancestors came over on the *Mayflower;* there are blacks descended from indentured servants, some descended from those who bought their freedom. We find examples of these families in the local New Jersey area surrounding Rutgers University, in places like Princeton, New Brunswick, and Somerville.

The development of the ghettos in the United States came about in this general way: After the Civil War—a revolution that saw the defeat of a slaveholding class by an industrial class—there was set in motion in this country a chain of migration into the industrial complexes of the North. Blacks moved in three specific waves: directly north, up the Mississippi River into Chicago and St. Louis; southwest, into Texas and California; and, of course, to the eastern seaboard.

An interesting thing about this migration and population shift is the similar economic and social patterns of the poverty ghettos—black *and* white—which resulted. Responding to the increasing pace of industrialization caused by the demands of the Civil War and the railroad-building boom of mid-nineteenth-century industry, the industrial class which had seized power in the United States began to import poor whites from eastern Europe. In case some of you young white readers have delusions about your origins and your history, you must recognize that most of you came out of eastern Europe, and that your grandparents were brought into this country to feed the industrial giant then a-borning. They, too, settled in and around the industrial concentrations, bringing with them the habit of rearing large families, as they had done in Europe. I mention this since size of family is often held against poor blacks. Not only are children valued in the rural cultures from which ghetto inhabitants come, but there is also an awareness that only a proportion will survive to manhood in the ghetto.

But the blacks were not able to gain a place in the northern industrial concentrations because of discrimination, and they became relegated to the service industries. They became the maids, the servants, the porters. To the extent that they did get into industry, it was heavy, backbreaking industry. The lowest categories in the industrial complexes were the ones occupied by blacks.

It then came about that blacks were left behind when, in the early 1930s, the immigrant whites of European background moved to organize against conditions that affected them—conditions that were the worst this country has ever seen. This class or stratum of people from Europe had ideological leaders and an organizational structure, and therefore it moved for the eight-hour day, the forty-hour week, and unemployment compensation. All the social legislation that most of us still live under came out of that period—a vicious, bloody period of labor organization in the United States, a period that saw deep social change take place. One particular stratum of the working class became elevated, while in its wake were left the black migrants occupying the ghettos. Blacks were left to occupy those rat-infested houses and garbage-strewn streets that the immigrant whites had moved out of—a continuing pattern that we are all familiar with today.

Stratification of the Black Ghetto

When discussing stratification in the black ghetto, one must also remember that the total American population is stratified. I would prefer to use the term "class society" to describe American conditions. The black ghetto is no exception. I will describe this stratification in very general terms before going on to discuss its political implications.

Within the framework of the black ghetto, there is a small (extremely small) number of industrialists. By and large, the few industries that have been developed by blacks in the past have been soon lost, as a result of monopolized industrial trusts or the inability to compete. Some of these businesses developed around the manufacture and sale of hair products, and are now developing around the *daishiki* shops and other Africa-related products. But it is a truism that profit-making businesses in the ghetto belong to whites.

The second group that is part of the upper crust or elite of the black community consists of the black professionals: the doctor, the lawyer, the undertaker, and so on. The professional unit of the black community is developing now and is getting to be an extremely powerful section of it. Black professionals are beginning to dominate certain parts of the educational structures. They are beginning to develop political power; and given existing population patterns, we can now predict that sixteen of the major cities in the United States will soon have black majorities. In cities such as Newark, Cleveland, and Chicago, it is reasonable to assume that the seat of power will be sought and developed by this particular section of the black community. It is not likely to be the working-class blacks—the 80 or 90 percent of the black population—who will first move to power.

There is also a small-business group that belongs to this top stratum, in that its ideology is the same and that it evidences the same feeling of wanting to "make it," to become a part of the system.

Next are the black people who work in the major industries, such as the Ford Motor Company and many of the chemical industries—the black blue-collar workers. At this point they are part of the trade-union movement, racist as it is. They have become recipients of the gains of unionism and are the most highly successful working units of the black community.

Another group consists of those who occupy the lower jobs in industry and agriculture: the migrant farm workers, the plastics and toy factory workers, for example—the multitude of unorganized black workers, plus many who are organized but who continue to live in exploited conditions because of the weaknesses and racism of the union movement at this point in time.

There is another layer of the black community which includes those who are unemployed on the basis of periodic layoffs, who are shifting from one section of the community to another, attempting to gain stability in the economic structure. They join with the last unit, the chronically unemployed—people who have been unemployed for long periods because of police records, because of welfare regulations which have forced them to leave their homes; and of course this last group includes the "dregs of society," as people call them—the drug addicts, the prostitutes, etc. The members of this group are fashionably called the "hard-core unemployed."

Now when we look at these various groups within the community scientifically and realistically, it is impossible to claim that in all cases—or even in most—what affects one group is going to affect the others, or that the solutions advanced by one group are in fact solutions that can be accepted by the others. Let us take the civil rights movement as an illustration.

The Civil Rights Movement as Serving the Elite

The civil rights period in the United States which saw the thrust of blacks in coalition with whites moving to integrate lunch counters, hotels, golf courses, and you name it, was primarily a thrust of the elite sections of the black community. These sections had become economically stable, and the only thing they found wrong with society was racism. Economically they were in good shape; they could have tea and cookies with whitey on an individual level. But when they went to conferences with their briefcases, with their ties and shirts on, they were humiliated by the very nature of the scene, as well as by signs on the streetcars saying, "Nigger, get in the back!" This insulted them.

At this point there was a commonality of feeling among all blacks, because most black people in the United States grow up experiencing such indignities. There are stories told all over of how blacks went back on visits to the South with big greasy bags full of chicken and big dishpans full of potato salad, carrying enough water so they would not have to stop for anything but gas. But even so, there are other stories about what happened when they stopped simply for gas. These became tales told around mealtimes, tales told at wakes and funerals, about the conditions black people faced when they went South. So, on this level, one has to see and feel the universality of it all.

Nonetheless, the integration issue was raised and introduced by the elite section of the community, who were faced with discrimination primarily on the social level. The lower sections of the black community—surely the vast majority of blacks in the United States—were faced with rat-infested houses, no gas or no jobs, or a sell-out union; but the civil rights struggles of the fifties were fought out purely along integrationist or social lines.

This is not to make an indictment of those struggles, but to take a realistic view of who led them and in whose interests they were fought. This is both sensible and realistic when we attempt to assess the future direction of the black struggle and to look beneath the surface. Let us do this with regard to current movements and ideologies.

Stratification and Political Ideology

Without going into great detail about the organizational

268

structure of the black community, I want to argue that the groups represented by the National Association for the Advancement of Colored People, the Urban League, the newly developing nationalist movements, the church structures, and so on reflect the various strata I have named. If you look at any one of the black leaders in America and begin to note the position he identifies with, the solutions he proposes to the common problems, you can almost tell what stratum he comes from. For example, take "black capitalism" as a solution. As I see it, this slogan means, "Whitey, get away from those stores. Leave those industries to us so that we can exploit the black people." The important question is, Whose interests does such a solution represent—the interests of the multitude of oppressed black people in America, or of a stratified section of the black community that has agreed to pattern itself after the capitalism of white America?

In considering the political leadership of the black community, it must be remembered that blacks have had very little traditional political patronage, because of racial discrimination. There weren't the appropriate number of municipal sewer-authority appointments, housing authority and welfare board appointments, and other such positions to go to the black community. The black political leader's base was made more slippery because he could not pass on the favors and appointments for his constituency that would enable it to develop a sound political organizational structure in the ghetto. Those of you who want to examine this question further might look at Kenneth Clark's *Dark Ghetto*, in which he deals with the political patronage that falls to the black community. Clearly, the unique exception of Adam Clayton Powell only highlights the rule.

The black community has suffered greatly precisely because it has accepted as solutions to its problems the patterns which the major social system and ideology decreed as solutions. Let us take the city of Newark, New Jersey, as an illustration. Here we can see the relationships of ghetto structure and the dominant American political ideology operating in a specific community.

In 1970 there was a battle in Newark for control of the

city. For the first time there were three black candidates for the position of mayor—Kenneth Gibson, George Richardson, and Harry Wheeler—in addition to the white incumbent, Hugh Addonizio. But none of these men could really be called a significant reformer. While some of Gibson's statements indicated that he might be capable of relating to the lower strata of the population that I mentioned, it is more important to examine the campaign issues that were raised—or not raised—and who was supporting whom. Within the black community the Gibson campaign came down basically to the argument that he should be supported because he was black. The mask of color could be used to obscure the basic economic questions which must be raised about Newark or any other ghetto city. As for Richardson, he was talking about being attacked and about his party headquarters being bombed, and he was calling for the governor to protect the Newark mayoralty race. And the town blacks and the old-line "give-me-some-coffee-and-scratch-me-on-the-back-of-the-head" niggers were backing the Addonizio administration.

I maintain that this campaign should be recognized as a struggle between representatives of the same economic stratum and ideology for a larger share of the existing pie. Such incidents as the explicit and widely publicized support of Addonizio by a group of forty-four black ministers further supports this thesis. My reading of their position suggests that while some few of them may have represented the churches of the lower economic groups, they—as the so-called leadership—had in fact been bought off by the Addonizio machine and had been part of it for the last eight to ten years.

So if anybody wants to still advance the notion that we are all brothers as blacks, and that this can be the basis by which we take over the control and distribute the power of cities such as Newark, I say he is dealing in folly. He may be right once in such an election, maybe even twice. But basically, and over the long haul, the real struggle will have to be for fundamental economic and social changes, and any candidate who thinks a slogan of black unity will long substitute for those changes is out of his cotton-picking mind. Gibson, as the first black mayor of Newark, will have an opportunity to find this out.

The Significance of Racism

I would like to raise what I consider fundamental questions about racism and oppression. One of the fallacies that has developed and has been a problem in the black community is uncritical assessment of the significance of racism. Racism still takes its vicious toll of the total American society and of the brains of black people. There are those who argue that the fundamental question facing black people is racism, and that if we stamp it out we shall have solved the basic problem of American society. Blacks who believe this haven't really come to grips with the fundamentals of the American social system. Racism has been a tool; it has been introduced into the social system as a tool to oppress and divide, so that the power structure in the United States could isolate the multitudes of working-class people in the country from each other.

Racism is *not* the underlying issue facing black people. The basic question, as it faces all oppressed people across the world, is one of imperialism and the colonization of peoples. The division of people into classes and strata has always been the fundamental question facing the multitudes of people on the face of the globe, and America is no exception. If blacks are to rid themselves of oppression, they must stamp out the system which developed and which perpetuates oppression.

I charge that the issue of color has been used on black people to the extent that it has created oppressive and self-mutilating psychological complexes. This must be looked at straight. I want to deal with it, in spite of the fact that it is a highly unpopular approach with some of the brothers. I have to do so because, while we can shake hands and do all the funny things we do when we talk about unity, the minority position has to be put forth, whether it is accepted at this time or not. You remember that the man who said the earth was round, and not flat, was jailed, and the man who said doctors were killing people in hospitals because they didn't wash their hands was put in a mental institution! So . . .

Now, the black community is unaware that, in itself, it has become oppressive to itself. In many instances it is crutching on its blackness. To see the question of color as being over and above the fundamental question of oppression is to have something wrong with one's head. The oppressive nature of the system against blacks was not developed simply because they were black; the question of color was used as a tool.

I remind you that the nation was developed as a result of immigrants moving to the United States in conscious attempts to gain certain freedoms. And yet within the same period slavery was introduced and maintained. Now obviously there is a contradiction here. How did the American nation justify this contradiction? What, in fact, happened was that Americans rationalized that contradiction by arguing that the blacks they were enslaving were not really humans, but subhumans. They institutionalized this belief. The churches institutionalized it with the curse of Ham, the educational system did it with Sambo, and many other examples could be given right down through the years. The justification of slavery became acceptable to almost every free person in the United States.

Malcolm has pointed this out; it is not new. All of the nationalist groupings very correctly pinpoint the question of how racism was introduced into the country to keep black people oppressed. But what has to be seen, and what blacks in many communities fail to see, is that at the same time this society was also oppressing other people in the lower economic classes. The majority of the oppressed in the United States happen not to be black. Seventy percent of the Americans in poverty are white. They are the very old, the very young, those with bad schooling and few skills. They are, in other words, those whom the economic system can't use.

The additional burden that falls on the backs of black people and keeps the division going among the working class is the question of color. You can see white sharecroppers and black sharecroppers in the southern part of the United States both starving to death. They can't develop a common interest against those who oppress them simply because no matter how bad conditions have been for the white share-cropper, he just "ain't a nigger." It is surprising how easily this simple division has kept the oppressed of the nation apart, and has kept them from struggling against the system that oppresses them. So we must recognize racism as a tool, not as the fundamental question across the globe.

The fundamental question facing the colonialized people of Africa isn't one of color; it has never been one of color. The real issue is who is to control their natural resources and world markets, and the enemy happens to be imperialism. If we stamp out imperialism, obviously we stamp out the control of nations by other nations, and therefore we stamp out colonial rule.

The Vacuum of White Working Class Leadership

Although the white working class is an oppressed group, with numerous just causes for acting in its own behalf, it lacks an effective leadership. As a black I can grab any black off the street when somebody's done something to me, raise the question of color, and get some unity. But if you are white, working class, and unemployed, you are in trouble. There is no organization that is really leading these people, so their thinking is up for grabs. With no ideological leadership to provide a framework for their thinking, to provide a counterweight to the deceptive "solutions" being offered to their problems, their thinking has gone racist—more racist, in fact, than most other sections of the white population. Therefore, as blacks begin to compete for the same jobs and to set up their own organizational structures, contradictions and struggles will be created.

Some of these struggles are going to be over the question of color. Trade-union members are reacting to blacks who are beginning to move in and exert themselves, saying, "Hey, man, we coming through here." Union leadership is unable to recognize that the total working class shares a common position because the leaders are off at the race track. The working-class whites are not even leading their own, so it is certainly impossible for them to think of coalitions with blacks. But we still have to look ahead from the present situation to see what may develop in the future.

What must be focused on is the white working class leadership's failure to recognize the similarity in position of all members of the working class and to take positive action based on an accurate assessment of the situation. I would charge that this failure—particularly among union leadership—to analyze the situation and to move in it is caused by the leadership's opportunistic search for personal gain and satisfaction, rather than a commitment to the freedom of the group it is supposed to represent.

Let me give you a few examples of what I mean. In spite of the fact that 65 percent of the American working people are organized, there are large groups, such as migrant farm workers, that are not. In fact, the majority of black workers in the United States are unorganized, and they could—and should—be the bastion of the American trade union movement at this point in time. You know, when you really look at the factory, you're looking at a damn prison—the regimentation, the time clock, the guard checking the badge. But you have to take the workers to the bricks to win the right to freedom from force of habit in this social system.

It takes money to organize migrant farm workers (or anyone else), and a lot of time and effort and struggle. And during that organizing period, the union leader is worrying about whether or not he is going to get his $30,000 salary next year if he upsets too many time-clock punchers. Having a personal history in the trade-union movement in New Jersey, I can attest that the majority of workers, black *and* white, in the small shops controlled by white trade union leadership have been sold out. The contracts are negotiated with the boss on the golf course and then brought back to the union meeting and handed out. No struggle, no growth—and no real movement out of that factory prison.

To take another example of mistaken union leadership, let me talk about the Ocean Hill-Brownsville school dispute in New York City, in which the union, in my opinion, played a very vicious role. The issue basically was the question as to whether the community of people most concerned with the children—parents, teachers, and others—could create new institutional structures responsive to their own experienced needs or whether the existing power structures and institutions would continue to control the scene.

Instead of recognizing their common interest with the community and moving to strengthen it, the leaders of the white teachers' union thought it was to their advantage to divide the community by charging that blacks (the parents) were anti-Semitic. Now, we know that anti-Semitism runs rampant in American society, and to the degree that it exists it is shared by blacks. So the question to be battled is the question of anti-Semitism, not simply its existence among black parents. Once again, in Ocean Hill-Brownsville, the white trade union used racism as a tool to divide and conquer.

You may wonder whether white workers—hard hats, teachers, and others—could ever lose their racist attitudes, lose their faith in the system's ability to serve them, and ally themselves with blacks in the building of new institutions. In other words, what are the necessary conditions for the kind of alliance I am suggesting?

Basically, in my opinion, it will only be when the white working class begins to develop a struggle within its own ranks, when it repudiates its own opportunistic and ineffective leaders, that it can begin to talk about joining blacks in a common thrust. Growth is experiential; that is, it results from encounter after encounter with the hard facts of experience. And therefore, struggle is the key to growth.

Stages in the Liberation Struggle

In terms of the struggle of the black community, however,

I would like to review what I have said and implied about struggle in general, and make some predictions for the future. We must recognize that struggle—or call it change, or movement, or process—is a sign of life and growth. In the context of this discussion, the driving force of that struggle is the lower economic community that is hungry—indeed, often starving—and determined to break out of that damned box. We have seen over and over again that a force for change on one side tends to create and stiffen a counterforce of opposition. It is in these terms, therefore, that the structure of the ghetto gives many clues as to the stage of revolution we are presently in, and we can make some predictions about the future of these struggles from a scientific view of the ghetto scene.

First of all, I predict that across this nation there will be a sharp increase in conflict, and that in many instances the struggle will become extremely violent. The struggle will be, first, by blacks against the power structure to control the conditions and destinies of the ghettos in which they are the major forces; and, second, by blacks within their own communities, over control of these communities by contending groups. The early period of the second phase will involve primarily a conflict among the elite groups of the black community—among various black leaders, such as in the Newark mayoralty race, as to what section or which individuals within that elite are to be in control.

At the same time, while that struggle is going on, there will also be rapidly developing an American brand of guerrilla warfare; in fact, I would say that it has already begun. By this I am referring to the riots in many cities, which marked the spontaneous reaction of lower economic class blacks—ghetto blacks—against the conditions that put them in the ghetto and keep them there.

This spontaneous reaction signifies a certain kind of struggle in its embryonic stage, when consciousness is just beginning to ripen, when the masses of blacks are just beginning to lose their submission to authority. The struggle has not yet become scientific—and by this I mean that the people have not yet begun to analyze what mistakes they have made, to examine other areas of struggle and alternative actions. They are still, now, at the stage of thinking about whether they should have thrown the Coca-Cola bottle, the ginger-ale bottle, or the five-gallon can of gasoline. But the analysis will develop very rapidly once it begins. This is, in fact, already happening in certain sections of the United States.

My second prediction about the future is that as this process occurs, new institutions will be created and grow in the black community. Now, the black church is representative of the kind of stratification in the ghetto that I indicated earlier. There are upper Baptists and lower Baptists—and maybe even middle Baptists. You must know that the black church has historically and traditionally served to take the minds of black folk off their troubles in the kitchen and put their minds to rest on the glory road. But while on the one hand it has played an extremely negative role by getting people to look for something from on high, "pie in the sky," it has also provided an avenue of expression and an organizational structure for which we had no substitutes. The late Dr. Martin Luther King, Jr., and the Reverend Ralph Abernathy are good examples of what can be done by the new kind of black minister, who recognizes the process and logic of struggle for change. So, I would predict that as blacks begin to recognize that the only thing that is going to cure their damnable conditions is struggle, they're going to stop dropping down on their knees, praying for somebody to throw a ham in the window, and start taking control of their community. And as soon as we rid ourselves of that black preacher who has to buy those long Cadillacs and those fancy shoes, the emotional needs that the church has served will be taken up in struggle, rather than in playing behind the pew.

Third, I predict that the black community will become increasingly scientific in its approach to life. The movement in the church shows that religion is undergoing the same kind of revolution that the whole society is undergoing. Soon man will know all there is to know beyond the moon, and will begin to realize his own powers over his own life. And as he searches for this scientific assessment of his world, he will be forced to arrive at a political consciousness which places him within the globe, as part of the total scene. In other words, an individual will have to develop, first, a global perspective; second, a national perspective; and, third, a perspective on the particular interest group that he identifies as being the key, the most significant section of the community. Before he can devise any real tactics or strategy for change, he will have to ask: "In whose interests do I fight? When I talk about liberation, whose liberation do I mean? Am I looking for self-liberation, or the liberation of the elite sections of the community, or the liberation of the mass of people?"

An individual's answers to these questions will place him in a category, either as part of that leadership core that is advancing the interests of the mass or as part of those who are advancing the interests of a small limited group to which they belong. The middle class is going to be forced to divide itself, to take a position. One section of it will line up with the power structure. The other section will line up with the oppressed and become part of the oppressed group's leadership.

I think you have to see that the wrenching of concessions from the power structure is the first stage in the dynamic of a major realignment. The changes that students have been courageously advancing all over this country, legislative and administrative innovations such as the Office of Economic Opportunity, and the new institutions of Community Action Programs—these stand as real examples of the power and the determination of that lower economic community to break out of the box I spoke of earlier. For instance, I now hold the position of executive director of the Community Action Program in Somerset County, New Jersey. For a black man without a degree, that would have been unthinkable five or ten years ago. It is the lower economic class throwing that Coca-Cola bottle that has forced such doors open, and we must recognize it. Change does not come merely because someone wants it—if that were the case, we would have had freedom a hundred years ago; it comes through the struggle that produces the necessary conditions and the leadership required to lead the masses.

What we do with the concessions we have won is the key. If we use them to build institutions in our communities, and if we defend them with our lives, then we will begin to change the habits and structure and thinking patterns of our constituency. And as we go through the experience of being black and chasing integration and knowing that "it ain't working," and then going on to the next attempt, we are going through a series of experiences. What will the blacks who are now taking a nationalist position be saying three years from now? Not too long ago I myself wore a *daishiki* and saw it as an extremely important thing to do, and I still wear one occasionally. I no longer think as strongly about the *daishiki* as I did in the past, because I find that no matter how many times I wear it, the conditions are still the same and the struggle must still take place. So now there is the idea not only of wearing it and identifying with it, but of taking it off and kicking someone in the behind when you have to.

These are the experiences required to prepare us for a new stage in our development. And as the struggle ripens and develops, the question of color will become less important in the black—and in the white—community, and the question of class and strata will become the more pronounced question. And that struggle is the task at hand.

16

SAMUEL D. PROCTOR

Survival Techniques
and the
Black Middle Class

One of the unresolved issues facing the black community is how to engage those who have "made it" more fully in the black liberation struggle. A serious loss to the movement is a massive manpower pool comprising hundreds of thousands of blacks who have discovered survival techniques for themselves but who have not found a way to articulate these techniques in the revolutionary causes that engage many younger and more vocal black protagonists.

It is natural and inevitable that those blacks who have earned college degrees, who have fought and cried and sweated their way through the wilderness of racial hostility and the morass of poverty, will be inclined to guard their gains jealously, find each other, form friendships, congeal into a class, marry attractive women, make money and spend it, join the same clubs, live near each other, party together, worship together, and hence erect a defense against the erosion of their social gains. Most of them were born in the midst of the Great Depression or earlier. Many were educated on fifteen-cents-an-hour campus jobs, washed cars for a quarter, shined shoes for a nickel, and waited on table for two dollars a meal plus tips. They had their education interrupted for a two-to-four-year stint in a segregated army and left buddies buried in Tunisia and Burma and on the islands of the seas.

Many came from homes where there were several children who could not get a college education and from communities where few adults did anything except domestic or menial labor. They have escaped an awful fate by dint of endeavor, investing their own ingenuity, time, talent, and labor in the pursuit of a dream of one day really being somebody.

One young man comes to mind who entered college in 1937. His father worked on the docks in a southern port city. His mother was a helpless diabetic. They lived in a rented, three-room row apartment. The toilets were outhouses. In order to stay in school this young man arose at daybreak and hauled ice for an hour or so to fill all the water coolers on campus. After classes he practiced football for two hours to keep his scholarship, and for extra money he washed dinner dishes and scrubbed the dining-room floor. Then came the war. Four years out. After the war he began to move, reaching a very good position in education. One day, while mowing the lawn that surrounded his new brick ranch house, he blew a blood vessel and died. At his funeral were hundreds of his friends, whose careers were very much like his own.

They are still around—school principals, government specialists, physicians, coaches, businessmen, social workers, clergymen, professional soldiers, lawyers, morticians, and, indeed, a few who live well without known sources of income. This is the black middle class, in which family incomes run from $15,000 to $50,000 a year. It can be found in any urban center of 150,000 people or more, especially in the South, the East, and the Great Lakes cities, and on the West Coast.

As is the case for the middle classes everywhere, the habits of life that brought these people success may be described as low-risk. These people are prudent. And their habits of life are incompatible with the spirit of revolution. They made it on safe bets, hard work, self-confidence, skillful manipulation, and brutal competitiveness. It will not be easy to get them to gamble their status on a program based on political theories and social hypotheses.

They own their homes, pay their taxes, support their families, educate their children, attend church, vote, support good causes, and keep good credit. At best they constitute a social threat to those whites who wonder how long they can perpetuate a black stereotype if this crowd swells. At worst they fail to involve themselves fully enough in the movement to alter institutional life in America so that thousands of blacks, who are far worse off than they, may enjoy an increasingly better standard of living.

One of the saddest commentaries on the black experience is the conversation among educated middle class blacks as they assess their present image in relation to the leaders of the vocal black militant movement. They congregate in paneled recreation rooms, in motel suites, in corners of formal downtown hotel ballrooms, and quiz each other on their posture vis-à-vis the black revolution. They nod in assent to those simplistic propositions that promise a continuation of their status undisturbed.

They get tight-jawed about programs that threaten to leave them unemployed, incarcerated, or otherwise separated from the flow of "goodies" to which they feel entitled. They feel that they have "beaten the system" and that their patterns of operation should be emulated by the young. They deplore the way the press celebrates activists who call for the hastening of major changes, the iconoclastic destruction of old institutions and customs, and the consequent displacement of the black middle class.

If these men and women felt guilty that would be one thing, but their awareness of their own life histories absolves them of guilt feelings. They have no notion at all that their behavior is remiss in any way. They see no relationship between their style of life and the causes of poverty, ignorance, hunger, and disease among the black masses. As a matter of fact, they are more inclined to indict those who call for the sudden reordering of the society as dreamers, hustlers, cranks, and psychotics.

It is this reality that denies power and momentum to the black revolution, that leaves it sputtering and groaning with fresh starts and, really, without the spread and depth of disciplined leadership. Like many college football games, the teams have shallow benches, because the beef, speed, and endurance are in the stands.

How, then, and on what terms can this depth of talent, discipline, intellect, and means be reappropriated and placed at the disposal of serious and sustained drives for basic and enduring social, political, and economic change?

Involvement and Utilization of the Middle Class

There is really no way for the black community to consolidate its gains or to alter permanently its status in America if the pressures upon it have the effect of hopelessly dividing its talented, resourceful, and enterprising elite from the masses who bear the burden of poverty and low self-esteem. The young, the college students, the unemployed, and the poor are unable to effectuate a thrust to erase racism and injustice against an entrenched, powerful majority that is indifferent to change; these groups of blacks cannot absorb the casualties and the penalties concomitant to success in such a struggle. There must be found a strategy that will make it possible for the black middle class possessors of brains, money, energy, and discipline to selflessly identify their interests with those of the black lower classes.

It is simply not true that middle-class blacks do not know and feel racism. They can rap with the best on what needs to happen in America. They are not stupid. They make no mistake about the depth and pervasiveness of injustice in our society. The question is one of strategy and tactics.

Moreover, the young militants may have written off the black middle class too soon. They may not be as impervious, as indifferent, as callous, as their present posture may suggest. Given the picture as presented, their deeper involvement may not be precluded. There is evidence that when openings appear that are compatible with their approaches, they do rally and move in. There is even more evidence that more openings need to be found that can call forth their style of effort.

The confrontations with the establishment that the grass-roots leadership frequently calls for often require the involvement of the better trained and career oriented black from the middle class to follow through and make a temporary success a long-term gain. Take the community health services centers sponsored by the federal antipoverty program. This program alone promises to raise the standard of medical care in the black ghettos. At one of these centers in the deep South the big problem was ophthalmology. A shortage of experts exists in this field. Black people need to see. Expensive eye specialists are not available to clinics for the poor. But out of Meharry Medical College came one young man with a specialty in ophthalmology, ready and available and black. In other words, when the rhetoric of the revolution is reduced to deeds, orators need technicians to follow through. And this manpower pool is in the reservoir of the middle class.

Class Divisions and Black Progress

Another important aspect of the talented, successful black

middle class is its intellectual resourcefulness. Because it is largely a product of the ghetto and the rural South, it is very familiar with the needs of black people. One of the principal criticisms of the black middle class is that its program is too slow, too deliberative, and too individualistic. It is alleged that it is shot through with apathy, cowardice or both. But the black middle class is not quite that naive. It does not purport to have a program. It has only a survival strategy. Middle-class blacks looked up a long time ago and found injustice and racism rampant and due process of law applicable only to whites; the state police and the county sheriff were aligned against them, and they concluded that open confrontation with the system was futile. Peaceful protests like the sit-ins and the marches they could, and did, support, because they felt them to be timely and viable options. But the idea of a blood bath looked like genocide. They rejected it. And the rhetoric that left them with a narrowing of choices they rejected as well. This rejection is, and was, no program. It was a survival strategy.

The attitude of the middle class has not been understood by the young militants, because they have interpreted it as a refusal to do anything at all. There is a caricature of the middle-class black which is extant but which the middle-class black does not recognize at all. Similarly, most middle-class blacks cannot find themselves in E. Franklin Frazier's work. They don't know who those poker-playing black women are, and have never been to a social function where anyone "passed out." The black college president, perhaps, has been the most conspicuous target of criticism. Frazier drags him over the coals. The young blacks remember him as a "stone" Tom. Who is he, anyway, and what does he do?

He stands between the black youth and a faculty rejected largely by the white academic structure, on the one hand, and the white business and political leadership, on the other, seeking funds to accomplish among blacks what neither the politicians nor the individual leaders really want to see accomplished. How can he win? By the time he states his case palatably enough for the politicians and the magnates, he has ruined it for black youth. And vice versa. But what does he do beyond sweating out this ambiguous role? He continues to recruit, train, and send on 500 to 1,000 black students a year per campus, vaulting many of them out of the pit of poverty in the rural South or the urban slums of the North to meaningful, fulfilling careers in all directions, placing them in new income brackets, and, whether branding them as middle class or not, making it possible for them to break free from the filth, the indignities, the degradation that accompanied their early life. These presidents have enjoyed a little honor and prestige, but only a few of them have deserved the slanderous criticisms that have been heaped upon them. Following one such president around, an observer would note that time after time, in city after city, a person came up and thanked him for finding him a scholarship, squeezing another job out of the budget, making calls for this or that job or graduate assistantship.

The gap that is alleged to exist between the black masses and the "bourgeoisie" is largely a myth and a lazy description of a complicated phenomenon. Many of the black bourgeoisie are first-generation urban dwellers, a bachelor's degree away from squalor, welfare, and the whole bit. Very few black families were well off enough in the twenties to be more than two generations deep in the middle class. And before the twenties, forget it.

This real proximity to the ghetto and the farm means that it is a fiction that the middle-class black is insulated from the problems, the attitudes, the needs, and the hungers of his black brothers. But the American class structure, the media, and the messiahs operate as insulating agents. However, the wall is thin indeed, and it takes little effort on the part of the middle-class black to get cheek to cheek with his less affluent brothers. Indeed it is imperative that he should, because it is his skill and savvy that are needed.

When an Urban Coalition program gets going in a large metropolis, who is better prepared to deal with the planning, the management, the strategy-ing than one who has the training and the peripheral vision of the black who has traveled the whole distance from brutal poverty to a decent level of literacy and sufficiency? He needs to pay his dues, and a way must be found to co-opt him.

When Virginia blacks began to get their "thing" together and to put some blacks on the city councils and in the legislature, the ones who were ready included young Henry Marsh in Richmond, a lawyer married to a dentist who is a physician's daughter and whose sister teaches medicine at Howard University. When the Racine, Wisconsin, blacks wanted a candidate there was Jack Bryant, a dentist, with two sisters married to dentists and another married to a corporation lawyer. Again, in the Virginia legislature we find Ferguson Reid, a board-certified surgeon whose brother is a dentist, and Bill Robinson, Ph.D., whose mother was for years secretary to Howard's president, Mordecai Johnson. In Washington, D.C., Channing Phillips, in 1971 a candidate for Congress from the District, is the mover—his father holds three degrees, his three brothers hold two degrees each, his sister is married to a man holding two degrees, and he is matched by Walter Fauntroy, holding a Yale graduate degree. Doug Wilder in the Virginia senate holds two degrees; Jesse Jackson, Leon Sullivan, and Wyatt T. Walker, three men actively engaged in programs of service to black communities, are all expert in several areas. Wyatt Walker was reared in a parsonage. He is not bad at chemistry, music, golf, and carpentry. Gifted and tough. Leon Sullivan was a West Virginia State College basketball ace, and Jesse Jackson was quarterback and president of the student government at North Carolina A and T State University. Mayor Kenneth Gibson of Newark is a product of the ghetto who went to night school for eight years for an engineering degree; another mayor of a New Jersey city, Matthew G. Carter of Montclair, worked his way through every inch of two degrees at Virginia Union University. This is the stuff of which the black middle class is made. These men are not spineless Toms. They are courageous and involved. Others are likewise, in less conspicuous ways. And there is a deep stratum of such talent waiting to be unearthed. It is folly for the young blacks to allow the press and the class structures in America to divide the blacks down the middle at the end of their first century out of slavery and chase the black strivers into a safe corner of middle-class comfort, leaving the black talent pool decimated and fragmented in a time of great opportunity.

The whites are often busy at the mischievous game of grading blacks "conservatives," "moderates," "activists," and "radicals." These tricks serve to scatter black strength and divide black power into controllable proportions. Whatever may be the agony and the pain of compromise, the black middle class has a role in the process of change, and a polarization in the black community is simply the cause of delay.

No black was more middle class than Martin Luther King, Jr. Yet no black was more sensitive to the needs of black America. And, as is the main point of this essay, no black has brought more talent to bear on the problem than did King. When Adam Clayton Powell was in his prime, he, too, brought from a middle-class background (Colgate University!) the same measure of talent and concern.

Let's face it, there are places where we need blacks that can be filled only with blacks who may be classified as middle class. The Westinghouse Broadcasting Company has several all-news stations with powerful outlets reaching millions on highways and in kitchens, where radios stay on. Simeon Booker and Carl Rowan are among their commentators. Knowing them both, one would conclude only that here again are middle-class blacks "doing their thing," not merely by being middle-class achievers, but by investing their talents where they were needed!

The Ford Foundation has recently "darkened" its staff and board. There were some "rams in the bush" ready. Sam Cook, Ph.D. in political science and professor at Duke University, was black and ready for a tough staff slot. Vivian Henderson, a Ph.D. in economics whose brother is vice-president of North Carolina Mutual (middle class!), was ready for Ford's board.

The revolution is not here yet. But until the details are clearer, one basic need is to harness the power of the middle-

288

class black and find a place for this power in the black struggle. The antithesis is to continue to set the tone of the rhetoric of revolution at a high pitch, to continue the name-calling and the gullible acceptance of simplistic class labels, and to allow the middle-class black to drift off, frustrated and torn, because he cannot find his role.

The Economic System, Race, and Education

Let us face the fact that much of the contempt that the young militant holds for the black middle class is a part of his contempt for the economic system that operates to benefit the few so bountifully and deprive the many so cruelly. It is the extent to which the black middle class has been co-opted by the system that the young militant finds hard to take. He also finds the system hard to take because it is designed for such materialistic goals.

In other words, there is an American middle class that lives well. It is buttressed by the system that allows the weak to be crushed and to go without advocacy. The middle class has effective representation at the council tables, but the poor are scattered, leaderless, and defenseless. Much of the student left is a direct result of students' awareness of this cruelty. Bad housing at high costs, higher prescription fees, higher auto insurance premiums, higher interest rates, cheap clothes at high prices, neighborhoods overrun with dope and prostitution and victimized by weak law enforcement, poor legal defense, and the worst public services and consumer protection—all these are the lot of the poor. This goes on and on. Instead of good politics correcting these conditions, a kind of tacit understanding prevails that everybody who is fit will escape this bottom and leave it as is.

Therefore, the young black sees his middle-class brother as having left the bottom himself but left it unchanged. And the very nature of the system dictates that not everyone can leave the bottom. So, let us repeat, this business of one black success after another in a slow procession is no solution. But lacking the emergence of an immediate change, by violence or otherwise, let the blacks who have escaped become more than ornaments and self-indulgent creatures of comfort. Let them get involved and continue the search for ways of modifying the society so that the bottom can change faster than now appears to be the case.

The black community is divided critically because the class divisions in America are clear and rigid. The middle class tends to get better and better at guaranteeing its status and guarding its boundaries. Thus, any black who crosses over and gets the label "middle class" is regarded as an enemy, ipso facto, and no ally of the black masses.

This is all bad. Blackness is another issue entirely apart from class in America. No matter how affluent, educated, and mobile one becomes, his race defines him more particularly than anything else. Black people, therefore, have a common cause that requires attending to, and this course does not allow for the rigid class separation that is the luxury of the American whites. There is a sense in which every black man is as far from liberation as the weakest one if his weakness is attributable to racial injustice.

The whole problem is aggravated by the grudging manner in which advantages are distributed in America. If the achievements of some blacks seemed to be within reach of most, that would be one thing. But advantages are grudgingly shared in America. Observe the fact that the most reactionary elements in the society are those immigrants from small Balkan countries whose citizenship is young and whose status in America is most tenuous.

Because it is so tough to "get ahead in life," those who do so are fearful of sharing their advantages. School integration in the South is so hard to accomplish because whites know that blacks can and will learn, that they have a hunger for something more than wine and watermelon, and that they will seek positions of power and influence if they get better starts in school. The southern whites know that there is high risk in leveling out opportunity. It means a more equitable division of the social "goodies" sooner or later. It will be tantamount to revolution without a shot fired.

Young blacks are unimpressed with the size and influence

of the black middle class because the system guards the middle class so securely that it is hard for whites and harder for blacks to change status.

Higher education must assume a major responsibility for correcting this unfair distribution of advantages. Since a plan for complete social change may not be readily implementable, the path of change may have to be one of escalating the upward mobility of as many persons as we can in the present system and counting on them to humanize it; we will have to call upon the universities to be more vigorous than they have been in broadening opportunity.

In a technological society, formal education turns out to be the most effective lever for lifting one out of the bottom. It works fast and its effect is hard to reverse. One is given not only skill and certification, but there is implanted within him a contempt for poverty, a built-in resistance to parasitic dependency upon public largesse, and an insatiable appetite for all those physical and aesthetic benefits that give him control over his destiny.

Education, therefore, becomes more than a conduit for culture; it becomes a powerful intervention agent for the alteration of the culture. As far as the black community is concerned, education has to be far more of the latter than the former—an agent of change rather than a lacquer.

Higher education bears the heavier burden because, in addition to preparing other professionals, it prepares the professional teachers, the molders of the young, the shapers of the future. How and where are the shapers shaped and the molders molded? Universities have a critical role at the very cutting edge of the problem of race. This means more than equalizing opportunity—it means equalizing results, doing what's necessary not only to *admit more black medical students* but to *produce more black surgeons*; it means more than opening up admissions—it means opening up the campus, the minds of department heads, and the attitudes of dorm directors, coaches, curriculum planners, and policy makers.

Within the past four years, since Upward Bound, the previously all-white schools have expanded black enrollment.

And the first thing they found out was that blacks would not be attached as unwanted appendages, but insisted on *more* black students. These mostly-white schools were cold and inhospitable. The black students demanded more than token black faculty and administrators, and they wanted a curriculum revision that would reflect the black experience from Timbuktu in the fourteenth century to Harlem in the twentieth.

It took the blacks no time to discover that a merely perfunctory admission to four years of role-playing would leave them with a weaker self-image, a schizoid approach to life, and an empty status symbol. They screamed out for change, and they got a great deal of it. They are not satisfied, however, because even a great deal of change does not meet the real need. No one really knows where all of this will lead, for nowhere else in the wide world are so many blacks and whites living in such proximity, with similar goals and objectives, and over so long a period with presumed equality as is the case on the newly desegregated American campuses. This is brand-new.

One may speculate that it may sensitize the whites to black needs, but a prophecy more to the point is that while this doubtless will happen, thousands more blacks every year will enter the fields of engineering, finance, the fine arts, political science, and government, thus finding places in the machinery of government and business that have heretofore been devoid of black faces. These graduates are going to go somewhere. Many say they are going back to the ghetto. And they will. But the ghetto has limited capacity to absorb these new redeemers, however well intentioned they may be. Where will they go? They will follow their white classmates into good jobs and join the middle class.

The issue is this: will they take on the snobbishness and the callousness of the middle class, or will they join the movement to alter conditions for the less fortunate blacks? Will the movement make a place for them and give them a chance to "do their thing" and "pay their dues"?

One or two moral issues surround the needed transformation of the white schools and the consequent enlargement of the black middle class. Where are the black teachers and administrators coming from? At the moment they are being taken from black colleges, even though black colleges have just as much of a challenge to face as they did a century ago. They are overflowing. More blacks are finishing high school, and a higher percentage have found out that the revolution is not going to happen tomorrow. They have found out also that the revolution may have to take a different style in urban, technological America; it may be smarter to be a computer programmer than a hurler of Molotov cocktails. So black colleges are bulging, while white schools are taking their faculty.

The answer to this dilemma lies in two directions. First, the black schools will have to use more white faculty. During these days of struggle for black identity and racial pride, they may serve best in fields other than the social sciences and the humanities; but the black college teaching pool will have to be expanded among whites if the white schools are going to raid black college faculties.

Second, any white school that employs top blacks on its faculty is obligated to reproduce tenfold the supply of black students who might have been the progeny of these faculty members had they remained at a Fisk University, a Morehouse College, or a Virginia Union University.

This is called a moral issue because it is: it has to do with fairness, justice, and choice.

Another issue that may seem to be purely intellectual, but is also moral, is the following: should black students be allowed to demand the substitution of black courses for other general-education courses? They should. The literature and the history of the West need not be totally supplanted. This is important to black Americans. But until they are retold in more broadly inclusive terms—"told like it is," including the black and the brown and the red and the yellow stories as well as the white, accentuating the true human sojourn rather than the story of European Christendom—there will be a need for substitute courses. European Christendom sponsored slavery and the colonizing of Asia, Africa, and Latin America. The glorification of this tradition is too much for the black students to swallow. Until the humanities have been revised, these students deserve well-articulated, well-planned, well-taught black studies.

The middle class black ranks are likely to expand, and it would be disastrous if this meant the widening of the chasms in the black community. The solidification of a snobbish, indifferent black middle class would be one of the worst ironies of history. One of the most gratifying novelties in history would be the emergence of a sensitive, creative black avant-garde sophisticated enough to know that their freedom is a farce until their brothers are free.

Cultural spokesmen for two generations: *Left,* Imamu Amiri Baraka (LeRoi Jones), contemporary poet, playwright, and novelist. *Below,* Langston Hughes, poet, playwright, and novelist of the Harlem Renaissance.

(Wide World Photos; The Schomburg Collection, New York Public Library)

Left, Reginald Gammon, "Hommage to Henry O. Tanner, Painter," acrylic on board.

Below, Benny Andrews, "Dinnertime" (1965), oil.

(Museum of the National Center of Afro-American Artists, photo by Doug Harris; courtesy of the artist)

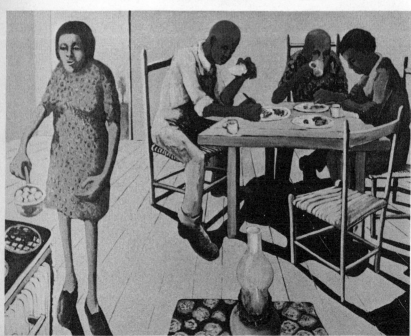

Lloyd Toone, "Life," collage.
(Courtesy of the artist)

294c

Right, James Denmark, "The Struggle" (1969), wood. *Below,* Bill Rivers, "Eclipse," oil on canvas.

(Museum of the National Center of Afro-American Artists, photos by Doug Harris)

17

JAMES DENMARK

Black Artists
in the
United States

Time and the ocean separate black people from their gifted ancestry. The dark era of the slave trade brought many people from the continent of Africa to the United States of America, separating them for centuries from their true identity and cultural heritage.

The black people who were brought to this continent as slaves had among them many who had been particularly gifted in Africa. However, in this country they found themselves at the mercy of ruthless slave traders, flesh-value-orientated slave dealers, and in most instances cruel masters. This, along with the forced dissolution of traditional family and tribal life, as well as the hard-faced day-by-day realities of slavery, debilitated, distorted, and in many ways stalemated the natural vitality and inherited creative forces that had developed and flourished among the black peoples of Africa for many centuries.

The complete oppression of black people by the slave masters and plantation owners left them little time to exploit their natural abilities. Under this oppression, and in this state of almost subhuman existence, along with being assigned backbreaking labor and every type of domestic service, black people found that the natural life style they had brought to this country was severely altered. They were not able to cultivate many of the artistic gifts that they had inherited. However, they could sing while doing their daily chores, while picking cotton, while acting as servants. The particular kind of music they enjoyed and invented was a music that was deeply spiritual, a music of hope and of looking to freedom. This music was charged with a dramatic spirit and dynamic force that is found today in rock and roll, in the blues, and in jazz. It is well known that the early forms of it developed into some of America's most creative and original music.

Without time to sculpt, without time to paint, without time to practice free expression in many art forms, black people did find another artistic outlet in the form of craftsmanship. Carved tools, furniture, metalwork, and pottery were some of the items created. In the area of New Orleans there was a concentration of master blacksmiths, men who were gifted at working in metal. They could take an idea from a patron and create masterworks in wrought iron and steel. Some of the works of these early black artisans survived the Civil War and are now the property of the Museum of Modern Art in New York City and the National Gallery of Art in Washington, D.C.

After the Civil War, there appeared many free black artists who earned their livings at other jobs while painting and sculpting in their spare time. The most notable achievements were those of Robert M. Douglas, Jr., and David Bustill Bowers. Both Douglas and Bowers earned livings as sign painters in Philadelphia during the 1800s. They both achieved recognition as artists of merit.

The first black artist to gain wide notice as a result of exhibitions and prizes won was Edward M. Bannister. Bannister was born in Nova Scotia in 1828. He exhibited regularly around Boston and won a prize for his painting "Under the Oaks" at the centennial exposition of 1876 in Philadelphia.

The economic security achieved by a number of black artists of this period who successfully struggled for recognition was overshadowed by social conditions in this country and by the feeble economic structure of the artists' own communities. There were also other barriers that had to be faced. One was the need for formal training and an environment that would allow for the freedom and ease of living that most artists find necessary for a productive and creative life. The alternatives were few. Many black artists exploited the advantages of being considered exceptions to their people and lived outside of their communities, while others chose exile, going to live and work abroad. Some of those who did so included Edmonia Lewis, Robert Duncanson, Meta Warrick Fuller, and Henry O. Tanner. Tanner is perhaps the most famous of this group and, indeed, of the black artists of his period. Henry O. Tanner was born in Pittsburgh in 1859, the son of a Methodist bishop. He studied at the Pennsylvania Academy of the Fine Arts, where Thomas Eakins was one of his instructors. After graduation Tanner took a job at Clark University in Atlanta, Georgia. He worked there for several years and then left for Paris to study further. After living and studying in Paris for some time, he journeyed to Palestine. This journey inspired a series of paintings based on biblical themes, which brought Tanner international acclaim. One of them, "Resurrection of Lazarus," was purchased by the French government for the Luxembourg Gallery collection.

Tanner's most important works, including those which comprise this famous biblical series, remain for the most part in European museums and collections. The Chicago Art Institute collection and the Grand Central Art Galleries in New York City also contain some of his work.

After this period of exodus there appeared on the scene a group of artists who decided to remain in the United States, and they painted largely in the tradition of other American artists. This group included William A. Harper, Édouard Scott, Edward Harleston, Archibald Motley, and Laura Wheeling Waring. Some of them succeeded in gaining general recognition, in having their work included in art exhibitions and galleries along with that of white artists.

This group was followed by still another wave of black artists, who formed, for the first time, a major creative force. During the 1920s and the early 1930s we experienced the era known as the Negro Renaissance. This renaissance was centered around Harlem, reflecting a new awareness of, and need for, a definition of black culture. Countee Cullen, Langston Hughes, and other noted poets contributed to this development. Among the best known artists of the period were Charles Alston, Eldzier Cortor, Allen Freelon, Earnest Chrichlow, Malvin Gray Johnson, William H. Johnson, Hale Woodruff, Georgette Seabrook, Norman Lewis, Romare Bearden, Horace Pippin, Hughie Lee Smith, Jacob Lawrence, and Charles White. Almost all of these artists have been represented by major galleries and have their works in the major museums and important collections of this country.

There are other men who are outstanding as artists and yet play a vital role as art professors and teachers in colleges and public schools: Jimmy Mosley, at Maryland State College; Hale Woodruff, at Atlanta University and New York University; James Porter, at Howard University; James Lewis, at Morgan State College; Howard E. Lewis, at Florida A & M University; Gregory Ridley, at Tennessee A & I State University; Hayward Oubre, at Alabama State College; Harper Phillips, at Bergen Community College. These artists have aided immensely in the development and encouragement of the careers of a considerable number of those who are now in the center of the "Black Arts movement."

After the period of the Negro Renaissance, there was a great interruption in artistic development and recognition. Political, social, and economic conditions in this country caused black artists to break their stride. But today we find another renaissance, a black renaissance.

Though the direction of today's Black Arts movement disperses into many forms of creative expression, there are evident in many works traces of a rich African heritage. For instance, many of today's artists are revealing as never before, and with very strong convictions, the expressive power of true "Blackness." Many are dealing with subject matter and expressive forms powerfully related to the black experience. In this group, Harper Phillips and Gregory Ridley have painted very strong neoprimitive forms that emerge and disappear in spaces of color and abstraction. Others like Robert Carter, Reginald Gammon, Lloyd Toone, Faith Ringgold, and Vincent Smith strike with compelling force at the political, social, economic, and cultural issues of today. Benny Andrews, Russ Thompson, and the late Bob Thompson reveal in their works the unique ability to express the commonly unseen and subconscious realities of the black experience.

In some of the nonrepresentational work, such as that done by Tom Lloyd, artists are able to convey a place and time by simply dealing with objects, forms, and colors. Their works frequently provoke a feeling of city life, a feeling of the bombardment of the design by their use of posters, billboards, debris, and the environment of the ghetto. Place and time may be as dramatically represented in such works as are figures or persons in others.

In Reginald Gammon's painting of the late Malcolm X we see a very powerful way of representing a person. Mr. Gammon does a very, very striking, very, very dramatic painting of a man who was a prophet for black people. We notice that distortions are used around the nose, the forehead, and the lip area to convey all of the intensity, all of the strong

belief and intentions, of a person who believed in an important social philosophy of the times. The artist, Mr. Gammon,
is currently artist-in-residence at Western Michigan University, and his paintings are beginning to win critical acclaim.

Indeed, a number of black artists are experiencing a wide
range of acceptance and are being included in national and
international exhibitions. Collectors and corporate buyers
are seeking their work. Major museums are including more
black artists in their exhibitions and at the same time are
considering their work in the category of important pur-
chases. Notable among the black artists who are achieving
wide recognition and who are having their work extensively
shown are: Richard Hunt, Sam Gilliam, Romare Bearden, Alvin D. Loving, Jr., Charles White, Tom Lloyd, Faith
Ringgold, Daniel L. Johnson, Joseph Overstreet, Raymond
Saunders, Lynn Bowers, and Benny Andrews. In spring 1971
the Whitney Museum of American Art presented a major
show of contemporary art by black artists, and at approximately the same time the Museum of Contemporary Art in
Geneva gave a similar exhibition. The spring 1970 presentation of the work of black artists at the Boston Museum of
Fine Arts received widespread attention. So black artists
are finally beginning to feel rewarded and respected both
by their own people and by the society in which they live.

Today we find many black artists still going abroad, not
now to escape, but to go back to the Motherland, to go back
to Africa. They are going back to try to bridge, somehow,
that time gap; to try to reinforce and regenerate the creative power that was lost by time, by slavery, by the breaking
up of families, by the breaking up of groups. As I talk to
these artists, I find that they have great belief in how much
there is to be done in the area of fine arts by black artists.
I think that we are going to see in the near future a whole
renaissance of painting, of sculpture, of interest in the arts,
not only by this nation, but by the world. As a result of
changing economic conditions, as a result of new programs
and new attitudes, artists are finding time to do things, find-

ing time to express themselves, finding time to cultivate a lost culture. Journeys to Africa tend to bring a new dynamic to the home front, a new awareness. The various programs by museums that I mentioned are giving courage to the lost generation of artists who had no place to go, no place to show. They are now working, producing, coming to the forefront with great, fresh, and exciting new ideas. Those of us actively participating in today's Black Arts movement are enthusiastic about the future.

SOURCES

"The Black Artist in America: A Symposium," *The Metropolitan Museum of Art Bulletin,* vol. XXVII, no. 5, January 1969.

DOVER, CEDRIC, *American Negro Art.* New York, Graphic Society, 1960.

LOCKE, ALAIN, *Negro Art Past and Present.* Washington, D.C., Associates in Negro Folk Education, 1936.

———*The Negro in Art.* Washington, D.C., Associates in Negro Folk Education, 1940.

Negro Artists: An Illustrated View of Their Achievements. New York, Harmon Foundation, Inc.

PORTER, JAMES A., *Modern Negro Art.* New York, Dryden Press, 1943.

18

FRANK BOWLING

Is Black Art
About Color?

The pressure of cultural nationalism on a global drift has given rise in the United States to a passionate, confused, but fashionable black nationalism, and with it a justified if shrill cry for cultural distinctiveness. The dilemma of adequately defining differences and giving them concrete form in aesthetic terms cannot be overstated, and is formidable due to confusion, urgency, and historical nearness. Objectivity about art is always a tall order, but a vested interest by whites and blacks in black art deepens the situation to near opacity. In any attempt to shed a little light on the sweeping generalizations about cultural distinctiveness that are currently being disseminated, such generalizations and the positions taken by their proponents must be seen for what they are: sincere attempts to define blackness, but not within the context of sculpture and painting. The question still is, Is black art to be appraised for its blackness or its artistic merit?

Most of the noises being made about black art sound, on the first few hearings, completely concerned with the *conception,* not the actual delivery *(the actuality!)* of a positively articulated object, set of objects, or thing. Such concern with intent begins to run contrary to the criterion, the accustomed yardstick which aesthetic judgment demands broadly and which such disciplines as painting and sculpture inherently need particularly. The heart of the matter seems ultimately to rest on the irony that what is being called for in such disciplines as painting and sculpture is, at bottom, really a set of ideal potentialities whose true model of being is purely semantic. It exists, if at all, only in principle, and is therefore waiting for an ideal interpretant.

We begin to run into more difficulty when we recognize that in recent years the standards—artistic standards, to be sure—applied to works being touted under the black label in black shows have disintegrated. That the black shows have, for the most part, been disheartening, dishonest, and questionable, has been seen not only by white critics and mixed audiences, but also by the black artists and their interested black supporters. In fairness it should be stressed that the white critics have been accused, justly or not, with prejudice, lack of equipment, and lack of any clear understanding of the issues involved, and, therefore, of being incapable of unbiased critical assessments. If the people who held the positions of ultimate arbiters and who have long resisted black participation now do exhibit the work of black artists, they do so with the burden of uncertainty.

A Comparative Perspective
on the Problem of Standards

The situation touches on more than we must necessarily confine ourselves to. Consider, for example, some statements from *Writing in England Today,* an anthology put together by Karl Miller, the current editor of *The Listener,* the official journal of the British Broadcasting Corporation, and the erstwhile literary editor of both *The New Statesman* and *The Spectator,* considered the most influential organs of the left and right wing of British politics, in that order. In his introduction to this anthology Miller writes that his book is "less an attempt to show the best pieces and the best people than to offer something like a corporate description or evocation. . . . It seemed right that Commonwealth fiction should be represented." "All over the world," he goes on to say, "writers have been reared in the *tradition of English literature* and it looks as if their hour has come. [Italics are mine.]"

There are a few very positive and significant reasons for our touching upon Miller's drift. In the first place, it seems that in this debonair, catholic broadside of an introduction, Miller adopts (perhaps it would be better to say echoes) very much the establishment attitude of giving "black endeavor" an "airing." That Miller is fortunate in having such a convenient term as "Commonwealth" (as a euphemism to include nonwhites) should not blind us to how meaningless this term is on close scrutiny. The situation in the United Kingdom in Miller's opinion, calls forth "less an attempt to show the best . . . than . . . a corporate description or evocation." Or to put it another way, perhaps a trifle more extreme, what this statement actually amounts to is: let us first, not only accept at last that they are one of us, but second, lower our standards to accommodate them.

That this attitude is extant to a very large degree here in the United States hardly needs underlining. What is painful, though, and frustrating to a degree, is the ever widening and distorted curves of the circles as larger and larger pebbles —now rocks—are dropped into the pool. The increased *quantity* of works by black artists seems to do little more than compound the demonstrable irony inherent in the contradictory attitudes in this lust for accommodation. That the works may not have true and valuable distinctiveness, which can only be substantiated by *quality,* is something which constantly worries black people—artists and others. The question in short is, By what absolute standards are these works being measured?

The difficulty encountered when trying to answer this question can perhaps be seen in greater definition if we pursue Miller's volume a little closer, but without too much specifying, for it is not my intention to hold up Miller's book as a racist tract. That it might be so is not incumbent upon me to prove; my task is to point up confusion—possibly my own.

Since none of the pieces in this anthology are dated later than 1966, one can assume that by the mid-sixties Miller (who is, incidentally, a Scotsman) and people like him were already aware of far-reaching ethnic differences in the corporate body of English expression. In fact, at about the same time certain wheels must have set into motion the now notorious, nation-shaking event at the Metropolitan Museum of Art, the "Harlem on My Mind" exhibition. Too much has been written about that misguided fiasco for me to add to it here, but it is a landmark in that it was the introduction to —perhaps it would be more accurate to say "the first brush" with—the official establishment for many a black artist. (See Benny Andrews in *Arts,* Summer 1970.) The editor of the exhibit's catalog included a quite distinctly racist declaration by a black high school girl, and this, like the wholesale giving in to black nationalist pressure, was unprecedented.

For anyone interested in the history and politics of the present situation, the difference in the British and the American attitudes on accommodation due to recognizing ethnic differences would seem quite clear. But their point of collaboration, on what is good for and meaningful to the present consciousness of ethnic difference, is misleading. Hence, they are of great importance to the present essay. The Miller book and the catalog are not equal. For our purpose, where they converge is on touching this common cultural dilemma and in the attitude which informs them: Establishment. If we argue on Establishment terms, then Miller's book is something of a success, and the exhibition and its catalog was a relative disaster. The arbitrary choice of these works (and the other choices that follow) is only permissible in that what we are discussing is education, and not essentially the individual books or attitudes. For this reason we can compare Miller's attitude and the Metropolitan's. On the one hand Miller reveals himself as an old-fashioned pedagogue, while the exhibition and its catalog was a wrong-headed attempt at public education from a contemporary point of view.

Included in Miller's book is an essay by Frank Kermode discussing William Golding's novels, in which Kermode says, "the best course for sympathetic critics is to be a shade more explicit, to do what the novelist himself perhaps cannot do without injury to the books, which grow according to imaginative laws and cannot be adjusted to the extravagant needs of readers." If this is true for books, it is even more so for works of painting and sculpture. In discussing black art, it is therefore necessary to try avoiding what is potentially misleading and to "be a shade more explicit."

White America has been seen to be historically racist, and black endeavor is about to suffer from overexposure, bringing in its wake, I suggest, much the same criteria by which this art has always been judged; the criteria of racism. Because the British do not have to deal with cultural differences on a strictly one-to-one, black-white basis, tokenism is rampant. For example, no critic who says Victor Naipaul (who is included in Miller's anthology) is an important modern writer can think that literature should embody contemporary life in terms of both form and content. These critics cannot understand the writer's drive to reshape the world (a world found pretty rotten) in his own image within the context of his given discipline. What, in fact, they are concerned with are National Morals and the upholding of these morals by clearly described, if old, often mothball-covered axioms, such as "the Englishness of an English writer."

It is perhaps proper to restate at this point a belief that the urgency to define "black," and hence to lay bare, to articulate the passionate essence throbbing therein, is not strictly an American phenomenon. It is quite simply that historically this task fell to us, and that socially, economically, and hence politically we are, if anybody, best placed to deal with what, after all, has been described as the only relevant problem of the twentieth century. At the same time the discussion, with its emphasis on education, will have to be centered on the United States, however much the concerns are global.

The following observations are essentially part of a continuing dialogue brought about by the prevailing pressures, fascination with, and committed interest in art done by black people. Hannah Arendt (whose essay "Reflections on Violence" is uppermost in my thoughts and must influence this work in more ways than I can acknowledge) has written:

> The danger of being carried away by the deceptive plausibility of organic metaphors is particularly great where the racial issue is involved. Racism white or black . . . objects to natural organic facts—a white or black skin—which no persuasion or power could change; all one can do, when the chips are down, is to exterminate their bearers.

It follows that any discussion within this context would be indulging in the contemporary rhetoric of violence and would be relevant only because it is the fashion.

The Distinctiveness of Black Art

Dealing with black art is a bridge-building process. As a painter, one soon discovers that art comes out of and feeds off art; thus, much of what is being painted is ancestor worship of one sort or another. This is nothing new to add to what we already know about the traditional African in general and the traditional African artist in particular. In the case of black art, a distinction will just simply have to be taken for granted between what is black now, what was traditional African then, and what is contemporary African

307

now. What has molded the contemporary entity labeled "black" is consistently and irrevocably intertwined with that which has brought about what we now understand as the United States—which simply means that, unlike negritude, blackness finds its energy centers somewhere in the heart of American (Western) society, while trying on the mantles and adjusting to, as well as mainly influencing, the global brotherhood of subject peoples and shared ethnic roots.

It is idle to suggest, as some do, that the black American is (exactly?) like any other man of color. It is a fact that what distinguishes him is, however grudgingly acknowledged, his complex inheritance of more than just his African beginnings in America, and this he shares with few, if any other, national types. Culturally, if the black American is not a Western man, he is not an African man either. He is a new man, the nearest and most culturally rich hybridization of the wheels of eternity. This is perhaps the distinction which blocks the door of full comprehension. But the word "hybridization," though convenient, is highly out of place here. "Black" is a round, total entity. An indisputable fact. This forces one to push past the oversimplification of the identification with just simply skin coloring and to seriously rummage into the philosophical and psychological content of all the influences. The prospect of this is mind-blowing, and the fact that it has probably not been done is another story, but it must not delay us.

The acceptance of inherited ethnic particulars and cultural diversity in the fabric of other disciplines, notably music and dance, is very rarely questioned now; yet the same situation is hardly ever advanced, much less upheld, in the plastic arts. The explanations for this are many-sided. Many say that the continuing bond between the African and the black American was ruptured by slavery, and that the mark-making abilities peculiar to blacks were lost once they came to America. That there is little evidence of a continuing tradition brought from the fatherland might be a consequence of the outrage (slavery), but it is more likely to be a consequence of the scarcity of research done in this area. The second assertion, that the Africans' mark-making abilities were lost on the journey across, is to me patently absurd. The little evidence extant, however, does indicate that a statement such as that made by William T. Williams in the *Metropolitan Museum of Art Bulletin* (January 1969)—"It seems to me that one of the underlying things is that basically we come from a non-visual culture"—is very far from the truth.

It is quite obvious that the education, if not the entire training, of blacks was left in the hands of white people. The numerous books on art, whether traditional African or European, that have come down to us or are now being produced are mainly by white people. A random selection of recent books that have come to my notice includes the Mentor-Unesco Art Books, introduced by William Fagg; *Tradition and Creativity in Tribal Art,* edited by Daniel Biebuyck; *African Art: Its Background and Traditions,* by Rene S. Wassing; *African Sculpture Speaks,* by Ladislas Segy; *Art in Africa,* by Tibor Bodrogi; and, in a different category, *Black Studies in the University,* edited by A. L. Robinson and others, which includes, among other things, Robert Farris Thompson's essay "African Influences on the Art of the United States."

The increasing number of these books, their content, educational value, and the fact that they are all written by white people is a constant source of vexation and fatigue, and one cannot fret away the dilemma. However, the point I want to emphasize is that they vary, and just as well, too, from the really atrocious effort by Mr. Segy to the excellent and scholarly *Tradition and Creativity*. It is legitimate to ask the people who are putting out these books whether they are conscious of, and are dealing with, the problem of what constitutes black art, for it is slippery and perplexing. At the same time, one is encouraged. In an essay in the *New York Review of Books,* one of the contributors to *Tradition and Creativity,* Professor Robert Goldwater, mentions the "collector," among other things (see my article in the spring 1970 issue of *Two Rivers*), and talks at length about acculturation, that is, the influence on the contemporary practicing African artist of the affluent world—broadly speaking, the white world. This business of the "collector" does have enormous bearing on the issue of education. Though the difference between the contemporary African artist and the black artist is an obvious, often cited, and important one, and for our purpose a different discourse, what is of real significance is that the teaching and opportunity for training sources have an equivalent in that they were European-steered (educated). For example, there is the case of Oshogbo, the history of whom is described in Uli Beier's book *Contemporary African Art*. The book shows a really frightful example of well-intentioned European meddling in the education of African artists, to judge from the evidence of the works illustrated in the book. When last heard of, Mr. Beier was off to the South Seas, no doubt to discover more native, unspoiled talent.

That painting and sculpture "grow according to imaginative laws and cannot be adjusted to extravagant needs" is just the point that the warring factions tend to miss, and consequently they try to stretch painting and sculpture to meet such needs. It is accepted that the experience of traditional African works contributed largely to modernism via cubism, surrealism, and other styles. But the reason for the relative lack of contributions, with any distinctive stamp, by the "natural" inheritors—those who, as LeRoi Jones describes them, "finally looked up in some anonymous field and shouted, 'Oh, ahm tired a dis mess, Oh, yes, Ahm so tired a dis mess,'"—is yet to be given. (See this contributor's discussion, "Black Art I and II," in *Arts,* April and May 1969.)

The difference between the African and the Afro-American is what happened when the latter looked up and realized he wasn't going back to Africa. This was traumatic, for "one of the main points of the [Melville] Herskovits book [*The Myth of the Negro Past*] is that most of the attitudes, customs, and cultural characteristics of the American Negro can be traced directly, or indirectly, back to Africa," observes LeRoi Jones in *Blues People*. He adds that this is compounded by the fact that "the African, because of the . . . differences between what was native and what he was forced to in [Western European] slavery, developed some of the most complex and complicated ideas about the world imaginable." Just as all this may go a long way in explaining why the black artist hesitated to take up the talisman of his rightful inheritance (and *Blues People* is as worthy as any account of the spirit of the rerouting), it fails to take the measure of what Black Art there is. Furthermore, the art that has been presented as black art is questionable, more characterized by some of the observations in Miller's foreword and in the Wilder declarations in the exhibit and catalog of "Harlem on My Mind." Or it is presented with basically humanist arguments, which Jones and a lot of other Americans (blacks) advance. Since the publication of *Blues People,* Jones's statement, "The idea that Western thought might be 'exotic' viewed from another landscape never presents itself to most Westerners," has been put in doubt by the publication of a book by Cottie A. Burland called *The Exotic White Man: An Alien in Asian and African Art.* Thus, at this point there is nothing so "mysterious" about the black experience.

I am not for one moment suggesting that the arguments so lucidly and passionately presented in Jones's book are discredited. On the contrary, the muscular prose with which his points are driven home, as with a pneumatic sledgehammer, serves as something of a physically twitching awakening for me with each reading. However, I resist the niggling humanist thread which weaves its way through this work, for I know of no precedent in traditional African expression and no equivalent with which I feel comfortable or admire in black modern literature and painting. In fact, what attracts me to certain examples of Antillean and African expression is a certain irony—even cynicism—and real realism. We mustn't lose sight of the fact that in a sense black art, like any other art, is a posture. Thus, in the polemic marketplace the posture is a postulate to be supported, redefined, restated within its individual and contextual world. It means that what hones and essentially distinguishes black art is the spirit that informs the activity inside its separate and special disciplines. It is completely intrinsic to artistic expression.

Knowledge About the Development of Black Art

The suppression of the inquisitive disposition in blacks born in the New World has never been sufficiently discussed. There is a relative dearth of any mention or suggestion of artistic life in the existing literature. But the blacks' investigation into what would have (*must have*) appeared alien and strange in artistic terms must have been forcing newer art forms and greater or different ranges of expression. Black people went through a process of understanding through what must be described as the *white stages* (alas! for want of a better term with which we could distinguish this essential process of growth) and then on to the development of this new entity *black*. The process must have involved—as with learning the new language and musical instruments—a thorough, unique grasp of all the axioms and issues involved to have climaxed in full-blown expression. Since black people are born to this natural cultural inheritance, the logical conclusion is that the trails left behind lack a thorough investigation. In my recent reading only Robert Farris Thompson has ventured a suggestion of this, and it is largely substantiated by my own limited experience in the South.

This spirit, of its very nature, is hard to define in simple language if one recognizes that one is dealing with nonverbal expression, i.e., painting and sculpture. It may simply be that recent criticism, if such it can be called, has recognized that the various thematic conflicts expressed in black artistic endeavor are remarkably tenacious. However, this criticism has, in general, either emphasized the ingenious and highly complicated manner by which such conflicts finally resolve themselves (by ignoring them) in accomplishment, or has reflected upon the fact that these conflicts are a stock set of attitudes defined (or perhaps "recognized") within a certain intellectual and social history. This is essentially either a refusal or an inability to "define" them. In the final analysis a certain unified *theme* (Historylessness, Rupture, Bondage Neurosis, Outrage, Pride, etc.) is *elucidated,* whose familiarity belies the ferocious intensity that the conflicts generate and from where they arose. These attempts do little more than demonstrate critics' basic arbitrariness.

It is best, therefore, to go back into the familiar to take issue with the techniques or processes which give rise to or articulate the thematic conflicts in order better to bring up whatever distinctions there exist. In this way the matter of ultimate resolution, if not entirely discredited, will, I hope, at least recede.

To go back to Kàrl Miller's anthology: in his introduction he talks a good deal about the 1950s. "They were tired of the international experimental avant-garde . . . mandatory modernity . . . they were democrats . . . 'Exit the hero' . . . they painted themselves battleship grey and were called 'The Movement' . . ." Well, the painters were in uniforms as well. The order of the day was wearing hobnailed boots and overalls, and they were all into "Expression," be it with thick paint or "drawing" with paint straight out of a tube. Miller continues that even though much of " 'The Movement' involved . . . reversions to ordinary speech and moral earnestness . . . not uncommon in English literature . . . the novelty of its programme" was the distinguishing factor. But, as Clement Greenberg says, "novelty as distinct from originality, has no staying power." Exaggeration caused The Movement as such to dissolve in England. There is no near equivalent in the United States of any parallel grouping, but there are sociological connections.

Leaving aside but not forgetting the previously mentioned racist diatribe in the "Harlem on My Mind" catalog, the catalog's heading, "1950–1959," is described as: "Frustration and Ambivalence." While there was an equivalent of this feeling in the intense immigration and buildup in the United Kingdom of black people from the West Indies and other parts of the British Empire, culturally there was a reflection of this black surge, but no recognition of it. Much as Miller can talk about Commonwealth literature having its hour in the 1960s, he cannot be blind to the fact that some of the people active and working during the 1950s were very properly Commonwealth, if that term has any meaning (and I don't think it has). Doris Lessing and Dan Jacobson are southern African and included in the anthology, but I doubt whether, in talking about "Commonwealth literature," Miller had them in mind. The case of Colin MacInnes is pertinent, too. Brought up in Australia, his sense of understanding more than Little England is well-known. However, his novel *City of Spades* (published in 1957) was widely discussed— but not because it was about a *city of spades*.

From all this and more, one is forced to concede that the real consciousness of black distinctiveness ripened in an amorphous past (as reiterated countless times) but actually coalesced, actually took place, during the sixties, in Britain as it did here. This leads me to believe that the arguments surrounding black art are structured somewhat on a framework akin to the conflict between The Movement and modernism—a revolutionary, elusive framework be it so.

Rather than dealing with modernist ideology with its elitist implications, lone-ing it, etc. (the connection between this and the witch-doctor sorcerer figure should not be missed, but must not detain us), there is today's rhetoric of militancy and the more accessible identification with the people. This turns out to be a signal social-climbing device, the perils of which were amply demonstrated by The Movement (but less by their generational equivalent, the Beats). The works and the personalities revealed through their black rhetoric prove grasping and desperately unpleasant.

An Examination of Some Selected Works

In an important essay, "On Expression and Expressionism," published in *Art and Literature* (summer 1964), Richard Wollheim discusses Marion Milner's *On Not Being Able to Paint* and observes:

> . . . to talk of putting a particular feeling or emotion into
> a subject or activity is highly metaphorical: unless . . .
> we take the phrase . . . and use as our criteria for its ap-
> plication the fact that after the x-ing the feeling or
> emotion is no longer experienced [Marion Milner wrote,
> ". . . when the drawing was finished . . . the original
> anger had all vanished."] She put the feeling into a
> picture, as one might a cat in a box.

This last sounds very much like Benny Andrews' rationale
for his painting "The Champion," as published in his letter
to the Sunday *New York Times* of June 21, 1970. This painting had recently been seen in an exhibition at the Boston
Museum of Fine Arts. Wollheim goes on to say: "the phrase
'when the drawing was finished . . . the original anger had
all vanished' obviously has no relevance. . . . Art is not simply
made by discarding life." Obviously, in the case of "The
Champion," the cat jumped out of the box again, for the
work, though painted, has little expressive of paint and does
not investigate the use of paint. The design of this work is
ordinary and does not engage interest, and the papier-mâché-
collage-and-rope turns out to be a moribund brumal-like effort
hailed upon with tactile rhetoric. In fact, it is a sort of
funereal, disengaged journalism.

Further, Wollheim invokes Wittgenstein:

> At one point Wittgenstein asks us if we can imagine
> ourselves using one phrase and meaning another by it
> (e.g., saying "It's cold here" and meaning "It's warm
> here") . . . our explanation would probably take the form
> of alleging that as we say the word "cold" out loud, we
> say the word "warm" to ourselves. [Not even that, I
> venture!] Or that we treat our utterance . . . as though
> it were a slip of the tongue. . . .

Every dweller in the black ghetto (community?), from
junkie to jack-of-all trades, "knows" about these changes.
That is their life style. Says Wollheim:

> We might find here a suggestion as to how the present
> question about the limits of expression is to be answered.
> For it might seem that a man can express y-ness by x-

ing, only if x-ing stands to y-ness in a relation which is, or is analogous to, that of meaning. . . . Marion Milner failed to express her feelings in the Downland landscape . . . failed to because (roughly) the kind of picture she drew does not "mean" peace.

Thus (!!) Benny Andrews.

The case of Danny Johnson, too, is pertinent here. In the foreword to the catalog of his recent exhibition at French and Company, Margit Rowell disclaims any connection between Johnson's sculptures and the form of expression known as minimal art. She claims that "no formal adventures distract the eye." Even though one should not succumb to the temptation to speak of minimal art (the clear implication from Margit Rowell's statement), these painted pillars of wooden statuary could hardly be said to have started out to offer an alternative. These works, if not considered as minimal art, should tempt one into other formal deductions (adventures!) through the eye (distraction!). But Margit Rowell is perfectly right: *They do not!* Nor are they a "vehicle or support for colour." (This last quote is an ironic betrayal of how often art content in black endeavor is assumed "outside" the relevant disciplines.) As such they do not deal with the problem of "anchoring" (Margit Rowell: "solidly anchored to the ground"). In fact, as I recall, they were not anchored even literally to the gallery floor. As works, they possessed little beyond fussy decoration, rather like old-fashioned knitting.

That these works failed to "express" most of what was inferred in the catalog's foreword is inherent in their posture. Works in the plastic arts are a structured exposure of emotion in time and space, of the self undergoing a series of critical changes (hence criticizing!); that is, artistic episodes leave behind aesthetic trails, brought about by intensely wrought decisions through the artist's engagement with his medium—painting, sculpture, etc. Cathartic emptying, reminiscent of "release," but release held together! The evolution of the act (of painting, sculpture) is a first-order activity: a forceful reminder that IT is made by a single individual with a potential of natural conveyance to a wider audience.

In sculpture the static forces of a solid body do not depend on the "quantity" of the mass (one thing sculpture just simply has to deal with is gravity)—that is, on "anchoring." Line as a direction and an affirmation of depth defines actual space (not mimetic space), but does not necessarily usurp it within the static rhythms. Static rhythm, as the only element of plastic and pictorial content, incorporates aspects of kinetic rhythms as the basic forms of our perception of real time, i.e., engaging the imagination. Sculpture shares with painting the time it takes to connect up with, be engaged by, and perhaps walk toward and past, but hardly around, the work. This is not discounting the fact that the engagement might be a lasting one, like the potential of any relationship. Sculpture's self-sufficiency unaccompanied by the baggage rhetoric of a chorus must now be so established as to not need mentioning. However, in the sense that sculpture occupies "man" space, Johnson's work was particularly troubling. His sculptures were "in the road," not underfoot, but in one's path with that particular negative, flat, indifferent heaviness. What saved the exhibition, if anything, were mirrors that engaged one in image play and as such had little to do with sculpture. The sculptures functioned not at all as sculpture, but as props in silent theater. They expressed nothing of sculptural interest—more accurately, nothing of personality (or emotion) through sculpture—but were altiloquent about play, which needed no special circumstances. As for all the talk about music, about jazz, who ever heard of a meticulously painted piece of carpentry playing jazz, except with the aid of electronic devices, or a jukebox.

In contrast, the artist Jack Whitten is driven to real painterly investigation. His earlier pictures have structures which are visually reminiscent of *the street* in a kaleidoscopic manner: circuses, carnivals, church, beaches, and swimming pools. He draws parallel conclusions about the species, caricaturing it with an exuberant, spontaneous handling equal to the imagined style (life style) of the brothers. The obvious speed with which these pictures have been done has produced a masterful ciliagraphic brush handling—paint applied and a sodden, brushed-in action, dry and direct. At times the strokes are a dense, quivering mass, filling in the entire picture plane. In other instances there is a contrast of free patches large enough to create the feeling of distinct compositional divisions. The colors are always engaging and intense, as the painter leaves delectations of nondescribed or nonspecific times and places; clothes neutral, automobiles, active; suggestions of Jackson Pollock's later misattempts. The flaws in Whitten's work begin to recede as he aims at the essential possibilities of paint. Ugliness and absurdity in measurable human terms begin to operate as paint, as mass, as line: success in portraying it (paint) as such. This is the kernel of Whitten's work, but the message has previously been governed by the stilted mannerisms of inherited dogma. Now that the anxious gesture has changed, the manner is directed at *paint,* hinging and hanging on paint's possibilities; the approach of his new phase repeats itself to such an extent that one wonders if this work has not begun, and will not end, in the full swoop of his secret and nondefinable *blackness.* This is the dilemma of Potential!

Of the older artists, apart from Jacob Lawrence, Romare Bearden is probably the best known. Bearden's work consistently tends to look better in reproductions; except perhaps his prints, of which I have not seen very many. The two most outstanding painters of this generation are, without hesitation, Norman Lewis and Bill Rivers. Lewis, whose painting at last seems to be finding an individual glow, has been long in developing. His best works seem to lie in the area of muted greys and blacks. Bill Rivers, on the other hand, is very much at home with primary colors and thick paint. Always attracted by the substance of paint, Rivers in his earlier works tended to be overwhelmed by a sort of European lushness. Comparatively small easel paintings, these works were overlaid with so much that has come to be identified with that candy-icing-lemonade school of Paris, stemming from Georges Braque and Henri Matisse after the war. (The best, and I daresay the most lasting, of this particular trend must be the works of Nicholas De Stael.) A driving conflict which seemed to arrest and bury most of Rivers' early work was the essential autobiographical nature of his imagination, the overlaying of a coloristic and pictorial thesis essentially neo-romantic-pessimistic in nature. This tendency to shore up pleasure by pandering to it in sweet color, slickness, and indifference which denied depth of feeling, was automatically anathema to an essentially mordant imagination which bites itself naturally into the acid yellows and flows with the reds and blues. Rivers' real cynicism and disillusionment smacked of an artificial, unconnected pictorial pleasure. Bordering on illustration, these works tried to deal with color and demonstrated fragmentation unreconstructed "located mainly in the exhilarating and more physical facts of luscious color . . . surfaces and decorously inflected design," in Clement Greenberg's words. Rivers' latest works are eminently satisfactory as statements rich in poise and declared intention.

Where Now?

The foregoing essay, admittedly not unbiased in its observations, is, I hope, clear enough to dissuade anyone who might think that I deliberately neglected to discuss the consistently increasing number of artists of merit whose efforts deserve as much space, if not more, than that allocated to the people who have been mentioned. There are people whose work I would have felt obliged to discuss, and I would have found pleasure, I'm sure, in doing so; some of them, like Joe Overstreet, Bill Williams, and Mel Edwards, I have written about elsewhere. But there are Ed Clarke, Malcolm Bailey, Chuck Bowers—to name a skimpy few.

Then there are a number of artists in Boston and Chicago with whose work I'm familiar. They work in what I consider an absurdly reactionary vein, but the power of their rhetoric and their committed seriousness to blackness cannot be gainsaid. If I consider the product of their efforts, and often their words about their work, to be nonsense, it is only because I cannot, I don't, see that being committed to black is quite the same as being a painter or sculptor. The two can

319

often exist in the same body, which is right, but with the maximum will in the world I cannot get past this skin-deep bombast. This is really beyond my powers.

In the seventies we can expect the continuing dialogue about black to be sustained with the measure of political license and tolerance existing or potentially in existence. Should works of painting and sculpture continue to be a black issue and not an art issue, it is my considered opinion that these works will suffer. It is easier to *say* than to *paint* the thesis that works from black hands and psyches have a distinct stamp. The measure of honesty an artist brings to his work cannot be too much stressed. An artist has to have something to be honest about, and here black artists have a distinct advantage. It is not as if "their hour has come." The fact is that they have a different perspective and view of the world long in history and short on recognition. The all-functioning role so amply filled by traditional African works is not an issue either; the world has changed. It has been seen to be the case that *black,* given our interconnectedness, universal interconnectedness, is to type as modernism is to culture. An unknown quantity with posture and potential! The question really is, Are black people missing many links, in dealing with modernism? Since a prevailing aesthetic expression in paint is completely identified with whites, the honest answer is that were we not afraid in many ways of being considered white, we would be truly black. We would be wholly black (this new entity) and tackle our "instruments" and language the way the leading jazz musicians and writers do, and with whom we are constantly being equated to our detriment—like Say It Loud, I'm Black and I'm Proud.

SOURCES

ANDREWS, BENNY, "On Understanding Black Art," *The New York Times,* Sunday, June 21, 1970.

————."The Black Emergency Cultural Coalition," *Arts Magazine*, summer 1970.

ARENDT, HANNAH, "Reflections on Violence," *New York Review of Books* (special supplement), February 27, 1969.

BEARDEN, ROMARE; Gilliam, Jr., Sam; Hunt, Richard; Lawrence, Jacob; Lloyd, Tom; Williams, William; and Woodruff, Hale, "The Black Artist in America: A Symposium," *The Metropolitan Museum of Art Bulletin*, vol. 27, no. 5, January 1969.

BEIER, ULI, *Contemporary African Art*. New York, Frederick A. Praeger, Inc., 1968.

BIEBUYCK, DANIEL, *Tradition and Creativity in Tribal Art*, vol. 2. Berkeley and Los Angeles, University of California Press, 1969.

Black Studies in the University, see Thompson, R. F.

BOWLING, FRANK, "Black Art; Talking About Books," *Two Rivers*, spring 1970.

————."Discussion on Black Art I and II," *Arts Magazine*, April and May 1969.

GOLDWATER, ROBERT, "Black Is Beautiful," *New York Review of Books*, December 18, 1969.

JONES, LEROI, *Blues People*. New York, William Morrow and Company, Inc., 1963.

MILLER, KARL, *Writing in England Today: The Last Fifteen Years*. Middlesex, England, Penguin Books, Ltd., 1968.

ROWELL, MARGIT, Foreword to catalog, French and Company exhibition of work of Daniel Larue Johnson.

SCHOENER, ALLON, ed., *Harlem on My Mind; Cultural Capital of Black America*. New York, Random House, Inc., 1968.

THOMPSON, ROBERT FARRIS, "African Influences on the Art of the United States," *Black Studies in the University: A Symposium*. New Haven, Yale University Press, 1969.

WOLLHEIM, RICHARD, "On Expression and Expressionism," *Art and Literature*, summer 1964.

19

CECELIA HODGES DREWRY

Black Theatre: An Evolving Force

> *"Yeh, just add up his saids and his dids and you get his 'is's' whoever he is. Whatever he is."*
> —Jason, in *The Monster*
> by RONALD MILNER

Essays, articles, and books on black theatre today are engorged with discussion concerning the black aesthetic, the capability of white critics to judge black plays, the need for a National Black Theatre, and limitations imposed on black theatres by the acceptance of foundation monies. White critics (Martin Gottfried and others) are still wrestling with the question of the black actor in white roles; of black critics for black plays; of, indeed, the very validity of a black theatre. Charles Gordone (*No Place to Be Somebody*), in the theatre section of *The New York Times* of January 25, 1970, declares, "I am a black playwright. . . . But in the last analysis, I do believe there never has been such a thing as 'black theater.'"

This article will eschew the intricacies of the controversies, for they are developed amply and often in *Negro Digest* (now *Black World*), *Journal of Black Poetry, Black Theatre: A Periodical of the Black Theatre Movement,* and in other literary and academic periodicals. Such issues are significant, and the debates they engender should be assessed by students of black theatre, but the urgency of the plight of black people in America today demands understanding and utilization of every phenomenon that concentrates on its easement. Black theatre is such a power. Just add up its "saids" and it "dids" and you will see where it is and where it is likely to go in the struggle for black fulfillment. As the new black dramatists develop, a pattern to this struggle for fulfillment emerges; a plan is evident in the course many black playwrights are following. The key to an understanding and assessment of black theatre today is in recognition of the plan: seeing current black dramatic activity "whole." This is the thesis of this paper.

Certain assumptions support the ideas that will be presented here. The first is the fact of black theatre. Whether one agrees with its premises and directives or not, a substantial corps of work written by blacks, for blacks, and about blacks has grown since the early sixties. In a comprehensive investigation of the field, study of earlier periods of Afro-American theatre (tensely identified as Negro drama in this current period of stark distinctions) would be imperative. In fact, I have never lectured on this topic without attention to the early works; they illuminate the fierce disenchantment with white America that infuses current black writings. Equally as important is the fact that material has been ignored or treated patronizingly too long by academicians, critics, and even by dilettantes. The giants

—Langston Hughes, Richard Wright, James Baldwin, and others—have received passing note in general college lectures and no attention through special courses. Most secondary school curricula have ignored the works completely.

Even though this picture has improved to some degree through agitation for black studies within the last two years, the student of black drama needs the early works for other reasons. He will enjoy the plays as plays; he will observe the breadth of style and content; he will identify with (or reject, or begin to understand) the agony of living as a hostage in a hostile land and the consequent emerging of the "black psyche," described by novelist John O. Killens. However, because of the number of plays that must be discussed, and because our concern here is for current, incomplete interpretations of the purpose and method of black theatre, and because some judgment will be made on the future role of black drama, we shall confine this discussion to current black plays.

Why consider this question, why attempt to diagram the plan emerging in black drama? A dual significance seems apparent, cultural and political in aim and seminal in effect. The academician, reared in the tradition of research and discovery of new insights, dissects his material with objectivity and thoroughness. He may lecture on Ralph Ellison's *Invisible Man* or write a piece on Elizabethan drama. For maximum effectiveness, however, the author or playwright must be discussed in the context of his times and of his aims. Neglecting to do so *damages* the validity of the conclusions on the subject; in the case of black drama, it seems to me, neglecting to do so *destroys* the validity of conclusions. Before attempting to place black theatre in context and to trace the plan of its development, let us define terms as they will be used in this article.

Every lecturer who has prepared a new course in Black American Writers, or Afro-American Literature, or Black Theatre has had to decide which of the "mixes" would be his guide: Literature on black themes by black writers? Black themes by white writers? "Universal" themes by black writers? Any theme using black characters?—and so on. The type of play to be discussed here has been defined—and the definition quoted often—by Ameer Baraka (LeRoi Jones) in his essay "The Revolutionary Theatre" in the collection *Home*. Even though it is readily familiar, let us review it for its directness and clarity:

> The Revolutionary Theatre should force change; it should be change. . . . The Revolutionary Theatre must EXPOSE! Show up the insides of these humans, look into black skulls. White men will cower before this theatre because it hates them. Because they themselves have been trained to hate. The Revolutionary Theatre must hate them for hating. For presuming with their technology to deny supremacy of the Spirit. They will all die because of this.
>
> . . .
>
> It should stagger through our universe correcting, insulting, preaching, spitting craziness—but a craziness taught to us in our most rational moments.
>
> . . .
>
> The Revolutionary Theatre must Accuse and Attack . . . The Revolutionary Theatre must take dreams and give them a reality. It must isolate the ritual and historical cycles of reality. . . . It is a political theatre. . . .
>
> Our theatre will show victims so that their brothers in the audience will be better able to understand that they are the brothers of victims, and that they themselves are victims if they are blood brothers. And what we show must cause the blood to rush, so that pre-revolutionary temperaments will be bathed in this blood, and it will cause their deepest soul, to move, and they will find themselves tensed and clenched, even ready to die, at what the soul has been taught.

In addition, black theatre is defined, by Ed Bullins, Barbara Ann Teer, and other outstanding writers and directors in the field, as material written by black people, for black people, about black people, and it is aimed at teaching them about themselves. These are the plays to be discussed.

Not only revolutionary plays that have been labeled as such will be included, therefore, but the plays dealing with the daily experiences of black people will be considered as part of the picture.

The Aims of Black Drama

The aims of current black playwrights, as described above, grow out of the oppressive treatment of the race in America ever since the first African slave was hauled ashore. They are inextricably bound up with the necessity to bend every energy and talent to survival. Ron Karenga leads in the emphasis on the utilitarian end of art when he explains, "Black Art must be for the people, by the people and from the people. That is to say it must be functional, collective and committing [*The Quotable Karenga*]."

Black theatre is often categorized as Revolutionary Theatre or the theatre of Black Experience. This discussion will investigate the subdivisions emerging from these areas, however, and note interrelationships among the types. In the period from the early sixties to the present, four emphases seem to recur: plays of instruction, of confrontation, of revolution, and, now, of ritual. Instruction has been in history, behavior, political and social philosophy, and the deeds of memorialized leaders. Of a subtler nature has been the instruction born of illustration; the plays detailing the frustrations of daily life have often been the more telling. Obviously these categories are not inviolable or mutually exclusive; they are set up for the sake of convenience.

Instruction

The historical pieces have had wide billing, the most searing being LeRoi Jones's *Slave Ship*. The keening *Aiiiiiieee-eeeeee* of slave women packed together in the stinking hold wrenches the viewer from his seat; his instruction in his heritage begins in tears and ends in fury. He is exposed to the enemy—white slavers and black "toms." The juxtaposition of slave-ship scenes with plantation and church vignettes underscores the selling out of the black man through history and illuminates the equation of a "tom" with a slaver.

In two comparative passages the "tom sells out," first to massa Tim, then to Mister Tastyslop. Through the skillful parallelism of the scenes, the playwright underscores not only the treachery of both deeds but also their equally heinous nature. First, the slave overhears plans for a revolt by the other slaves, led by Reverend Turner. In seven short lines, almost a litany, Slave 1 poses the critical question, "Reverend what we gon' do when massa come," and Slave 2 promises that his throat will be cut. The question and answer are given three times. Then the traitor is seen describing the plans for " 'volt" to the master. Jones's subtext is rich here, for even though the scene is short the implications are vigorous. Not the least of these is the use of the Reverend in both scenes but with a shift in his stand in the second. His strength is in silence in the slave scene; only others speak. In the second scene, however, he has become the "tom," and he promises that his congregation "will be non-violenk [sic]."

The playwright's conclusion is harsh and candid: dealing in nonviolence is tantamount to blackmail and treason. There is the indication, also, that the Preacher is doubly despicable because of his nonviolent "doubletalk" ("Of course diddy rip to bink, of vout juice. And penguins would do the same") and because he springs from a line of men who had challenged the enemy, physically, in the past. He and his white god must die, and only then can the cast and audience join and "dancing starts for real."

Ben Caldwell's *Mission Accomplished,* included in the Black Theatre issue of *The Drama Review* (summer 1968), teaches the same grim lesson from history. With the arrival of a priest and two singing-dancing nuns in the Kingdom of Baboza, "a long-flourishing kingdom," the destruction of the black people is begun. In two pages they are seduced and subjugated.

> *Priest:* What did he [King] say this time?
> *Interpreter:* He says he doesn't believe it. No one can walk on water.

Priest: Get the pictures, girls, quick! They're interested! We've got 'em!

. . .

Priest: You see. Jesus walking [on] the water. *He comes behind the* KING *and strikes him with the cross, knocking him senseless.* There! that oughta civilize him! Get the chains!

The message to black people is clear.

The history of the black woman is sensitively spun out in Sonia Sanchez' *Sister Son/ji,* whose time is "age and now and never again." She moves through the trials of Mississippi life, of young womanhood, of loss of her man, death of her children, and solitary old age—all in a monologue that is personalized, yet meshes with experiences of black women throughout the ages. Through the sister's memories, one sees long reaches of women who "dared to pick up the day and shake its tail until it became evening. a time for us. blk/ness. blk/people." The instruction is sharp: "Anybody can grab the day and make it stop . . . will you?" This play is found in Ed Bullins' anthology, *New Plays from the Black Theatre,* with what would be an excellent companion piece for an evening's presentation, Salimu's *Growin' Into Blackness.*

Appearing first in a 1969 issue of *Black Theatre,* the latter play bore no subtitle, but the later anthology describes it as "Life dedicated to building the Black Nation"—that is, instruction in the role or behavior of black women. The story is simple: if Lolita does not give up her natural and straighten her hair, her mother will put her out. So she leaves home to continue studying "about bein black" and to dedicate her "life to Black people." Many of the plays in this category give positive examples of conduct, but equally as many derive the lesson from negative observations.

Two of the most effective are Ed Bullins' *The Electronic Nigger* (published in his *Five Plays*) and William Wellington Mackey's *Family Meeting* (printed in *New Black Playwrights*). In the former, Mr. Carpentier, a student in a creative-writing class, sends the class off the stage cawing like crows by the end of the first class meeting. It is an adult evening class; Carpentier is an arrogant, loquacious fool who speaks in endless circumlocation: "What I'm saying is this . . . with our present cybernetic generation it is psycho-politically relevant to engage our socio-philosophical existence on a quanitatum scale which is, of course, pertinent to the outer-motivated migration of our inner-oriented social compact. Yes! . . ." Worse than this is his profession: wiretapper for the government—representing the black writer's contempt for those who would martyr their own, again. Jones, the instructor, in a rare opportunity to complete a sentence during the evening, chastises, "But, sir, speaking man to man, how do you feel about your job? Doesn't it make you uneasy knowing that your race, I mean, our people, the Negro, is the most victimized by the police in this country? And you are using illegal and immoral methods to . . ." All is lost in the welter of Carpentier's pomposities and interruptions, however, and the confusion of "crows" exits at the end of the play. There is humor here, but, in the larger scheme of things, the play seems to propel the revolution for the minds of men that is the thrust of black theatre. Crowing? For what, when sanity has been destroyed?

More intricate in form and perhaps a greater delight for the symbol-searchers is Mackey's *Family Meeting*. Warning against adoption of false values is made visual and aural through the interchange of white and black characters from act to act, through use of film projections and music. The subtext is enriched by insertion of a scene from one of Richard Wright's short stories ("The Man Who Was Almost a Man") into the first act of the play. The Love family takes pride in color, wealth, position, neighborhood, fraternal organization —almost every whim that has corroded black progress in the past. They are satirized roundly, and contempt for their choices is exacerbated through imagery and contrast.

If one ignores the instructions of *Family Meeting*, he will meet them again in the brief, hard-punching plays *How Do You Do* (Ed Bullins) and *The Monster* (Ronald Milner). Each attacks witless pompousness similar to Carpentier's, but the monster, a black college dean who feeds on white

values and sabotages the strivings of black students, is murdered (by his love of those values). No case is made for
him, as is for the fawning college president in Ellison's *Invisible Man*. He is mesmerized into suicide—with a white
coed. His student gives the moral for the day in his closing
lines: ". . . add up his saids and his dids and you get his 'is's' "
—the cardinal instruction in behavior shared by black dramatists with black audiences.

In fact, this is one aspect of the political and social philosophy that infuses all of the plays. We need not attempt to
isolate the area of instruction, for at the core of almost every
black play are the messages:

"Think Black."

Erase white values from your life style.

Help and teach and love your own black people.

Destroy all that impedes these aims and/or progress
toward full manhood.

Reclaim your African heritage.

Women, love and support your men.

Men, protect and cherish your women.

The last use of obvious dramatic instruction to be discussed occurs in the recent black plays that are memorials
to lost leaders: Malcolm X, Marcus Garvey, Otis Redding.
These men speak from the grave to protect their living
brothers.

Finally, how does the theatre of black experience fit into
the revolution for the minds of men? What teaching does
it offer? Among these plays, I should include all but one of
those so listed in the 1968 issue of *The Drama Review*: Bill
Gunn's *Johnnas*, Dorothy Ahmad's sensitive *Papa's Daugh-*

ter, Ed Bullins' *Clara's Ole Man,* and certainly his *A Son, Come Home,* as well as his *In the Wine Time,* and *In New England Winter,* all published elsewhere. Charles Fuller's *The Village: A Party,* presented Off Broadway as *The Perfect Party* and perhaps not written for a black audience exclusively; Lonne Elder's *Ceremonies in Dark Old Men,* a prize-winning play; and Douglas Turner Ward's *Happy Ending* are all dramatizations of the black experience in America. Young Johnnas is destroyed by a mother who insists on his similarities to all humankind and a teacher who points out the differences. Papa's daughter Mae assumes her dead mother's role in her household almost permanently, as does Adele in *Ceremonies.* With strength and delicacy Mae makes the necessary break with her father. Clara's stab at a small freedom is thwarted by Big Girl, who is her "ole man." The premiere presentation of *The Village* at Princeton University probed the validity of interracial marriage in today's society. Ward's *Happy Ending* (along with its satirical companion piece, *Day of Absence*) has enjoyed so many Off Broadway and television performances that it is probably familiar to the reader. As is true of both of these plays, his *The Reckoning* shows black folks outwitting white folks.

Ceremonies in Dark Old Men limns the black experience in "un-huh" detail. Yes, that's how it is to be black—and Mr. Parker, vaudevillean-turned-barber; his sons, Theo and Bobby; and his daughter-mother-wife, Adele, tell it well. Each one has his "scene of recognition" when the gut Gordian knot of his life tugs tighter than ever as he spits out its description in pain and anger at the inevitability of the outcome. Adele, after months of being the only working adult in a household of men; Adele, who wants to marry; Adele, who wants to hold on to a sense of wonder in life, explodes:

> I thought it would be my duty to free all of us, but who the hell ever told every black woman she was some kind of damn saviour! That can cause your body to grow cold until pain becomes a pleasure. . . . Sure this place was

built for us to die in, but if we're not very, very careful, Theo—that can actually happen. . . .

Her father's battle against the destructive power of "doing the right thing" has been great:

> You go downtown, looking and believing you can get a job as an elevator operator in one of those high buildings, and when they send you to the basement with a broom, you still don't believe it, . . .
>
> I got sour the day my legs got so trembly sore on the stage of the Strand Theatre . . . it took me three weeks to talk to Doris about it. And you know something? She didn't say a word—she just went out and got a job—she did it as if it was her duty . . . I just couldn't run downtown to meet the man the way she did—not after all those years of shuffling round like I was a dumb clown . . . my head patted . . . back of the bus . . . front of the train, yassah, nosuh, grinning when I was bleeding to death! . . . Sure, I felt sick for having to depend so much on my wife, and my daughter here—but if I had done the right thing—just think about that now, the right thing!—it would have blinded my eyes forever, ruptured my heart, and broken every bone in my soul.

But Mr. Blue Haven really tears at the black viewer's mind and memory when he rehearses the litany of man and woman, father and son, fear and determination:

> . . . so I took him [his son] home, and watched him fall asleep. Then I grabbed his mother, and put her into bed, . . . I put my hands on her, and before long, our arms were locked at each others' shoulders, and then my thighs moved down between her thighs. . . . After that, we just laid there, talking soft. I would tell her she was the loveliest bitch that ever lived, . . . It got quiet, I sat up on the edge of the bed, with my head hanging long and deep, trying to push myself out of the room, and back into it at one and the same time. She looked up at me, and I got that same question all over again—will you marry me? Will you be the father of your son? I tried to move away from her, but she dug her fingernails into my shoulders—I struck her once, twice, and again, and

again—with this hand! And her face was a bloody mess!
I put my clothes on and I walked out into the streets,
trembling because I knew, for the last time, I was gonna
have to go back and save that little boy from being a
bastard all the days of his life.

I'm going to get married, and that gets me to shaking
all over! The last time I trembled this way, *I killed a
man!* I can't ever let that happen again [excerpted from
version in *New Black Playwrights,* edited by William
Couch, Jr.].

Read that passage carefully; reread it for its screaming
illumination of the struggle against "controls" and the intertwined desire of a father to stand tall before his son. We
were not able to applaud these speeches, in formal fashion,
on the night my Douglass College students and I saw the
play (some of us for the second time); we could merely mur-
mur, in sisterly recognition, "Un-huh, yes, yes."

Each of the other plays in the didactic category distills the
substance of black family life in a special way. They are
outstanding works, but since reviews and critiques are
accessible and because thorough consideration of their interrelationships could be a study in itself, I suggest careful
review of each and its commentary. *A Son, Come Home* plays
flashback against the present in very effective fashion. *In
the Wine Time* and *In New England Winter* give the reader
opportunity for an extended view of the black experience, for
they are the first two plays of a projected trilogy. *In New
England Winter* carries forward the story of Cliff Dawson,
the convicted murderer of the first play. He has been released, and he plays out the need for "sympathy, tenderness,
compassion" with his half-brother, Steve.

Ed Bullins' "instruction" reminds black people of "how it
is." One critic has complained that the Bullins plays merely
mirror our problems but offer no guides to solutions. If ab-
solutely true, this seems to me their special significance.
When the revolution for minds has been totally won, and
the "dreams given reality," revolutionary theatre will have
lost its reasons for being, but the theatre of black experience will continue to remind and comfort and enrich.

333

Confrontation

A second area of attention by black dramatists is that of confrontation. In an essay entitled "Ideological Forces in the Work of Negro Writers" (in *Anger, and Beyond,* edited by Herbert Hill) Horace R. Cayton describes confrontation as "a direct face-to-face meeting of people or peoples with conflicting interests, ideas or values which must be resolved . . . by a synthesis of these conflicting ideologies or beliefs or it may result in avoidance, isolation or violence. A confrontation is always a tense, meaningful and fateful phenomenon." As a practical strategy this tactic has been nonviolent, and more recently it has contrived, through purposeful goading, to elicit violence from, or assure weakness of, the adversary.

In dramatic context, however, destruction of any black man who is weak has been the result. Clay's fantastic defense comes too late in LeRoi Jones's *Dutchman,* and so Lulu murders him. Her goading has been constant, but he has been slow to anger. The crowd-police confrontation in *Riot Sale or Dollar Psyche Fake Out* by Ben Caldwell (in The *Drama Review,* 1968) ends in destruction as the crowd abandons revolution to scoop up antipoverty money shot from cannons. *Take Care of Business* by Marvin X portrays another awakening that occurs too late: after a son goads him into acceptance of responsibility, a father dies of a heart attack. (This play, which is also published as *Flowers for the Trashman,* is in the *Drama Review* issue also, as are the following two discussed.) In Jimmy Garrett's *And We Own the Night* the female counterpart of the father in *Take Care of Business* refuses to acknowledge the goading of her son's friend. He berates her for lauding white compassion when her son lies dying in a revolutionary encounter. She will not hear, and so must be shot by her son's own hand. And the most degraded of the "losers" in confrontation is the black policeman in *Police,* by LeRoi Jones. He is even unable to shoot himself and must beg the very woman who castigates him for treachery to kill him.

Confrontation without inflexible determination, however,

is ineffective. If the adversaries are not of equal strength, the outcome is waste and—more important—"right" will be predicated on the assumption that, ultimately, revolution is inevitable.

Revolution

Revolutionary black theatre, defined earlier, is best exemplified in the work of Ameer Baraka (LeRoi Jones): *Four Revolutionary Plays (Experimental Death Unit #1; A Black Mass; Great Goodness of Life;* and *Madheart), The Slave,* and *Home on the Range.* Critics (white) have been most outraged by *The Slave* and a brief work, *The Toilet,* whose setting *is* a high school toilet. Robert Brustein, writing in *The New Republic* ("Three Plays and a Protest," January 23, 1965), finds that "the decay of western culture—to which the playwright frequently alludes in *The Slave*—is nowhere better exemplified than in the unwarranted favor this culture has lavished on LeRoi Jones because he has shown little theatrical purpose beyond the expression of a raging chauvinism, and few theatrical gifts beyond a capacity to record the *graffiti* scrawled on men's room walls." George Dennison, in his article "The Demagogy of LeRoi Jones" *(Commentary,* February 1965), echoes these acid sentiments. He finds the play more than offensive and "part of the rot of America," because, he claims, Jones panders to topicality and opportunism; he accuses the playwright of "dragging in race by the ears." A strange accusation to make against one who lives in a country where race is being "dragged in" constantly as a motive for degradation and condescension, and against one whose avowed intention is to EXPOSE, to "stagger through our universe correcting," to "Accuse and Attack!"

This type of comment by white critics is included here to underscore the motivation for the "black-critics-judging-black-plays" school of thought. Black critic Larry Neal, writing about the black revolutionary who figures in *The Slave,* understands that his "only salvation lies in confronting the physical and psychological forces that have made him and his people powerless." Toni (Cade) Bambara understands that he portrays "the crisis drama within the 'native.' " The comments of the white critics and the breadth of the support they receive make necessary the diagraming of the thesis of this paper: that black theatre, in the strictest sense, is an evolving phenomenon, that each of the playwrights engaged in its unfolding brings a separate emphasis to the total pattern, and that the pattern emerges from a concept of the utilitarianism of all art. If this is so, *The Slave* serves a special purpose in the development of black art and black emancipation: it and the other revolutionary plays batter the white man, yes—but, what is more important, they carry forward the "revolutionizing" of the mind of the black man. He sees that the step from confrontation to revolution must be taken, but that it, too, is doomed if not firm and unswerving.

A brief summary of *The Slave* will illustrate this. Walker, a black revolutionary, enters the home of Grace, his former wife (white), while street fighting is in progress. When Grace and her present husband return, the three engage in arguments about the state of the world and of art; there are recriminations and taunts. Walker drinks himself to sleep, thereby allowing the husband, Easley, to attack him. Walker recovers and kills Easley. Grace is killed by a falling beam during one of the bombardments. Walker limps from the house, declaring that his two daughters, who have been asleep upstairs, are dead. He reverts to the gait and posture of an old man (field slave) that he had assumed in his prologue to the play. At the same moment, a child is heard crying.

Unanswered questions and tirades notwithstanding, the play makes its "revolutionary" point: total commitment is the single road for the black man. Return to old white haunts or dallying away from the battle—even if the destruction of the enemy does occur belatedly—is not good enough. One is still in bondage then—a calculating field slave rather than a fawning house nigger, but in bondage all the same. Walker will fight another day (as the field slaves rose from time to time), but he is not totally "revolutionized" in his desires and values. The insanity of which Grace accuses him will blunt the agony of this self-knowledge, somewhat.

Intellectual and physical confrontation and revolution occur in each of the *Four Black Revolutionary Plays. Experimental Death Unit #1* warns the reader that the revolution (physical) is at hand: two white degenerates and their black prostitutes die! *A Black Mass* warns the reader that the horrible white beast, created by Jacoub, a black magician, must die. It has no regard for human life, and its vomit and slobber contaminate the black beings it touches. These contaminated "offspring" escape into the audience, screaming, "White! . . . White! Me! White!" They must be killed. The Black Man in *Madheart,* a third play in the collection, declares a similar obligation when his sister and mother run mad in desire for whiteness: "They'll die or help us, be black or white and dead. I'll save them or kill them. That's all." Finally, in *Home on the Range* a blabbing white family is attacked by black criminals. The whites speak a gibberish that emphasizes their animal traits and their noncommunication with blacks. They are mindless, television-addicted automatons. When the black intruders overcome them, one sister compliments her black brothers, "Good Morning, *Men.* Good Morning."

Ritual

Having won the minds of black audiences and assaulted the minds of whites, black theatre is ready to become ritualistic. In fact, traces of ritual appear in the latter plays discussed above. Jacoub's incantations and "solutions" (*A Black Mass*) and the masked Devil Lady's hold on Mother and Sister (*Madheart*) suggest otherworldly perceptivity. The essence of ritual, however, is the creation of powerful forces for change or reinforcement. When this phase of black theatre emerges fully, the developing evaluation of new theatrical forms and the revolution for the minds of men will have reached a peak. Director Robert Macbeth discusses this in the 1969 issue of the periodical of the New Lafayette Theatre, *Black Theatre.*

Of what significance is the preparation for ritual theatre? The phases of black theatre being dealt with today are concerned, primarily, with instruction, confrontation, and revolution as survival tools for living in America. Rituals based on African archetypes demand *careful* study of the psyche and mores from which they emanate. This required study adds layers of authentic information to the black man's knowledge of his heritage. When this *shall* have occurred, the stage will be set for the ritual form of theatre to expand from its present experiments with American themes. Pure African ritual can be presented, but more pertinent will be the new form that can evolve from Afro-American combinations. Content may influence form; the dramatic and religious and organizing power of ritual can reach greater numbers of people, since everyone participates; the political and cultural aims of black people can be supported by the energy and intensity of ritual theatre; the fullest experience in discovery of self and heritage could occur.

If the development follows normal proliferation, black drama should become (in its most highly developed state) a new form using elements of method and style distilled from the revolutionary plays, the plays of black experience, and the rituals. The one-dimensional brevity of a piece like *Arm Yrself or Harm Yrself* (LeRoi Jones) may inject itself into a section of a full-flowing ritual to foster contrast and emphasis. The pageant approach may become the most popular. Attempts at prediction are not profitable but the points to be made are:

(1) Black theatre, based on political motivations, is in an evolving stage.

(2) Several ways of accomplishing its aims are being used by black playwrights today.

(3) The full fruition of the form will not be apparent until all of its political dicta have been presented.

(4) These dicta are being presented all at once, but the overall effectiveness cannot occur until each level of

the mind's receptivity has been passed and the next guide offered.

(5) The business of black theatre is cultural reawakening, political direction, and self-enlightenment.

(6) When this "business" has been accomplished, black theatre will be free to:
  (a) develop as a less-restricted art
  (b) evolve special form (s) based on all those that have preceded.

The significance of a review such as this seems to lie in the following three conclusions:

(1) Black theatre is not merely propaganda or agit-prop theatre, as has been charged, for it is concerned with the whole life experience of the black man, not merely his fair pay or his right to education. Secondly, it is directed to the victims, primarily, not to the consciences of the perpetrators of injustice.

(2) To judge current works, critics need to hold in mind the large pattern and evaluate according to the place of the work in that scheme.

(3) It is likely that the standards of judgment pertinent to black theatre will be deduced from the "new forms"; they may well have some of the classic criteria among them.

One must wait and see. In his first book of published poems, one of my former Princeton University students, Julius Thompson, has summed up the matter in this way:

> *"Black Art"*
>
> *Only time*
> *Can tell*
> *What has*
> *Been stolen.*

—and, one must add, what is yet to be unearthed.

SOURCES

BOOKS

BARAKA, AMEER. *See* LeRoi Jones.

BULLINS, ED, *Five Plays*. New York, The Bobbs-Merrill Company, 1968.

_____ *New Plays from the Black Theatre*. New York, Bantam Books, Inc., 1969.

COUCH, WILLIAM, JR., *New Black Playwrights*. Baton Rouge, Louisiana State University Press, 1968.

GAYLE, ADDISON, JR., ed., *Black Expression*. New York, Weybright and Talley, Inc., 1969.

HILL, HERBERT, ed., *Anger, and Beyond*. New York, Harper & Row, Publishers, 1966.

JONES, LEROI, *Dutchman* and *The Slave*. New York, William Morrow and Company, Inc., 1964.

_____ *Four Black Revolutionary Plays*. Indianapolis and New York, The Bobbs-Merrill Company, 1969.

_____ *Home: Social Essays*. New York, William Morrow and Company, Inc., 1966.

_____ and Neal, Larry, eds., *Black Fire*. New York, William Morrow and Company, Inc., 1968.

KARENGA, MAULANA RON, *The Quotable Karenga,* ed. Clyde Halisi and James Mtume. Los Angeles, US Organization, 1967.

THOMPSON, JULIUS, *Hopes Tied Up in Promises*. Philadelphia, Dorrance and Company, 1970.

TURNER, DARWIN J., and Bright, Jean M., eds., *Images of the Negro in America*. Boston, D. C. Heath and Company, 1965.

WARD, DOUGLAS TURNER, *Happy Ending* and *Day of Absence*. New York, Dramatists Play Services, Inc., 1966.

PERIODICALS

Black Theatre: A Periodical of the Black Theatre Movement, ed., Ed Bullins, nos. 2 and 3, 1969. New York, New Lafayette Theatre Publications.

Commentary, "The Demagogy of LeRoi Jones," by George Dennison, February 1965.

The Drama Review, vol. 12, no. 4, summer 1968. New York University.

Negro Digest, Chicago, Johnson Publishing Company, vol. 16, no. 6, April 1967.

The New Republic, "Three Plays and a Protest," by Robert Brustein, January 23, 1965.

20

Black Students Speak: Three Views on Black Studies

I

The Effect of Afro-American Studies on Attitudes of Black People

AUDREY C. ARTHUR

There can be little doubt that there have been many different types of reactions by Afro-Americans in this country, the young as well as their parents, to the emergence of a renewed focus on the African contributions and heritages so much a part of Black America. These different reactions have developed out of the rekindling of Black national interest in Afro-American studies, on every academic level. The current strains which are bursting forth from sensitized Blacks in this country are not "new" in the sense that they are original. Such concepts as Black equality, Black unity, Black expression, Black history, Black purpose, were all voiced before by such outstanding men as Frederick Douglass, Martin R. Delaney, Henry M. Turner, Edward Blyden, and George Washington Williams. The important difference between these men and the Black leaders of our time is that the latter are advantageously placed in a time period when widespread, well-planned, *well-funded* Afro-American Studies programs are not only accepted, but very often encouraged, by whites in power positions in universities and high schools. The time and setting are just prime for the revival of interest in African heritage in the 1960s.

Black Students

Since I am living in this critical time for Black self-awareness, I shall concentrate on the effects experienced by young Blacks in the ten years between 1960 and 1970.

There are just so many things for a newly enlightened Black student to learn and digest in his consciousness about himself and his heritage as an Afro-American. As an "american," the Black student found himself throughout his childhood being bombarded by propaganda designed to strip away all hints of a background outside of America. Can you comprehend the magnitude of erasure necessary to accomplish that? It is fantastic how society, white and Black, has—or had until 1960—successfully erased any attachment a Black child might have felt for Africa or her achievements. As a matter of fact, I can recall becoming enraged when a childhood playmate called me "black." For, at that time in my life, to be called "black" was just about the worst insult anyone could hurl. How times have changed! Now, when the Black student is exposed to the achievements and contributions of Afro-American society, he absorbs this knowledge like a dry sponge. While absorbing facts about his past, he becomes acutely aware of the fact that he, too, belongs in history—like the Jews, Italians, and Germans with whom he has come in contact all his life. This awareness is the linchpin for his social development from then on. His mind gradually becomes extremely sensitive to the literature about Afro-America, her people and her goals, and he begins to grow into that "sensitized" person to whom I referred earlier. He begins to think more and more about what he can do to help alleviate *his* people's problems on some level: economic, social, or political. He now realizes that he does have a people; Afro-Americans are his people and they are distinct, not simply an amalgamation or prototype created by the white society. Afro-Americans represent a reality to him and, most vital of all, they owe no thanks to European culture for their existence, as do "negroes" in the United States, who are products of the white imperialistic slave mentality.

One thing that becomes increasingly obvious to students of Afro-American history, as well as american history, is the inherent "un-americanism" of the Blacks living in this country today. There have always been two distinct societies in america—one white, the other, Black. Most Black people have been aware of this for generations and find it comical when whites discover it. This is true despite the fact that the white "plantation mind" saw it necessary to "de-Africanize" its slaves. White society replaced, as best it could, the natural freedoms of the African with the false promises and idealisms of america, and the African became the "gray-colored" Afro-American he is today.

I consider the "American" part of the racial description to be the burden of the white society in 1970. This is the pledge, the promise, as it were, that white society made to Black people when it took them from their African titles and privileges and forcibly replaced these with the pseudo-equality inherent in the word "american." I, for one, am still searching to determine what it means for me, a Black woman,

343

to be an american. I'm quite aware of the definition as it applies to the white American, but "Black america" is still waiting.

Finding no value, at least no definitive value, in being an american, the Black student finds himself searching back via the Afro-American Studies programs to discover just who he is, where he comes from, where he is going culturally. There is no question as to the value of the various sociology, history, and literature courses dealing with Afro-America. They have been the branching-off point for further study by Black students and have given us the necessary background and bibliographic information. For instance, through studying the development of Afro-American art and music, Black men and women find new ways of expressing the moods and feelings which hitherto have not been given their justice through the conventional European means. An analogy would be trying to play an African chant on a piano. Likewise, how can the sensitivities of Afro-Americans be fully utilized unless through their natural means? There are numerous other ways in which Afro-Americans stand to benefit from wide-scale Afro-American studies.

However, the main thing to be gained from studying Afro-American history is, as the Honorable Adam Clayton Powell said in his address to the Eighty-ninth Congress, "a sense of pride in being black." Throughout the history of the american Black, he has been taught that "blackness is evil, and Negroes 'no-good,' . . . only 'white is right,'" that Negroes with "white blood" in their veins were better, as Alvin F. Poussaint points out in his article in *The Black Power Revolt*. The most damaging result of this brainwashing has been that the Black man has adopted his self-image from the dictates of the white racists. Consequently, we have a long history of Black men and women learning to hate themselves because of their blackness. This "cancer of the mind" ate away, generation after generation, until the Black child emerged as an exact duplicate of his forefathers, hating himself and resenting his blackness. It has been substantially shown that the self-concepts of children are formed at

344

a very early age, from their own experiences and their relationships to their environments. The negative self-concept
takes hold early in life; if it is not guarded against, the child
evidences it in his expressions, his art, his vocabulary—in
short, his entire life style.

With the assistance of the full-scale Afro-American Studies program throughout all educational levels, these negative
self-concepts may be changed. Only in this way will Black
people ever achieve a *permanent* position of psychological
equality. Afro-American studies programs will provide the
means to achieve equality; the natural drive and persever-
ance of the people, the will. Black people will begin to find
ways of expressing themselves within the framework of Black
definitions, by Black standards, instead of according to what
white society dictates.

One of the secondary effects of Afro-American Studies
programs is a "polarization" of Blacks and whites so long
held together, however loosely or tenuously, by integration
groups such as the NAACP. The two societies are now being
drawn away from each other sociologically. While these two
parts of society have always existed on two distinct levels,
it is within the last ten years that they have begun moving
apart on a larger scale. The social and historical awareness
resulting from careful study of Black history has had the un-
mistakable effect of driving the wedge deeper and deeper between whites and Blacks. It is clear to me that before there
can be any social interaction of meaningful proportions between whites and Blacks, we Black people must be resocial-
ized, via our studies, and must emerge as "Black People"
with a capital *B*, united and racially proud.

This is a difficult time for Blacks and whites because it is
one of readjustment. Whites must accept the harsh fact that
Blacks do not want their paternalistic assistance, or their
liberal ideas. To be sure, this rejection is going to be a
"slap in the face" to many so-called liberals. Ironically, a situation is reversing itself; the day is approaching when whites
will find themselves saying, "We shall overcome" in relation
to their dealings with Blacks. They shall just have to be

"patient," to use a much worn out phrase, until Blacks are ready to meet them without expressing the hatred and animosity generated by the inequalities and brutalities we have endured and, in fact, continue to endure in America.

II

Black Studies vs. Black Studies

DEBORAH BANKSTON

Whenever I seriously consider why such a thing as Black Studies exists in a white university, a contradiction comes to my mind. Should I think that whites really want blacks to realize their black identity in terms of themselves, their history, their culture? Should I really believe that they (whites) are going to allow their institutions to be directed toward this end? These questions are erased from my mind when I seriously examine the purpose of education in this country in the first place. Just as the Russians teach communist ideology to all their young minds in order for their society to perpetuate itself, our American government must instill in the minds of its people democratic ideology. It is reasonable to assume that the people of a given society must be programmed somewhat to that society's beliefs in order for that society to survive. What better way to program a people than through its educational system—the only system that gets us at three or four and keeps us until we are at least sixteen.

In his article in *Black Studies in the University* Maulana Ron Karenga speaks to this question of recognizing the educational institution as a political institution:

> Everything moves in terms of political power, because without that power nothing is accomplished. The educational institution . . . one of the institutions that the power structure maintains, in order to reinforce its own position. One learns to be a "better American," I assume, by going to an American university; where else could one learn to be a better American than in a university? What

you have to understand is that you should not fool yourself by thinking that education is an academic thing; it is basically a political thing, and it provides identity, purpose, and direction within an American context.

If you are a white institution, for example, and blacks come in here, then the blacks come out "white," too, unless they have some different identity, purpose, and direction to shield them from all of this.

Now, if this is so, then how can it be that a white university would teach those things which would be nonwhite or non-American? To be more explicit, let me maintain that the American university, as a *supporting column* to the political structure whose policy is that of oppression and racism, must teach its students to support that political structure. Here lies the contradiction: the university cannot teach black identity and culture in terms of the truth while at the same time teaching American political ideology. One is the antithesis of the other. Therefore, I have come to this conclusion about Black Studies in a white university: Black Studies is white studies, and can only act as a placating agent for black students.

Culture: The American culture is set up so that the black man "is not recognized as a man but still as a boy," says Yusef Iman in *Something Black*. The boys are supposed to be integrated into the social, economic, and political structures of this country. I say integrated out of politeness when I really mean tolerated. Blacks were never really meant to have a share in the power structure. They (blacks) were only meant to be oppressed in this country. These were, and are, the overall goals of our political system, and education is the means used to enforce the system. Black Studies programs keep blacks wrapped up in humanities. (The ironic thing about that is that whites have the audacity to think they can teach these things which they know nothing about.) You see, the whole theme involved here is tolerance of our presence under your control. If you teach us economics, it is only for the benefit of making capitalism seem correct to the black man. In history we are still taught "who discovered what," when the black man had no business fighting the Indians to discover Chicago. Black Studies does not get black people through the door of a golf club. Black Studies still placates us. It still teaches us white values, which gets us nowhere. It turns out the Sally Sue type of Negro character portrayed by Deanne Harris in "The Saga of Sally Sue":

> *Sally Sue Emerson WAS a*
> *Very Bright (?) young lady.*
> *She was*
> > *The First Colored secretary of the Urban League*
> > *The First Colored to have a desk in an*
> > > *Exclusive, Equal Opportunity Office that was*
> *So HIGH up downtown that*
> *Birds never peeked in her*
> *Sound-dust-germ-people-proof window.*
> *Oftentimes—times Sally Especially enjoyed—*
> *She was The Only Negro at Exclusive parties,*
> *(With the exception, Of Course, of the menials who*
> *prepared food and drink . . .)*

Sally Sue had a rude awakening when she found herself treated like a "nigger" by some "friendly" policemen who arrested her in a raid. The poem concludes:

> *After ONE night in the jail*
> *With one friendly policeman after the other,*
> *Sally Sue Emerson was no longer*
> > *The Only Colored*
> > *in the office*
> > *in the Park Ridge apartments:*
> *Sally became—to the disappointment of her parents*
> > > > *the Urban League*
> > > > *and friends (?)*
> > > > *BLACK!*

You see, a black man can imitate the white man and "fit in" the economic, political, and social structures, but still be kicked in his ass! Blacks, then, cannot let Black Studies in white universities placate them. Blacks, then, cannot let Black

Studies make black scientists work in the laboratories to make an atomic bomb. This happens when Black Studies is white-controlled.

Black in Black for Black

Since white universities will only allow Black Studies to be taught from a white point of view, it is obvious that blacks need *an alternative system of education.* This means Black Studies in a Black Setting for the Benefit of the Black Community. The alternative for blacks is to set up black institutions which will perpetuate the system of *black nationalism,* not white racism. The purpose of the alternative system of education will be to establish a black value system in the minds of black people which would become "the first line of COLLECTIVE DEFENSE against white cultural oppression," to use John H. Johnson's phrase. The Institute of the Black World in Atlanta, the Communiversity in Chicago, Malcolm X College in Chicago, the Center for Black Education in Washington, and Malcolm X Liberation University in Greensboro, North Carolina, are some of the institutions in existence now for the purpose of making a black nation.

Culture (according to Malcolm X, in *Malcolm X Speaks*):

> The political philosophy of black nationalism means that the black man should control the politics and the politicians in his own community. . . . The economic philosophy of black nationalism . . . means that we could control the economy of our community. . . . The social philosophy of black nationalism . . . means that we have to get together and remove the evils . . . that are destroying the moral fiber of our community.

The black universities are advocating the cause of black liberation, which in turn means black independence. Their programs are designed to teach black people how to build a nation in terms of how to control the three factors Malcolm spoke of. The Black Studies program of Malcolm X Liberation University, as described in the March 1970 issue of *Negro Digest,* is a typical example of how these institutions

349

approach the problem. The three main areas of concentration are: goods and services, consciousness, and mechanisms of force and violence—simply because these things are essential in bringing about independence. The curriculum is divided into two sections. One, dealing with ideology, is designed to make the student understand the historical, social, economic, and political framework of black experience in the world. The other section deals with basic skills needed by blacks to build a nation, especially in the areas of science, medicine, and engineering.

Using education in this way to create a thing of beauty, black nationalism does away with the schizophrenic Sally Sues and those black men who discovered Chicago. Rather, it produces this end result:

Result: Little Malcolms and little H. Rap Browns, little sisters and brothers who know they are black warriors in this land of evil. Nationalism produces mothers who know that their children and their grandchildren will inherit the earth. African peoples will once more be on top of that 360-degree circle, once more regain their position as kings and queens on this earth while the white man destroys himself. Blacks will be in control of their own destinies because they will control their own power structure, which will only benefit black people. The black infant will no longer be confused and think that the policeman is there to protect him (the child) from evil. The child instead will inherently know that the policeman is the evil.

III

Black Studies and Liberation, or Know the Real/Enemy

KAREN PREDOW

"Harvard and schools like that have ruint more niggers than bad whisky."   —JESS B. SIMPLE

Most readers of Langston Hughes's works are familiar with the wit and wisdom of his character Jesse B. Semple

(Simple), who has spoken a bit of philosophy on almost every subject from feet to the causes of World War II. As far as traditional institutions of higher education developing Black people in our struggle for liberation are concerned, Brother Simple's conclusion is very accurate; the scars of an inadequate educational base are deep. One response to this educational dilemma has been an attempt by Black students on many college campuses (and within many high schools) to develop Black Studies programs. Within this movement there are many crucial questions facing Black people regarding both the feasibility of establishing such programs within the traditional educational system and exactly where such programs would be beneficial if established—at predominantly white colleges in the North or at predominantly black colleges in the South.

This paper will attempt to present some of the questions and problems being dealt with in terms of the task and definition of Black Studies within the liberation struggle.

According to Professor Alphonso Pinkney, increasing expressions of Black nationalism within the Black liberation movement were manifested in the demand for departments and institutes of Black Studies at traditional colleges and also in independent Black education centers. For Black students (and Black faculty) the demand for, and attempt to develop, Black Studies programs have necessitated a serious scrutiny of the task and purpose of "white" educational institutions (both predominantly white and predominantly Black colleges) and the education that Blacks receive at these institutions.

One Black student, Theodus Jowers, Jr., has described the political nature of education as executing the three C's: control, concepts, and conditioning. He states that in order to establish and maintain white nationalism, "the educational system must deal totally with the society in its projection of the positive images of whiteness: concepts, values, beliefs, attitudes, history, world view, and power relationships." In considering the need to change traditional educational systems, Black students in large numbers have reached a similar

351

analysis. It has become increasingly clear through the protracted struggle for liberation by Black people that it is necessary to regain, reorganize, and rebuild a cultural base from which Black people can begin a point of reference (in terms of the struggle and the Black experience) and analysis. This is the essence of Black Studies.

Harold Cruse, in *The Crisis of the Negro Intellectual*, succinctly delineates the necessity of developing a Black cultural base, especially as one reviews and analyzes the past experiences of protest by Black people and realizes the crucial issues of the movement. He states:

> . . . the truth is that the more practical sides of the Negro problem in America are bogged down organizationally and methodologically precisely because of cultural confusion and disorientation on the part of most Negroes. *Thus it is only through a cultural analysis of the Negro approach to group "politics" that the errors, weaknesses, and goal-failures can cogently be analyzed and positively worked out.*

As Brother Pinkney points out, many Black nationalist organizations have begun to establish and build a cultural base for Black people through their activities and ideologies. In a speech to the Black Power Conference held in Philadelphia in September 1968, Brother Imari Abubakari Obadele, I, of the Republic of New Africa stated: "Brains demands the imagination to take the basic mass literacy of our people and rapidly lift the masses free of the slothful brain-washing, self-doubt, and self-abasement which living in America has brought us." However, through the experiences Black students have encountered in attempting to set up Black Studies programs, it has become increasingly clear that traditional institutions cannot and/or will not begin to deal with the program as it must be handled to be of benefit to Black people. Nor is the need for Black Studies viewed in the same perspective by Black students and college administrators.

Black students take the position that most educational experiences in traditional institutions leave Blacks in that state of "cultural confusion and disorientation" that Cruse states is "bogging down" the movement. Such institutions have "colonized," and continue to colonize the minds of Black people into the stream of thought promoted by white America. The task that is necessary for Blacks is thus to retrain the thinking of Black minds.

Donald Henderson, in his paper "Black Determination on Campus," prepared for the March 1969 Conference of Black College Administrators on Predominantly White Campuses, explains:

> The point is that the approaches to history, among other subjects, as exemplified in standard college courses do smack of racism, whether by design or simply through neglect. In this context, the activities of black students have "pulled the cover off" an unacknowledged aspect of racism fostered by the conventional university educational process. Moreover, if seen in the broad perspective of the American social system, in order to rectify this state of affairs it is necessary to do precisely as the black students have suggested—namely "decolonize the black mind."

The recognition of the need for Black Studies grows out of an awareness of the continued physical and mental violence upon Black people as demonstrated by the Orangeburg, South Carolina, massacre in 1968 and the overt attacks against the Black Panthers. It also is a result of the experiences of the Civil Rights movement, for if one seriously studies the beginnings of the Black Studies demand, it is based in the movement activities of the fifties. Legally, the Civil Rights movement achieved its goals: school desegregation rulings, legislation providing for open housing, voting rights, use of public facilities. The Civil Rights movement also brought to light the inability of white America to give, legislate, donate, or program Black people into equality and liberation. Now Black people do not simply view their oppressed position as merely a result of de facto segregation, but as a result of neo-colonialization.

As Preston Wilcox wrote in his article "Black Studies as an Academic Discipline," in the March 1970 issue of *Negro Digest:*

353

The thrust for Black Studies Programs developed not on white college campuses but at Selma, Birmingham, and the March on Washington. It was on the civil rights battlefield that Blacks learned that an appeal to the white conscience had to be replaced by an appeal to Black consciousness; that the alternative to white oppression was not integration but the mounting of Black Power; that white people could not save Black people from exploitation and degradation as long as white people benefited from them.

It is for this reason that Black Studies must embody more than the mere alteration of an American history course with the incorporation of the deeds of Crispus Attucks and Matt Henson, for essentially that remains a white history course. Black Studies must do more than survey Black history (in terms of events defined by white history), drama, art, and music; it must also, in restudying the history of Black people in Africa, Latin America, and North America, develop its world view and opinions in terms of the experiences of Black people. Preston Wilcox provides a general definition of Black Studies when he states: "Black Studies . . . is that body of experience and knowledge that Blacks have had to summon in order to learn how to survive within a society that is stacked against them."

The task of Black Studies is to enable Black people to be able to start their analysis, organization, and fight for liberation from a base point that is clear in analyzing what has been done, and is being done, to Black people. It is necessary to change our way of thinking. Poet Don L. Lee, in his work "a poem to complement other poems," gives an accurate picture of the task of Black Studies. In part, he says:

> change. i say change into a realblack righteous
>   aim. like i don't play
> saxophone but that doesn't mean i don't dig
>   "trane." change.
> change.
> hear u coming but yr/steps are too loud. change.
>   even a lamp post changes nigger.

354

change. stop being an instant yes machine change.
niggers don't change they just grow that's a
   change; bigger & better niggers.
change, into a necessary blackself.
change, like a gas meter gets higher.
change, like a blues song talking about a righteous
   tomorrow.
   change, like a tax bill getting higher.
   change, like a good sister getting better.
   change, like knowing wood will burn. change.
   know the realenemy.
                    . . .
   change change your enemy change change
   change change your change change change.
your
mind nigger.

In view of the previously discussed source, definition, and task of Black Studies, it becomes clear that the dual questions of the feasibility of developing such a program within established schools; and if feasible, exactly where, when, and how this should take place, are confronting black students, scholars, parents, and teachers. That such a program must be extensive and intensive in content is recognized; that time is almost nonexistent is a pressuring factor. Some black scholars have proposed the development of several programs at the predominantly Black colleges in the South, combined with cooperative programs in the predominantly white schools in the North which will cut back on the drain of black brainpower and resources.

Others maintain that it is indeed imperative to begin programs at predominantly white colleges because of the type of education these schools produce, the growing urban population in the North, and the increasing number of Black students enrolling in these colleges as a result of integrationist demands of current Black students.

An alternative to developing extensive programs in educational institutions (and hence avoiding the dilemma of where, when, and how, and the fight against the three C's while at-

tempting to deal with a Black Studies Program) is the establishment of independent educational centers throughout the country and the world. Currently on the increase are the number
of preschool liberation centers in Black communities and af-
ter-school or Saturday sessions in Black education sponsored
by various organizations. Several independent institutes and
colleges have been formed in Black communities, e.g., Malcolm
X Liberation University, the Center for Black Education, the
Communiversity, and the Institute of the Black World. All
these centers work to pool the talents of Black scholars,
teachers, students, parents, and community people to participate in and develop an educational process and course of study
which is based on the experience of Black people and which
enables them to recognize and deal with the real issues surrounding the power of their oppressors in the United States
and throughout the world. Most of the people working within
these centers feel that Black Studies within "white" educational institutions will not develop programs to deal with such
concrete issues. The reasons are clear; white educational systems are working for, and based on, the neo-colonialist power
structure.

A paper prepared by the staff and students of Malcom X
Liberation University, presented in October 1969, states:

> Black Studies is neo-colonialistic in that it seeks to ob-
> fuscate the real issues of generating an analysis of the
> power structure and its ever expanding colonization proc-
> ess, and in its stead, seeks to keep Black people exposing
> themselves for the benefit of the colonial forces. So we
> see then that the goal of Black Studies is to take some
> of the best minds in the Black community and make them
> dependent and addicted to the colonizer's system.

Students, staff members, and parents of the Communiversity in Chicago have outlined the purpose of an independent
educational system as:

(1) To help Black people understand what is being
done to them and reveal the drama of everyday
local, national, and international events.

356

   (2) To help Black people understand the relationship of the Black colony in America to the white metropolitan society in America.

   (3) To aid confused Black professionals.

   (4) To help Black students achieve a proper frame of reference.

   (5) To help community organizations with organizational tasks and mobilizations.

Such a program is geared to development of the basic point of reference for Black people so as to eliminate the "cultural confusion" that cripples a colonized people in its attempts to overthrow the colonizer. It is a program to liberate the mind so that the actions of Black people will consistently deal with the real problem, the real enemy. Indeed it seems that much of the development of this program of Black Studies must and will be done in the immediate future outside of the "white" educational system, for any program designed to develop a cultural base different from the guiding base upon which an institution is built is in direct contradiction to that institution. Such a program is therefore in danger of co-optation and oppression or suppression at the decision of the school's administrators. That Black students and faculty members will continue to develop programs within the system is also a reality. The question is which will be most beneficial to the largest number of Black people in the shortest amount of time. As Malcolm X stated:

> *This generation,* especially of our people, has a burden more so than any other time in history. The most important thing that we can learn to do today is think for ourselves. *If you don't do it, you'll always be maneuvered into a situation where you are never fighting your actual enemies, where you will find yourself fighting your own self.*

With the art, drama, poetry, history, research, organization, and planning within the movement, Black Studies as a part

357

of liberation must make Black people not only deal with the confusion and contradictions of our own oppressed existence, but must enable a colonized people to study and know the real enemy.

SOURCES

PUBLISHED WORKS

BARBOUR, FLOYD B., ed., *The Black Power Revolt*. Boston, Porter Sargent, Inc., 1968.

CRUSE, HAROLD, *The Crisis of the Negro Intellectual*. New York, William Morrow and Company, Inc., 1967.

_____ *Rebellion or Revolution?* New York, William Morrow and Company, Inc., 1968.

IMAN, YOSEF, *Something Black*. Newark, N.J., Yusef Iman, 1969.

LEE, DON L., *Don't Cry, Scream*. Detroit, Broadside Press, 1969.

LITTLE, MALCOLM, *Malcolm X Speaks*. New York, Grove Press, Inc., 1966.

Negro Digest, September 1969 and March 1970 issues.

OBADELE, IMARI ABUBAKARI, I, *Revolution and Nation Building*. Detroit, The House of Songhay, 1970.

ROBINSON, ARMSTEAD; Foster, Craig C.; and Ogilvie, Donald H., *Black Studies in the University*. New York, Bantam Books, Inc., 1969.

SANCHEZ, SYLVIA, *Home Coming*. Detroit, Broadside Press. 1969.

WALTON, SIDNEY, *The Black Curriculum: Developing a Program in Afro-American Studies*. East Palo Alto (Nairobi), Black Liberation Publishers, 1969.

UNPUBLISHED PAPERS

"Critique of a Colonizing Program," staff and students of Malcolm X Liberation University, October 1969.

FURNISS, W. T., "Black Studies Programs and Civil Rights Violations," American Council on Education Report, April 8, 1969.

HENDERSON, DONALD, "Black Determination on Campus, "prepared for Conference of Black College Administrators on Predominantly White Campuses, March 21, 1969.

JOWERS, THEODUS, JR., "The Politics of Education: How We Get an Education and Don't Get Educated," March 1970.

STRICKLAND, WILLIAM, "The Race Revolution: Reflections on a Dying Republic."

WITT, WILLIAM, "Racist Myths About Africa and Africans," prepared for People Against Racism (PAR).

_____"Racist Myths About the Period of Reunion and Reaction," prepared for PAR.

21

LENNOX S. HINDS

The Relevance
of the Past
to the Present:
A Political
Interpretation

> "Those who cannot remember the
> past are forced to repeat it."
> —HAROLD CRUSE

While Afro-Americans struggle toward a formula, a strategy, a methodology, for complete structural change of the oppressive political, economic, and cultural American institutions, new leaders have emerged, tactics have changed, and such labels as "integrationist," "nationalist," "moderate," "accommodationist," "radical," "militant," and "revolutionary" have been given new definitions consistent with the prevailing emotional climate. Within the past decade the cry has changed from the "Freedom Now" of Martin Luther King's "Negro evangelism" to the advocacy of urban guerrilla warfare and armed struggle by the Black Panther party. As Harold Cruse points out in *The Crisis of the Negro Intellectual*, "It was historically unfortunate that the American Negro created no social theorists to back up his long line of activist leaders, charismatic deliverers, black redemptionists, and moral suasionists." The fact is that the self-appointed and establishment-created national black leaders represent a disorganized and dysfunctional array of individuals and groups in pursuit of selective black goals. To a large extent this confusion stems from either these leaders' superficial analysis of, or inability to analyze, Afro-American history, thereby failing to synthesize political, economic, and cultural premises that are conceptually tied to historical antecedents.

The history of the black experience in North America reveals two unresolved issues that have transcended a century of struggle under changing slogans and leaders:

First: Whether black separatism as a social philosophy should be pursued as a political, economic, and cultural solution to black oppression in America.

Second: Whether significant structural changes in the economic, political, cultural, and administrative institutions in America can be accomplished through evolution or revolution.

Historical Antecedents

Of these two issues, the former has historically dominated the scene until recently. During the pre–Civil War period some Afro-Americans were strongly advocating a black separatist position. Among the leading proponents of such a position was Martin R. Delaney, a Harvard graduate physician.

Delaney stated: "Africa is our fatherland and we its legitimate descendants. . . . I have outgrown, long since, the boundaries of North America, and with them have outgrown the boundaries of their claims."

These words could be those of any contemporary black nationalist advocate. Howard H. Bell, in his introduction to Delaney's book *Search for a Place; Black Separatism and Africa,* notes that an examination of the underlying premises of both the contemporary movement and that of the Delaney era, although separated by the Civil War and more than a century of unkept promises, have more in common than at first meets the eye. Both have elements of pride in race, which have too often been lacking among the oppressed. Both look to the black man as the means of salvation, not only for Africa but also for America. Both are aggressively aware of black unity, which scoffs at claims of white superiority but is ready to accept black superiority. Both demand the fulfillment of economic and social equality. Both are disdainful of white-led or even white-participating efforts at betterment of conditions for blacks. Both demand black leadership for black projects. Both have failed to conceptualize a political and ideological frame of reference that is applicable as a solution to the exploitation and oppression of blacks within the United States.

It is important to note that the black nationalist movement represents a spectrum of social consciousness ranging from cultural nationalism to revolutionary black nationalism. Maulana Ron Karenga, chairman of US, articulates some general propositions of the cultural nationalists in the following quotations (from his selection in *The Black Power Revolt):*

> There is no such thing as individualism, we're all Black. The only thing that saved us from being lynched like Emmett Till or shot down like Medgar Evers was not our economics or social status, but our absence. . . .
>
> US is a cultural organization dedicated to the crea-

tion, recreation and circulation of Afro-American culture. . . .

If by primitive you mean more natural, we need to be
more primitive. . . .

Blacks must develop their own heroic images. . . . To
the white boy Malcolm X was a hate teacher—to us he
was the highest form of Black Manhood in his generation.

Another cultural nationalist, Josef Ben-Jochannan, describes black power as "that power which black peoples had
in Africa before the invasion and domination of Africa by
the Europeans under the guise of 'taking Christianity to the
heathen Africans.' "
It appears that the underlying philosophy of the cultural
nationalists is reduced to the generation of race pride,
through the eradication of self-hindering psychological complexes of blacks in respect to self-assessment and cultural
heritage. This is accompanied by a rejection of European
aesthetics and assertion of African life styles, manifested in
the assumption of Arabic and African names, the wearing of
African garments, and the speaking of African languages.
Institutionalized responses include the development of social-
science literature—history, philosophy, and political science
—from a black perspective.
Aligned to cultural nationalism is religious nationalism.
These two movements afford an essentially psychic escape
valve by changes in names and cultural symbols. The most
influential and dynamic religious nationalistic organization
in Afro-American history is the Black Muslims. Unlike most
of the contemporary movements, the Muslims underwent a
development predicated upon a systematic analysis by Farrad Mohammad (founder of the sect) of the economic and
political frustration of blacks in the Detroit area. This frustration had resulted from the effects of the Depression and
the vacuum created by the death of Noble Drew Ali, leader
of the Moorish Science movement, and the deportation of

Marcus Garvey. Farrad was able to capitalize on the Moorish and Garveyite passions and to transform them into a new force in which religious and political energies were fused.

C. Eric Lincoln, in *Sounds of the Struggle,* expresses the rationale underlying *why* Muslim recruits become believers. The group's aims were expressed by a Muslim minister as follows: "To get the white man's foot off our neck, his hand out of our pocket, and his carcass off our back. To sleep in our own bed without fear and to look straight into his cold blue eyes and call him a liar every time he parts his lips."

It is interesting to note that Farrad built his movement around the sociopolitical consciousness of the black poor. He appealed to the Judeo-Christian ethic of blacks by preaching extensively from the Bible and at the same time utilizing the writings of Joseph F. Judge Rutherford, leader of Jehovah's Witnesses, and varied literature such as James H. Breasted's *The Conquest of Civilization* and Hendrik Willem Van Loon's *Story of Mankind.* The Muslims were the vanguard of all contemporary black nationalist groups because they analyzed the historical antecedents that gave rise to mass movements among blacks and solved the problems of the succession of leadership endemic to earlier movements. No other movement has made a more significant impact on the race consciousness of black and white America than the Muslims through their most effective spokesman, Malcolm X. The Muslims' essentially reformist ten-point program was adopted and modified by the Black Panther party, the most radical black (or white) organization on the contemporary scene.

In the Muslims' economic and political program one can see the influences of both Garvey and Booker T. Washington. Unlike Garvey, who advocated emigrationism linked with Pan-Africanism, the Muslims called for territorial separatism, on the grounds that this country was built upon 350 years of unrequited toil of blacks without due compensation or benefits of the resulting wealth. Garvey radicalized Booker T. Washington's conservative nationalism, but the basic tenets of Washington's program were adopted by the Muslims through Garvey. Washington said, in 1900:

364

. . . brains, money, property, education—plenty of good schools and good teachers—tone down worthless civil rights protests. . . . Let us build our group economic power. . . . Let us have good farms, good businesses, thriving cooperatives. . . . Let us establish these things for ourselves and all civil rights will be added as a matter of course, for we will then be truly equal.

One may ask, what is the significance of all this to my present discussion? Simply this: the current advocates of black power have not internalized the reasons for the failure of Booker T. Washington's program, nor have they fully analyzed the socioeconomic forces that generated the Black Muslim movement among a poor, working-class constituency. Therefore, SNCC and CORE on the contemporary scene again imagine that basic structural changes in the economic, political, and cultural institutions can be accomplished by:

> Giving up "integration" efforts . . . de-emphasizing civil rights protests . . . stop agitation for more worthless . . . civil rights bills. . . .
> Let us go back into the black communities and build our own economic, educational, and political institutions. . . .
> Let us build Black Power! Then we will be equal.

The concepts articulated by both SNCC, CORE, and their historical antecedent, Booker T. Washington, are essentially bourgeois reformist—that is, they express the belief that within this politically pluralistic society, conflicting race, class, and political interests can be resolved through the process of democratization. Cruse makes a point, in *Rebellion or Revolution,* that

> Bourgeois-oriented Negroes . . . clutter up the Negro civil rights movement with their strident protests and really believe that American capitalism is going to grant them racial equality, while they remain in blithe ignorance of the inner workings of American capitalism.

Both SNCC's and CORE's transition from integration-fo-

365

cused movements to an essentially nationalist stance reflects the historical conflict that has existed throughout a century of struggle against the exploitation of blacks. It is doubtful whether these organizations recognize the historical dynamics of this conflict as it manifested itself in the personalities of Delaney and Frederick Douglass, and later in the conflicts between Booker T. Washington and W. E. B. Du Bois, Marcus Garvey and Du Bois, Elijah Muhammad and Malcolm X, and most recently Stokely Carmichael and Eldridge Cleaver.

The issue remains the same—whether integration or black separatism is the social philosophy providing a solution applicable to the political, economic, and cultural oppression of blacks in America.

In general, the black nationalist movement has been characterized by ambiguity. Except in the cases of direct emigrationist movements such as the Delaney and Garvey movements, the philosophy of separatism has been advocated as a means of winning full acceptance of blacks in American society.

Whether the stated ultimate goals of either black capitalism or a separate nation will be accomplished by their respective advocates is unlikely at worst and problematical at best. In an ideological, rhetorical, and programmatic sense, most of the features of the contemporary black nationalists have been seen before: cultural nationalism, territorial separatism, emigrationism, religious nationalism, economic nationalism, and revolutionary nationalism.

The Integrationist Sentiment

One of the few black intellectuals who internalized the full dynamics of the conflict between the integrationist and separationist tendencies was W. E. B. Du Bois. His deep insights into the dilemma are evidenced in the following excerpts from "Striving of the Negro People," first published in the August 1897 edition of *The Atlantic Monthly* and reprinted in a number of other sources:

> . . . One ever feels his twoness,—an American, a Negro;
> two souls, two thoughts, two unreconciled strivings; two
> warring ideals in one dark body, whose dogged strength
> alone keeps it from being torn asunder.
>
> The history of the American Negro is the history of
> this strife,—this longing to attain self-conscious man-
> hood, to merge his double self into a better and truer
> self. In this merging he wishes neither of the old selves
> to be lost. He would not Africanize America, for Amer-
> ica has too much to teach the world and Africa. He
> would not bleach his Negro soul in a flood of white Amer-
> icanism, for he knows that Negro blood has a message
> for the world. He simply wishes to make it possible for
> a man to be both a Negro and an American without
> being cursed and spit upon. . . .

From the above statement made by Du Bois it is clear that
he recognized the pivotal relationship between cultural
identity and the development of political and economic philosophies. As long as the Afro-American's cultural identity
is in question or open to self-doubts, there can be no positive
identification within the demands of his political and economic existence. It is this awareness that distinguishes Du
Bois from the broad spectrum of integrationist advocates,
ranging from the nonviolent activists of the Martin Luther King heritage to the proponents of violent, armed struggle in the Black Panther party. To clarify the issue it will
be necessary to define integration. As E. Franklin Frazier
notes in *On Race Relations,* the generally accepted meaning
of the term "integration" involves the acceptance of blacks
as individuals into the political, economic, and social organizations of American life. Implicit in this is a cultural negation of black institutions—that is, a call for the gradual dissolution of the black community, the decline and eventual
disappearance of the associations, institutions, and other
forms of associated life which constitute the black experi-
ment in America. This represents the prevailing school of
thought that is adhered to by welfare organizations such as
the Urban League, which are content to suck the tit of white
philanthropic groups, and the staunch defenders of Amer-

ican values in the NAACP. However, it identifies only part of the integrationist ideology and serves to obscure the historical conflict between the integrationist and nationalist forces. Furthermore, this narrow interpretation of integration makes the Black Panther party's "class analysis" approach appear to be a revolutionary black nationalist position rather than a revolutionary integrationist philosophy.

For the purposes of this discussion, then, I will define the integrationist philosophy as reflecting the aspiration of groups, organizations, and individuals who perceive the problem of the exploitation and oppression of blacks as a *total* American dilemma. An implicit assumption of the integrationist, then, is that only through the concerted action of divergent societal, class, and racial groups, organized through commonality of interest, can significant structural changes be made in the political, economic, and cultural institutions. While specific remedies, procedures, and strategies vary from organization to organization, the underlying premise remains the same.

Heretofore, the major proponents of the integrationist philosophy have been members of the black middle class. As a group they evidenced a propensity toward conformity to dominant norms, morals, beliefs, and values which demonstrated an implicit or unconscious striving to become assimilated into the dominant culture. To accomplish this, the price exacted from this group was abject conformity of thinking.

Recently we have witnessed a growing identification of intellectuals and middle-class students with cultural nationalism, which in the past has had its primary appeal to lower-class blacks, who viewed the impediments to integration as being insurmountable and therefore never envisioned it as a viable goal. To a large extent the growing identification of students with cultural nationalism has resulted from the recent development of race-consciousness. Another factor has been the disillusionment of blacks with the integrationist philosophy, and a revolt by black youth against the old respectable and conventional leadership which was the main conduit of conformist attitudes and outlooks.

368

The whole civil-rights fight, at least as it envisions integration as a goal, is a middle-class fight. The NAACP, CORE, the Urban League, and followers of SCLC are all ostensibly middle class. The tenets of these organizations are founded on the myth that black Americans, like previous waves of Euro-Americans, can be assimilated systematically into the American, i.e., the capitalist, system. Each of those waves of white immigrants were assimilated essentially at the expense of blacks, and also at the expense of other white immigrants who followed them from Europe. The integrationist leaders have shown little development of their political perspectives beyond their Frederick Douglass, pre–Civil War, abolitionist antecedents. The validity of their philosophy is established by the resistance of whites to their demands. Because they have been stalwartly refused entrance into the ruling power groups in the American system, bourgeois blacks feel justified in making assimilation into these groups their goal. They never bother to make an analysis of the desirability of maintaining the existing order of things. In their assimilationist zeal, these defenders of American ideals of fair play and pluralism actually believe that black Americans can be merged into the general American community, accepted and fully mobile in every area of social and cultural intercourse through legal, legislative, and educational programs.

Implicit in the above approach and strategy is the belief that racial exploitation can be eliminated and social change implemented by judicial decrees, administrative rulings, and legislative acts. An analysis of American jurisprudence affords little foundation for this premise. In 1954 the *Brown* v. *Board of Education* decision was hailed as a landmark decision. It supposedly validated the law as a viable mechanism against de jure racial segregation. Sixteen years after this decision, President Nixon is proceeding with all deliberate speed to assist southern states in working out details for compliance with the court order. As a result of the 1964 Civil Rights Act, an Office of Economic Opportunity was formed, with a specific mandate to wage a war on poverty.

Why not a war on the rich? Why not a war on the military-industrial complex siphoning off 46 percent of the national resources? These reforms in the form of civil rights bills are palliatives. They are part of the national pacification program designed to co-opt the exploited and oppressed into believing that through pluralism and the adversary system the Constitution of the United States protects the rights and liberties of all Americans. What the NAACP–Urban League–SCLC wing fails to recognize is the fact that the Constitution was written on the premise that black people were not even people, let alone citizens. As Loren Miller writes, in an essay entitled "Race, Poverty and the Law":

> . . . every Fourth of July and every Bill of Rights Week, orators shout themselves hoarse and teachers exhaust themselves telling Americans, adults and children, that the original Constitution and the Bill of Rights protected the rights and liberties of all Americans. This myth has no foundation in American jurisprudence. The fact is that the equalitarian guarantees explicit and implicit in the Constitution and amplified in the Bill of Rights offered absolutely no protection to the blacks. As Chief Justice Roger B. Taney said in the Dred Scott case decided in 1857, "The Constitution was made by and for white men." He noted that blacks were not even in the minds of the framers of the Constitution when they were conferring special rights and privileges upon the citizens of a state in every other part of the Union.

The Civil War amendments were passed to rectify these inequities. After the ratification of the Thirteenth Amendment in 1865, Congress enacted the first Civil Rights Act of 1866 in response to the threat of the Black Codes to reduce blacks to semislavery. Congress codified the sweeping legislative command for equality as contained in the 1866 Civil Rights Act in the constitutional shorthand of the Fourteenth Amendment, ratified in 1868. In 1870 it proposed and secured the ratification of the Fifteenth Amendment. This congressional action culminated in the Civil Rights Act of 1875. (There was no similar legislation until 1957.)

The Supreme Court now took over, and in court decision after court decision—from the Slaughterhouse Cases, in which it restored the Dred Scott doctrine that there are two categories of citizenship, national and state, to *Grovey* v. *Townsend,* in which it decided that state political parties could exclude blacks—it pushed the frontiers of legal reform backward to the philosophy of white racists: blacks have no rights which the white man is bound to respect. The net result of the Court's post–Civil War decisions was to return blacks to a modified second class citizenship.

These historical facts, with their intrusions into current thinking, must be borne in mind when one assesses the impact of the *Brown* v. *Board of Education* decision and the 1964 Civil Rights Act. Unfortunately, the proponents of social change through judicial decrees, administrative rulings and legislative acts have not internalized the fact that the most important decisions that this country will be faced with will not turn on law, but on considerations of power. Consequently, proponents of the judicial system must understand where the law stops and where power begins.

Advocates of Revolutionary Change

Within the context of the integrationist forces, the proponents for complete structural changes in the political, social, and economic institutions in the United States have been faced with the issue of determining whether these changes can be accomplished through evolutionary or revolutionary means.

The situation becomes more confused as individuals and groups attempt to apply classical Marxist socioanalytical premises mechanically, without examining the dynamics and uniqueness of American capitalism and its oppressive racial and class underpinnings. From an international perspective, the struggles of most oppressed people can be characterized by their class character, or as a struggle between the "haves" and the "have-nots." But in the United States, blacks constitute a disproportionate number of those living below the poverty line, simply because blacks are locked out of economic institutions by virtue of their skin color. A serious defect is implicit in most Marxist socioanalytic approaches in that they fail to recognize the fact that blacks are kept at the bottom of the economic ladder by *both* the capitalistic system and the exploitation of blacks by whites—resulting in white people being either active or passive recipients of the benefits derived from this relationship. It would be a tragic mistake to believe that if the economic system (capitalism) were destroyed, the exploitation of blacks would cease immediately. Racism is an oppressive force which is nurtured by the rulers of the economic system and digested by the masses of white society. As relevant as it is, the question of racism and its eventual elimination is too complex to deal with summarily, and must be reserved for a later paper.

White Marxists find themselves frozen into a dialectical frame of reference that mechanically espouses the outmoded and obsolete concept that the working classes will be the generating mechanism of the socialist state. While I do not raise any serious questions as to the validity of Marx's premises as applied to the social forces at play more than a hundred years ago in Europe, they are inapplicable to the American scene for at least two reasons. First, Marx predicted that the inner contradictions between the methods of production and the social relations of production, i.e., capital versus labor, would generate "class struggle," resulting in the working class overthrowing the capitalists. But the role of social forces is constantly changing. An examination of the reality of contemporary American capitalism reveals a coalition between the "hard hats" and the establishment, between white labor and white capital, to the detriment of blacks.

Secondly, an examination of basic Marxist tenets discloses that Marx did not foresee a socialist revolution in American countries. His premises were based upon the social dynamics of the highly industrialized nations with organized working classes whose interests conflicted with those of the capitalist classes of owners. He envisioned that class struggle and eventual expropriation of the capitalist owners would result from the owners exploiting labor, and thereby becoming richer and more concentrated. This was related to the development of monopolies. Conversely, the poor would be pushed further into the clutches of poverty to the point of revolution. The fact of the matter is that this theoretical model has never been verified. No social revolution since, and including, the Russian Revolution has taken place in an advanced industrial nation. In fact the only successful social revolutions have occurred in industrially backward, agrarian, semicolonial, or colonial counties. It is therefore ludicrous to mechanically apply classical Marxian socioanalytical models to the unique power relationships in the United States. I state the foregoing because the revolutionary integrationist forces have rhetorically advocated a mechanical "class" approach without analyzing numerous historical antecedents suggesting that this approach is obsolete, because the "working class" is identified with the industrial-military complex. Hardly a single white worker has joined the black struggle. The only whites who joined the struggle came from the middle class and were those who were most economically secure: college students, professionals, intellectuals—individuals who represent no significant social force. James Boggs, in *Racism and the Class Struggle,* observes that the white workers are, in fact, mobilizing to resist blacks. Not since the 1930s and the organization of the unions has there been such a mass mobilization among white workers. He further notes that the working class, aided and abetted by the large numbers of the middle class who have come from the working class, represent the bulk of the counterrevolutionary force against the black liberation movement.

Given this reality, why is revolution the only viable mechanism for social change within the context of the United States? To a large extent the methods employed to bring about social change are dictated by the goals and objectives of the movement for change and the reaction of the establishment. For example, the NAACP–Urban League civil righters are seeking racial equality within the context of the established order. While the realization of this goal or objective might dictate the use of revolutionary means, its realization is mitigated against by the procapitalist ideology of these groups, representing a basic contradiction. They are not seeking to change the political, economic, and social institutions of the system. In fact, they are struggling for an opportunity to become capitalists. They would be satisfied if racial equality was achieved within the oppressor class as well as the oppressed class. Some have argued that the achievement of total integration would require revolutionary means, since it represents a threat to the established order of power relationships.

The school of thought to which I subscribe maintains that the establishment is prepared to allow a few blacks into the ruling class, to form alliances with black exploiters under the guise of black capitalism. United States capitalism, like an oyster, is able to absorb abrasive material within its system, secrete digestive juices, and transform it into a "pearl." This was exemplified by Roosevelt's social reforms in the 1930s, popularly called the New Deal. The New Deal demonstrated the ability of the establishment to pacify, neutralize, and absorb the most radical concepts advocated by the Communist revolutionaries from the 1920s to the present; yet the basic foundations of the system (private property relationships) have remained the same. Ghetto uprisings are being planned for, and handled, either as natural disasters or as predictable reaction-products of the system. We conclude that the reality of evolution as a method for changing the economic, political, and social structures within the United States is not supported by a single historical antecedent.

On the other hand, historical analysis of the conflicting sociodynamic forces and the reactions of the established political order associated with certain revolutions suggests that the navigators of capitalistic growth within the United States are being placed on a self-destruct circuit by the most revolutionary force within the country, the black movement. While we do not maintain that this force can, or

374

will, unilaterally bring about the envisioned structural changes, we note that it has been the prime mover for social change in the last quarter of a century; it has set the tone and developed the strategies for change and has exposed the contradictions of the system—providing the wedge for other movements, such as Students for a Democratic Society and the feminists, to chip away at its foundations.

James Boggs, in *Racism and the Class Struggle,* makes the following observation:

> Blacks in the United States constitute the only revolutionary social force at this stage both because they have been systematically damned to underdevelopment inside this economically most advanced and politically most backward society, and because, having been made expendable by technological advances, their very survival depends on their creating a new society in which politics rather than labor will be the socially necessary activity giving the system its rationale and order. This means that the black revolution must create a kind of society which goes far beyond any that have been achieved by revolutions in the past.

Boggs further notes that the leadership of the American revolution can only come from blacks: first, they constitute the only social force who, as a mass, cannot be incorporated into the system; and second, since they have been systematically excluded from Western civilization and culture for so many generations, they are not prisoners of Western methods of thought. He then concludes that they are therefore the ones best able to do what the Asian revolution has done—exploit the weakness of Western strategy, which is ultimately based on Western methods of thought, and defeat the counterrevolution.

The navigators of the establishment have counted on the efficacy of specific social reforms to act as palliatives in their pacification of the black movement. The 1964 Civil Rights Act and the resulting war on poverty with its manpower training and retraining programs for the "hard-core unemployed" manifest this strategy. The establishment has therefore been puzzled by the ghetto rebellions over the past few years. James C. Davies, in *Processes of Rebellion: The History of Violence in America,* makes observations that reveal the inevitability of increased rebellion by blacks and other alienated social forces, leading ultimately to revolutionary struggle. He notes that there is a general pattern of change that precedes rebellion, and he illustrates similarities in the French Revolution, the American Civil War, the Nazi revolution, and the uprisings of black Americans in the 1960s. He observes that in all these cases, revolt was preceded by a long period of improvement in conditions followed by a more or less sharp decline. In other words, as a result of increasing socioeconomic or political satisfactions, expectations of continued improvement are generated. If such expectations are substantially frustrated for many people, group conflict is likely to increase, and popular uprisings occur.

Revolutionary change involves the complete structural rearrangement of the political, economic, and social institutions. Implicit in this is the transfer of power and a war on the part of the powerless to take power by all means necessary. The establishment's planners and strategists are cognizant of the social dynamics that determine revolution. They recognize, as James C. Davies observes, that revolution is most likely to take place when a prolonged period of rising expectations and rising gratifications is followed by a short period of sharp reversal, during which the gap between expectations and gratifications quickly widens and becomes intolerable. The planners and strategists are caught in the dilemma of devising pacification programs designed to keep the gap between what people want and what they get at a tolerable level. At the same time, proponents of revolutionary change are raising the social consciousness of the population to higher levels. Therefore, what was heretofore envisioned as a "privilege" or "benefit" is demanded as a "right."

To understand the revolutionary potential of the recent black rebellions, one must examine their historical antecedents as they relate to general propositions concerning the role of social dynamic forces preceding rebellion and revolution.

An examination of history suggests that those who must concentrate on survival usually do not revolt: they are too hungry. At the end of the Civil War blacks were preoccupied with survival to the exclusion of all other interests. They could concern themselves only with the satisfaction of their physical needs. Blacks were fair game for racist whites. Lynch mobs were used, rather than lawful or institutionalized methods of oppression. Between 1882 and 1941 there were approximately 5,000 lynchings. This diminished to approximately three to five per year between 1937 and 1948. To a large extent as a result of the attack on the judicial process waged by the NAACP, the establishment began to pass legislation designed to break the institutionalized strongholds that had relegated blacks to the lowest level of survival within the social system. The FEPC (Fair Employment Practices Committee) was implemented by President Roosevelt to eliminate discrimination in the defense industries. In 1946 the CIO and AFL took the edge off desperation by extending token membership to blacks. By 1948, FEPC legislation had been passed in six states. Symbolically, in 1947 the first black was admitted to major league baseball. By 1951 there were fourteen blacks in major league baseball. By 1954 all but three of the sixteen major league teams had been integrated. Concessions were won in the integration of low-cost public housing. In 1956 all public housing in Washington, D.C., was desegregated. In 1962 President Kennedy issued an order prohibiting discrimination in any housing that was either financed or had mortgage insurance under a government program.

These advances created the delusion that systematic assimilation into the mainstream of America was possible. As a result of the acts of legislatures, courts, and administrative agencies in their efforts to equalize opportunities for black people, the expectation levels of blacks as to the viability of the system to address itself to their needs became excessively optimistic. On the other hand, between 1950 and 1960 increased violence by whites against blacks was evidenced. After the 1954 *Brown* v. *Board of Education* decision, more

377

than 534 cases of bombings, burnings, and intimidation of parents and children were recorded. Schools, churches, and the homes of black leaders were bombed, and many people were killed in these bombings. In fact, starting in the mid-1950s increased white resistance and violence were experienced by the black movement. Every time the white reactions impeded or threatened progress, the gap widened between black expectations and gratifications. Davies notes that the time sequence of events preceding the black rebellions in the 1960s was consistent with that of major historic revolutions —that is, a rather long period of rising expectations followed by a relatively brief period of frustration that struck deep in the psyches of black people.

Given this analysis, it would appear that, to be successful, the planners and strategists have only to steer along this fixed course of "minimizing the gap between the expectations and achievements of blacks," but this essentially locks them into an endless merry-go-round, with the demands increasing both in intensity and frequency.

As blacks demand more fundamental changes through extralegal methods, reactionary forces will make the establishment respond through legal violence. Then hatred of oppression and the oppressors will be imprinted in the consciousness of the rebels. This hatred will linger and deepen like embers in a dry tinder after firefighters have tried to beat to death a small fire. To the extent that there are other social forces (such as women and radical white youth) who are experiencing frustration of different basic needs and who can focus their frustration on the government, then the seeds for the revolution exist. People deprived of jobs may join in revolt with people who are exploited by employers, landlords, police, or military troops. Within the context of the United States the catalytic force of the American revolution will be revolutionary blacks. They are the ones who have brought to the fore the inner contradictions of the system. The cities will be the battleground of the struggle; the techniques to be used and strategies to be outlined will be dictated by the objective conditions there. As blacks who are concentrated in these areas move, agitate, and struggle for control of basic institutions that mold their lives, they will invariably recognize that the economic, political, and social control of institutions operating within the black communities is situated outside of their communities. While the election of black mayors in Cleveland, Newark, Gary, and Fayette may satisfy an emotional need of blacks, the basic premises of power remain intact—that is, the foundations of property relationships within capitalism. Invariably blacks will recognize that the very structure of the economic, political, and social systems must be changed.

Black revolutionary leadership needs the insights of social theorists who have analyzed the uniqueness and dynamics of American capitalism, thereby synthesizing political, economic, and cultural premises that are conceptually tied to historical antecedents. Simplistic solutions cannot take the place of such synthesis and analysis. Hopefully the present black leadership will not continue to be blinded by the immediacy of contemporary events to the lessons of Afro-American history.

SOURCES

BARBOUR, FLOYD B., ed., *The Black Power Revolt*. Boston, Porter Sargent, Inc., 1968.

BOGGS, JAMES, *Racism and the Class Struggle*. New York, Monthly Review Press, 1970.

BRACEY, JOHN H., JR.; Meier, August; and Rudwick, Elliott M., *Black Nationalism in America*. Indianapolis and New York, The Bobbs-Merrill Company, Inc., 1970.

CRUSE, HAROLD, *The Crisis of the Negro Intellectual*. New York, William Morrow and Company, Inc., 1967.

_____ *Rebellion or Revolution?* New York, William Morrow and Company, Inc., 1968.

DAVIES, JAMES C., *Processes of Rebellion: The History of Violence in America*. New York, Bantam Books, Inc., 1969.

DELANEY, MARTIN R., and Campbell, Robert, *Search for a Place:*

Black Separatism and Africa, introduction by Howard H. Bell. Ann Arbor, The University of Michigan Press, 1969.

DU BOIS, W. E. B., "Striving of the Negro People," *The Atlantic Monthly,* August 1897. Reprinted in John H. Bracey, Jr., et al., *Black Nationalism in America* (q.v.) .

FRAZIER, E. FRANKLIN, *Black Bourgeoisie.* New York, The Free Press, 1957.

———— *On Race Relations.* Chicago, University of Chicago Press, 1968.

LINCOLN, C. ERIC, *The Black Muslims in America.* Boston, Beacon Press, 1961.

———— *Sounds of the Struggle.* New York, William Morrow and Company, Inc., 1967.

MILLER, LOREN, "Race, Poverty and the Law," in Ben B. Seligman, ed., *Aspects of Poverty.* New York, Thomas Y. Crowell Company Inc., 1968.

SELECTED BIBLIOGRAPHY

Suggested by the Authors

BOOKS

Aptheker, Herbert, ed., *A Documentary History of the Negro People in the United States,* 2 vols. New York, Citadel Press, 1951.

_____ *American Negro Slave Revolts.* New York, International Publishers, 1943.

_____ *Nat Turner's Slave Rebellion.* New York, Grove Press, Inc., 1966.

Arendt, Hannah, *The Origins of Totalitarianism.* New York, Harcourt, Brace & Company, 1951.

Baraka, Imamu Amiri, *see* Jones, LeRoi.

Barbour, Floyd B., ed., *The Black Power Revolt.* Boston, Porter Sargent, Inc., 1968.

Bascom, William R., and Herskovits, Melville J., eds., *Continuity and Change in African Cultures.* Chicago, The University of Chicago Press, 1959.

Biebuyck, Daniel, *Tradition and Creativity in Tribal Art,* vol. 2, Berkeley and Los Angeles, University of California Press, 1969.

Billingsley, Andrew, *Black Families in White America.* Englewood Cliffs, N.J., Prentice-Hall, Inc., 1968.

Bodrogi, Tibor, *Art in Africa.* New York, McGraw-Hill Book Company, 1968.

Bontemps, Arna, ed., *American Negro Poetry.* New York, Hill and Wang, Inc. 1963.

Botkin, B. A., *Lay My Burden Down.* Chicago, The University of Chicago Press, 1945.

Bracey, John H., Jr.; Meier, August; and Rudwick, Elliott M., eds., *Black Nationalism in America.* Indianapolis and New York, The Bobbs-Merrill Company, 1970.

Brown, H. Rap, *Die Nigger Die!* New York, Dial Press, 1969.

Brown, Sterling A.; Davis, Arthur P.; and Lee, Ulysses, eds., *The Negro Caravan.* New York, Dryden Press, 1941.

Bullins, Ed, ed., *New Plays from the Black Theatre.* New York, Bantam Books, Inc., 1969.

Carmichael, Stokely, and Hamilton, Charles, *Black Power: The Politics of Liberation in America.* New York, Random House, Inc., 1967.

Chapman, Abraham, ed., *Black Voices: An Anthology of Afro-American Literature.* New York, New American Library, 1968.

Clark, Kenneth, *Dark Ghetto*. New York, Harper & Row, Publishers, 1965.

Cleaver, Eldridge, *Soul on Ice*. McGraw-Hill Book Company, 1968.
_____ *see* Scheer, Robert, ed.

Cornish, Dudley Taylor, *The Sable Arm: Negro Troops in the Union Army, 1861-1865*. London, Longmans, Green and Company, Ltd., 1956.

Courlander, Harold, *Negro Folkmusic, U.S.A.* New York, Columbia University Press, 1963.

Cox, Oiliver C., *Caste, Class, and Race*. New York, Doubleday & Company, Inc., 1948.

Cruse, Harold, *The Crisis of the Negro Intellectual*. New York, William Morrow and Company, Inc., 1967.

_____ *Rebellion or Revolution?* New York, William Morrow and Company, Inc., 1968.

Curtin, P. D., *Africa Remembered*. Madison, University of Wisconsin Press, 1967.

Daley, Charles U., ed., *Urban Violence*. Chicago, The University of Chicago Center for Policy Studies, 1968.

Dark, Phillip, *Bush Negro Art*. London, Alec Tiranti, Ltd., 1954.

Davies, Kenneth G., *The Royal African Company*. London, Longmans, Green and Company, Ltd., 1957.

Donnan, Elizabeth, ed., *Documents Illustrative of the History of the Slave Trade to America,* 4 vols. Washington, Octagon Books, 1930-35.

Draper, Theodore, *The Rediscovery of Black Nationalism*. New York, The Viking Press, 1970.

Du Bois, W. E. B., *The ABC of Color*. New York, International Publishers, 1970.

_____ *Autobiography*. New York, International Publishers, 1968.

_____ *Black Reconstruction in America*. New York, Harcourt, Brace & Company, 1953.

_____*The Souls of Black Folk,* 1903. Reprinted: New York, New American Library, 1969.

Duignan, Peter and Clendenen, Clarence, *The United States and the African Slave Trade, 1619-1862*. Stanford, Calif., Hoover Institution on War, Revolution, and Peace, 1963.

Ellison, Ralph, *Shadow and Act*. New York, The New American Library, 1966.

Essien-Udom, E. U., *Black Nationalism*. Chicago, The University of Chicago Press, 1962.

Fagg, William, *Art of Central Africa*. New York, New American Library, 1967.

_____ *Art of Western Africa*. New York, New American Library, 1967.

Feldman, Susan, ed., *African Myths and Tales*. New York, Dell Books, 1963.

Franklin, John Hope, *From Slavery to Freedom*, New York, Alfred A. Knopf, Inc., 1956

Frazier, E. Franklin, *Black Bourgeoisie*. New York, The Free Press, 1957.

_____ *The Negro Church in America*. New York, Schocken Books, 1963.

Garvey, Marcus, *see* Jacques-Garvey, Amy, ed.

Gayle, Addison, Jr., ed., *Black Expression*. New York, Weybright and Tally, Inc., 1969.

Hernton, Calvin C., *Sex and Racism in America*. New York, Grove Press, Inc., 1965.

Herskovits, Melville J., *The Myth of the Negro Past*, 2nd ed. Boston, Beacon Press, 1958.

_____ *The New World Negro*. Bloomington, Indiana University Press, 1969.

Hill, Herbert, ed., *Anger and Beyond: The Negro Writer in the United States*. New York, Harper & Row, Publishers, 1966.

Howard, Warren S., *American Slavers and the Federal Law, 1837-1862*. Berkeley, University of California Press, 1963.

Hughes, Langston, *Simple Speaks His Mind*. New York, Simon & Schuster, 1950.

_____ and Bontemps, Arna, eds., *Book of Negro Folklore*. New York, Dodd, Mead & Company, 1958.

Jacques-Garvey, Amy, ed., *The Philosophy and Opinions of Marcus Garvey*, New York, The Humanities Press, 1963.

Jeffers, Camille, *Living Poor*. Ann Arbor, Mich., Ann Arbor Publishers, 1967.

Johnson, Charles S., *Shadow of the Plantation*. Chicago, The University of Chicago Press, 1934.

Jones, LeRoi, *Blues People*. New York, William Morrow and Company, Inc., 1963.

_____ *The System of Dante's Hell*. New York, Grove Press, Inc., 1963.

_____ and Neal, Larry, eds., *Black Fire*. New York, William Morrow and Company, Inc., 1968.

Karenga, Maulana Ron, *The Quotable Karenga.* Los Angeles, US Organization, 1967.

King, Martin Luther, Jr., *Stride Towards Freedom.* New York, Harper & Brothers, 1958.

Lester, Julius, *Black Folktales.* New York, R. W. Baron Publishing Company, 1970.

Leuzinger, Elsy, *Africa; The Art of the Negro Peoples,* translated from the German by Ann E. Keep. New York, McGraw-Hill Book Company, 1960.

Malcolm X and Haley, Alex, *The Autobiography of Malcolm X.* New York, Grove Press, Inc., 1965.

Marine, Gene, *The Black Panthers.* New York, New American Library, 1969.

Mayer, Milton, *The Art of the Impossible.* A Center Occasional Paper, vol. 2, no. 3, April 1969, published by the Center for the Study of Democratic Institutions, Santa Barbara, Cal.

McPherson, James M., ed., *The Negro's Civil War: How American Negroes Felt and Acted During the War for the Union.* Princeton, N.J., Princeton University Press, 1964.

Meier, August, and Rudwick, Elliott M., *From Plantation to Ghetto: An Interpretive History of American Negroes.* New York, Hill and Wang, Inc., 1966.

Meltzer, Milton, ed., *In Their Own Words: A History of the American Negro,* 3 vols. New York, Thomas Y. Crowell Company, 1964, 1965, 1967.

Myrdal, Gunnar, *An American Dilemma.* New York, Harper & Brothers, 1944.

Oliver, Ronald, and Fage, J. D. *A Short History of Africa.* Baltimore, Penguin Books, Inc., 1962.

Proctor, S. D., *The Young Negro in America, 1960-1980.* New York, Association Press, 1966.

Quarles, Benjamin, *The Negro in the Civil War.* Boston, Little, Brown and Company, 1953.

Robinson, Armstead; Foster, Craig; and Ogilvie, Donald, eds., *Black Studies in the University,* New Haven, Yale University Press, 1969.

Scheer, Robert, ed., *Eldridge Cleaver: Post-Prison Speeches and Writings.* New York, Random House, Inc., 1969.

Seale, Bobby, *Seize the Time: The Story of the Black Panther Party and Huey P. Newton.* New York, Random House, Inc., 1970.

Segy, Ladislas, *African Sculpture Speaks.* rev. ed., New York, Hill and Wang, Inc., 1969.

Silberman, Charles, *Crisis in Black and White*. New York, Random House, Inc., 1964.

Stampp, Kenneth M., *The Peculiar Institution: Slavery in the Antebellum South*. New York, Alfred A. Knopf, Inc., 1956.

United States National Advisory Commission on Civil Disorders, *Report of the National Advisory Commission on Civil Disorders*. New York, Bantam Books, Inc., 1968.

Van den Berghe, Pierre L., *Race and Racism*. New York, John Wiley & Sons, Inc., 1967.

Wassing, Rene S., *African Art: Its Background and Traditions*. New York, Harry N. Abrams, 1968.

Wiley, Bell Irvin, *Southern Negroes, 1861-1865*. New Haven, Yale University Press, 1938.

Wright, Richard, *White Man, Listen*. New York, Doubleday & Company, Inc. (Anchor paperback), 1957.

Young, Whitney, *To Be Equal*. New York, McGraw-Hill Book Company, 1964.

ARTICLES, PAMPHLETS, AND NEWSPAPERS

The Black Panther Newspaper. Official paper of the Black Panther party, Ministry of Information, Black Panther party, Box 2967, Custom House, San Francisco, Calif. 94126.

Bowling, Frank, "Discussion on Black Art, I and II," *Arts Magazine*, April and May 1969.

Browne, Robert S., "The Case for Black Separatism," *Ramparts*, December 1967.

——— "The Case for Two Americas—One Black, One White," *The New York Times Magazine*. August 11, 1968.

Congress of Racial Equality, "Black Self-Determination—the Only Alternative" (mimeographed).

Ferry, W. H., "Farewell to Integration," *The Center Magazine*, March 1968.

Muhammad, Elijah, *Message to the Blackman in America*. Chicago, Muhammad Mosque of Islam, No. 2, 1965.

Rodney, Walter, *West Africa and the Atlantic Slave Trade*. Nairobi, East Africa Publishing House, 1967. Pamphlet, Northwestern University Press, 1735 Benson Avenue, Evanston, Ill. 60201.

Sherrill, Robert, "Birth of a Black Nation." *Esquire*, January 1969.

ABOUT THE AUTHORS

RALPH DAVID ABERNATHY is an internationally known civil rights leader. He was the closest associate of the late Dr. Martin Luther King, Jr., and succeeded him as president of the Southern Christian Leadership Conference. Dr. Abernathy is also pastor of the West Hunter Street Baptist Church in Atlanta, Georgia.

EMILY ALMAN, chairman of the Douglass College sociology department, has done research in the areas of poverty and social change. Chairman of the college's Equal Opportunities Board, she earlier helped to develop mechanisms for university-wide recruitment of black, Puerto Rican, and other minority group students.

HERBERT APTHEKER is the author of more than twenty books in the areas of history, sociology, and philosophy, including *A Documentary History of the Negro People in the United States* (1951) and *American Negro Slave Revolts* (1943). He is the Literary Custodian of the late Dr. W. E. B. Du Bois, teaches history at Bryn Mawr College, and is director of the American Institute for Marxist Studies. He has edited *The Correspondence of W. E. B. Du Bois,* published in 1971.

AUDREY C. ARTHUR was born and raised in New Brunswick, New Jersey. She was a member of the Black Students' Congress at Douglass College and graduated from Douglass in 1970.

DEBORAH BANKSTON graduated from Douglass College in 1971, where she was student chairman of the Afro-American House and assisted in the development of the African and Afro-American Studies program. She has taught in the New Brunswick Liberation School and helped organize a children's program in Newark.

FRANK BOWLING is assistant professor of art at Massachusetts College of Art, where he teaches contemporary art. He is a painter and writes art criticism, and has exhibited his work here and abroad. Born in Guyana and educated in London, he is a regular contributor to *Arts Magazine* and other art journals. His paintings are included in several public and private collections in the United States and Europe.

RONALD S. COPELAND has devoted much of his time to the direction

386

of a youth-development program in Franklin Township, New Jersey. He was chairman of Somerset County CORE and has served in varied official and unofficial community roles, all dedicated to the liberation struggle. He is employed by the New Jersey Office of Economic Opportunity.

JAMES DENMARK is an artist who works in varied media, including painting, drawing, printmaking, ceramics, and welded sculpture. He has taught at schools and colleges in Florida and New York and has exhibited widely in the past few years.

CECELIA HODGES DREWRY has taught Black Theatre at Douglass College, where she was a member of the drama department and chairman of the African and Afro-American Studies program. She has presented staged readings to theatre, radio, and television audiences and has taught as guest lecturer at Princeton and Columbia universities. She is presently Assistant Dean of the College at Princeton University.

HENRY N. DREWRY teaches courses in Afro-American history at Princeton University, where he is also director of Teacher Preparation and Placement. He is coauthor with Frank Freidel of a high school text in United States history, and with Cecelia Hodges Drewry of the recently published *Afro-American History: Past to Present.*

GEOFFREY HENDRICKS, associate professor of art at Douglass College, studied African art at Columbia University with Paul Wingert and has taught African and Oceanic art. He is a practicing artist, involved in intermedia and happenings, and has exhibited widely in the United States, Europe, and Japan.

LENNOX S. HINDS gave up a career in research chemistry to enter Rutgers Law School, where he is now president of the Association of Black Law Students. A community activist and past officer of several community action groups, he has been teacher and consultant at community agencies and colleges, particularly in programs serving disadvantaged urban youth.

ESI SYLVIA KINNEY has concentrated her research activities mainly in West Africa and in urban centers of the United States. She is a performer, has written several articles concerning the functional aspects of African music and dance, and is an assistant professor of ethnomusicology in the anthropology department at Livingston College, Rutgers University.

A

NN

J. L

ANE

teaches recent American history and Afro-American history at Douglass. She is the author of *The Brownsville Affair* and the editor of *The Debate Over "Slavery": Stanley Elkins and His Critics,* both published in 1971.

C

OLIN

P

ALMER

is from Jamaica. He recently completed his doctoral degree at the University of Wisconsin and teaches history at Oakland University in Michigan. He is currently writing a book on Negro slavery in colonial Mexico.

W. M. P

HILLIPS

, J

R

., sociologist, is an associate research professor with the Center for Urban Social Science Research of Rutgers. From 1968 to 1970 he was on leave organizing and serving as director of the Office of Research and Development of the New Jersey Department of Education. Author of articles on race relations and education, he is currently principal investigator of a National Institute of Mental Health-financed study of educational decision-making in Newark, New Jersey.

A

LPHONSO

P

INKNEY

has written three books, including the widely adopted *Black Americans,* published in 1969, and many scholarly articles on ethnic relations in the United States. He is professor of sociology at the University of Chicago and at Hunter College. His latest book, *The American Tradition of Violence,* was published in 1971.

K

AREN

P

REDOW

served as chairman of the Douglass College Black Students' Congress and in numerous official and unofficial capacities in university programs focused on the needs of black students, on black studies, and on black culture. She graduated from Douglass College in 1970 and is a counselor in the Rutgers urban-university department.

S

AMUEL

D. P

ROCTOR

is professor of education at the Graduate School of Education at Rutgers. A past president of both Virginia Union University, of which he is an alumnus, and North Carolina A & T University, he also served as administrator in the Peace Corps in Nigeria and Washington. Author of a number of articles, he wrote

The Young Negro in America 1960-1980, which was published in 1966.

THEODORE TAYLOR is executive director of the Community Action Program in Somerset County, New Jersey, where he pursues a long-time dedication to the development of community control by local residents. A former union organizer, he also established the Heritage Foundation to promote the appreciation of the black heritage. Taylor has played a prominent role in local politics.

IVAN VANSERTIMA is from Guyana. He is the author of a book of poetry, *River and the Wall,* published in 1958, and of a volume of critical essays, *Caribbean Writers,* published in 1968, and has had his work included in a number of anthologies. He is also the compiler of a Swahili dictionary of legal terms. For many years he was broadcaster from England to the Caribbean on Commonwealth affairs. He teaches oral tradition and Swahili literature in translation at Douglass College.

JULIUS M. WAIGUCHU is a citizen of Kenya who did his college and graduate work in the United States, mainly in the field of comparative politics. He recently received his Ph.D. from Temple University and presently teaches in the Institute of Black Studies at Paterson State College in New Jersey. His essay on nation-building in Kenya appears in *Administration of Change in Africa,* edited by E. Philip Morgan, published in 1971.

Index

Abernathy, Ralph D., 183-185, 190-197, 202, 204-205, 242-e, 277
abolitionists, 2, 107, 116-117, 135, 137-139, 142, 149-152, 171, 174
Account of the Slave Trade, 95-96
acculturation of U.S. blacks, 73-75, 309-310
admissions, college, 214-218, 220, 222, 224-225, 229, 231

Africa (*see also* art, culture, folklore, languages, music, missionaries, separatism, slave trade, individual countries), 15-16, 18-19, 40-42, 125, 218-219, 230, 231
African Art, 309
African Institution of Boston, 80
African Intelligence, 69

Index

Index

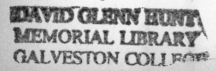